PRIVATIZATION AND ITS DISCONTENTS

In *Privatization and Its Discontents*, Matthew Titolo situates the contemporary debate over infrastructure in the long history of public–private governance in the United States. Titolo begins with Adam Smith's arguments about public works and explores debates over internal improvements in the early republic, moving to the twentieth-century regulatory state and public-interest liberalism that created vast infrastructure programs. While Americans have always agreed that creation and oversight of "infrastructure" is a proper public function, Titolo demonstrates that public–private governance has been a highly contested practice throughout American history. Public goods are typically provided with both government and private actors involved, resulting in an ideological battle over the proper scope of the government sphere and its relationship to private interests. The course of that debate reveals that "public" and "private" have no inherent or natural content. These concepts are instead necessarily political and must be set through socially negotiated compromise.

Matthew Titolo is Professor of Law at the West Virginia University College of Law. Professor Titolo researches nineteenth-century American legal and political history and teaches American legal history as well as commercial law courses.

Privatization and Its Discontents

INFRASTRUCTURE, LAW, AND
AMERICAN DEMOCRACY

MATTHEW TITOLO
West Virginia University College of Law

CAMBRIDGE
UNIVERSITY PRESS

Shaftesbury Road, Cambridge CB2 8EA, United Kingdom

One Liberty Plaza, 20th Floor, New York, NY 10006, USA

477 Williamstown Road, Port Melbourne, VIC 3207, Australia

314–321, 3rd Floor, Plot 3, Splendor Forum, Jasola District Centre, New Delhi – 110025, India

103 Penang Road, #05–06/07, Visioncrest Commercial, Singapore 238467

Cambridge University Press is part of Cambridge University Press & Assessment, a department of the University of Cambridge.

We share the University's mission to contribute to society through the pursuit of education, learning and research at the highest international levels of excellence.

www.cambridge.org
Information on this title: www.cambridge.org/9781108475679

DOI: 10.1017/9781108683456

© Matthew Titolo 2023

This publication is in copyright. Subject to statutory exception and to the provisions of relevant collective licensing agreements, no reproduction of any part may take place without the written permission of Cambridge University Press & Assessment.

First published 2023

A catalogue record for this publication is available from the British Library.

A Cataloging-in-Publication data record for this book is available from the Library of Congress.

ISBN 978-1-108-47567-9 Hardback
ISBN 978-1-108-46876-3 Paperback

Cambridge University Press & Assessment has no responsibility for the persistence or accuracy of URLs for external or third-party internet websites referred to in this publication and does not guarantee that any content on such websites is, or will remain, accurate or appropriate.

To my wife and daughter.

Contents

Acknowledgments		*page* ix
Introduction		1
1	Early Liberalism, Adam Smith, and the Seeds of the Infrastructural State	33
2	Forging the Infrastructural State: 1787–1837	55
3	"A Wilderness of Turnpike Gates": Roads and Public Authority in Antebellum America	87
4	The Panic of 1837 and the Infrastructure Crash	111
5	"The Ground under Our Feet": The Birth of Public Utilities	134
6	The Death of Laissez-Faire and the Rise of Infrastructure in the Cold War	169
Conclusion: "Our Crumbling Infrastructure"		199
Index		211

Acknowledgments

This book is the culmination of several years of research and thinking about American political development, the public–private problem, and infrastructure. I first became interested in these issues when I started reading about privatization of public services in the United States, which a friend of mine once called "a niche issue." This book is my effort to explain the historical importance of that niche issue as a central feature of American political economy. The problem of privatization seemed to me a missed opportunity to revisit American legal and policy history. It struck me as I researched the book that the voluminous literature on infrastructure across academic disciplines had not grappled with the intersection of law and politics in a way that captured central themes in American history: attitudes toward government and the fiscal order, the public/private divide in law, and public discourse around infrastructure. This book is my opportunity to make a point that others have made before me: While we commonly view the market and the state as separate entities, they are in reality entangled networks of governance. Infrastructure is a nice frame for these issues because it resonates with contemporary policy questions that everyone recognizes.

Writing a book like this is definitely not a solo project. Over the past several years, I have received support from my family, friends, and West Virginia University, all of whom have helped me bring this project to fruition. My wife, Tania de Miguel Magro, has encouraged my work on this book over the last couple of years in many ways, including reading drafts as well as by inspiring me to complete this manuscript as she finished her own. My seven-year-old daughter Ximena has kept me on track toward the harried end stage of the project by monitoring my daily writing progress, as well as giving me welcome respite from its burdens. Good friends and mentors over the years, including Steven Pfaff, Greg Jackson, Chris Sagers, and Vince Pecora, have influenced the outlook that gave the book whatever intellectual weight it has. Chris Sagers helped me formulate this project in its earliest stages, for which I am very grateful. Particular thanks also to Greg Jackson for reading and critiquing early drafts of the book, providing substantial feedback. Giorgi Heiko rendered invaluable assistance with research and preparation of the manuscript for publication. West Virginia University College of Law has lent support by encouraging me to pursue a scholarly project of this scope, despite the fact that it would take several years to complete. I have also received financial support in the form of several Arthur B. Hodges College of Law grants that have helped me focus on writing this book. Finally, Matt Gallaway at Cambridge University Press was generous and patient with my slow progress with this manuscript during the pandemic years, when homeschooling for my daughter took up so much of my energy.

Introduction

Building infrastructure is an inherently political act of creation. Every investment choice lays the foundation for a future that could have been otherwise. Yet, infrastructure needs are typically presented as dispassionate, objective facts. In truth, infrastructure is the physical manifestation of both political power and social values.[1]

I INTRODUCTION

I would like to begin this book with the term "infrastructure" itself, a word that turns up over a billion hits on a simple Google search. From this fact one might conclude that infrastructure has always been with us, like the air, sea, or water. But although it is ubiquitous today, infrastructure is really a very recent term in English. It entered our common vocabulary only in the late twentieth century, although it had been in use by military planners and development economists since the 1950s. Despite the fact that we now use the word all the time, infrastructure is a notoriously ambiguous word that has been defined in different ways at different times.[2] When we use the word today we might mean something like "[t]he underlying framework of a system; esp., public services and facilities (such as highways, schools, bridges, sewers, and water systems) needed to support commerce as well as economic and residential

---

[1] Kevin DeGood, *Infrastructure Investment Decisions Are Political, Not Technical*, CENTER FOR AMERICAN PROGRESS (April 14, 2020), www.americanprogress.org/issues/economy/reports/2020/04/14/483084/infrastructure-investment-decisions-political-not-technical/.

[2] *See*, for example, Jeffrey M. Stupak, *Economic Impact of Infrastructure Investment*, CONG. RSCH. SERV. 1, 1 (2018): "Although infrastructure spending has garnered increased attention recently, there is no generally agreed-upon definition of infrastructure. In general, the term refers to longer-lived, capital-intensive systems and facilities. Some restrict the definition to include systems and facilities that have traditionally been provided by the public sector, such as highways and water treatment facilities. However, others include predominantly privately owned systems and facilities, such as those involved in electricity production and distribution. The definition of infrastructure can be extended even further to include research and development expenditures, as they add to the stock of technology and information available for use by private individuals." Binyamin Appelbaum, *Why the Meaning of "Infrastructure" Matters So Much*, N. Y. TIMES OP. (Apr. 26, 2021), www.nytimes.com/2021/04/26/opinion/infrastructure-definition-history.html.

development."[3] Modern usage by economists and policy analysts focuses on "core" infrastructures that increase economic output (e.g., "roads, railways, airports, and utilities"), but it might exclude other types of structures that do not reflect how economists measure output such as "hospitals, schools, and other public buildings."[4] When figured this way, infrastructure measures the "public capital" that makes the private economy of goods and services function.[5] Physical infrastructure is both an economic indicator and a force multiplier, enabling modern economies either to "take off" or stagnate, flourish or decline.[6]

Before it was a modern economic term, however, infrastructure was a nineteenth-century French engineering word that slowly migrated into broader English usage in the twentieth century.[7] As Ashley Carse writes: "[I]nfrastructure was initially an organizational and accounting term used to distinguish the construction work that was literally conducted *beneath* unlaid tracks (roadbeds) or was otherwise organizationally *prior* to them (surveys, plans, bridges, tunnels, embankments) from the *superstructure* of roads, train stations, and workshops that was situated *above* or constructed *after* the tracks."[8] In this sense, infrastructure refers to the prior state investment required to build transportation systems: for example, the surveys, dredging and blasting, which are precursors to commercializing the railway hardware typically owned by the private contractor. In contrast, "superstructure" is the railway itself, privately owned and operated. The original definition identifies a persistent feature of infrastructure in liberal market economies: public investment is often a

---

[3] Infrastructure, BLACK'S LAW DICTIONARY (11th ed. 2019). For another attempt at a definition, see BRETT M. FRISCHMANN, INFRASTRUCTURE: THE SOCIAL VALUE OF SHARED RESOURCES 4 (2012) (emphasis in original): "Familiar examples of 'traditional infrastructure' include (1) *transportation systems*, such as highway systems, railway systems, airline systems, and ports; (2) *communication systems*, such as telephone networks and postal services; (3) *governance systems*, such as court systems; and (4) *basic public services and facilities*, such as schools, sewers, and water systems."

[4] Stupak, *Economic Impact of Infrastructure Investment*, supra note 2, at 13.

[5] See William J. Rankin, *Infrastructure and the International Governance of Economic Development, 1950–1965*, in INTERNATIONALIZATION OF INFRASTRUCTURES: PROCEEDINGS OF THE 12TH ANNUAL INTERNATIONAL CONFERENCE ON THE ECONOMICS OF INFRASTRUCTURES 61, 61–75 (Jean-François Auger et al. eds., 2009); Pedro Bom & Jenny Ligthart, *What Have We Learned from Three Decades of Research on the Productivity of Public Capital?*, 28 J. ECON. SURV. (2014).

[6] Wouter Thierie & Lieven De Moor, *The Characteristics of Infrastructure as an Investment Class*, 30 FIN. MKT. PORTFOLIO MGMT. 277, 278 (2016): "Adequate infrastructure is a driver of a region's comparative advantage..., economic growth..., its productivity..., and contributes to quality of life and welfare"; Surbhi Gupta & Anil Kumar Sharma, *Evolution of Infrastructure as an Asset Class: A Systematic Literature Review and Thematic Analysis*, 23 J. ASSET MGMT. 173, 173 (2022): "Infrastructure is considered as the linchpin of economic growth of any nation."

[7] Ashley Carse, *Keyword: Infrastructure: How a Humble French Engineering Term Shaped the Modern World*, in INFRASTRUCTURES AND SOCIAL COMPLEXITY: A ROUTLEDGE COMPANION 27, 27–39 (Penelope Harvey et al., eds., 2017); see also H. William Batt, *Infrastructure: Etymology and Import*, 110 J. PRO. ISSUES ENG'G (1984); Larry Beeferman & Allan Wain, *Infrastructure: Defining Matters*, January 12, 2016, available at SSRN: https://ssrn.com/abstract=2714308 or http://dx.doi.org/10.2139/ssrn.2714308.

[8] Carse, *Keyword: Infrastructure*, supra note 7, at 29–30.

precondition for the flow of goods and services produced by private corporate firms, not to mention a precondition for life as we understand it in the modern world.

With this simple word, French engineers were dividing the world into public and private spheres – a division that has been re-enacted countless times in the infrastructures of modern life down to our own era. Like the word "system," infrastructure implies a relationship between parts and a whole, with infrastructure providing the necessary and prior support for a larger project or purpose.[9] Infrastructure also implies first- and second-order activities where certain underlying forms are required to enable some essential or desirable activity.[10] Railroads, for example, cannot be built without surveys, digging, and blasting. But digging and blasting are not the main purposes of the railway system; the main reason for railways is the movement of goods and people across territories. Although the term infrastructure has changed meaning since it was first used by French engineers in the nineteenth century (it is now a much more comprehensive term), some version of the infrastructure concept is necessary whenever we divide up the world into primary and secondary activities, which we view as interconnected, but where we want to distinguish functions and purposes across layers or nodes in a system.

Infrastructure in its original sense links together public and private networks into an engineering framework in which the state is responsible for doing the ground-clearing work that allows for economic development. Infrastructure's beginnings suggest another larger point that this book will explore: modern capitalism has always involved an entangled network of public and private actors subsidized and regulated by the state. The concept of infrastructure suggests a financialized public–private network that entails governance across space and requires legal and political regulation, as well as public subsidy, to support economic development. As I will argue throughout the book, the categories of "public" and "private," however difficult to define precisely, are central to how we frame politics through infrastructure across the *longue durée* of American history.

Infrastructure, or its cognate concepts such as public utilities or public goods, divide up the world into market and non-market activities across the space of the "economic," implicitly assigning responsibility to state and non-state actors (such as corporations) in ways that generate political contestation around republican governance and the public good; interest group dynamics; land rights; struggles over resources and ecological challenges; competing legal rationales; the division between public and private; and a host of other political issues. These larger

[9] *Id.* at 27.
[10] Rankin, *Infrastructure and the International Governance of Economic Development*, *supra* note 5, at 62: "Infrastructure involves a separation of human activity into two categories: the supportive and the supported. The boundaries of infrastructure are thus defined in terms of a vertical, gravitational metaphor: infrastructure is fundamental, basic, foundational, and it is as necessary for its superstructure as a solid foundation is for a building. Karl Marx used a similar metaphor for describing society in general, where an economic base determines the nature of the cultural-political superstructure. The modern category of infrastructure, however, is more complex than this, as it blurs the distinction between physical and metaphorical support. The support provided by railroads and hydroelectric plants is undoubtedly metaphorical, yet immaterial infrastructures (such as standards) seem in turn to refer, metaphorically, to the physicality of steel and concrete."

questions cannot be solved in the final instance by appealing solely to narrow economic rationales. How we parse out what are primary and secondary, private and public, plays an important role in mapping the relationships between state and market and to imagining political possibilities in the present.

Infrastructure in policy discourse has been even more malleable than its use in technical economics, where it appears as "social overhead capital" or related terms. If you are a national security bureaucrat, for example, "critical infrastructure" might encompass structures that stretch across much of the American economy, which would certainly fall outside of a narrow understanding of "public works infrastructure."[11] For national security purposes, if perhaps not at other times, infrastructure is critical when its vulnerability to attack highlights the dependency of the entire national polity on interconnected systems of production and circulation. Moreover, infrastructure can include both physical and nonphysical assets – where "assets" can even be defined as techniques of management.

As an example, consider the comprehensiveness of the following definition from the National Research Council's *Infrastructure for the 21st Century: Framework for a Research Agenda* (1987):

> In this report, the term "public works infrastructure" includes both specific functional nodes – highways, streets, roads, and bridges; mass transit; airports and airways; water supply and water resources; wastewater management; solid-waste treatment and disposal; electric power generation and transmission; telecommunications; and hazardous waste management – and the combined system these modal elements comprise. A comprehension of infrastructure spans not only these public works facilities, but also the operating procedures, management practices, and development policies that interact together with societal demand and the physical world to facilitate the transport of people and goods, provision of water for drinking and a variety of other uses, safe disposal of society's waste products, provision of energy where it is needed, and transmission of information within and between communities.[12]

"Public works facilities" fits squarely within anyone's definition of "infrastructure." "Facilitate" shows us that infrastructure provides the supporting structures that we generally take for granted in modern societies (e.g., transportation, water provision, waste disposal, energy, and information transmission). However, "operating procedures, management practices, and development policies" shifts the frame away from

---

[11] "There are 16 critical infrastructure sectors whose assets, systems, and networks, whether physical or virtual, are considered so vital to the United States that their incapacitation or destruction would have a debilitating effect on security, national economic security, national public health or safety, or any combination thereof." CYBERSECURITY & INFRASTRUCTURE SECURITY AGENCY, CRITICAL INFRASTRUCTURE SECTORS, www.cisa.gov/critical-infrastructure-sectors; *see also* JOHN MOTEFF ET AL., CRITICAL INFRASTRUCTURES: WHAT MAKES AN INFRASTRUCTURE CRITICAL? (Report for Congress RL31556, Congressional Research Service, Aug. 30, 2002), https://digital.library.unt.edu/ark:/67531/metacrs3176/.

[12] NATIONAL RESEARCH COUNCIL, INFRASTRUCTURE FOR THE 21st CENTURY: FRAMEWORK FOR A RESEARCH AGENDA 4 n.1 (1987).

objects to *policies* and *governance rationales* that define an important aspect of the infrastructure idea. In the simplest sense, governance rationales can mean the justifications that are offered in favor of public investment in infrastructure. Frequently these have included military preparedness, commercial and residential development, nation-building, and economic competitiveness.[13] In more recent years, those governance rationales have expanded to include a host of other concerns such as sustainability, equity, and resilience in human-designed systems.[14]

Infrastructure is also a frequent theme in politics, as has been the case in America since the debates around "internal improvements" in the nineteenth century (a subject taken up in Chapter 2). Infrastructure stages long-standing American debates regarding the scope of federal power under the Constitution; the power of financial markets to control public resources; the role of government in providing public services; and the role of private interests and the corporation in developing and maintaining the basic infrastructure of society, among many others. Initially, we can identify two familiar patterns. On the one hand, many have worried about "boondoggles" that waste taxpayer money on large projects perhaps better left to the private sector, if they are needed at all. Since infrastructure investment inevitably involves channeling public money into private hands, it is always open to charges that it is really just "corporate welfare," which is a critique with a long vintage in U.S. history.[15] Concerns about the fiscal imprint of infrastructure harken back to fears of out-of-control government debt that have shaped the republican imaginary since the eighteenth century. Such fears, for example, were an important aspect of Adam Smith's views on public works (discussed in Chapter 1) and continue to be an important theme in American politics. We hear echoes of this today in calls to outsource government functions to the private sector, or arguments in favor of more public–private partnerships to reduce the fiscal footprint, public bureaucracy, or labor costs for infrastructure (discussed in the Conclusion).

---

[13] "The argument is straightforward: projects that will contribute substantially to political and economic stability or military preparedness must override narrow, self-interested concerns of individual localities. In the public works field, political and military claims have historically been crucial in legitimating government action. The French national government saw fit to subsidize Haussmann's reconstruction central Paris primarily because of such considerations, and public works spending has since been linked with governmental concern over unemployment-caused political instability." Sy Adler, *Infrastructure Politics: The Dynamics of Crossing San Francisco Bay*, 10 PUB. HISTORIAN 19, 21 (1988).

[14] See, for example, ORG. FOR ECON. CO-OP. & DEV., OECD RECOMMENDATION ON THE GOVERNANCE OF INFRASTRUCTURES (OECD/LEGAL/0460, July 16, 2020), www.oecd.org/gov/infrastructure-governance/recommendation/: "Quality of public governance is essential to achieve national and international commitments on sustainable and inclusive economic growth, and to ensure equal opportunities and access to services for citizens. In particular, Infrastructure investment and delivery are important tools for the economic and social recovery efforts from the COVID-19 crisis. Infrastructure governance will be crucial to ensure that public investments contribute to a sustainable rebound while strengthening infrastructure resilience, in particular for challenges such as climate change and inclusive growth."

[15] For recent attacks along these lines, see David Blackmon, *Infrastructure Bill Implements Green New Deal Via Corporate Welfare*, FORBES (Aug. 10, 2021), www.forbes.com/sites/davidblackmon/2021/08/10/infrastructure-bill-implements-green-new-deal-via-corporate-welfare/?sh=6f9c2f63ebd0.

On the other hand, infrastructure is attractive for Progressives who want to revive the idea of the public good in an era dominated by neoliberal politics. Today you are likely to find a Progressive vision tied to a sense that the federal government should be doing more to invest in the American future. In fact, infrastructure can be synonymous with "the public good," "the commons," or simply "crucial objects worthy of government investment," for those arguing against the reduction of all political values to market values. This is typically coupled with calls to make infrastructural goods more widely available, more just and more sustainable:

> There is a long overdue need for major new federal investments in infrastructure – but increasing federal spending alone is not enough. To ensure the benefits of federal investments are shared broadly, an infrastructure bill should include policies designed to protect labor rights; fight workplace discrimination; set high standards for wages and benefits; and support high-quality training and apprenticeships. Additionally, federal funds should be targeted to those communities facing the greatest need as well as redress the unequal burden of pollution and geographic isolation that neglectful and discriminatory investment policies and projects cause.[16]

The need for more federal investment has been a common theme since the 1980s, when the philosophy of public investment turned in a more conservative direction. Tying infrastructure into other policy questions (labor rights, discrimination, ecological concerns, etc.) can be traced back to the 1970s, when liberals began to turn against the New Deal state on a number of grounds, such as its corporatism; its bad record on environmental, labor, gender, and racial issues; its support for the military–industrial complex; and so on. When Progressives talk about infrastructure today, however, they nevertheless turn to the past for inspiration, speaking in terms of a "Green New Deal" that would enact programmatic investment in American society.[17]

You will also find many noting the difference between physical and human infrastructures, a distinction with roots in development economics beginning in

---

[16] Kevin DeGood, et al., *Building Progressive Infrastructure: How Infrastructure Investments Can Create Jobs, Strengthen Communities, and Tackle the Climate Crisis*, CENTER FOR AMERICAN PROGRESS (Jan. 31, 2019), www.americanprogress.org/article/building-progressive-infrastructure/ (2019).

[17] For the range of issues that get bundled together under the rubric of "infrastructure" in contemporary politics, *see*, for example, WHITE HOUSE, FACT SHEET: THE BIPARTISAN INFRASTRUCTURE DEAL (Nov. 6, 2021), www.whitehouse.gov/briefing-room/statements-releases/2021/11/06/fact-sheet-the-bipartisan-infrastructure-deal/ ("This Bipartisan Infrastructure Deal will rebuild America's roads, bridges and rails, expand access to clean drinking water, ensure every American has access to high-speed internet, tackle the climate crisis, advance environmental justice, and invest in communities that have too often been left behind. The legislation will help ease inflationary pressures and strengthen supply chains by making long overdue improvements for our nation's ports, airports, rail, and roads. It will drive the creation of good-paying union jobs and grow the economy sustainably and equitably so that everyone gets ahead for decades to come."); *see also* HOUSE COMMITTEE ON THE BUDGET, STRONG INFRASTRUCTURE AND A HEALTHY ECONOMY REQUIRE A FEDERAL INVESTMENT, Oct. 29, 2019, https://budget.house.gov/sites/democrats.budget.house.gov/files/documents/Infrastructure%20and%20the%20Economy%20-%20Post-Hearing%20Report%20-%20FINAL.pdf.

the 1950s, when the term "infrastructure" first began to be widely used by planners and high-level politicians and bureaucrats.[18] During the debates around President Biden's infrastructure package in the fall of 2021, for example, Senator Bernie Sanders tweeted out his support for the bill in these terms: "Rebuilding our crumbling physical infrastructure – roads, bridges, water systems – is important. Rebuilding our crumbling human infrastructure – health care, education, climate change – is more important. No infrastructure bill without the $3.5 trillion reconciliation bill."[19] In another tweet, Sanders answered the question "[w]hat is infrastructure in this country" with a bullet point list: "roads, bridges, our energy grid, broadband, childcare, dental, vision, & hearing care for the elderly." He concluded: "Now is the time to begin addressing our physical infrastructure as well as our human infrastructure. Let's get it done."[20]

There is also a sense of urgency in contemporary infrastructure politics. Consider the modern phrase "our crumbling infrastructure," which appears frequently in media reports, white papers, and political discourse and has been in use at least since the 1980s.[21] There are several senses in which we can understand this phrase. First, in the literal sense, crumbling infrastructure comes to our attention in myriad ways in everyday life: blackouts caused by aging power systems and stressed power grids; transportation delays due to inadequate public transport or road construction, etc. Frequent reports since the 1980s have highlighted the physical decay of infrastructures: "The United States now has more than four million miles of roads and bridges,

---

[18] For recent examples, see, for example, Elizabeth Carr-Hurst, *Human Capital Infrastructure Is Essential to Addressing Our Nation's Physical Infrastructure*, NATIONAL LEAGUE OF CITIES, www.nlc.org/article/2021/04/27/human-capital-infrastructure-is-essential-to-addressing-our-nations-physical-infrastructure/ (last visited Jul. 9, 2022); *see also* The World Bank's Human Capital Project, www.worldbank.org/en/publication/human-capital (last visited Jul. 9, 2022).

[19] Bernie Sanders (@SenSanders), TWITTER (Sept, 2, 2021, 7:28 PM), https://twitter.com/sensanders/status/1433572638014640128?lang=en.

For some scholarly uses of human infrastructure see, AbdouMaliq Simone, *People as Infrastructure: Intersecting Fragments in Johannesburg*, 16 PUB. CULTURE 407, 407–29 (2004); Gabriel Rosenberg, *Youth as Infrastructure: 4-H and the Intimate State in the 1920s Rural United States*, *in* BOUNDARIES OF THE STATE IN US HISTORY (James T. Sparrow et al., eds., 2013).

[20] Bernie Sanders (@SenSanders), TWITTER (Apr. 6, 2021, 11:00 AM), https://twitter.com/berniesanders/status/1379448812146679809.

[21] *See*, for example, WHITE HOUSE, FACT SHEET: THE BIPARTISAN INFRASTRUCTURE DEAL, *supra* note 17 ("For far too long, Washington policymakers have celebrated 'infrastructure week' without ever agreeing to build infrastructure. The President promised to work across the aisle to deliver results and rebuild our crumbling infrastructure"); Aaron Klein, *Time to Fix Our Crumbling Infrastructure*, BROOKINGS (Oct. 6, 2016), www.brookings.edu/research/time-to-fix-our-crumbling-infrastructure/; Daniel Speer, *Our Crumbling Infrastructure Is Failing Small Businesses*, U.S. CHAMBER OF COMMERCE (Oct. 18, 2019), www.uschamber.com/infrastructure/transportation/our-crumbling-infrastructure-failing-small-businesses; Joan C. Szabo, *Our Crumbling Infrastructure*, NATION'S BUS. 16, 16–24 (Aug. 1989). The sense of urgency has been the source of some frustration for libertarians. *See*, for example, David Harsanyi, *Our Infrastructure Is Not "Crumbling." Repeat: Our Infrastructure Is Not "Crumbling*," REASON MAGAZINE, Feb. 9, 2018, at https://reason.com/2018/02/09/our-infrastructure-is-not-crumbling-repe/.

much of which was built for an earlier time, is now in poor repair, and continues to become more and more congested."[22] The fragility of infrastructure is also brought painfully to public awareness in moments of catastrophic failure: when bridges collapse, levees break, water systems fail, and dams crumble, we are made aware that the structures and systems we depend on are much more precarious than we imagine.[23]

But I want to suggest that this phrase also has a great deal of force in modern politics because of its metaphorical resonance. Infrastructure can act as a powerful symbol of the collective social life that infrastructure literally makes possible. The infrastructure is "ours" in the popular phrase because it is imagined as the shared property of a political community. When infrastructure crumbles, it is not just the brute physical stuff like cement and asphalt that we worry about (although it is that too). Rather, it is the nation itself that is at risk of collapsing through a failure of political will and imagination. Everyday infrastructure discourse in our times reflects a widely shared sense of national decline that many attribute to a failure of government to live up the mid-century promise of New Deal social investment.[24] Infrastructure rhetoric fuses the economic and the ideological into a vision of vitality and national renewal, tapping into the postwar politics of growth to imagine a prosperous collective future.[25]

Infrastructure has long worked as a meditation on the national interest. Published for the bicentennial, for example, the *History of Public Works in the United States* (1976) nicely illustrates the view of infrastructure as a national patrimony: "The vast network of public works facilities which extends from coast to coast provides the life-support systems for the most productive nation in the world. Two-hundred years after its founding, the United States stands second to no other country in terms of wealth and power – characteristics which are both liked and disliked abroad. Each, however, is generally considered essential for protecting the interests of Americans, increasing their standard of living, and assisting the people of other nations in obtaining a better way of life."[26] For the American liberal imaginary, infrastructure

---

[22] Henry Pestroski, The Road Taken: The History and Future of America's Infrastructure 9 (2016); Loren Thompson, *How a Decaying Surface Transport System Is Endangering U.S. Security and Economic Strength*, Forbes (Nov. 4, 2017), www.forbes.com/sites/lorenthompson/2017/11/14/how-a-decaying-surface-transport-system-is-endangering-u-s-security-and-economic-strength/?sh=71629403b3c4.

[23] Eric Klinenberg, Palaces for the People: How Social Infrastructure Can Help Fight Inequality, Polarization, and the Decline of Civic Life 14 (2018); *see also* American Society of Civil Engineers, Infrastructure Report Card, https://infrastructurereportcard.org/making-the-grade/ ("Our nation is at a crossroads. Deteriorating U.S. infrastructure is impeding our ability to compete in the global economy, and improvements are necessary to ensure our country is built for the future").

[24] Matt Blitz, *When America's Infrastructure Saved Democracy*, Popular Mechanics (Jan. 23, 2017), www.popularmechanics.com/technology/infrastructure/a24692/fdr-new-deal-wpa-infrastructure/.

[25] Robert M. Collins, More: The Politics of Growth in Postwar America (2000).

[26] American Public Works Association, History of Public Works in the United States, 1776–1976, 6 (1976).

is a tangible example of government-led nation-building that stands in for a politics of the public good. Infrastructure offers widely credible evidence of the need for Government action in a time of market dominance, and acts as a metaphor for the social or the collective in an era of market-centered neoliberalism. For many today seeking to revive social democracy, infrastructure is the ultimate word to conjure with.

Along these lines, some have connected infrastructure to a normative vision of American democracy. Infrastructure used in this way is often credited to a speech by Ronald Reagan to the British Parliament on June 8, 1982: "The objective I propose is quite simple to state: to foster the infrastructure of democracy – the system of a free press, unions, political parties, universities – which allows a people to choose their own way, to develop their own culture, to reconcile their own differences through peaceful means."[27] Reagan is using the term in one of the senses that it acquired during the Cold War, to mean civil society and the institutions of liberal democracy. The phrase has long since migrated into general usage to the point where it is now a commonplace. In their defense of President Biden's infrastructure package, for example, Christopher Jones & David Reinecke make the connection explicit between a normative vision of American democracy and infrastructure: "To be a full-fledged citizen able to achieve the American Dream," they write, "requires access to infrastructure."[28]

Others have lent their support to Biden's infrastructure bill by appealing to the infrastructure-American democracy link:

> With a once-in-a-generation investment in infrastructure just passed by Congress and awaiting the president's signature, we have a unique opportunity to ensure these dollars are spent in a participatory and inclusive capacity, bringing Americans together across differences to revitalize the practice of democracy. In addition to our roads, tunnels, and bridges, we can allocate these dollars through channels that also strengthen our civic infrastructure. Ultimately, the goal is to use federal infrastructure dollars in ways that also support our democracy.[29]

When used in this way, it is clear that we are a long way from the roads, bridges, and subways we need to for our daily commute. We are closer to a sense of imagined community, a civic culture of democracy materialized through massive federal investment.[30] After news reports publicized the billions of dollars the American

---

[27] Ronald Reagan, U.S. President, Address to Members of the British Parliament (June 8, 2022), archived at Ronald Reagan Presidential Library & Museum, www.reaganlibrary.gov/archives/speech/address-members-british-parliament.

[28] Christopher Jones & David Reinecke, *Infrastructure and Democracy*, 33 ISSUES SCI. & TECH. (2017), https://issues.org/infrastructure-and-democracy/.

[29] Hollie Russon Gilman, et al., *Use Infrastructure Dollars to Support Our Democracy*, THE HILL (Nov. 8, 2021), www.amacad.org/news/use-infrastructure-dollars-support-our-democracy.

[30] BENEDICT ANDERSON, IMAGINED COMMUNITIES: REFLECTIONS ON THE ORIGINS AND SPREAD OF NATIONALISM (2016); Gilman et al. *Use Infrastructure Dollars, supra* note 29 ("In addition to our roads, tunnels, and bridges, we can allocate these dollars through channels that also strengthen our civic infrastructure. Ultimately, the goal is to use federal infrastructure dollars in ways that also support our

government was spending on rebuilding Iraq and Afghanistan, many Americans responded with a call for "nation building at home" through infrastructure investment.[31] It is clear, then, that we speak of infrastructure in both ideological and practical senses. Infrastructure is not just limited to physical things that move people and goods from point A to point B. It invokes normative commitments to governing in the public good and a vision of investment in the nation. Moreover, infrastructures call upon us to resolve thorny questions that have been central themes in American political history: the proper role of government; federalism; the role of the corporations as a government actor doing public work; histories of racial exclusion inscribed into the material infrastructures of modern life; the possibility for corrupt collusion between public and private sectors; and public attitudes toward taxes, debts, deficits, etc.

In our times there is another reason that infrastructure widely resonates: the privatization of infrastructure has become a major public issue since the Reagan years.[32] "Privatization" can mean different things in different contexts. In some parts of the

democracy"); Derrick Johnson, *American Democracy's Infrastructure Is Crumbling*, CNN OPINION (Aug. 2, 2021), www.cnn.com/2021/08/02/opinions/voting-rights-crumbling-american-infrastructure-johnson/index.html; Jill Blair & Malka Kopell, *Twenty-First Century Civic Infrastructure: Under Construction*, THE ASPEN INSTITUTE (Spring 2015), https://aspencommunitysolutions.org/wp-content/uploads/2013/06/21st-Century-Report-FINAL-NoBlanks.pdf.

[31] *See*, for example, President Barack Obama, Remarks by the President on the Way Forward in Afghanistan (June 22, 2011), https://obamawhitehouse.archives.gov/the-press-office/2011/06/22/remarks-president-way-forward-Afghanistan ("Over the last decade, we have spent a trillion dollars on war, at a time of rising debt and hard economic times. Now, we must invest in America's greatest resource –our people... We must rebuild our infrastructure and find new and clean sources of energy ... America, it is time to focus on nation building here at home"); *see also* Lawrence J. Korb & Alex Rothman, *Nation Building at Home*, CENTER FOR AMERICAN PROGRESS (Sept. 26, 2011), www.americanprogress.org/article/nation-building-at-home/; see also Stephen M. Walt, *Nation Building at Home: Why We Need Roads, Bridges, and Boring Stuff Like That*, FOREIGN POLICY (Nov. 27, 2012), https://foreignpolicy.com/2012/11/27/nation-building-at-home-why-we-need-roads-bridges-and-boring-stuff-like-that/ ("So here's a basic strategic principle that we've largely forgotten over the past seventy years, but which would serve us well today: Let's first make sure our leaders have done all we can to improve the lives of Americans – you know, the citizens who work and pay taxes to support the government – before they take on various international projects whose primary purpose is to benefit someone else"); Keith Magee, *It's Time for America to Do Some "Nation Building" at Home*, CNN OPINION (Sept. 7, 2021), www.cnn.com/2021/09/07/opinions/america-needs-to-nation-build-at-home-magee/index.html.

[32] Witold J. Henisz, et al., *The Worldwide Diffusion of Market-Oriented Infrastructure Reform, 1977–1999*, 70 AM. SOCIO. REV. 871, 871–97 (2005). Privatization has been extensively debated since the 1980s. *See*, for example, John B. Goodman & Gary W. Loveman, *Does Privatization Serve the Public Interest?*, 69 HARV. BUS. REV. 26–28, 32, 34–36 (1991); *see also* GOVERNMENT BY CONTRACT: OUTSOURCING AND AMERICAN DEMOCRACY (Jody Freeman & Martha Minow, eds., 2009); Chiara Cordelli, THE PRIVATIZED STATE 23–44 (2020); PRIVATISING DEVELOPMENT: TRANSNATIONAL LAW, INFRASTRUCTURE, AND HUMAN RIGHTS (Michael Likosky ed. 2005); THE CAMBRIDGE HANDBOOK OF PRIVATIZATION (Avihay Dorfman & Alon Harel, eds., 2021); ALON HAREL, WHY LAW MATTERS (2014); Craig Anthony Arnold, *Privatization of Public Water Services: The States' Role in Ensuring Public Accountability*, 32 PEPP. L. REV. 561, 561–604 (2005); Alex Kozinski & Andrew Bentz, *Privatization and Its Discontents*, 63 EMORY L. J. 263, 263–82 (2013); Chris Sagers, *The Myth of "Privatization,"* 59 ADMIN. L. REV. 37, 37–78 (2007).

world (e.g., Europe and Latin America), it might mean selling off large state-owned enterprises to the private sector. The United States, on the other hand, does not have large state-owned enterprises, so the debate has centered on outsourcing government services to the private sector, "government by contract," and now most recently, state and municipal privatization efforts. Many have written about privatization in the context of market-based governance under what has come to be called neoliberalism.[33] National and local media have reported widely on this phenomenon, often expressing concerns about the loss of control over public infrastructures, possibilities for corruption, accountability, and other risks in leasing or selling public assets to the private sector.[34] Defenders of privatization point to the potential for cost savings, efficiency, flexibility, and historical pedigree of public–private cooperation.

Once "infrastructure," rather than say "public works," becomes the nomenclature, it becomes a technocratic issue of sound management and loses its connection to government. The "public–private partnership" terminology, for example, frames infrastructure as a problem to be solved across the government–corporate divide. From this perspective, there are not compelling reasons why infrastructures should be controlled directly by public agencies. In fact, there may be good reasons to move infrastructures off government balance sheets, where they can appear as liabilities, whereas a public–private lease arrangement, for example, can at least in the short term appear as an asset. Privatization and infrastructure are also a natural conceptual pairing because public infrastructures are today the logical object for the global privatization industry: They are often massive structures built during the heyday of direct public expenditures in the mid-century infrastructure boom, now often undercapitalized because of the fiscal revolution in the 1970s. In other words, much of what is "public" and in need of private capital can also be categorized as infrastructure.

The pushback against privatization and arguments for more government investment in infrastructure is founded on a specific historical vision of the twentieth-century welfare state as an embodiment of democracy and the rule of law. Jon D. Michael's *Constitutional Coup: Privatization's Threat to the American Republic*, for example, lays out the case for privatization's pivotal connection to public–interest liberalism and democracy:

> [This] book takes us back in time to explore the project of twentieth-century administrative governance as a normatively and constitutionally virtuous one. It describes the almost evangelical denunciation of that project, as evidenced by what

---

[33] *See*, for example, THE NEOLIBERAL DELUGE: HURRICANE KATRINA, LATE CAPITALISM, AND THE REMAKING OF NEW ORLEANS (Cedric Johnson, ed. 2011).

[34] *See*, for example, Seymour Melman, *Looting the Means of Production*, N.Y. TIMES, op-ed page (July 26, 1981), www.nytimes.com/1981/07/26/opinion/looting-the-means-of-production.html; Emily Thornton, *Roads to Riches: Why Investors Are Clamoring to Take Over America's Highways, Bridges, and Airports – And Why the Public Should Be Nervous*, BUSINESSWEEK (May 7, 2007), www.nbcnews.com/id/wbna18396534; Jenny Anderson, *Cities Debate Privatizing Public Infrastructure*, N.Y. TIMES (Aug. 26, 2008), www.nytimes.com/2008/08/27/business/27fund.html.

is now a multigenerational campaign to refashion public governance in the image of a Fortune 500 company, if not now something straight out of the new gig economy. And it explains how dangerous, distorting, and destructive this campaign has been—and why the operational challenges and democratic imperatives of the twenty-first century compel us to redeem that original, and long beleaguered, administrative project.[35]

While this view has much to commend it and many defenders today, the purpose of this book is different: not so much to critique privatization or defend public infrastructure, which has so ably been undertaken elsewhere, as an attempt to bring infrastructural history in the United States into clearer focus. Privatization is of our moment, to be sure, but it also reflects long-standing entanglements of public and private in government, economy, and law throughout American history. This book will suggest that our framing of the world into state and market, public and private, is foundational to liberal politics and economics in ways that have been open to contestation, redefinition, and debate.

However malleable a term, I argue that some version of infrastructure, whether called "internal improvements," "public works," "public utilities," or something else, has been central for liberal development models based on political commitment to economic growth anchored in state governance, investment, and regulation. Arguments about who builds, owns, and controls infrastructure, and what its purposes are, also implicate debates about the meaning of democracy within liberal capitalist modernity. The terminologies at play may be different, but they all suggest a common thread: infrastructure troubles liberalism's categories of public and private because it links the two domains together in a literal sense – governments are often involved on a massive scale in subsidizing corporate ventures – but also along the dimensions of law and ideology, because the categories of public and private, while hardwired into modern liberal capitalism, are nevertheless fluid and permeable. Infrastructure demonstrates the stubbornly political nature of economic life while also complicating models that imagine self-sustaining market systems.

II INFRASTRUCTURE STUDIES

Scholars across academic disciplines have made infrastructure an object of study since the 1990s.[36] Since it is a key concept for nation-building and what we now call economic development, infrastructure can also be a way of understanding the material embodiment of state governance and Enlightenment rationality, which have been both celebrated and contested throughout modern history. Infrastructures

---

[35] JON D. MICHAELS, CONSTITUTIONAL COUP: PRIVATIZATION'S THREAT TO THE AMERICAN REPUBLIC 4 (2017).
[36] See, for example, INFRASTRUCTURES AND SOCIAL COMPLEXITY: A COMPANION (Penn Harvey et al., eds., 2017).

allow the state to tally up, codify, and exploit the resources within its territories (and beyond) for the purposes of the resource extraction at the heart of developmental governance.[37] Along these lines, Foucauldian approaches emphasize the disciplinary "biopower" that infrastructure represents in the modern world, which means at a minimum control over territories and populations. Some have explained how the police power (discussed in Chapter 1 and elsewhere) was the pivotal legal technology that allowed states to modernize transportation and communication networks.[38] Infrastructure in the critical tradition is a technology of power that permeates the governance of everyday life in modern societies. Others point to the resonances of infrastructure with Marxian concepts of base/superstructure.[39]

With the return to the state in political theory in the 1980s, scholars began to explore state structures as semiautonomous forces in their own right.[40] Michael Mann's essay "The Autonomous Power of the State: Its Origins, Mechanisms, and Results" explored the extensive reach of modern states through their pervasive "infrastructural power," which he compares to the much more limited "despotic power" of pre-modern states. The pre-modern state, he argues, had strong despotic powers but relatively narrow reach. Modern liberal democracies, on the other hand, operate through law, institutions, and bureaucracies that in theory at least are less despotic but enjoy a much more pervasive power apparatus. For Mann, public and private networks embody the deeper reach of the state apparatus in the modern world and civil society groups and other non-state entities multiply the reach of the state through indirect mechanisms based on the model of a dispersed network, which he calls "infrastructure." So for Mann, the category "infrastructure" would include literacy, money, weights and measures, transportation networks, etc., which store power in a dispersed network, creating capacities available for use by the state.[41] Moreover, "[i]nfrastructural techniques diffuse outwards from the particular power organizations that invented them."[42] Thus states might appropriate technologies developed elsewhere and conversely might lose

---

[37] *See*, for example, JAMES C. SCOTT, SEEING LIKE A STATE: HOW CERTAIN SCHEMES TO IMPROVE THE HUMAN CONDITION HAVE FAILED (1998). While I do not necessarily share Scott's viewpoint, his analysis nevertheless provides valuable insights into how states operate as they tally up and liquidate resources toward the ends of modern governance.

[38] Pasquale Pasquino, *Theatrum Politicum: The Genealogy of Capital – Police and the State of Prosperity*, in THE FOUCAULT EFFECT: STUDIES IN GOVERNMENTALITY 105–19 (Graham Burchell et al., eds., 1991).

[39] *See* CHRISTOPHER BREU's recent overview of infrastructure as a concept within the critical tradition in *Biopolitics and/as Infrastructure*, in BIOTHEORY: LIFE AND DEATH UNDER CAPITALISM 119, 119–35 (Jeffrey R. Di Leo & Peter Hitchcok, eds., 2020).

[40] See, for example, BRINGING THE STATE BACK IN (Peter B. Evans et al., eds., 1985); *see also* THEDA SKOCPOL, PROTECTING SOLDIERS AND MOTHERS: THE POLITICAL ORIGINS OF SOCIAL POLICY IN THE UNITED STATES (1992).

[41] Michael Mann, *The Autonomous Power of the State: Its Origins, Mechanisms and Results*, 25 EUR. J. SOC. 185 (1984).

[42] *Id.* 41, at 194.

control of infrastructural technologies as they diffuse through the broader society, sometimes directly subverting state power. Likewise, historians have turned to infrastructure to explain the elaboration of infrastructural power through transportation networks, power grids, and other technologies.[43] New histories of capitalism and globalization have also contributed to our understanding of infrastructure's political economy, suggesting its larger logistical purpose: "Global trade depends on cheap and efficient transportation, which, in turn, requires networks of canals, roads, airports, pipelines, railroads, dredged rivers, harbors, ports, and telecommunications facilities."[44]

Some have argued for the importance of infrastructures as a neglected aspect of modern politics, perhaps suggesting the value of infrastructure as an organizing theme for a constructive program. One of the problems of an infrastructural politics is that functioning systems are often taken for granted in the modern Western world. Of course, it is a remarkable achievement of modern infrastructural states that over time their ordinary functioning can fall into the background of everyday life. Nevertheless, one of the challenges when arguing for more investment is that infrastructure is one of the many quotidian features of modern life simply too boring to think about in a sustained way. As Susan Leigh wrote in the late 1990s, however, attentiveness to infrastructure is "a call to study boring things," the "unstudied" material, and informational structures that shape modern life.[45] As she notes, by studying such things we bring to light the hidden codes that inform important distributional questions: "Study a city and neglect its sewers and power supplies (as many have), and you miss essential aspects of distributional justice and planning power.... Study an information system and neglect its standards, wires, and settings, and you miss equally essential aspects of aesthetics, justice and change."[46] In a similar vein, cultural critic Bruce Robbins suggests that infrastructure has often been culturally invisible precisely because it is taken for granted, as in the case of public utilities infrastructure:

> Public utilities drop off the radar because they seem to constitute a minimum threshold, an earth-bound zone in which the large irresolutions of politics can for once be ignored and decisions safely left to the technocrats. Indeed, public utilities are often figures for a desired political minimalism, as in [Ezra] Pound: "Some one ought to be employed to look after our traffic and sewage, one grants that. But a superintendence of traffic and sewage is not the sole function of man. Certain stupid and honest people should, doubtless be delegated for the purpose. There politics ends [for] the enlightened man." Yet there has never been a moment when

---

[43] See, for example, JO GULDI, ROADS TO POWER: BRITAIN INVENTS THE INFRASTRUCTURE STATE (2012).

[44] ASHLEY CARSE, BEYOND THE BIG DITCH: POLITICS, ECOLOGY, AND INFRASTRUCTURE AT THE PANAMA CANAL (2014), preface.

[45] Susan Leigh Star, *The Ethnography of Infrastructure*, 43 AM. BEHAV. SCI. 377, 377–91 (1999).

[46] *Id.* 45, at 379.

everyone possessed such public goods as access to clean water and efficient sewers. These are, as they have been, objects of political struggle.[47]

The contempt that Ezra Pound expresses toward infrastructure invites the rejoinder that infrastructure is not something we can actually take for granted. Not only is access to infrastructure not distributed equitably, but even if it were, interconnected technologies also multiply risks across infrastructures in ways that highlight collective dependencies and vulnerabilities.[48] Or as the American Publics Works Association puts it: "There is a general tendency to take public works facilities and services for granted, not realizing how much people are actually dependent upon such systems…"[49]

Modern infrastructure can inspire faith in modernity and progress, with all of the normative baggage those ideas carry with them: "The provision of infrastructures is so intimately caught up with the sense of shaping modern society and realizing the future … [that] possession of electricity, railways, and running water came to define civilization itself."[50] Likewise, Brian Larkin describes the "political address" of infrastructure as an important facet of

> the way technologies come to represent the possibility of being modern, of having a future, or the foreclosing of that possibility and a resulting experience of abjection. In this view, roads and railways are not just technical objects then but also operate on the level of fantasy and desire. They encode the dreams of individuals and societies and are the vehicles whereby those fantasies are transmitted and made emotionally real. Infrastructures are the means by which a state proffers these representations to its citizens and asks them to take those representations as social facts.[51]

---

[47] Bruce Robbins, *The Smell of Infrastructure: Notes toward an Archive*, 34 BOUNDARY 25, 31 (2007). For literary scholarship on "infrastructuralism" see, for example, THE PROMISE OF INFRASTRUCTURE (Nikhil Anand et al., eds., 2018); John Durham Peters, *Infrastructuralism: Media as Traffic between Nature and Culture*, in TRAFFIC: MEDIA AS INFRASTRUCTURES AND CULTURAL PRACTICES 31–49 (Marion Näser-Lather & Christoph Neubert, eds., 2015); Michael Rubenstein, *Infrastructuralism: An Introduction*, 61 MOD. FICTION STUD. (2015); Michael Rubenstein, PUBLIC WORKS: INFRASTRUCTURE, IRISH MODERNISM, AND THE POSTCOLONIAL (2010); Patricia Yaeger, *Dreaming of Infrastructure*, 122 MOD. L. ASS'N 9, 9–26 (2007); Julia Elyachar, *Next Practices: Knowledge, Infrastructure, and Public Goods at the Bottom of the Pyramid*, 24 PUB. CULTURE 109, 109–29 (2012); Marshall Sahlins, *Infrastructuralism*, 36 CRIT. INQ. 371, 371–85 (2010).

[48] For example, STEPHEN GRAHAM, DISRUPTED CITIES: WHEN INFRASTRUCTURE FAILS (Stephen Graham ed. 2010) focuses our attention on how disaster risks are managed, or mismanaged, by fragile and networked infrastructures. KELLER EASTERLING'S EXTRASTATECRAFT: THE POWER OF INFRASTRUCTURE SPACE (2014) is concerned with the public–private networks binding together contemporary global capitalism.

[49] AMERICAN PUBLIC WORKS ASSOCIATION, HISTORY OF PUBLIC WORKS, *supra* note 26, at v.

[50] Paul N. Edwards, *Infrastructure and Modernity: Force, Time, and Social Organization in the History of Sociotechnical Systems*, in MODERNITY AND TECHNOLOGY 185–225 (Thomas J. Misa et al., eds., 2003); *see also* GEOFFREY C. BOWKER & SUSAN LEIGH STAR, SORTING THINGS OUT: CLASSIFICATION AND ITS CONSEQUENCES (1999).

[51] Brian Larkin, *The Politics and Poetics of Infrastructure*, 42 ANN. REV. ANTHROPOL. 327, 333 (2013).

But the infrastructural dreams of modern societies always have a dark side, on which scholars have elaborated extensively: they displace vulnerable populations, inflict ecological harm, sweep up massive resources, create corporate power centers, and otherwise expand the repressive capacity of Capital and State. As an embodiment of state power, infrastructure appears as a common theme within modern academic discourses of colonialism, postcolonialism, and empire.[52] The scholarship around the subject figures infrastructure as a tangible representation of the materiality of power in the modern world. Infrastructures are often monumental, ideologically conflicted projects that shape our lives and define the bounds of the political, and not always for the better. Along these lines, scholars emphasize ruins, reparation, resilience, and decay in their accounts of infrastructure.[53]

Privatization and Its Discontents elaborates the ways that infrastructures have been objects of investment, subsidy, and regulation that span the boundaries between public and private. One of the major themes of the book is that, despite national mythologies of a laissez-faire past, American governments at every level have been involved in infrastructure for purposes of commerce, territorial control, and defense, as well as urban and regional development. The approach taken here reveals important implications of infrastructure for American political history and suggests that today's policy problems have deep roots within the modern liberal order. For example, American government has typically built up its infrastructures by using corporations to supply them. This has sometimes seemed like a routine fact of life, but has often been controversial across the political spectrum, attacked by anti-corporate, populist, or socialist critics. Nevertheless, because of its quasi-public nature, the corporation as a legal entity is a perfect emblem for infrastructure in the modern world, because the corporation is itself a hybrid public–private entity that

---

[52] *See*, for example, MICHAEL TRUSCELLO, INFRASTRUCTURAL BRUTALISM: ART AND THE NECROPOLITICS OF INFRASTRUCTURE (2020) for a recent focus on the destructive aspects of infrastructure; *see also* DANIEL R. HEADRICK, THE TOOLS OF EMPIRE: TECHNOLOGY AND EUROPEAN IMPERIALISM IN THE NINETEENTH CENTURY (1981); JULIE GREENE, THE CANAL BUILDERS: MAKING AMERICA'S EMPIRE AT THE PANAMA CANAL (2009); REBECCA TINIO MCKENNA, AMERICAN IMPERIAL PASTORAL: THE ARCHITECTURE OF US COLONIALISM IN THE PHILIPPINES (2017); ERIC RUTKOW, THE LONGEST LINE ON THE MAP: THE UNITED STATES, THE PAN-AMERICAN HIGHWAY, AND THE QUEST TO LINK THE AMERICAS (2019); Aditya Ramesh & Vidhya Raveendranathan, *Infrastructure and Public Works in Colonial India: Towards a Conceptual History*, 18 HIST. COMPASS 1, 1–10 (2020), https://doi.org/10.1111/hic3.12614; Deborah Cowen, *Following the Infrastructures of Empire: Notes on Cities, Settler Colonialism, and Method*, 41 URB. GEOGRAPHY 469, 469–86 (2019); Miriyam Aouragh & Paula Chakravartty, *Infrastructures of Empire: Towards a Critical Geopolitics of Media and Information Studies*, 38 MEDIA, CULTURE SOC'Y. 559, 559–575 (2016); Colin McFarlane, *Governing the Contaminated City: Infrastructure and Sanitation in Colonial and Postcolonial Bombay*, 32 INT'L J. URB. REG'L RSCH. 415, 415–35 (2008); THE PROMISE OF INFRASTRUCTURE (Nikhil Anand et al., eds., 2018).

[53] *See*, for example, CHRISTOPHER R. HENKE & BENJAMIN SIMS, REPAIRING INFRASTRUCTURES: THE MAINTENANCE OF MATERIALITY AND POWER (2020); *see also* Stephanie Wakefield, *Infrastructures of Liberal Life: From Modernity and Progress to Resilience and Ruins*, 12 GEOGR. COMPASS 123, 123–77 (2018), https://doi.org/10.1111/gec3.12377.

has been responsible for much infrastructure development. The book's contribution is to suggest that public–private entanglements mapped by contemporary scholars have a longer pedigree than we typically acknowledge. The pages that follow draw our attention to the genealogy of public and private at the center of infrastructure's complex history in American law and politics.

III STATE, PUBLIC AND PRIVATE

The book's framing of infrastructure through law and development owes much to historians of the American state. There has been much debate about the development of the American state, especially in the nineteenth century. The competing views can roughly be summarized as follows. On the one hand, there are those who argue that the nineteenth-century developmental state was minimal compared both to other industrial societies in the period and to the large American state of the twentieth century.[54] Of particular concern for this book, the small-state story is sometimes coupled with a second one regarding the "laissez-faire" nature of American law and policy, especially before the Civil War. As Kimberly S. Johnson argues in *Governing the American State* (2007): "For many Americans who worry about the size, complexity, or responsiveness of the American government, the nineteenth century is a lost Eden of Jeffersonian agrarian democracy. In this idealized perspective, nineteenth-century American government was limited and orderly, a great machine overseen by a night watchman state and held in check by an active yeoman citizenry."[55] Here is the historian Sidney Fine making a similar point in 1956:

> The doctrine of the negative state was one of singular vitality in that agrarian America which had proclaimed its independence in 1776 ... The result both of American experience and of American conditions, hostility to government action was promoted in the sphere of ideas by the doctrine of natural rights, by the faith of Americans in the self-sufficiency of the individual, and, to a lesser extent, by the teachings of classical political economy. The existence of a 'law of nature' that was superior to man-made law had been vigorously affirmed in seventeenth-century England and had been imported thence to the American colonies.[56]

On this view, individualism, the market, entrepreneurialism, and laissez-faire fuel the rise of capitalism, the American nation, and liberal democracy. This has been an enduring narrative of American development, which took root in the late

---

[54] For an origin story that locates the emergence of the American State after the Civil War, see RICHARD BENSEL, YANKEE LEVIATHAN: THE ORIGINS OF CENTRAL STATE AUTHORITY IN AMERICA, 1859–1877 (1990).
[55] KIMBERLEY S. JOHNSON, GOVERNING THE AMERICAN STATE: CONGRESS AND THE NEW FEDERALISM, 1877–1929 (2007), 1.
[56] SIDNEY FINE, LAISSEZ FAIRE AND THE GENERAL WELFARE STATE: A STUDY OF CONFLICT IN AMERICAN THOUGHT 1865–1901 3 (1956).

nineteenth century, and afterward inspired influential writers to formulate a general account of American liberal culture organized around anti-statist themes.[57] From this point of view, a powerful story about American constitutional development comes into focus, where "[s]tates' rights advocates won the day" and as a result "the nationalist vision was expunged from the American political tradition. In the nineteenth century, 'governance in Washington barely mattered in the lives of ordinary Americans,' and the federal government dwindled to become no more than a laughing matter, the ludicrous spectacle of 'a midget institution in a giant land.'"[58]

Historians have explained how the "market revolution" of the antebellum period ushered in a new age of industrial and financial capitalism that accelerated the decline of republican norms on the path to market society.[59] For example, John Lauritz Larson's *The Market Revolution: Liberty, Ambition, and the Eclipse of the Common Good* (2010) tells the story of the nineteenth century as one of decline from the republican culture of the American revolution toward the laissez-faire of the Gilded Age (and by extension our own). On this view, the failure of early republican aspirations to the general welfare and the common good yield to the crush of interests and disintegrative energies of market capitalism. At the level of political ideology and discourse, nineteenth-century Americans, no less than today, frequently spoke the language of laissez-faire, self-reliance, and the unregulated competition of the marketplace: "Before Charles Darwin even published the theory of evolution that would be perverted into a harsh sociology, the principal tenets of 'social Darwinism' – laissez-faire and the survival of the fittest – could be seen taking root in the economic culture of mid-nineteenth-century America."[60]

The Jacksonian era and the market revolution are an especially important chapter in the story of antebellum laissez-faire. As the story goes, the "Jacksonian Democrats ... canonized the doctrine of laissez-faire" and "made war upon governance itself ... Convinced by ideology that governance was unnecessary, a people empowered by their Revolution to set the agenda and govern themselves on behalf of the common good chose instead to dismantle the state. In the resulting vacuum, America's nineteenth-century entrepreneurs understandably wrote their own rules and imposed order to suit their comfort and convenience."[61] Jackson's attack on the Bank of the United States and the Federalist's state-building legacy lend credence

---

[57] See, for example, LOUIS HARTZ, THE LIBERAL TRADITION IN AMERICA: AN INTERPRETATION OF AMERICAN POLITICAL THOUGHT SINCE THE REVOLUTION (1955).

[58] MAX M. EDLING, A HERCULES IN THE CRADLE: WAR, MONEY, AND THE AMERICAN STATE, 1783–1867 18 (2014).

[59] CHARLES SELLERS, THE MARKET REVOLUTION: JACKSONIAN AMERICA, 1815–1846 (1991).

[60] JOHN LAURITZ LARSON, THE MARKET REVOLUTION IN AMERICA: LIBERTY, AMBITION, AND THE ECLIPSE OF THE COMMON GOOD 138 (2010).

[61] LARSON, THE MARKET REVOLUTION IN AMERICA, *supra* note 59, at 177.

to the view that government receded in the antebellum era, ushering in a new age of industrial and financial capitalism that planted the seeds of a mass democracy and eventually a middle-class commercial society.

These accounts make important contributions to our understanding of the American past. Laissez-faire ideas circulated widely within the writings of political economists, in broader print culture and among elites in antebellum culture, just as they do today. However, there has always been an element of hypocrisy to laissez-faire arguments as well as selectivity to how they are applied in the world of policy. As Kathleen G. Donohue writes: "at the center of classical liberal theory [in Europe] was the idea of laissez-faire. To the vast majority of American classical liberals, however, laissez-faire did not mean no government intervention at all. On the contrary, they were more than willing to see government provide tariffs, railroad subsidies, and internal improvements, all of which benefited producers. What they condemned was intervention on behalf of consumers."[62] Donahue's observation applies as much to market theories of our own age as it does to those of the past. As the rest of the book chronicles, there has always been more state and more public regulation in the American tradition than the laissez-faire story suggests. To see this clearly requires that we jettison our preconceptions about laissez-faire and a state-market dichotomy.

Historians have provided substantial evidence that the American state was not conceived as a hands-off enterprise designed to hobble government action. Max M. Edling's A Revolution in Favor of Government (2003), for example, makes the case that pressing concerns with national defense and fiscal power in the late eighteenth century produced a Constitution that was designed for energetic governance.[63] Brian Balogh's A Government Out of Sight (2009) provides a comprehensive account of the strong but indirect presence of the federal government in the economy since the early days of the Republic.[64] William J. Novak has been a consistent proponent of theory that American law was generally more protective of

---

[62] KATHLEEN G. DONOHUE, FREEDOM FROM WANT: AMERICAN LIBERALISM AND THE IDEA OF THE CONSUMER 2 (2003).

[63] MAX. M. EDLING, A REVOLUTION IN FAVOR OF GOVERNMENT: ORIGINS OF THE U.S. CONSTITUTION AND THE MAKING OF THE AMERICAN STATE (2003); see also William Novak, The Myth of the "Weak" American State, 113 AM. HIST. REV. 752, 752–72 (2008).

[64] BRIAN BALOGH, A GOVERNMENT OUT OF SIGHT: THE MYSTERY OF NATIONAL AUTHORITY IN NINETEENTH-CENTURY AMERICA (2009); Desmond King & Robert C. Lieberman, Ironies of State Building: A Comparative Perspective on the American State, 61 WORLD POL. 547 (2009); Daron Acemoglu et al., State Capacity and American Technology: Evidence from the Nineteenth Century, 106 AM. ECON. REV. 61 (2016). Although somewhat outside our infrastructure purview, scholars have provided helpful accounts of public–private governance in the United States. See, for example, Elisabeth S. Clemens, Lineages of the Rube Goldberg State: Building and Blurring Public Programs, 1900–1940, in RETHINKING POLITICAL INSTITUTIONS: THE ART OF THE STATE 187, 187–215 (Ian Shapiro et al., eds., 2006); see also JENNIFER KLEIN, FOR ALL THESE RIGHTS: BUSINESS, LABOR, AND THE SHAPING OF AMERICA'S PUBLIC-PRIVATE WELFARE STATE (2003).

the public good in the antebellum era than is suggested by stories about laissez-faire or American statelessness.[65] As Novak argues: "[W]hile the despotic power of the American state (until recent times) might have been limited, the scale and scope of its infrastructural power is and always has been extensive."[66] This book has also benefitted substantially from the existing literature on "internal improvements" in the United States, as well as from other histories of American infrastructure development.[67] The book also builds on the skepticism about the claimed laissez-faire American approach to development first elaborated in the mid-twentieth century, when scholars began documenting the many ways that states were active in advancing development goals.[68]

In framing infrastructure history in America around the public–private divide, *Privatization and Its Discontents* enters a lively debate that has only intensified in the years since the rise of neoliberalism the decline of the American welfare state. Political and legal theorists have challenged the myth of the market as a realm of noncoercive freedom set against the power of the state. Bernard Harcourt's *The Illusion of Free Markets* (2011), for example, shows that markets themselves have always been highly regulated phenomena and traces the operations of power and

---

[65] WILLIAM J. NOVAK, THE PEOPLE'S WELFARE: LAW AND REGULATION IN NINETEENTH-CENTURY AMERICA (1996); see also William Novak, *Public–Private Governance: A Historical Introduction*, in GOVERNMENT BY CONTRACT: OUTSOURCING AND AMERICAN DEMOCRACY 23–40 (JUDY FREEMAN & MARTHA MINOW, eds., 2009).

[66] NOVAK, THE MYTH OF THE "WEAK" AMERICAN STATE, *supra* note 63, at 763; *see also* Michael Mann, *The Autonomous Power of the State*, *supra* note 41.

[67] *See*, for example, JOHN LAURITZ LARSON, INTERNAL IMPROVEMENT: NATIONAL PUBLIC WORKS AND THE PROMISE OF POPULAR GOVERNMENT IN THE EARLY UNITED STATES (2001); ZACHARY CALLEN, RAILROADS AND AMERICAN POLITICAL DEVELOPMENT: INFRASTRUCTURE, FEDERALISM, AND STATE BUILDING (2016); RONALD E. SHAW, CANALS FOR A NATION: THE CANAL ERA IN THE UNITED STATES, 1790–1860 (1990); Bruce Seely, *The Saga of American Infrastructure: A Republic Bound Together*, 17 WILSON Q. 18, 21 (Winter 1993); Jonathan Gifford, *The Saga of American Infrastructure: Toward the Twenty-First Century*, 17 WILSON Q. 40–47 (Winter 1993); Udo Sautter, *Government and Unemployment: The Use of Public Works before the New Deal*, 73 J. AM. HIST. 59–86 (1986); Paul Chen, *The Constitutional Politics of Roads and Canals: Inter-Branch Dialogue Over Internal Improvements, 1800–28*, 28 WHITTIER L. REV. 625 (2006); Harry N. Scheiber, *Government and the Economy: Studies of the "Commonwealth" Policy in Nineteenth Century America*, 3 J. INTERDISC. HIST. 135–51 (1972); CARTER GOODRICH, GOVERNMENT PROMOTION OF AMERICAN CANALS AND RAILROADS, 1800–1890 (1960); JOHN D. MAJEWSKI, A HOUSE DIVIDING: ECONOMIC DEVELOPMENT IN PENNSYLVANIA AND VIRGINIA BEFORE THE CIVIL WAR (2000); SEAN PATRICK ADAMS, OLD DOMINION, INDUSTRIAL COMMONWEALTH: COAL, POLITICS, AND ECONOMY IN ANTEBELLUM AMERICA (2004); RYAN DEARINGER, THE FILTH OF PROGRESS: IMMIGRANTS, AMERICANS, AND THE BUILDING OF CANALS AND RAILROADS IN THE WEST (2015).

[68] *See*, for example, LOUIS HARTZ, ECONOMIC POLICY AND DEMOCRATIC THOUGHT: PENNSYLVANIA, 1776–1860 (1948); MILTON HEATH, CONSTRUCTIVE LIBERALISM: THE ROLE OF THE STATE IN THE ECONOMIC DEVELOPMENT OF GEORGIA TO 1860 (1954); OSCAR HANDLIN & MARY FLUG HANDLIN, COMMONWEALTH: A STUDY OF THE ROLE OF GOVERNMENT IN THE AMERICAN ECONOMY: MASSACHUSETTS, 1774–1861 (1987).

punishment from Jeremy Bentham to the Chicago School.[69] Harcourt explains the regulated nature of "laissez-faire" markets, while pointing out that the rhetoric of free markets has nevertheless enjoyed continuing ideological power. Whether objects or practices are classified as public or private is a defining question for liberal legal regimes, which seek to enshrine property and other private rights while at the same time operating within a developmental state. Early thinkers in the liberal tradition, such as John Locke, grounded the emergent governance project in the priority of private rights over public power and the state, which exists to protect those rights. From this political tradition we have inherited operative categories public and private, with law and politics policing the boundary between them. The public/private divide is also inscribed into our pervasive understandings of the state/market dichotomy. Legal scholars, however, have been debating the public–private divide since the early twentieth century, exploring its boundaries, limitations, and permeability.[70] *Privatization and Its Discontents* adopts the view that "[f]ar from being either natural, necessary, or the way things have been from time out of mind, the public-private antinomy and judicial balancing are surprisingly recent and contingent human creations, social constructions of a particular historical moment."[71]

Infrastructure illuminates the book's central claim that the "private economy" of our contemporary imaginary, with all the normative associations carried with it (efficiency, optimality, liberty, etc.) is and always has been grafted onto public

---

[69] BERNARD HARCOURT, THE ILLUSION OF FREE MARKETS: PUNISHMENT AND THE MYTH OF NATURAL ORDER (2011); *see also* MARIANA MAZZUCATO, THE ENTREPRENEURIAL STATE: DEBUNKING PUBLIC VS. PRIVATE SECTOR MYTHS (2015); PETER K. EISINGER, THE RISE OF THE ENTREPRENEURIAL STATE: STATE AND LOCAL ECONOMIC DEVELOPMENT POLICY IN THE UNITED STATES (1988); JACOB S. HACKER & PAUL PIERSON, AMERICAN AMNESIA: HOW THE WAR ON GOVERNMENT LED US TO FORGET WHAT MADE AMERICA PROSPER (2016). In recent years, many have challenged laissez faire stories from different perspectives. For example, Ha-Joon Chang's BAD SAMARITANS: THE MYTH OF FREE TRADE AND THE SECRET HISTORY OF CAPITALISM (2008) challenges the common economic parables about free trade's role in the rise of capitalism that underpin modern market theories. Others have focused on the relationship between the State and the financial system that makes capitalism possible. *See*, for example, CHRISTINE DESAN, MAKING MONEY: COIN, CURRENCY, AND THE COMING OF CAPITALISM (2014).

[70] David Ciepley's *Beyond Public and Private: Toward a Political Theory of the Corporation*, 107 AM. POL. SCI. REV. 139–58 (2013) is especially helpful for understanding the corporation as a basic legal and political technology of governance; *see also* Harry N. Scheiber, *The Road to Munn: Eminent Domain and the Concept of Public Purpose in the State Courts*, 5 PERSPS. AM. HIST. 329–402 (1971); Carol Harlow, *"Public" and "Private:" Definition without Distinction*, 43 MOD. L. REV. 241 (1980); Duncan Kennedy, *The Stages of the Decline of the Public/Private Distinction*, 130 U. PA. L. REV. 1349 (1982); Karl E. Klare, *The Public/Private Distinction in Labor Law*, 130 U. PA. L. REV. 1358 (1982); Morton Horwitz, *Santa Clara Revisited: The Development of Corporate Theory*, 88 W. VA. L. REV. (1986); Pauline Maier, *The Revolutionary Origins of the American Corporation*, 50 WM. & MARY Q. 51–84 (1993); William Novak, *Law, Capitalism, and the Liberal State: The Historical Sociology of Willard Hurst*, 18 L. & HIST. REV. 97 (2000); William Novak, *The American Law of Association: The Legal-Political Construction of Civil Society*, 15 STUD. AM. POL. DEV. 163–88 (2001).

[71] William J. Novak, *Common Regulation: Legal Origins of State Power in America*, 45 HASTINGS L. J. 1061, 1068 (1994).

structures of sovereignty, law, and state. Indeed, much of what we classify as the private economy is parasitical on preexisting public infrastructures, sovereign government powers (e.g., eminent domain, military force, government loans, subsidies, and tax incentives), or dependent on direct public investment. Infrastructure proves to be a pivotal concept to sort out these issues, because it complicates liberalism's commitment to an independently existing economy by reinforcing how dependent that economy is on the state.

IV CHAPTER BREAKDOWNS

Chapter 1 begins at the origins of modern political economy with a discussion of Adam Smith's *Wealth of Nations*. The narrative of American political development traditionally begins with 1776, the year both the Declaration of Independence and *Wealth of Nations* were published. Under a conventional view, these two texts announce the arrival of the twin forces of political freedom and free market capitalism, together defined as "classic liberalism." Our analysis of infrastructure's history begins with Smith because of a surprising feature of early political economy: while we imagine classical liberalism as hostile to the state, and to frame the worlds in terms of a state-market dichotomy, Smith positions the state as central to infrastructure and to the "take off" of market economies.

Public works, Smith argues, are necessary for commerce and national development. They are the preconditions of a trading system and also a material representation of progress and civilization. However, they will not be adequately supplied by private firms acting on their own without involvement by the state. Thus, while Smith is chiefly remembered for his argument in favor of an invisible hand of a self-regulating market, he understood that market economies cannot supply "public works" through private action alone. *Wealth of Nations* argues that "public works" are integral to establishing the national framework for an emergent capitalist economy. To develop this line of argument, Chapter 1 introduces the concept of the police power, which is important for understanding the legal construction of public governance in the modern world, and central for understanding the idea of the economy. The concept of police power (or just "police") finds its roots in Greek *politeia* and cognates such as "polis" and "policy." William Blackstone's influential *Commentaries on the Laws of England* (1765–69) describes police as a technology of order: "By the public police and economy I mean the due regulation of domestic order of the kingdom: whereby the individuals of the state, like members of a well-governed family, are bound to conform their general behaviour to the rules of propriety, good neighborhood, and good manners; and to be decent, industrious, and inoffensive in their respective stations."[72]

---

[72] William Blackstone, Commentaries on the Laws of England, Vol 4 (1979) (1753), 162.

Police is the legal technology for "seeing like a state" and describes the state's jurisdiction over regulation of health, safety, and welfare (which is why Foucauldian scholars have taken such an interest in it).[73] As such, *police* was of central importance for the construction of markets and public spaces in the modern order. Smith discusses police in earlier works such as his *Lectures on Jurisprudence* (1763), where he describes its domain as "cleanliness, security, and cheapness or plenty." The concept migrates into American usage in the nineteenth century, eventually marking the proper domain of legislative power in the constitutional order. By the time we reach *Wealth of Nations* ten years after the lectures, however, there is little discussion of police, which makes it possible to read Smith as a straightforward advocate for an unregulated marketplace. But I argue that despite the shift in vocabulary, *police* has not disappeared in *The Wealth of Nations*. It has instead changed form from an arbitrary power to set prices levied by the mercantilist state, to a cost-internalizing norm of prudence that would be superintended by a government acting on new economic principles.

Because infrastructures would require government involvement, this meant a large fiscal footprint, especially considering the scale of infrastructures in the modern world. Without proper oversight, this could enable the nimble hand of the tax collector to pick the pockets of society at large. But Smith's tax aversion should not be mistaken for "statelessness." I argue that if we read Smith's theories of costing and fiscal probity carefully, we can see that he is not making an argument in favor of a stateless society. Smith is advocating that infrastructures be governed by cost-internalizing principles represented by what would later be called "self-liquidating infrastructure," which means that public goods should as much as possible pay their own way and offset their own costs.

Smith, for example, argues that public works should be financed with tolls and fees in order to commit proceeds to the specific projects that those revenues support, rather than swelling the public coffers with general revenues, which only makes a tempting target for rent extraction by parasitical state elites. Tolls and fees would also ensure that infrastructures receive the necessary upkeep and would be efficiently managed. Thus, we can observe a certain fiscal conservatism at the heart of infrastructural politics at their modern origins that remains with us today. In an important sense, I would suggest, our privatization controversies today are latter-day echoes of problems that were already in play in the eighteenth century. These costing and fiscal questions will likely always be an intrinsic aspect of public infrastructure politics.

Reading Smith is also helpful because his theories of money, public finance, and trade yield important insights into infrastructure's relationship to the fiscal order. Smith's views about the "economy" essentially prefigure later views of infrastructure

---

[73] *See*, for example, Markus Dirk Dubber, The Police Power: Patriarchy and the Foundations of American Government (2005).

in which the world is divided into primary activities (production and trade) and secondary yet necessary forms of governance (the state, infrastructure, money). The division of the world into primary economic activity and secondary enabling activity has a profound implication for what counts as worthy of investment and what doesn't. In Smith's classical model and its modern inheritors, there is a real private economy of production and trade and an infrastructural framework that turns out to be a precondition of it, with the latter working as an exception to the rule of market competition. Whether we are talking about sovereign debt, money, or infrastructure, Smith develops his analysis across primary and secondary domains and is always concerned to prevent the secondary domain from swallowing up the primary one (this was his view of the natural tendency of mercantilism, for example). Private trade and production are the driving forces behind the new capitalist growth paradigm. But these drivers of growth are impossible without the infrastructure of the state, which always needs to be policed by self-limiting principles provided by the new field of economics.

Chapter 1 concludes by discussing Smith's ideas about natural monopoly, which supplied an important exception to the general rule of market competition, and would become important in shaping our modern ideas of infrastructure. On the one hand, Smith criticizes monopolies, just as he criticized the joint-stock company, because they threaten to exclude new competitors from the field, drive up prices, and encourage rent-seeking behavior. To be sure, Smith thinks that some limited monopoly protections may be necessary to incentivize companies to undertake risky and valuable enterprises. But he is generally wary of monopolies unless they are limited and absolutely necessary. Monopolies created by law (e.g., guilds) can degenerate into shakedown rackets, the type of special privilege that only inures to the benefit of small classes at the expense of the general public. This line of attack has been an enduring theme in America due to its heritage of political republicanism.

On the other hand, Smith makes an important exception for "natural monopolies" (although he does not use that term himself), which exists for Smith when some feature of natural geography makes competition infeasible (e.g., a winemaker situated on a unique piece of land should enjoy a monopoly on producing a particular vintage). Later in the nineteenth century, however, the idea of natural monopoly expanded to new networked technologies (trains, telephony, water, and power systems) and would form the basis for public utility infrastructure. Liberal political economy invented the concept of natural monopoly as a carve-out to market logics, which created the seeds that grew into public utility at the end of the nineteenth century.

Chapter 2 evaluates the internal improvements period in the United States as an important moment that prefigures later infrastructural politics in America. Nineteenth-century Americans used the term "internal improvements" rather than our term infrastructure to refer to canals, roads, harbors, lighthouses, railroads, and other technologies of national, regional, and local development. This chapter argues against the laissez-faire thesis of early American development and posits in its place that the fiscal state pioneered by Alexander Hamilton created the stability for later public investment and expansion. Thus, it is to Alexander Hamilton, not Adam Smith, to whom we should look as a foundational figure for understanding early American political economy. Chapter 2 emphasizes the state-building aspects of the U.S. Constitution and argues that America's founding document was not meant to create a hands-off state. The text of the Constitution gave broad powers to Congress to build up the infrastructures of a market state and those powers were used throughout the nineteenth century (though not without controversy and not in ways that its most enthusiastic advocates hoped).

Infrastructure investment was one of the most important issues of the day, and debates over internal improvements became some of the defining conflicts of the era. On the one hand, Americans were eager for improved roads, harbors, lighthouses, and other infrastructural improvements. They petitioned their representatives frequently for government support of new projects. On the other hand, direct federal investment in infrastructure faced many obstacles, and internal improvements continued to be controversial well into the nineteenth century. There were a number of reasons for this. The first difficulty to achieve national objectives through specific infrastructure projects was competition and rivalry within Congress for development money. Each specific canal or road project, after all, would benefit some regions at the expense of others, potentially diverting traffic from a politician's state or region to that of a rival. There was thus every incentive to block projects that could stymie commercial growth in a politician's home state.

The second was that there was partisan disagreement between Federalist and Republican visions of the proper scope of the national infrastructural power. To begin with, southerners objected to a national infrastructural power because they feared the possibility that northerners would use that power to emancipate slaves. Moreover, there were political disagreements over whether the Constitution allowed for federal internal improvements in the first place. Federalists read the Constitution as providing ample justifications for infrastructure development at the national level. They pointed to powers implied by "necessary and proper" clause of Article I, Section 8, and other provisions such as the Postal Clause, to support their claim that the Constitution intended a wide field of government action. Strict constructionists on the other hand demanded that projects be supported by specific authorization, which was not to be found in the Constitution's text. Despite these disagreements, however, the federal government remained active in internal improvements throughout the nineteenth century, but not always to the extent or in the manner that developmentalists hoped.

Alexander Hamilton's theories of money and debt are also important because they offer an alternative vision to Adam Smith's idea of a system of trade prior to government. Hamilton's vision is one where the national government creates the foundations for a market state. In the sovereign debt crisis after the Revolutionary

War, Hamilton argued that the federal government should assume the outstanding war debts incurred by states. There were several problems at play. The first was that the new nation was cash poor and lacked a reliable circulating medium for trading and investment. The second was that the new nation was deeply in debt and lacked adequate fiscal resources to escape it. Hamilton's debt assumption plan would fix both problems at a stroke by turning the existing state debts into a national asset, establishing the nation's reputation as a reliable debtor for foreign investors and creating a liquid trading market in government bonds. Alexander Hamilton was thus the architect of the modern American debtor state, one that would support capitalism by maintaining an active role in stability and growth. Anti-Federalists (later Republicans) took a view that was more in line with Adam Smith and a republican tradition that believed sovereign debt was a source of national ruin, although they struggled to maintain this commitment in the nineteenth century (or any other).

Secretary of the Treasury Albert Gallatin published an important document for the history of American infrastructure: The *Report of the Secretary of the Treasury on the Subject of Public Roads and Canals* (1808). Gallatin's plan was to create a federally subsidized system of roads and canals from the east into the interior. The report is a very modern document, filled with detailed financial and engineering specifications and is framed as a project of nation-building. Notably, Gallatin proposes a model that Adam Smith would have approved of: his projects would be self-liquidating and would partially pay their own way with tolls and fees. His idea reflected republican themes of prudence and fiscal responsibility and forecast an important aspect of infrastructure's future. Despite the fact that Congress did not act on the plan, there were other attempts to revive it under the idea of the "American System," but the plan met with only limited success. Nevertheless, the federal government continued to support internal improvements, often acting indirectly through land grants and other forms of subsidy and support.

Chapter 3 turns to the state level and the legal construction of public space, explaining that turnpikes were an early example of "public–private partnerships," forms of self-liquidating infrastructures that would in theory defray their own costs through tolls. I argue that despite their mixed public–private character, the legal order nevertheless treated turnpikes as quasi-public instrumentalities of government. While there were some successes with turnpikes, their quasi-public nature created a problem for them as business ventures in the long run because turnpikes involve the unpopular enclosure of customary spaces, and legislatures were often unwilling to allow turnpikes to raise their tolls to provide an adequate return on investment.

Chapter 3 explains that the law of the "highway" was a powerful tool for government development with deep roots in the common law. Roads have defined public space since the early modern period, and keeping the roads open was considered a central feature of sovereignty (John Locke, for instance, uses the example of traveling on the highway as evidence of our "tacit consent" to sovereignty in his *Two*

Treatises on Government (1689)). And the link between sovereignty and public roads was a commonplace in later American law. Tennessee's high court made the point succinctly in 1847: "The power to open roads is a prerogative of sovereignty; it has been delegated by the legislature to the county courts in this state, and is exercised by them, not as a judicial, but municipal, function."[74] This would have been evident in antebellum law, because "highway" had a broad definition and would have included turnpikes, plank roads, railroads, bridges, ferries, and canals. The legal formulation of the highway gave a broad construction to public power.

However, with turnpikes and other franchised infrastructure, legislatures also had to balance their power over public spaces with due regard for the private interests of the turnpike companies. To make this point clear, Chapter 3 reads an Ohio turnpike statute of 1840, using its provisions as a hermeneutic key to explain how states created the regulatory framework for turnpike development. The 1840 statute exerted control over how the roads were built and what the tolls would be; required oversight by commissioners; included anti-fraud provisions; provided many toll exemptions; and provided for the eventual reversion of turnpike roads to the state. Chapter 3 argues that while the law favored public–private infrastructure development, it sought to protect the rights of the public in ways that curtailed the power of private infrastructure companies, ultimately making it difficult to run them as private businesses.

Moreover, the publicness of turnpikes also took other forms, including popular resistance, which included "shunpiking," defined as the practice of toll evasion by moving around the turnpike gate or creating an alternative route. This was so common that William Blackstone warned against it in his magisterial *Commentaries on the Laws of England* (1765–1770). Due to their sometimes-controversial nature, legislatures were not willing to do much to stop toll evasion. An inherited culture of political republicanism also led some to decry the privatization of public spaces, as when Thomas Paine used turnpikes as an anti-republican metaphor: "The duty of man is not a wilderness of turnpike gates, through which he is to pass by tickets from one to the other."[75] The chapter concludes by examining decisions from state courts that, while certainly not as radical as Paine's prescription, nevertheless suggest a republican approach to turnpikes and other franchised transportation as a form of public highway, despite the fact that they were operated by a corporate franchise.

Chapter 4 marks an important turning point for infrastructure development in the United States. In the absence of sufficient direct federal investment in infrastructure, and inspired by the success of the Eerie Canal, states launched their own development programs in the 1830s. Americans had had long experience with state-level economic development, as scholars began uncovering in a series of important

---

[74] Franklin & Columbia Tpk. Co. v. Cnty. Court of Maury, 27 Tenn. 342, 354 (1847).
[75] THOMAS PAINE, RIGHTS OF MAN (1971) (available in THE WRITINGS OF THOMAS PAINE, Vol. II (Moncure Daniel Conway, ed.) at www.gutenberg.org/files/3742/3742-h/3742-h.htm).

works in the 1940s–1960s. While courts were initially protective of the vested rights of older infrastructure ventures, the Supreme Court signaled a new direction in the 1830s with decisions that opened the way for state-led development of new infrastructure ventures. States were in a good position to step in where the federal government had not, because states could charter corporations and create the legal and financial framework for new infrastructure investment in their own regions. States also had their own banking systems and could charter banks and infrastructure companies with strings attached; they could, for example, charter a bank only on condition that it agree to capitalize an infrastructure project.

States could also offer direct and indirect support to new infrastructure ventures. States offered tax breaks and other incentives; they also granted the power of eminent domain to speed construction. State courts also cleared the way for new building by tipping the balance of property rights away from landowners toward developers, for example, by making it more difficult to obtain damage judgements against developers for destruction of nearby land. States, as you would expect, taxed property owners to subsidize new development. But they also expanded on Adam Smith's idea of self-liquidating infrastructure to finance new development. They did this by engineering what economic historian John A. Dove calls "taxless finance." This worked in a number of ways, but essentially came down to the state selling its own bonds and using the proceeds to invest in a canal or a railroad, or permitting the company to market its own bonds to the public directly, with debt backed by the state. The idea was that this debt would be retired from the profits earned by the canal or railroad, thereby avoiding heavy taxation to pay off the debt.

The problem with this approach was that states borrowed irresponsibly, taking on more debt than they could handle. This caused a crisis of confidence among creditors, contractions on available sovereign debt for states, and ultimately precipitated a massive economic downturn in the 1840s. With this bitter experience in mind, many states amended their own constitutions to place various limits on state investment in infrastructure ventures. Some states, such as Michigan, barred state-financed internal improvements altogether: "The state shall not be a party to, nor interested in, any work or internal improvement, nor engaged in carrying on any such work, except in the improvement of or aiding in the improvement of the public wagon roads and in the expenditure of grants to the state of land or other property."[76] Other revisions required referenda to approve government debt, restricted the total dollar amount of debt or barred any investment other than one that had a "public purpose." State governments found ways around these limitations, for example by shifting infrastructure investment to the local level, since the constitutional amendments did not preclude them from investing in infrastructure. Courts did not prevent states from doing this when governments were sued by taxpayers under the

[76] MICH. CONST of 1850, art. 14, § 9.

language of the new state laws. Instead, they held that it was up to the state legislatures to decide what counted as a valid public purpose.

Chapter 5 develops an account of infrastructure after the Civil War that focuses on several issues. The first is the legal revolution of the 14th Amendment, whose Due Process, Equal Protection and Privileges and Immunities Clauses promised to expand federal rights to the states. Early on, the Supreme Court dampened hopes that the new amendments would be used to protect African Americans, women, and others who were seeking rights under the new order. The Court ruled that the police powers of the states were alive and well, even after the 14th Amendment's expansion of federal power. A series of major decisions developed a new jurisprudence of the police power of the states in the context of disputed fundamental rights that the 14th Amendment protected.

One of the first important decisions, *The Slaughterhouse Cases* (1873), involved a seemingly minor dispute over a Louisiana law that required butchers to ply their trade in a specific slaughterhouse in New Orleans. Butchers challenged this law and claimed that it abridged their fundamental right to pursue a trade as they saw fit. Justice Miller disagreed with the claim that the 14th Amendment codified a fundamental federal right to pursue a trade. The state's police power included the sort of ordinary regulation that was being challenged in the case. Notably, Justice Field's dissent developed a new theory of fundamental economic rights, in support of which he quotes Adam Smith's idea of property in one's own labor.

Railroads emerged as indispensable commercial infrastructure after the Civil War. Midwestern states began regulating railroad rates in response to populist protests against high shipping costs for agricultural goods. Four years later, in *Munn v. Illinois* (1877), the Court was confronted with challenges to this new spate of state regulation. The railroads challenged the regulations under the 14th Amendment's Due Process Clause and also under the Commerce Clause of the U.S. Constitution. The 14th Amendment forbids the government from "depriv[ing] any person of life, liberty, or property." The central question was whether the state of Illinois had "taken" the property of the railroad when it capped its rates. Chief Justice Morrison Waite reached into the canon of common law for an answer: the state's police power had always allowed it to regulate in the public interest, which included the power to set rates for public infrastructures. Justice Field provided an important dissent that found the majority's reasoning suspect because it disregarded the right of the railroads to turn a profit: "The principle upon which the opinion of the majority proceeds is, in my judgment, subversive of the rights of private property, heretofore believed to be protected by constitutional guaranties against legislative interference...."[77]

The period after the Civil War expanded the field of government action with new Progressive regulation, higher tax obligations, and governments that were much more

---

[77] 94 U.S. 113, 137 (1876).

active in regulating the economy. Many viewed the new order as a radical break with what they began imagining as a laissez-faire American past. Chapter 5 tracks the new laissez-faire legalism that sought limits on this expanded power to tax, spend, and regulate, limits that many saw in the Constitution and the American legal tradition. Christopher Tiedeman's *A Treatise on the Limitations of Police Power in the United States* (1886), and many other important works in the period, read the 14th Amendment as providing the foundation for new fundamental economic rights of property and contract against government interference.

These new economic rights were called "substantive due process" because they identified certain rights (most especially liberty and property) as so fundamental that they required judicial protection against legislative overreach. Substantive due process led to more stringent oversight of tax-subsidized infrastructure construction, just as the newly reinvigorated "public purpose" doctrine policed legislative tax subsidies for development. Henry J. Booth's *Treatise on the Law of Street Railways* (1911[1892]), provides an opportunity to examine the workings of the infrastructural police power at the local level, showing how courts attempted to balance public versus private rights.

Chapter 5 then focuses on two infrastructures – telegraphs and railroads – to illustrate the trend toward monopoly and federal regulation in the Progressive era. States regulated and taxed telegraphs and railroads on a piecemeal basis, but eventually networked infrastructures were the subject of federal regulation under the Commerce Clause. Major Supreme Court decisions such as *Pensacola Tel. Co. v. Western Union Tel. Co.* (1877) and *Wabash and St. Louis & Pacific Railway Company v. Illinois* (1886) resolved disputes over the proper regulatory regime for the new networked infrastructures. The future for networked infrastructures would be in regulated monopolies, overseen by new state and federal commissions and agencies, such as the Interstate Commerce Commission (1886). Finally, a new generation of reformers expanded the idea of public utility into the conceptual foundation for regulating in the public interest in the twentieth century. There was broad agreement at the time that infrastructures such as gas, water, and electricity were indispensable for modern life and that their provision could not be left to an unregulated free market. Innovations in science, technology, and public management worked together to produce a new technocratic frame for infrastructure. However, although there was much debate over the issue of municipal ownership, the future for infrastructures would be a mixture of public and private utilities.

Chapter 6 frames the rise of the modern infrastructure concept and the decline of laissez-faire as related phenomena of the mid-twentieth century liberal developmentalism. The chapter begins with recent reappraisals of the New Deal's legacy for American infrastructure, and explains why the New Deal has become a reference point for American political debates about the positive role that government can play in a revived social democratic liberalism. The growth of the administrative state led to debates about rule of law and bureaucratic overreach, as the classical liberal distinction drawn by Jeremy Bentham between "agenda" and "non-agenda" of government began to crumble. A new realism about the public/public divide in the 1920s and 1930s undermined the case for private rights that had featured in the *Lochne*r era as an obstacle to Progressive regulation of the worker–owner relationship. Realists attacked the case against regulation that was grounded in Lockean constitutionalism, represented by substantive due process. Moreover, debates within economics going back to the Progressive era suggested a new institutional direction for political economy that pointed to an active role for the state in managing economic affairs. Economic growth, expertise, and the public good would be the measures of the new order.

Infrastructure appears for the first time as a developmental concept in the late 1940s and 1950s. It became a keyword within modernization theory, which viewed societies as systems, and tended to downplay the idea of an independently existing economy that could develop without investment by governments. The successes of the Marshall Plan suggested that investment in rebuilding various sectors (such as "defense") would also have to include funding for the supporting systems that make the primary objective possible. The World Bank and NATO had been calling these secondary systems "infrastructure" since the late 1940s, and debates in Congress show the term being debated and defined in the 1950s as it makes its way from an obscure piece of engineering jargon to the central political term that it has become today. Walt Whitman Rostow's *Stages of Economic Growth: A Non-Communist Manifesto* (1960) supplied a classic account of societies moving through well-defined stages (from traditional to modern) before becoming fully mature market economies. Rostow uses terms like "social overhead capital" or infrastructure to describe the precursors to growth and development. Beginning in the 1940s, economic historians created a counternarrative of American history that normalized state investment in an era when state planning was often deeply controversial. They pointed to the American experience of internal improvements to substantiate the claims of state-led developmentalism that they viewed as central to defeating communism through economic aid to emerging economies. During the 1960s and after, we see a liberalism that prefers a broad vision of social infrastructure competing with a more conservative vision that reasserts the priority of hard infrastructures and the private sector.

The Conclusion tracks the re-emergence of infrastructure as a political theme in the 1980s. At the moment when the federal government was investing less money in state and local infrastructures, books and reports with titles like *America in Ruins: The Decaying Infrastructure* (1983) and *Fragile Foundations: A Report on America's Public Works* (1988) capture a sense of decline and a call to action to reinvest in public goods. Economic growth remains at the center of arguments for more infrastructure investment: "Putting aside public safety concerns, infrastructure investment is critical to keeping an economy functioning. The problem is that old bridges, roads, and equipment keep working until they fail. This phenomenon encourages decision makers to put off what most observers would acknowledge as necessary investments in sustaining the future of economic activities."[78] Privatization and public–private partnerships have played an important role in the debates over infrastructure financing since the 1980s, which fits into an overall approach to more businesslike government that has prevailed since the Reagan era. However, these arrangements remain controversial in ways that would have been recognizable to earlier generations concerned about the possibility for undermining democratic governance when private companies have too much control over public resources.

Infrastructure continues to implicate important normative questions about the public good in market society. Themes of historical memory begin to surface in the 1980s in a time of retrenchment, reminding readers of the past achievements of a more ambitious liberalism. Infrastructure also becomes a campaign theme in the 1980s and appears in almost every Democratic and some Republican party platforms between 1980 and the most recent election. The book closes with the Infrastructure Investments and Jobs Act, President Biden's signature social investment legislation. The debate around the infrastructure plan replays themes around "big government" that have preoccupied American politics for half a century. Many mainstream journalists have praised the plan for its ambitious scope, comparing it to past liberal achievements, most especially the New Deal. The legislation also brought the infrastructure concept back into public consciousness, and commentators wrote articles and think pieces explaining the range of meanings that infrastructure has held across history.

The debate has pitted left-liberals against conservatives, with Progressives calling for broader investment in social infrastructure, expanding the concept beyond concrete and steel, while conservatives insist on the narrow definition of hard infrastructure investments. Historians criticize the narrow definition as the exclusive meaning of the term as judged by the American experience: "But this narrow definition of infrastructure and fear of public investment in multiple facets of the U.S. economy at a time of great need does not square with the nation's history…. As Roosevelt demonstrated, the infrastructure of a nation is much more than paved roads or physical structures. It includes the social and economic well-being of its people and the building of a society that provides a clean environment and equal opportunity for all."[79] When President Clinton reassured conservatives in 1996 that "the era of big government is over," he caught the prevailing mood of a liberalism enchanted by technology and the corporate economy. Subsequent events have called that consensus into question and the neoliberalism that took ambitious social investment off the table seems to be fraying around the edges.

---

[78] WILLIAM R. THOMPSON, AMERICAN GLOBAL PRE-EMINENCE: THE DEVELOPMENT AND EROSION OF SYSTEMIC LEADERSHIP 139 (2022).

[79] David B. Woolner, *Biden Wants to Go Big on Infrastructure: History Says That's the Right Call*, THE WASH. POST (Apr. 7, 2021).

1

Early Liberalism, Adam Smith, and the Seeds of the Infrastructural State

1.1 INTRODUCTION

Let us begin with one of the most fortuitous coincidences in the history of liberalism: both the Declaration of Independence and *The Wealth of Nations* were published in 1776, a date to conjure with if there ever was one. Here is the economist Mark Skousen in 2007 echoing a fairly standard view of 1776: "Certain dates are turning points in the history of mankind. The year 1776 is one of them. In that prophetic year, two vital freedoms were proclaimed – political liberty and free enterprise – and the two worked together to set in motion the industrial revolution."[1] Skousen's comment reflects a fairly standard view of "classical liberalism," an idea that embodies a belief in the small state, the rule of law, private property, and a guarantee of various rights of free expression. This definition will do just as well as any other: "'Classical liberalism' is the term used to designate the ideology advocating private property, an unhampered market economy, the rule of law, constitutional guarantees of freedom of religion and of the press, and international peace based on free trade."[2] American independence and laissez-faire were born together in a moment of revolutionary fervor that tore down the old order and birthed the new project of democratic capitalism.

On the one hand, Adam Smith's *Wealth of Nations* provides some evidence for this view of classical liberalism. Smith's magnum opus famously argued that an end

---

[1] MARK SKOUSEN, THE BIG THREE IN ECONOMICS: ADAM SMITH, KARL MARX AND JOHN MAYNARD KEYNES 5 (2015) (originally published in 2007).

[2] Ralph Raico, *What Is Classical Liberalism?*, 11/1/2018, https://mises.org/library/what-classical-liberalism (last visited May 26, 2022); *see also* CHRISTOPHER W. CALVO, THE EMERGENCE OF CAPITALISM IN EARLY AMERICA 9 (2020) ("For practical discursive purposes, and in full recognition of the risks of oversimplification, 'liberal economics' is defined here as the intellectual system originating with Smith that aims to expand individual economic freedom while simultaneously restricting state intervention within a market-based (capitalist) economy"). For negative and positive liberty in the liberal tradition, see Isiah Berlin's classic Cold War essay *Two Concepts of Liberty, in* LIBERTY 1–54 (Henry Hardy ed., 2004). A useful account of liberalism's history from the point of view of a left-liberal, see EDMUND FAWCETT, LIBERALISM: THE LIFE OF AN IDEA (2d ed., 2018) (2014). For an intellectual history of the market, liberalism, and capitalism, see JERRY Z. MULLER, THE MIND AND THE MARKET: CAPITALISM AND WESTERN THOUGHT (Anchor Books 2003); *see also* JOHN LAURITZ LARSON, THE MARKET REVOLUTION: LIBERTY, AMBITION, AND THE ECLIPSE OF THE COMMON GOOD 141–68 (2010).

to mercantilism and price regulations would unleash the power of private trade and production, leaving an invisible hand to direct a cycle of growth and prosperity under the natural law of competition. The natural laws he identified, human avarice and self-interest – doing what comes naturally – did not need any external locus of control or guiding morality: "It is not from the benevolence of the butcher, the brewer, or the baker that we expect our dinner, but from their regard to their own interest. We address ourselves, not to their humanity but to their self-love, and never talk to them of our own necessities but of their advantages."[3] Self-interest alone would lead to a generalized prosperity that no individual could have planned in advance. The government's role in this vision is largely limited to the protection of property, contract, and other private rights, as well as civil order and national defense. Our prevailing policy models, following Adam Smith and his neoclassical heritage, depict a competitive marketplace and a circuit of production and consumption that ideally function with minimal oversight by the state.

On the other hand, whether we call it infrastructure, public goods, or public works, liberal societies depend in practice on a class of useful things that cannot be adequately supplied by the market. In fact, modern societies have relied over time on larger and more technologically complex infrastructure systems to produce and deliver goods and services: transportation and communication, power grids, sanitation services, water delivery and purification, and so on. While these have often been "public–private partnerships," in practice much of what we now call "infrastructure" has been logistically impossible without state investment and oversight. As transportation, communication, water, power, and other systems grow larger, implicating millions of people, they are increasingly shaped by political questions of law and statecraft that challenge the picture of an idealized marketplace operating under its own laws. Infrastructures are enmeshed in regimes of urban, regional, and national governance, intimately tied to normative conceptions of the public good and struggles over the distribution of resources and shaped by uneasy tensions between market competition and public regulation.

Infrastructure has always held an uneasy place in the liberal order because it spans the boundaries between state and market, public and private – realms that liberal theory would prefer to keep separate. As such, infrastructure dramatizes the conflict between laissez-faire theories and actual governance practices within liberal capitalism.[4] Adam Smith's work reveals how early liberalism imagined

---

[3] ADAM SMITH, AN INQUIRY INTO THE NATURE AND CAUSE OF THE WEALTH OF NATIONS, Books 1–3 (2012).

[4] As discussed in the Introduction, the term infrastructure itself is a relatively recent one. Americans did not use the term in the nineteenth century, relying instead on "internal improvements" or simply "improvements." Calling something "public works" certainly suggests to us that the government has an obligation to supply it, while infrastructure is a machine or computational metaphor that seems more agnostic about who is responsible for it. But for now, I will use the terminology somewhat loosely in our modern sense for ease of communication.

infrastructural governance in the modern world. Reading Adam Smith's *Wealth of Nations* against the grain, Chapter 1 draws our attention to normative subtexts of state-market relations that are often neglected in idealized pictures of Smith's legacy. It finds that Smith's masterwork, *The Wealth of Nations*, so influential for its vision of a disembedded market and a night-watchman state, actually envisioned a more complex interplay between trade, commerce, and the state than we sometimes attribute to his thought. As Jo Guldi writes: "In more recent times, we have come to see eighteenth-century economists like [Bernard] Mandeville and Smith as critical of the state. In fact, these authors laid the foundation for considering how states could nurture their domestic economies by ensuring infrastructure."[5]

Indeed, Adam Smith carved out important exceptions to the logic of competition that his theory otherwise implies, including public works and natural monopoly. Thus, at the foundation of classical liberalism, we already find a blueprint for a society governed by law and statecraft. But although classical liberalism envisions a governed society, it is always haunted by fears of unsustainable levels of government debt. To keep the state in check, Smith writes "privatization" into his idea of self-liquidating infrastructure – public works that pay their own way through user fees, which anticipates the public–private infrastructural state we inhabit today. In the same vein, Smith's thinking about the nature of money, also influential on later economic discourse, suggests how deeply the logic of privatization is embedded in liberal governance models.

1.2 SELF-LIQUIDATING INFRASTRUCTURE, POLICE, AND LIBERAL GOVERNANCE

Adam Smith's *Wealth of Nations* (1776) remains the touchstone for the articulation of "the market" in classical liberal theory. His work was widely influential in the nineteenth-century transatlantic world and was an important source for the economic theories that shape our own policy imaginary. The standard account of *Wealth of Nations* taught in college classrooms usually begins with Smith's vision of human nature as essentially selfish.[6] This is still the foundational assumptions for modern economic theory: the free-market, rational-choice Adam Smith that is taught in schools and appears in the popular media. When a think tank wants to promote "using free markets to create a richer, freer, happier world," for example, it calls itself *The Adam Smith Institute*.[7] There is plenty to work with in Smith's writings to support this interpretation. As Smith writes in *Wealth of Nations*:

---

[5] JO GULDI, ROADS TO POWER: BRITAIN INVENTS THE INFRASTRUCTURE STATE 90 (2012).
[6] The passages on selfishness, for example, are among the most frequently underlined in my Kindle version of *The Wealth of Nations*.
[7] ADAM SMITH INSTITUTE, www.adamsmith.org/ (last visited May 27, 2022).

> Every individual ... neither intends to promote the public interest, nor knows how much he is promoting it ... he intends only his own security; and by directing that industry in such a manner as its produce may be of the greatest value, he intends only his own gain, and he is in this, as in many other cases, led by an invisible hand to promote an end which was no part of his intention.[8]

Of course, Smith elaborates on this message at length in *Wealth of Nations*.

For Smith, nobody in particular needs to "promote the public interest" precisely because *Homo economicus* generates the public interest, as a positive externality, just by doing what comes naturally: buying and selling, and producing and consuming. The "truck and barter" we get up to when we meet our basic needs generates a natural economic order that logically and historically precedes the state: "logically," because trade and commerce are the true locus of society's productive energies; "historically," because in Smith's view, "primitive" man already practiced commerce when he traded spears for grain in the barter economies of the distant past. Thus, under this classic view of Smith, competitive markets drive growth and prosperity in a largely self-regulating process, with minimal oversight by the government. Encouraging private trade, entrepreneurship, and production is the benchmark of sound social policy, but stifling those forces with excessive price controls and other regulation is not. In fact, if not kept within bounds, the state can be captured by elites who are adept at manipulating its complex machinery (taxes, public finance, corporations, and empires) to channel "rents" into their own coffers. The government left to its own devices is a parasite, battening on resources produced by an otherwise healthy organism. Freed from this parasitism by sound economics, a self-regulating commercial world would set its own developmental agenda. If we read Smith this way, it is unclear what, beyond minimal policing functions, the liberal state would be left to do.

All of this suggests that for Smith the state was a puzzle that needed to be solved. And indeed, that is true. But Smith did not solve the puzzle by eliminating the state or imagining an economy without governance. The stateless Smith of the invisible hand is an artifact of later economic thought with its own anti-regulatory agenda. Generations of economists have narrowed Smith's contributions to the invisible hand, self-regulating market, and spontaneous ordering. The economist and philosopher Amartya Sen has argued that the Chicago School and Cold War politics played an important role in popularizing a version of Adam Smith that fits with their own views on the appropriate role of government in the economy.[9] Christopher

---

[8] SMITH, THE WEALTH OF NATIONS, *supra* note 3, at Book 4, chapter 2. *See also id.* at Book 5.

[9] There has been a debate over Adam Smith's attitude toward laissez-faire since German scholars first articulated *Das Adam Smith Problem* in the nineteenth century. How could the man who wrote the *Theory of Moral Sentiments*, which extolled the virtues of sympathy, be the same person who wrote *Wealth of Nations*, where self-interest was the animating spirit of society? For a discussion of this debate, see James R. Otteson, *The Recurring "Adam Smith Problem,"* 17 HIST. PHIL. Q. 51–74 (2000). For a recent discussion of how Adam Smith's work was reinterpreted for modern economics,

Calvo suggests that, in the American context at least, historians have also simplified Smith's legacy in the nineteenth century: "In search of an intellectual paragon, historians have raised Smith into the pantheon of American political economy, retelling reductionist narratives or ignoring the nuances and complexities in the relationship between the *Wealth of Nations* and American economic thought."[10]

The *Wealth of Nations* tells a more complicated story than is suggested by our categories of "state" and "market," and when we read Smith's magnum opus, we learn that he was not as hostile to government as many today imagine. It remains true that classical liberals would insist, with Jeremy Bentham, that the state should carefully mark the boundary between its *agenda* and *non-agenda*.[11] However, Smith himself envisioned a positive role for the state to construct a governed market society through techniques of "public economy." And as an historical matter, actually existing liberal capitalism has tended to rely on tools of active governance, even if the infrastructural state uses corporations and "public–private partnerships" to achieve its ends.

The place to begin thinking about governance for Smith is his *Lectures on Justice, Police, Revenue and Arms*, also called *Lectures on Jurisprudence*, which combines a series of lectures that Smith delivered in the 1760s.[12] In those lectures, Smith previewed the system of political economy he would develop in *Wealth of Nations*. The *Lectures* demonstrate Smith's early understanding of governance and the basic function of law and "police" – a concept with a much broader and more basic meaning than our modern idea of the municipal security force. In legal discourse, *police* refers to the fundamental power of the sovereign to regulate for health, safety, and morality. The etymology of police is the Greek word *politeia* and its cognates, such as *polis*, politics, and policy.[13] It is so fundamental a concept that Smith calls "[p]olice …

---

see Glory M. Liu, *Rethinking the "Chicago Smith" Problem: Adam Smith and the Chicago School, 1929–1980*, 17 MOD. INTELL. HIST. 1041–68 (2020); David A. Reisman, *Adam Smith on Market and State*, 154 J. INST. THEORETICAL ECON. 357–83 (1998); Warren J. Samuels and Steven G. Medema, *Freeing Smith from the "Free Market": On the Misperception of Adam Smith on the Economic Role of Government*, 37 HIST. POL. ECON. 37 (2005).

[10] CALVO, THE EMERGENCE OF CAPITALISM IN EARLY AMERICA, *supra* note 2, at 28.

[11] See Jeremy Bentham, *A Manual of Political Economy*, in THE HISTORY OF ECONOMIC THOUGHT: A READER 203–4 (Steven G. Medema & Warren J. Samuels, eds., 2d ed., 2013).

[12] ADAM SMITH, LECTURES ON JUSTICE, POLICE, REVENUE AND ARMS (1896) (originally delivered at the University of Glasgow and reported by a student in 1763). For a positive assessment of Smith's theory of government elaborated in the *Lectures on Jurisprudence*, see BARRY WEINGAST, ADAM SMITH'S CONSTITUTIONAL THEORY (Working Paper, 2007), available at https://ssrn.com/abstract=2890639 or http://dx.doi.org/10.2139/ssrn.2890639. With respect to a common view that markets emerge of their own accord, Weingast writes: "This common view suffers from the *neoclassical fallacy*…; namely, that free markets can exist without government. Most economic models implicitly assume all the elements of Smith's 'liberty': security from violence; property rights and contract enforcement, and protection from government predation. Universally in today's developed world, governments provide this market infrastructure; and no market economy exists without it," *Id.* at 2.

[13] Santiago Legarre, *The Historical Background of the Police Power*, 9 UNIV. PA. J. CONST. L. 745, 748–49 (2007).

the second general division of jurisprudence." The jurisdiction of police is "cleanliness, security and cheapness or plenty."[14] As Bernard Harcourt notes: "Smith placed his entire discussion of public economy under the rubric of 'police' and he identified the principal task of 'police' as facilitating *bon marché* [the good market]."[15]

Police is connected to another fundamental concept: the "economy." The root of "economy" is *oikos* – the household – and economy therefore represents the study of sound household management. Political economists and jurists worked through the implications of this concept in the eighteenth century as they sought regulatory principles for the emerging liberal order. William Blackstone's *Commentaries on the Laws of England*, for example, figures the "public police" as a patriarchal technology of household management: "By the public police and economy I mean the due regulation of domestic order of the kingdom: whereby the individuals of the state, like members of a well-governed family, are bound to conform their general behaviour to the rules of propriety, good neighborhood, and good manners; and to be decent, industrious, and inoffensive in their respective stations."[16] *Police* is the legal rationale for governing the well-regulated patriarchal household of the republican imaginary.

Police was already in use in Colonial debates in the 1770s over Parliament's regulatory power in the colonies. The distinction became important as American colonists debated the power of the British government to tax the internal commerce of the colonies. There was broad agreement at the time that the British could tax external trade throughout its empire. But as the British government began to rely more on intrusive colonial taxation, such as the Stamp Act, American colonists argued more insistently that they enjoyed a right to "internal government" free from interference – understandings that were later incorporated into the state constitutions after Independence.[17] In the nineteenth century, state and federal courts began using the police power terminology in a variety of disputes over state regulatory power. One of the most common issues involved the conflict between state police power and the right of private property. Here, for example, in *Commonwealth v. Alger* (1851), Massachusetts Chief Justice Lemuel Shaw explains the scope of state police power vis-à-vis private property:

> All property in this commonwealth, as well that in the interior as that bordering on tide waters, is derived directly or indirectly from the government, and held subject to those general regulations, which are necessary to the common good and general

---

[14] *Id.*

[15] Bernard E. Harcourt, The Illusion of Free Markets: Punishment and the Myth of Natural Order 287–312 (2012). For an extended discussion of the police power as a patriarchal model of governance, see Markus Dirk Dubber, The Police Power: Patriarchy and The Foundations of American Government (2005), especially 47–153.

[16] William Blackstone, Commentaries on the Laws of England, Vol 4 (1979) (1753), 162.

[17] Legarre, *The Historical Background of the Police Power*, supra note 13; *see also* Jack P. Greene, *Empire Confronted: 1764–1766*, in The Constitutional Origins of the American Revolution 1764–1766 (2011).

welfare. Rights of property, like all other social and conventional rights, are subject to such reasonable limitations in their enjoyment, as shall prevent them from being injurious, and to such reasonable restraints and regulations established by law, as the legislature, under the governing and controlling power vested in them by the constitution, may think necessary and expedient.

This is very different from the right of eminent domain, the right of a government to take and appropriate private property to public use, whenever the public exigency requires it; which can be done only on condition of providing a reasonable compensation therefor. The power we allude to is rather the police power, the power vested in the legislature by the constitution, to make, ordain and establish all manner of wholesome and reasonable laws, statutes and ordinances, either with penalties or without, not repugnant to the constitution, as they shall judge to be for the good and welfare of the commonwealth, and of the subjects of the same.[18]

As William Novak writes: "Public regulation – the power of the state to restrict individual liberty and property for the common welfare – colored all facets of early American development. It was the central component of a reigning theory and practice of governance committed to the pursuit of the people's welfare and happiness in a well-ordered society and polity."[19] More generally, *police* was an organizing concept for early political economy as it attempted to establish a legal-conceptual framework for the emergent market society. Every U.S. state constitution, for example, has a police power clause that establishes the basic authority for state regulation. Police authorizes the multitude of laws and administrative regulations the sovereign might enact to ensure the peaceful and orderly management of people and resources in the kingdom. It is the legal technology that allows "seeing like a state." Furthermore, as an historical matter, *police* was fundamental to building state-led infrastructure networks in the eighteenth and nineteenth centuries.

The legal and constitutional questions surrounding the police power in America will be explored in later chapters. Returning to Smith for now, we see an interesting shift in his thinking around *police* and *economy*: By the time *The Wealth of Nations* is published ten years after the *Lectures*, "police" largely vanishes from Smith's vocabulary.[20] Because of this, and because so much of *Wealth of Nations* is concerned with elaborating a theory of private trade, it is easy to miss the governance elements that are tucked into the last few chapters. But we should not conclude from this shift in terminology that state-centered governance itself had disappeared from one of classical liberalism's foundational texts. *The Wealth of Nations* does not advocate for a stateless society, nor does Smith think that economies can function

---

[18] *Commonwealth v. Alger*, 61 Mass. 53, 85 (1851). For historical discussion of the police power in America, see D. Benjamin Barros, *The Police Power and the Takings Clause*, 58 UNIV. MIAMI L. REV. 471, 471–524 (2004).

[19] WILLIAM NOVAK, THE PEOPLE'S WELFARE: LAW & REGULATION IN NINETEENTH-CENTURY AMERICA 2 (1996).

[20] HARCOURT, THE ILLUSION OF FREE MARKETS, *supra* note 15, at 443.

absent state activity. The Smith of *Wealth of Nations* would agree with the *Lectures* ten years earlier that "the establishment of law and government is the highest effort of human prudence and wisdom...."[21]

The Wealth of Nation tells us, for example, that the circulation of goods and services ("commerce") would require public trust in government: "Commerce and manufactures," Smith writes, "can seldom flourish in any state in which there is not a certain degree of confidence in the justice of government."[22] Smith's state, therefore, will do more than just provide the minimal framework for securing private property and contract rights: it will use its regulatory powers (*police*) to the ends of national economic development. It will necessarily have an active agenda, one that would become increasingly expansive throughout the liberal nineteenth century. However, it is important to note that the jurisdiction of *police* has been diminished between the *Lectures* and *The Wealth of Nations*. Or to put it another way, police has been transformed from a direct governance mechanism into something more abstract: *a necessary precondition for the emergence of a market society*. A prudent government, in short, will embed *police* into the structures of a wisely administered developmental state.

From Smith's perspective, the agenda of the state will consist of three broad functions: military defense, the administration of justice, and "public works and public institutions."[23] Of the latter, Smith writes: "the duty of erecting and maintaining certain public works and certain public institutions which it can never be for the interest of any individual, or small number of individuals, to erect and maintain; because the profit could never repay the expense to any individual or small number of individuals, though it may frequently do much more than repay it to a great society."[24] Smith's "public works" is roughly equivalent to our modern vocabulary for infrastructure – although it is only *roughly* equivalent, as our use of "infrastructure" tends to be much broader and more abstract than "public works" would have been for Smith. As Smith envisions it, infrastructure cannot fall to the marketplace because it will not be profitable for any individual to do so. Despite the disappearance of the concept from *Wealth of Nations*, however, Smith hints that the building of infrastructure will be a natural function of *police*. He alludes to this during his survey of governance practices across the globe: "This branch of public police accordingly is said to be very much attended to in all those countries, but particularly in China, where the high roads, and still more the navigable

---

[21] SMITH, LECTURES ON JUSTICE, POLICE, REVENUE AND ARMS, *supra* note 12 (quoted at Loc. 3138 in Kindle Version).
[22] SMITH, THE WEALTH OF NATIONS, *supra* note 3, at 375 in Book 5.
[23] *Id.* at chapter I in Book 5.
[24] *Id.* at 205 in Book 5. *See also id.* at Book 5. For a discussion of Adam Smith's attitudes toward government, see MULLER, THE MIND AND THE MARKET, *supra* note 2, at 76–80. *See also* PETER MCNAMARA, POLITICAL ECONOMY AND STATESMANSHIP: SMITH, HAMILTON AND THE FOUNDATION OF THE COMMERCIAL REPUBLIC 11–92 (1998).

canals, it is pretended, exceed very much everything of the same kind which is known in Europe."[25]

Smith's discussion of "public works," which includes "good roads, bridges, navigable canals, harbors," provides an important insight into the relationships between infrastructure financing in the liberal state as imagined at their origins.[26] Public works infrastructure is valuable first and foremost because of the economic growth that it enables; indeed, for Smith, economic growth would be impossible without state-led infrastructure. Smith understands public goods infrastructure in terms of its costs and benefits to the larger society: "Good roads, canals, and navigable rivers, by diminishing the expense of carriage, put the remote parts of the country more nearly upon a level with those in the neighbourhood of the town. They are upon that account the greatest of all improvements."[27] But infrastructure also implicates a broader normative vision of "civilization," since infrastructure enables the development of a latent potential intrinsic to human nature: to develop our individual talents, to specialize within the division of labor, to raise the level of general material culture, and to thus augment the general "human capital" of our society. While we find echoes of this developmental approach in President Monroe's writings and speeches and the American System in the American nineteenth century, even in the late eighteenth century, Smith could see the need for development all around him: the isolated Scottish Highlands, after all, needed to be integrated into the British imperial economy so it could enjoy the bounty of general civilization. Isolation prevents the labor specialization that leads to more effective use of resources and more productive commercial exchange. Like "improvement," which could also mean spiritual and cultural growth, "commerce," could mean social exchange and communication and was not limited to financial transactions in goods and services.

The benefits of infrastructure were as clear to Adam Smith as they would be to Americans in the nineteenth century: Good transportation would create a networked society linking nodes of production and consumption into a common national project of economic development. This would benefit consumers by lowering the price of goods and boost sales volume, thus increasing aggregate national wealth. Infrastructure would also be an important weapon against manufacturing monopolies, because a more dispersed trade network would mean that regional producers could reach more remote customers and thus compete with incumbent

---

[25] SMITH, THE WEALTH OF NATIONS, *supra* note 3, at 235 and Book 5. For the influence of Chinese canal-building on the Eerie canal project, see Craig R. Hanyan, *China and the Erie Canal*, 35 BUS. HIST. REV., 558, 566 (1961): "The Chinese ideas which percolated the experience of New York's canal builders worked with equal subtlety, but with equal force. To a New York provided only with the inadequate works of the Western Company, China gave the vision of a government-built Grand Canal." Christian Parenti also notes the influence of China's Grand Canal on American canal builders in RADICAL HAMILTON: ECONOMIC LESSONS FROM A MISUNDERSTOOD FOUNDER 240–41 (2020).
[26] *Id.* at 230 in Book 5.
[27] *Id.* at 111 in Book 1.

firms, as the case of the isolated Scottish Highlands suggested to Smith. In the end, infrastructure would create a more competitive marketplace that challenged existing monopoly enterprises and lead to more cost-effective management practices within firms: "Though they introduce some rival commodities into the old market, they open many new markets to its produce. Monopoly, besides, is a great enemy to good management, which can never be universally established but in consequence of that free and universal competition which forces everybody to have recourse to it for the sake of self-defence."[28]

But while the benefits to good infrastructure are clear, the costs are harder to see, especially if those costs are bundled up in the general fiscal operations of the state. Thus it is the case that infrastructure, although necessary, should internalize costs to prevent waste and mismanagement. This was especially important for Smith because of the monumental scale of modern infrastructure projects, a point that becomes clear when Smith compared modern road systems with the more modest and less labor-intensive public works of the middle ages. The less extensive road systems of the "ancient monarchies of Europe," Smith argues, could be maintained by a simple labor tax, which was still in common use for road maintenance throughout the United States in the nineteenth century: "The labour of the country people, for three days before and for three days after harvest, was thought a fund sufficient for making and maintaining all the bridges, highways, and other public works which the commerce of the country was supposed to require."[29] As infrastructure technology becomes more capital-intensive and technologically sophisticated, however, it is more expensive to build and maintain. Therefore, modern states will of necessity have recourse to heavier taxation to achieve the same purpose.

Since the high cost of infrastructure was an important problem for modern societies, Smith spends considerable space in Book V elaborating on the basic purpose of infrastructure. He directs his readers to three basic questions: Why should infrastructure be built? where should it be built? and how should it be financed? Smith answers these questions with a single principle: Infrastructure will embody a logic of utility aimed at general economic development with minimum impact on the public fisc. The "why" of infrastructure tells us "where" it will be most useful. It is especially important that infrastructure only be built where it will assist commercial development. Here, Smith has in mind national and regional economic capacity, but he is also thinking of *commerce* and *improvement* in eighteenth-century terms, which is to say moral and cultural capacity as well as the development of material civilization. Thus, in a sense, our contemporary vocabulary of "hard" and "soft" infrastructure is already present in Adam Smith. "Hard" infrastructure means, for example, roads, post offices, and canals. "Soft" infrastructure, in contrast, means something like human capital, which in Smith's view also feeds back into

---

[28] Id. at 112, Books 1–3. *See also id.* at Book X.
[29] Id. at 302, Book 5.

commercial development. As Smith sees it, infrastructure exists to serve the public good, which is best served by increasing commerce, in its broader eighteenth-century sense, the traffic of persons, ideas, and goods that circulate within the prosperous nation, ideas that were also in evidence when Americans debated their own internal improvement policy in the early republic.

More generally, Smith views infrastructure as an enabling technology that will bring markets and commerce into existence, releasing hitherto unrealized possibilities for civilizational advance. Citing the example of the Scottish Highlands, Smith argues that isolation presents an obstacle to the natural division of labor that would likely occur in its absence. Certain kinds of occupations can only develop within large cities ("porter" is Smith's first example), and small towns do not provide opportunities to develop specialized skills necessary to capture the value created by division of labor: "In the lone houses and very small villages which are scattered about in so desert a country as the Highlands of Scotland, every farmer must be butcher, baker, and brewer for his own family."[30] Without infrastructure enabling people to travel outside the narrow confines of the provinces, it would be difficult to develop economic efficiencies, which would generally improve the human condition. Smith associates civilizational advance with good transportation infrastructure, suggesting infrastructure's intrinsic usefulness as a technology of empire. Smith is particularly concerned that nations develop "water-carriage" rather than remaining land-locked. The ancient empires, for example, built "navigable canals" and "inland navigation."[31] Smith compares the ancient seafaring empires favorably to "[a]ll the inland parts of Africa" and other isolated regions, which "seem in all ages of the world to have been in the same barbarous and uncivilized state in which we find them at present."[32] In short, infrastructure is a defining feature of civilization as it is figured by the developmental imagination.

Infrastructure's implication with government financing, however, means that it will require sound oversight to prevent siphoning off productive capital. Public works in the liberal state will need to be disciplined by accounting principles with an eye to reducing costs: "A magnificent high road cannot be made through a desert country where there is little or no commerce, or merely because it happens to lead to the country villa of the intendant of the province, or to that of some great lord to whom the intendant finds it convenient to make his court."[33] Smith voices a familiar concern here that public money will be spent building "bridges to nowhere," and otherwise lead to corrupt self-dealing. The same concern is expressed in another way when Smith discusses infrastructure pricing, which is just as important as purpose and place. Pricing should be calibrated as closely as possible to its true utility for aggregate

---

[30] *Id.* at 14 in Book 1.
[31] *Id.* at 15–16 in Book 1.
[32] *Id.* at 16 in Book 1.
[33] *Id.* at 231 in Book 5.

social welfare. To achieve this objective, infrastructure should couple a broad public purpose with a narrow logic of internalized costs. The balance must be carefully struck between government control and private ownership. On the one hand, Smith argues that "[t]he tolls for the maintenance of a high road cannot with any safety be made the property of private persons."[34] On the other hand, if government is simply allowed to set toll prices it will be tempted to use that money for purposes unrelated to repair and maintenance: "[I]f the tolls which are levied at the turnpikes should ever be considered as one of the resources for supplying the exigencies of the state, they would certainly be augmented as those exigencies were supposed to require. According to the policy of Great Britain, therefore, they would probably be augmented very fast. The facility with which a great revenue could be drawn from them would probably encourage administration to recur very frequently to this resource."[35]

Smith's sarcastic tone here forecasts public choice theories of the twentieth century, with their deep skepticism of the fiscal soundness and efficiency of the modern state. The risk of infrastructure for Smith lies in the near certainty that the government would use it as just another source of extracting rents while neglecting to invest in the necessary upkeep to make the infrastructure useful for commerce. The result would be bad roads, bad fiscal balance sheets, and sluggish commercial development. To prevent government abuses, Smith proposes tolls calibrated to the weight of the carriage passing over the road, as long as that money is earmarked for road maintenance rather than being absorbed by the general revenue of the state. Smith's elegant solution to the problem of financing public works infrastructure augured things to come. His concern with protecting the public fisc leads him naturally to the argument that infrastructure should defray its own costs with fees levied as much as possible on actual users of that infrastructure. Smith thus advocates for user-funded public works, or what contemporary public cost accounting calls "self-liquidating" infrastructure.[36] The idea is that infrastructure should pay for itself over time through bond issues or loans that can be retired with user fees such as tolls to avoid undue impact on the public fisc.[37]

---

[34] *Id.* at 232 in Book 5.
[35] *Id.* at 233–04 in Book 5.
[36] Robert D. Leighninger Jr., Long-Range Public Investment: The Forgotten Legacy of the New Deal 8–9 (2007). *See also* Realignment Project, *The Curse of "Self-Liquidation" – Direct Job Creation vs. Traditional Public Works (A Job Insurance Supplement)* (July 15, 2010, 12:44 AM), https://realignmentproject.wordpress.com/2010/07/15/the-curse-of-self-liquidation-direct-job-creation-vs-traditional-public-works-a-job-insurance-supplement/: "The idea of a 'self-liquidating' public works project – i.e., one that would generate sufficient revenue to pay back the cost of construction – is one of the most persistent policy ideas in modern history. It was dominant throughout the Western world for the whole of the 19th century, and especially in the 20th century leading up to the Great Depression. Self-liquidation became the gold standard for assessing the value and worth of public works, and it wasn't an accident that self-liquidation only calculates a narrow economic value without considering the social value of the project, or the economic impact on the workers and the businesses they patronize, or the inherent value of the worker's labor."
[37] Smith, The Wealth of Nations, *supra* note 3, at 230–36 in Book 5.

In order to keep expenses low and apportioned fairly, infrastructure should be paid for only by those who use it. Smith believes that this user-fee model might be widely extended, for example, to the administration of justice. To avoid having the legal system be "a burden on the general revenue of the society," and to defray its costs, Smith proposes that parties pay the costs of lawsuits themselves by "[a] stamp-duty on the law proceedings of each particular court."[38] More generally, Smith concludes: "It seems not unreasonable that the extraordinary expense which the protection of any particular branch of commerce may occasion should be defrayed by a moderate tax upon that particular branch."[39] Although this sounds reasonable on its face, it is worth considering what it means that the costs of infrastructure should be paid for by "that particular branch" of society that uses it. Smith envisions this infrastructure user fee as both a matter of equity – only those who use it pay for it – and a matter of efficiency.

On the one hand, it seems eminently fair for infrastructure users to foot the bill for only the services they use rather than distributing the cost widely across society. Why should Londoners pay for a road in the Highlands? On the other hand, of course, the question of "who should pay," is not a neutral question. A pay-as-you-go model of user fees, for example, seems strongly implied by Smith's theory of infrastructure. By our lights, such a model could be considered regressive, begging the important distributional questions that are raised by infrastructures in modern societies. Self-liquidating infrastructure, however, follows the liberal logic of internalized cost and general efficiency, coupled with a distrust of the government to manage public resources wisely. Broader questions of equity that shape real-world infrastructural politics are hinted at but not elaborated in Smith's model. By writing these principles into infrastructure, classical liberalism figures infrastructure as a secondary technology for the production of economic growth. As a secondary yet necessary undertaking, infrastructure is clearly marked off from more important economic activity and inscribed within the logic of balanced budgets. In Smith's analysis of costs, we see *police* written into the infrastructures of the modern liberal state itself, superintended by self-limiting economic principles.

Thus, while *police* seems to disappear as an organizing concept between the *Lectures* and *The Wealth of Nations*, it is more accurate to say that *police* merely changes form, evolving from the customary (and arbitrary) price-setting authority of mercantilism into a more technocratic conception of regulation with an eye to increasing economic output and the material advance of "civilization." In short, the state is still necessary in *Wealth of Nations*, but it will always be *dangerous* as long as it remains committed to its historic ethos of war, waste, and luxury. The state itself will need an external source of discipline that *police* imagines as the role of the wise patriarch: that source of discipline will now be economic theory itself,

---

[38] Id. at 228 in Book 5.
[39] Id. at 237 in Book 5.

which is just then emerging in the writings of Smith and classical economics. The sound management of *police* reappears in Smith as the fiscally prudent government learning to live within its means. In Smith's theory, the problem of public goods infrastructure could be solved by carefully balancing its costs against its general utility for commerce and development. But his argument implicates the uneasy tension between the broad logic of "improvement" and "commerce" that infrastructure enables and the narrower concerns of the cost-accounting principle written into self-liquidating public works. By discussing questions of equity, albeit in the margins, Smith implies distributional and equitable concepts such as fairness and legitimacy that have always surrounded economy and infrastructure.

As we shall see in subsequent chapters, the question of infrastructure financing and governance remained important questions throughout the nineteenth century. Albert Gallatin, for example, who had read Smith, followed his approach in his infrastructure plan in the early nineteenth century. Alexander Hamilton, on the other hand, rejected Smith's view of government debt and essentially reversed Smith's understanding of the relations between state and economy under capitalism. Hamilton substituted his own pragmatic and historical understanding of statecraft and development for Smith's model. These questions remain highly relevant today, as we debate the politics of user fees, state and local budgets, municipal debt and important distributional questions implicated in infrastructure provision.[40] Liberal governance models, committed to an idea of "the economy," remain conflicted about the relationship between the enabling structures of modern society and other, more valuable, activities that those structures exist to enable. Or to put this in a more pointed way: at its origins, public infrastructure has been inscribed within the logic of "privatization" that shapes our own infrastructural politics.

1.3 DEBT, GOVERNANCE AND THE LIBERAL HOUSEHOLD

We can sharpen our understanding of infrastructure within the liberal order by examining Smith's analysis of taxation, sovereign debt, and the nature of money. To begin with, Smith links money and infrastructure when he argues that bridges, canals, and the post office can add to the revenues of the state as a type of tax: "The coinage, another institution for facilitating commerce, in many countries, not only defrays its own expense, but affords a small revenue or seignorage to the sovereign. The post-office, another institution for the same purpose, over and above defraying its own expense, affords in almost all countries a very considerable revenue to the sovereign."[41] Seignorage is the surcharge or tax that sovereigns collect for turning

---

[40] For a recent treatment of this question, see DESTIN JENKINS, THE BONDS OF INEQUALITY: DEBT AND THE MAKING OF THE AMERICAN CITY (2021).
[41] SMITH, THE WEALTH OF NATIONS, *supra* note 3, at 230 in Book 5; CHRISTINE DESAN, MAKING MONEY: COIN, CURRENCY, AND THE COMING OF CAPITALISM 78–79 (2014).

bullion into coinage for general use by the public. Smith's use of "seignorage" here in the context of the post office is suggestive of a deeper link between infrastructure and the finances of the modern state. The state's monopoly power over coin represents its special role in providing infrastructures for commerce and development. Elaborating the linkages between money, state power, and infrastructure, Smith imagines a direct relationship between infrastructure and the sovereign power that enables it. This was not merely theoretical; it reflected the actual course of liberal statecraft in the United States. For example, using their corporate charter powers, American states could license corporations to (in principle) produce and distribute value across commercial society. The federal government also made liberal use of seignorage to connect money, land, banks, military power, and infrastructures in the nineteenth century.

Additionally, money, like law and other public-facing institutions, supplies an infrastructure of commerce superintended by the state even though it will involve multiple actors across a chain of public–private governance. But there is a catch: Smith believes we must be very careful before allowing the government too much license in using its infrastructural powers for "seignorage." The problem with infrastructure is that although it is socially necessary, it is very expensive to create and maintain; it is open to the public and will suffer wear and tear that must be repaired. Moreover, because the state will be involved in infrastructure, there is always a danger that public works will crush productive commerce with onerous taxation or rent-seeking behavior by the government or the elites who have captured it. The state, in other words, must undergo a "civilizing process" that weans elites from aristocratic habits of waste and luxury and orient them toward the prudential ethos of *police*.[42]

Concerns over sovereign debt, taxation, and the warfare state were endemic to political theory since the emergence of modern banking in the Italian city-states and are front and center in the story of infrastructure. Early states contracted large sovereign debts to engage in warfare, hire mercenary armies, distribute patronage, etc.[43] Niccolò Machiavelli had established the importance of sovereign debt for the political economy of the prince's household and state. These concerns carried over into the eighteenth-century British writers who observed a massive increase in sovereign debt connected to "empire, war, and parliamentary patronage."[44] David Hume, for example, worried throughout his life that public debt would spread ruin throughout the land. In "Of Public Credit" Hume issued a dire warning about the ultimate end point for the overly-indebted state: "The whole fabric, already tottering, falls to the ground, and buries thousands in its ruins. And this, I think, may be

---

[42] Although subject to much criticism, Norbert Elias's *The Civilizing Process* (1939) offers a still-valuable account of the disciplining of aristocratic elites that attended the development of the modern nation state.

[43] For an excellent history of sovereign debt see Kenneth Dyson, *The Evolution of Public Debt*, in STATES, DEBT & POWER: 'SAINTS' AND 'SINNERS' IN EUROPEAN HISTORY AND INTEGRATION (2014).

[44] *Id.* at 71.

called the *natural death* of public credit: For to this period it tends as naturally as an animal body to its dissolution and destruction."[45]

Smith, while not willing to go as far as Hume in banning public debt altogether, is likewise concerned that public borrowing, especially for war making, could lead to irresponsible public finance and national ruin. Smith, like Hume before him, draws a tight nexus between warfare, the fiscal state and what we would now call the "real economy." As Hume had argued in his essay *Of Commerce*, echoing Machiavelli, financing the war state had a direct effect on the common people whom early modern kings crushed with oppressive taxation: "When the sovereign raises an army, what is the consequence? He imposes a tax. This tax obliges all the people to retrench what is least necessary to their subsistence."[46] Warfare was one of the largest expenditures of the early modern state and supplies one of the most pressing rationales for good transportation infrastructure. But when the state needs to wage war, it requires much more revenue, which it supplies in the short term by expanding the public debt and resorting to onerous taxation. This is a drain on the private economy, caused by the state drawing off productive resources to fund war.[47]

The problem is that complex sovereign debt dynamics makes it possible to hide the real state of national indebtedness with accounting tricks. The "sophistry of the mercantile system," as Smith calls it, obscures the long-term financial health of the state because neither governing elites nor creditors has any incentive to be prudent. So, while it might *seem* logical to view sovereign debts as a matter of simply balancing the national account, in the long run unchecked sovereign debt is wasteful and destructive for the real economy. In the end, sovereign debt pits parasitic creditors and the profligate warfare state against productive enterprises that form the basis of a nation's true wealth.[48] Mercantilism leads, in other words, to institutional distortion and moral hazard. "But a creditor of the public," Smith writes, "considered merely as such, has no interest in the good condition of any particular portion of land, or in the good management of any particular portion of capital stock. As a creditor of the public he has no knowledge of any such particular portion. He has no inspection of it. He can have no care about it. Its ruin may in some cases be unknown to him, and cannot directly affect him."[49] Smith's attack here on the rentier class is designed to free up capital for more productive uses.[50] He is concerned that if we

---

[45] Maria Pia Paganelli, *David Hume on Public Credit*, 20 HIST. ECON. IDEAS 31, 31–48 (2012); John Christian Laursen & Greg Coolidge, *David Hume and Public Credit: Crying Wolf?*, 20 HUME STUD. 143, 143–49 (1994); J. G. A. POCOCK, THE MACHIAVELLIAN MOMENT: FLORENTINE POLITICAL THOUGHT AND THE ATLANTIC REPUBLICAN TRADITION 496–97 (1975).

[46] DAVID HUME, DAVID HUME ESSAYS: MORAL, POLITICAL, AND LITERARY (Eugene F. Miller ed., revised ed., Liberty Fund 2013) (1777) (quoted at Loc. 3852 in Kindle edition).

[47] SMITH, THE WEALTH OF NATIONS, *supra* note 3, at 387 in Books 4–5. *See also id.* at Book X.

[48] *Id.* at 387–88 in Books 4–5.

[49] *Id.* at 389 in Books 4–5.

[50] Not coincidentally, Smith levels this same criticism at joint-stock corporations. To avoid rent-seeking and misaligned incentives, Smith develops a stakeholder theory of corporate governance – one that

treat the payment of sovereign debt as simply the balancing of national accounts, governments will attempt to disguise their indebtedness by manipulating the money supply, demonetizing or debasing coinage, etc., or by resorting to expanding their tax base, especially in their vulnerable and disenfranchised colonies.[51] As discussed in Chapter 2, Alexander Hamilton's financial restructuring dealt with this problem by aligning the interest of large creditors to the federal government, a move that Republicans saw as antidemocratic and corrupt.

In Book V, Chapter III, "Of Public Debts," Smith lays out his concern for the oppressive growth of sovereign debt. The vocabulary he uses resonates with the republican themes common in American history about the sound management of the fiscal household: "The progress of the enormous debts which at present oppress, and will in the long-run probably ruin, all the great nations of Europe has been pretty uniform. Nations, *like private men*, have generally begun to borrow upon what may be called personal credit, without assigning or mortgaging any particular fund for the payment of the debt; and when this resource has failed them, they have gone on to borrow upon assignments or mortgages of particular funds" (emphasis added).[52] Smith repeats a similar point elsewhere to develop his account of national policy as prudent household management. When he does so, he uses language that invokes the patriarchal police power: "It is the maxim of every prudent master of a family, never to attempt to make at home what it will cost him more to make than to buy ... What is prudence in the conduct of every private family, can scarce be folly in that of a great kingdom."[53] In other words, nations, like private individuals, must balance their books. Here is the debate between Hamilton and Jefferson in a nutshell, a debate that has been remarkably persistent as an organizing theme of American political history, which will be explored in more detail in Chapter 2. As President Obama put it in 2010: "At a time when so many families are tightening their belts, [OMB director Jacob Lew] is going to make sure that the government continues to tighten its own."[54] It would be difficult to find a better contemporary example of an appeal to republican virtue than President Obama's sentiment.

But nations, of course, are not private individuals. They borrow on better terms and in general their debts are more generously forgiven.[55] And more fundamentally, they exercise important control over money and public finance that individuals do not, as Alexander Hamilton understood. Yet Smith's logic of the nation-as-household

has profound implications for infrastructure and state investment. *See* SMITH, THE WEALTH OF NATIONS, *supra* note 3, at 253–55 in Books 4–5.

[51] SMITH, THE WEALTH OF NATIONS, *supra* note 3, at 390–403 in Books 4–5.
[52] *Id.* at 375 in Books 4–5.
[53] *Id.* at 23 in Books 4–5.
[54] Quoted in Derek Thompson, *Obama: Loosen the Belt, Tighten the Speechwriting*, ATL. (July 15, 2010), available at www.theatlantic.com/business/archive/2010/07/obama-loosen-the-belt-tighten-the-speechwriting/59808/.
[55] For a discussion of the various paradoxes of sovereign debt, see JEROME ROOS, WHY NOT DEFAULT? THE POLITICAL ECONOMY OF SOVEREIGN DEBT (2019).

casts a continuing shadow over modern politics of budgets, public debt, and infrastructure. To see this point from another angle, it is helpful to examine Adam Smith's views on the origins of money. In his quest to reduce the state's power over trade, Smith asks us to imagine money as a convenience technology that enables preexisting commerce. To justify this claim in historical experience, he tells a just-so story about the emergence of money from barter. In Book One, Chapter IV, "Of the Origin and Use of Money," Smith develops his account of the division of labor developed in the first three chapters, in which we had learned about man's innate "propensity to truck, barter, and exchange one thing for another," using self-interest as the engine of commercial exchange and producing a natural inequality arising from differences in talent.[56]

Smith, picking up on Aristotle's account of money, elaborates an evolutionary story of money's emergence from preexisting barter economies. In the beginning, lacking money and credit, "primitive" man bartered for goods, swapping, say, cattle for wheat in a series of one-off trades. This process, however, has a design flaw: it would quickly succumb to the problem of *mutuality of wants*, meaning that in order for a true barter economy to work, individuals trading cattle would happen to need wheat just at the moment when that other party had it available. Money is then invented to make this process more efficient. States eventually monopolize the process of money production in order to make barter possible. Thus is the "economy" imagined as separate from, and prior to, the state – a view that still shapes our understanding of infrastructure as secondary to the real economy.

What is important here is that for Smith and for later economists, money is merely a passive register of value that is created elsewhere. The barter story is important for liberal models and the state-market dichotomy that shapes infrastructure's ideological and material life. One implication of the story is that barter *is* the real economy; it predates the state, laws, institutions, etc. Money is a passive register of value created by the productive half of a nature-politics divide. New studies of money's origins and functions, written in the shadow of the 2008 financial crisis, present serious challenges to Smith's just-so story – and with it the presumed priority of private over public in the economic imagination. In fact, all available historical evidence suggests that complex credit arrangements preceded the emergence of specie-money (i.e., coin). Money, in other words, is a product of a resource and taxing system produced by the state not an epiphenomenon of private trade. It is, as Alexander Hamilton understood, a governance project, albeit in Hamilton's account still bound to the narrative of creditworthiness, character, and virtue.[57]

---

[56] SMITH, THE WEALTH OF NATIONS, *supra* note 3, at 11–12 in Book 2.

[57] For an alternative story about money-creation as a project of state governance that imagines it as a "constitutional project," see DESAN, MAKING MONEY, *supra* note 41, at 24: "'Money' is invented when a community, acting through a stakeholder, denominates in a homogeneous way the disparate contributions received from members, and recognizes them as a medium and mode of payment."

Smith's story, which imagines money as simply a more convenient technology for preexisting barter, has had long-lasting consequences for our views about public finances and infrastructure. The barter story tends to downplay the state's role in trade and commerce, which are figured through natural law and Lockean property rights as prior to the state. As Scott Ferguson puts it: "[W]hether this story is adopted guilelessly, rejected outright, or accepted as a useful myth, the modern economic orthodoxy is retained in its basic structure and premises. In this drama, private exchange is the hero and government, a tag-along sidekick…. Though it may take part in the money relation, market exchange remains the economy's protagonist. Government is never the star of the show."[58] In other words, Smith and his inheritors essentially privatize money and represent the state as a wise custodian of preexisting resources created elsewhere. While Smith acknowledges the state's role in infrastructure provision, and in market creation and development, he writes a logic of austerity into the very infrastructures of modern life.

1.4 THE BIRTH OF INFRASTRUCTURE: NATURAL MONOPOLY, CORPORATIONS, AND PUBLIC UTILITY

The problem of monopoly and the corporation shaped liberalism's approach to infrastructure from the time of Adam Smith. Monopoly and the corporation were twin problems for Smith because unless carefully managed both could distort efficiencies that occur in the "natural" marketplace. Until the late nineteenth century, corporations in the United States were created by special acts of government, granting a monopoly over a specific trade, social function (e.g., poor relief), or what was considered commercially valuable and politically important activity (such as building infrastructure). As limited monopolies, corporations could serve a useful function as a temporary reward for a risky undertaking, such as, in Smith's words, "to establish a new trade with some remote and barbarous nation."[59] Smith is referring here to the East India company, but the corporation was indispensable as a type of proprietary governance model for the British empire that enabled the colonization of North America. Like patents and copyrights, the trade monopoly is necessary to encourage socially valuable but risky ventures.

One problem with corporate monopolies is that they can last for many years or even be granted in perpetuity, thus presenting an obstacle to new entrants. Moreover, a "perpetual monopoly" grants the monopolist the power to "tax" the public with higher prices by excluding competitors from the market: "A monopoly granted either to an individual or to a trading company has the same effect as a secret in trade or manufactures. The monopolists, by keeping the market constantly

---

[58] Scott Ferguson, Declarations of Dependence: Money, Aesthetics, and the Politics of Care 708–16 (2018) (quoted at Loc. 708–16 in Kindle edition).
[59] Smith, The Wealth of Nations, *supra* note 3, at 253 and Books 4–5.

under-stocked, by never fully supplying the effectual demand, sell their commodities much above the natural price, and raise their emoluments, whether they consist in wages or profit, greatly above their natural rate."[60] Monopolies also lock new entrants out of the market through special grants of exclusive rights by government – precisely the corrupt collusion of government and elite business interests that so incensed Americans in the nineteenth century.

Corporation, monopoly, and infrastructure thus share a common history within liberal governance. In the colonies and later United States, corporate monopolies were granted to companies that built and maintained bridges, roads, and ferries and other projects. Infrastructure monopolies were some of the most visible and familiar uses of the corporate form in the early United States, and governments typically granted exclusivity for transportation infrastructure to secure long-term returns on capital investment. Despite early liberalism's animus against monopolies, however, it sometimes made sense to leave monopolies undisturbed. If carefully circumscribed, exclusive monopolies could serve the ends of social utility. Smith thus exempted a certain class of enterprise from his general antipathy to corporate monopoly. These are enterprises enjoying some built-in advantage, which economists would later call "natural monopoly."

Natural monopoly would not always govern infrastructure. Smith for example thinks that competition could still govern infrastructure where providers undertook "routine" or "uniform" activities such as banking, insurance, and "the trade of making and maintaining a navigable cut or canal; and ... the similar trade of bringing water for the supply of a great city."[61] In Smith's time, as through the American nineteenth century, chartered companies supplied cities with water, built canals, and undertook other infrastructure projects. According to Smith, the more routine the activity, the more likely it was that joint-stock companies were perfectly capable of performing this work without being granted exclusivity. In other words, it made sense to Smith that there would be multiple and competing providers of water or companies dedicated to canal maintenance. And indeed, the historical record in America reflects that pattern.

A natural monopoly, on the other hand, exists for Smith where an industry enjoys advantages that accrued from its geographical situs or other special qualities arising not from artificial legal interference (e.g., the grant of exclusive franchise) but from nature itself. In other words, a natural monopoly enjoyed legitimacy over mere legal monopoly (e.g., guilds and other state-created monopolies) because it arose from some advantage that was intrinsic in the natural order of things. So, for example, certain European wine producers enjoy price premia for wines because of their unique situated vineyards, what French winemakers call "terroir." These vineyards enjoy a unique advantage that enable them to sell vintage wines at a large markup.

---

[60] *Id.* at 47 in Book 1.
[61] *Id.* at 254 in Book 5.

1.4 Natural Monopoly, Corporations and Public Utility

There was not enough high-quality wine produced to meet market demand, which meant higher prices. However strongly one felt about competition, though, there was no point in mandating that two regions create wine denominated as *Bordeaux* to ensure a good outcome for consumers. The French winemaker enjoyed a natural monopoly that there was no good reason to disturb.[62]

Classical liberalism's faith in the competitive joint-stock infrastructure venture would be sorely tested as technologies became more capital-intensive and complex throughout the nineteenth century. Eventually, the category of natural monopoly would broaden beyond just those enterprises that arose from geographical advantage. By the second half of the nineteenth century, the development of new networked infrastructure technologies (e.g., telegraph, water, gas, railroads, etc.) complicated Smith's assumptions about competitive infrastructure provision, and challenged the prevailing model of intra-firm competition in liberal political economy. Nineteenth-century liberals such as J. S. Mill were faced with the question of how to square new, capital-intensive, and networked infrastructures with the norm of competitive markets. In *Principles of Political Economy* (1848), John Stuart Mill used the examples of water and gas supplies in the city to make a case that such services should not follow the model of competition that he advocated for a market economy. He begins with the presumption that "voluntary associations" should be left to act as they see fit. But that does not mean that the government will not have an interest in control and regulation:

> This applies to the case of a road, a canal, or a railway. These are always, in a great degree, practical monopolies; and a government which concedes such monopoly unreservedly to a private company, does much the same thing as if it allowed an individual or an association to levy any tax they chose, for their own benefit, on all the malt produced in the country, or on all the cotton imported into it.[63]

There was little sense in duplicative capital investment in the case of the new networked infrastructures. It made little business sense, for example, for a water company to invest in new pipes where another company had already created the physical architecture for water provision. Infrastructure monopolies provide economies of scale, which are hindered or made impossible by multiple overlapping providers. J. S. Mill and other liberals would thus apply Smith's concept of natural monopoly (and later, public utility) to the problem of infrastructure provision in the new networked industries; by the end of that century natural monopoly and public utility seemed poised to swallow a good deal of the economic activity of cities, states, and regions.

---

[62] *Id.* at 117–18 in Book 1; Adam Plaiss, *From Natural Monopoly to Public Utility: Technological Determinism and the Political Economy of Infrastructure in Progressive–Era America*, 57 TECH. AND CULTURE, 806–30, 809 (2016).

[63] JOHN STUART MILL, PRINCIPLES OF POLITICAL ECONOMY (3d ed. 2017) (1848) (quoted at Loc. 8340–42 in Kindle edition).

As dense transportation and communication networks crisscrossed Europe and the U.S., political economists developed sophisticated theories of natural monopoly and public utility to exempt from market logic a wide range of objects, networks, and services that had previously been provided by competitive franchises. The expanded idea of natural monopoly, which tracked the networked technologies and urban density, would lay the conceptual foundation for public utilities law at the turn of the twentieth century. This was a byproduct of more sophisticated technological systems that developed between the time of Adam Smith and the time of the New Deal.[64]

1.5 CONCLUSION

Despite its reputation as a source for laissez-faire theory, *The Wealth of Nations* and related works of classical liberal theory are better understood as developing the framework for a market state – one that will be disciplined by the cost-internalizing principles embodied in self-liquidating infrastructure. Despite Smith's rejection of mercantilist regulations, his model for a commercial society requires careful calibration through *police*. The governments of the future will still "see like a state," harnessing resources, human capital, and money to the ends of improvement and development. On this view, a market society will still require the careful guidance of a state that learns to discipline itself with sound economics. However, when Smith acknowledges the need for regulation, *police*, and natural monopoly, he forecasts the problems that liberal governance models will face as they attempt to prioritize a private economy that is always parasitical on preexisting state structures and techniques of management. The networked infrastructures of the nineteenth century would extend ever further the reach of the government until by the end of the century they would threaten to swallow the private marketplace with a tide of expanded *police* that resembled nothing so much as the mercantilist regulations that Smith had hoped to banish.

---

[64] Manuela Mosca, *On the Origins of the Concept of Natural Monopoly: Economies of Scale and Competition* 15 EUR. J. HIST. ECON. THOUGHT 317–53 (2008).

2

Forging the Infrastructural State

1787–1837

"If Congress can make canals, they can with more propriety emancipate."[1]

2.1 INTRODUCTION: AMERICA'S COMPLICATED INFRASTRUCTURAL POLITICS

Alexis de Tocqueville was a great admirer of America's passion for improvement: "America is a land of wonders, in which everything is in constant motion and every change seems an improvement. The idea of novelty is there indissolubly connected with the idea of amelioration."[2] One of the most frequent complaints in Tocqueville's *Democracy in America*, however, was the terrible quality of American roads: "If ever the taste for travelling takes you, I do not counsel you to choose the part of America where I am now. The roads are fearful, detestable, the carriages are so rough that it's enough to break the toughest bones."[3] America's transportation system was in terrible shape in the decades after independence. Much travel on the seaboard was by boat or ferry; rivers frequently froze and made travel difficult or impossible. In *American Notes on General Circulation*, Charles Dickens reported the icy conditions and deteriorated roads that hampered his travels through Connecticut in the winter of 1840: "We went on next morning, still by railroad, to Springfield. From that place to Hartford, whither we were bound, is a distance of only five-and-twenty miles, but at that time of the year the roads were so bad that the journey would probably have occupied ten or twelve hours."[4]

As Tocqueville traveled throughout the country, he discussed many topics with the people he met, including the matter that was on everyone's mind: the difficulty

---

[1] Cited in DANIEL WALKER HOWE, WHAT HATH GOD WROUGHT: THE TRANSFORMATION OF AMERICA, 1815–1848 221–22 (2007).
[2] Alexis de Tocqueville, DEMOCRACY IN AMERICA (tr. Henry Reeve, 2009) (1840).
[3] Id.
[4] Charles Dickens, Worcester. *Chapter V The Connecticut River. Hartford. New Haven. To New York*, in AMERICAN NOTES FOR GENERAL CIRCULATION AND PICTURES FROM ITALY 60–67 (1913) (edition available on The Gutenberg Project).

of traveling across the eastern seaboard of the United States in the 1830s. George Wilson Pierson records the following exchange between Tocqueville and South Carolina politician Joel Roberts Poinsett on the subject of American roads:

Q. How are roads made and repaired in America?
A. It's a great constitutional question whether Congress has the right to make anything but military roads. Personally, I am convinced that the right exists; there being disagreement, however, practically no use, one might say, is made of it. It's the States that often undertake to open and keep up the roads traversing them. Most frequently these roads are at the expense of the counties. In general our roads are in very bad repair. We haven't the central authority to force the counties to do their duty. The inspection, being local, is biased and slack. Individuals, it is true, have the right to sue the communities which do not suitably repair their roads; but no one wants to have a suit with the local authority.[5]

Poinsett's response that roads were a "great constitutional" question refers to the roiling debate over "internal improvements," a term that Americans used (rather than "infrastructure") to talk about lighthouses and the postal system, as well as roads, bridges, canals, and other transportation and communication networks. While this sort of basic infrastructure may seem like the sort of unremarkable material stuff that defines modern societies, that was not the case in the early United States. Internal improvements remained politically controversial well into the nineteenth century, implicating early American divisions between North and South, Federalist and Republican as well as regional competition for development dollars in Congress. As John Lauritz Larson observes, "[w]ithin a decade of the ratification of the 1787 Constitution, all kinds of schemes for internal improvement – whether for universities, libraries, roads, canals, or river and harbor improvements – were engendering bitter debates about class rule, popular sovereignty, the virtues of agriculture or commerce, regional jealousy, states' rights, national consolidation, and the return of government corruption."[6]

The case of internal improvements at the federal level from 1787 to 1837, however, suggests that American governance patterns were pragmatic and utilitarian, rather than committed to laissez-faire theory of the small state. Federal power in a variety of ways to create a liberal capitalist state by building transportation and communication infrastructures. While the concessions in America's constitutional model to small-state Republicans often thwarted the more ambitious plans of the Federalist nation builders, it was not laissez-faire theory that prevented the use of federal power for nation-building projects. When government in the first half of the century wanted to promote economic development, "no overriding theory held government back."[7] The liberal forms of governance that developed in America were not the Lockean minimal state that Louis Hartz famously imagined to be America's continuous

---

[5] Quoted in GEORGE WILSON PIERSON, TOCQUEVILLE IN AMERICA 653 (1996) (1835).
[6] JOHN LAURITZ LARSON, INTERNAL IMPROVEMENT: NATIONAL PUBLIC WORKS AND THE PROMISE OF POPULAR GOVERNMENT IN THE EARLY UNITED STATES 5 (2001).
[7] LAWRENCE M. FRIEDMAN, A HISTORY OF AMERICAN LAW 177 (3d ed. 2005).

laissez-faire tradition.⁸ Rather, the American experience of internal improvements reveals the complicated entanglements of state, law, and capitalism in the nineteenth century and illustrates the continuing problems with neat categories of state and market, public and private to describe the political economy of capitalism.

Although the publication date of Wealth of Nations coincides with the Declaration of Independence, it is to Alexander Hamilton's developmental vision of public finance – not Adam Smith's notion of an invisible hand – which supply the sharpest insights into the early American market state. As Hamilton understood, the American fiscal state was a necessary agent to the economic, territorial, and military objectives of early nation-building. One signature laissez-faire policy, free trade, was rejected by Congress in favor of high tariffs and protectionism for much of the nineteenth century, much to the chagrin of Southern planters who wanted a regime of free trade in order to increase the volume of cotton sales abroad. Moreover, governments at every level of society exercised regulatory power to advance some version of the public good through infrastructure construction and regulation. As William J. Novak writes: "The nineteenth century was not an era of laissez-faire or statelessness where public inertia and political naiveté just happened to provide the perfect conditions for a burgeoning private market economy and a self-generating civil democracy."⁹ There was no generalized theory, whether republican, liberal, or otherwise that prevented the state and federal governments from taking an active role in growing an empire of law and capital and developing what we would later call "the economy" (a concept discussed in Chapter 6).

2.2 SEEING LIKE A STATE IN EARLY REPUBLIC

Road-building authority inherited from the colonial era had placed responsibility for roads on the local authorities, who were ill-equipped to handle the demands for new financing and construction. In his *Travels through the Western Country in the Summer of 1816*, David Thomas described the "shameful negligence" in failing to improve some roads.¹⁰ The roads crisscrossing the eastern states were small, local, and mostly unpaved outside of the largest towns and cities, as they had been in colonial times. Winter travel was difficult or impossible as detritus made them impassible, and in many places, ferries shutdown when rivers swelled, limiting travel where there were no bridges. As early industrial development got under way, a lack of good roads kept prices high and transportation costs often made inter-settlement trade prohibitive. Travel and trade in the tidewater coastal regions was often accomplished via boat and ferry, which was complicated by iced-over rivers. The new water-powered

---

[8] See LOUIS HARTZ, THE LIBERAL TRADITION IN AMERICA: AN INTERPRETATION OF AMERICAN POLITICAL THOUGHT SINCE THE REVOLUTION (2d ed. 1991) (1955).
[9] WILLIAM J. NOVAK, THE PEOPLE'S WELFARE: LAW AND REGULATION IN NINETEENTH-CENTURY AMERICA 235–36 (1996).
[10] DAVID THOMAS, TRAVELS THROUGH THE WESTERN COUNTRY IN THE SUMMER OF 1816 21–22 (2013) (1819).

energy sources needed to be located near falls, often far from settlements. The system of local road authority and financing inherited from Colonial times was not enough to accommodate the late eighteenth-century boom in trade and travel.[11]

Despite the obvious need for development, American infrastructure policy was complicated by the Constitution's approach to federal power, regional rivalries, and a lack of technology and engineering expertise. Internal improvements became a defining political issue of the age, functioning as a proxy for deeper disagreements over the scope of federal power and the relationship between citizen and state. Ordinary politics played a large role, too, with Congressmen often objecting to specific projects where they would benefit rival regions at the expense of their own. Suspicions of elite motivations also played a role in hampering infrastructure construction. George Washington and the Federalists may have been enthusiastic about building regional and national networks, on nation-building grounds. But it was also true that Federalist elites would personally profit from connecting the eastern seaboard to the trans-Appalachian west: "Virginia's Potomac route to the West *could* bind together the extremities of a rising empire," Larson points out, "but it surely *would* increase the value of George Washington's Ohio lands and nourish a great city close by Mount Vernon."[12]

Building transportation and communication infrastructure was in any event a matter of national survival. For the Federalists, a centralized approach was the best way to construct a nation-state capable of expanding and developing its own military and commercial powers. Roads, canals, and transportation infrastructure would serve as nodes in a network linking far-flung communities and territories into a coherent sociopolitical project that could develop economy in pursuit of national and global power. Hamilton and the Federalists looked to centralized European models and imagined a networked capitalist nation that could compete on the world stage with France and Great Britain. But centralization of power in a fiscal state was deeply controversial. After all, anti-statist sentiments formed a powerful current in early American politics and shaped the American Constitution and early American governance. In particular, the centralized European fiscal state, with its high levels of taxation and plenary police powers, inspired deep animus among many Americans, who wanted a clean break with European models. Jeffersonian Republicans notably saw in the Federalist dreams of fiscal centralization more a nightmare of despotic power that Americans had so recently fought a war to escape.

Moreover, there were regional divides that complicated infrastructure politics at the national level. Southerners generally (but not universally) opposed federally controlled internal improvements. This was for several reasons. First, Southerners did not expect to make much use of internal improvements; many planters were already happily situated on extant rivers and others lived by subsistence farming. Second, and more importantly, the threat of expansive federal control and

---

[11] *See* LARSON, INTERNAL IMPROVEMENT, *supra* note 6, at 26–30.
[12] *Id.* at 30.

jurisdiction implied by congressional improvement programs threatened the power of slaveholders to protect the lifeblood of the slave economy, reflecting growing fears of abolitionist intrusion. As North Carolina Senator Nathaniel Macon said to a friend: "If Congress can make canals, they can with more propriety emancipate."[13] At the federal level, debates about the Constitution's explicit authority for internal improvements became moves in a proxy war over federal power that would culminate in the Civil War (and in one form or another, continue to this day.)

Despite the obvious difficulties in forging a unified transportation policy, many petitions poured in pleading for roads, canals, and other transportation projects.[14] Internal improvements were also popular in Congress, who were eager to deliver improvements to their districts. After the American Revolution, however, it was unclear who would assume responsibility for the improvements that would enable territorial control and expansion. The Federalists argued that roads, bridges, canals, harbor improvements, railroads, and other projects would lay open a commercial and communication network – the physical media through which the nation itself would be constituted. Infrastructures were pivotal technologies that would allow the fledgling nation to "see like a state," James Scott's phrase for the "maps of legibility" that allowed the modern state to control and develop a vast territory for commerce, settlement, and military defense.[15] Drawing these maps of legibility would require large expenditure for surveys, inventories, cartography, manpower, and expert engineering, itself in short supply in the early republic.[16]

Section 2.2.1 shows that the Federalists' Constitution was far from a laissez-faire document that intended the federal government to do very little. The Constitution was instead intended to produce an active state capable of energetic and expansive governance. However, the Constitution was a compromise document from the beginning, and battles soon erupted over how to interpret key language that Federalists viewed as authorizing large projects, but that Republicans viewed as tending to lead to corruption and "consolidation." Moreover, debates over internal improvements embodied deeper political tensions between northern commercial interests and slaveholders. At the same time, infrastructure politics sowed the seeds of a distinctively American legal culture, shaped by perennial conflict between narrow and broad readings of the nation's founding document.

Section 2.2.2 argues that it was Alexander Hamilton's reforms that laid the foundation for the nation-building of the early nineteenth century. Hamilton's plan was the antithesis of Adam Smith's laissez-faire state. Hamilton did not share David Hume's view that sovereign debt would lead, by definition, to the ruin of the national household. Instead, if carefully managed, a centralized fiscal order, and a debtor state,

---

[13] Cited in HOWE, WHAT HATH GOD WROUGHT, *supra* note 1, at 221–22.
[14] *See* LARSON, INTERNAL IMPROVEMENT, *supra* note 6, at 54, 171.
[15] JAMES SCOTT, SEEING LIKE A STATE HOW CERTAIN SCHEMES TO IMPROVE THE HUMAN CONDITION HAVE FAILED 3 (1998).
[16] *See* HOWE, WHAT HATH GOD WROUGHT, *supra* note 1, at 216.

would help to create the financial framework that would enable nation-building. Section 2.2.3 discusses in detail the bitter constitutional controversy that shaped infrastructure politics in early America. Finally, Section 2.2.4 reads closely one of the most important state-building documents of the era, the Gallatin Report, discussing how Gallatin's business prospectus, which envisioned a partnership between business and government, laid out the basic approach to infrastructure in the years to come.

2.2.1 *The Federalist Constitution and the Fiscal State*

The Constitution has long been read as a document designed to say "no" to expansive government powers. Under this consensus view, the Constitution created a divided government of limited powers that protected individual liberties and property rights against state encroachment. The small-state Constitution embodied an exceptionally American animus against government resulting in an antebellum America that was uniquely "stateless" and laissez-faire. The small-state still features in popular accounts of the Constitution, whether lamented by left-liberals or celebrated by right-libertarians. The small-state Constitution was popularized by a Cold War liberalism eager to offer an American counternarrative to the "big government" alternatives of fascism, socialism, and communism. However, the small government theory does not accurately capture the state-building dimensions of the U.S. Constitution, either assuming, as the left does, that the Constitution has always been an obstacle to desired government policies, or as the right does, that the Constitution is a bulwark of liberty against overly energetic and expansive government. Both left and right, in other words, imagine a minimalist Constitution that is designed principally to check government power, a story with a long afterlife even after the end of the Cold War.[17]

Historians have known for a long time that the standard narrative is more than a little misleading. To begin with, the minimalist Constitution does not fit neatly with the actions of the early government. In the 1780s, the United States was vulnerable to hostile powers in possession of both the will and capacity to challenge the new nation's fragile hegemony in North America. As George Washington wrote to Benjamin Harrison of America's precarious military situation: "I need not remark to you Sir, that the flanks and rear of the United States are possessed by other powers, and formidable ones too; nor how necessary it is to apply the cement of interest, to bind all parts of the Union together by indissoluble bonds, especially that part of it, which lies immediately west of us, with the middle States. For, what ties, let me ask,

---

[17] For a recent treatment of this question, *see* Stephen M. Feldman, *Is the Constitution Laissez-Faire? The Framers, Original Meaning, and the Market*, 81 BROOK. L. REV. (2015); *see also* Bruce Seely, *The Saga of American Infrastructure: A Republic Bound Together*, WILSON Q. 18, 21 (Winter 1993); Jonathan Gifford, *The Saga of American Infrastructure: Toward the 21st Century*, WILSON Q. 40–47 (Winter 1993); Paul Chen, *The Constitutional Politics of Roads and Canals: Inter-Branch Dialogue over Internal Improvements, 1800–1828*, 28 WHITTIER L. REV. 625 (2006).

shou'd we have upon those people?"[18] The pressing questions of nation-building, national community, and national defense – Washington's "cement of interest" – highlighted the immediate need for adequate transportation and communication infrastructure.

Even during the U.S. Confederation of Congress, moreover, the new government was already preparing the field for future infrastructure policies. The Land Ordinance of 1785, for example, bound up new territory, military power, and finances into a public system to dispose of land to fund national defense and infrastructure: "Surveyors were ordered into the wilderness to run lines and carve up the country into numbered squares with fee-simple deeds and unique legal descriptions that could be bought and sold at a distance by anyone with money."[19] Importantly, the statute required cooperation between the land surveyors ("geographers"), the board of treasury, and the Secretary of War, the latter of which would take one-seventh of each lot "for the use of the late continental army," as remuneration for soldiers who served. The Board of Treasury would sell the remaining shares in lots for the benefit of the thirteen states. Portions of the land would also be reserved for future sale by the federal government and one-sixteenth of each "section" for public schools and the "maintenance of the poor."[20] The federal government also claimed one-third of "all gold, silver, lead and copper mines."[21] The future of the American infrastructural state would lie in the central government's sovereign power to create financial liquidity out of the property and land system created by its unique position as a sovereign power.

The Constitution should therefore be read in the context of nation-building and state formation in the long nineteenth century.[22] The Constitution was intended to consolidate a fiscal and military state that was capable of warfare and advancing development policies. Although the Constitution was designed to avoid the heavy administrative structures of European states, there is little evidence that the Constitution itself was intended to reproduce the same weak, decentralized governance model that had made the Articles of Confederation a dead letter in the decade after American independence. Rather, the American Constitution was intended to enable energetic government within the limits of what were possible given the antistatist republicanism that emerged out of America's colonial experience. As Max

---

[18] Letter from George Washington to Benjamin Harrison (Oct. 10, 1784), Founders Online, National Archives, https://founders.archives.gov/documents/Washington/04-02-02-0082. (Original source: 2 THE PAPERS OF GEORGE WASHINGTON, CONFEDERATION SERIES, 18 JULY 1784–18 MAY 1785 86–98 (W. W. Abbot, ed., 1992)).

[19] JOHN LAURITZ LARSON, THE MARKET REVOLUTION IN AMERICA: LIBERTY, AMBITION, AND THE ECLIPSE OF THE COMMON GOOD 15 (2010).

[20] Land Ordinance of 1785, reprinted in 2 THE TERRITORIAL PAPERS OF THE U.S., THE TERRITORY NORTHWEST OF THE RIVER OHIO 12–18 (Clarence Edwin Carter, ed., 1934).

[21] AMERICAN PUBLIC WORKS ASSOCIATION, HISTORY OF PUBLIC WORKS IN THE UNITED STATES 7–8 (Ellis L. Armstrong et al., eds., 1976).

[22] See, for example, MAX M. EDLING, A REVOLUTION IN FAVOR OF GOVERNMENT: ORIGINS OF THE U.S. CONSTITUTION AND THE MAKING OF THE AMERICAN STATE (2003); MAX M. EDLING, A HERCULES IN THE CRADLE: WAR, MONEY, AND THE AMERICAN STATE, 1783–1867 (2014).

M. Edling observes, "the Federalist argument was not a protoliberal call for minority rights and limited government but an argument about state formation, or state building. [The] Federalists tried to create a strong national state in America, a state possessing all the significant powers held by contemporary European states."[23]

Yet, arguments about *how* to build the infrastructures of the new nation-state were mediated by competing concepts of democracy, which were left unresolved by the Constitution. Fundamental issues of practical statecraft could not be answered by the Constitution's bare text, which left many important questions to be resolved by future generations (not the least of which was slavery). What, for example, was the "general welfare"? Was any congressional policy, by definition, aimed at the general welfare (as the Federalists sometimes seemed to argue)? What congressional powers, specifically, were included in the "necessary and proper" clause? How far could the Commerce Clause expand the reach of federal jurisdiction? Likewise, how broadly could one stretch the concept of "postal roads," since those were explicitly authorized in the Constitution? Were Congress's enumerated powers the only ones they had, or were there gaps in the Constitution that needed to be filled by judicial and political interpretation? The Constitution surely lent its newly expanded powers to the planters to preserve slavery with the fugitive slave clause, but would this clause be enforced, or would slavery's gradual abolition make it a dead letter? The bare text of the Constitution could not answer these questions, nor could it resolve the deep political divisions around the emerging infrastructural state.

Despite these unresolved issues, historians have concluded that the Constitution was a state-building document on many of the issues that mattered most to the Federalists. For example, questions of national revenue and wartime debts hung over the Philadelphia Convention of 1787, which brought together delegates from twelve states, many of whom believed that they were there to amend the existing Articles of Confederation.[24] James Madison and his Federalist backers, however, had already stacked the deck in favor of a more comprehensive agenda from the very beginning, and they achieved much of what they wanted at the Convention. The Federalist agenda had a more ambitious reach than merely amending the Articles of Confederation: to build a strong central state that could defend itself in a hostile world where competing empires could very well thwart the independence of the new country.

This would first require fixing the financial mess in which the new government found itself. The British had had many advantages in the war, including the ability to borrow massive sums of money on its public credit. The Americans enjoyed no such luxury. The United States ultimately spent $400 million on the War for Independence. Officially ending only four years prior, the new government was deeply in debt and lacked the fiscal base from which to extract revenue for either

---

[23] EDLING, A REVOLUTION IN FAVOR OF GOVERNMENT, *supra* note 22, at 4.
[24] For an excellent and accessible account of the convention, *see* RICHARD BEEMAN, PLAIN, HONEST MEN: THE MAKING OF THE AMERICAN CONSTITUTION (2009); *see also* MICHAEL J. KLARMAN, THE FRAMERS' COUP: THE MAKING OF THE UNITED STATES CONSTITUTION (2016).

debt servicing or for basic statecraft. In the absence of a sound fiscal basis, the Continental Congress printed money to cover the costs of war. In June 1775, the Congress decided to issue the Continental Dollar, which was pegged to the value of the Spanish Dollar, in order to finance the war. Congress continued to emit this currency until 1779, by which time it had issued $200 million. During this same period, however, the states were also issuing their own currencies rather than resorting to taxation. Congress requested that the states begin collecting taxes and paying that money to the treasury. But instead of paying these revenues to the treasury, the states for the most part spent that money directly. The Congress was thus forced to drastically increase the rate at which it printed the Continental Dollar to make up for the shortfall and the value of the Continental had drastically depreciated by the late 1770s: "The U.S. federal government entered the 1790s deep in the red, with $80 million in obligations, representing roughly 40 percent of the gross national product (GNP). Over $12 million of that was owed to foreign creditors, mainly France and Holland."[25]

Given these pressing concerns, it is not surprising that finance and debt would figure prominently in the debates at the Constitutional Convention. "Under a vigorous national government," Hamilton wrote in Federalist No. 11, "the natural strength and resources of the country, directed to a common interest, would baffle all the combinations of European jealousy to restrain our growth."[26] Only a centralized fiscal system could help consolidate federal power and enable a unified political nation-building project. For the Federalists, both the political credibility and financial liquidity of the young country would therefore rest on the same foundation: a strong financial system with state backing, monetized natural resources, and a fully serviced war debt. All of this was a tall order for a new country. This would require a fortified financial system and a different theory of money's relationship to the state than the one Adam Smith articulated in *Wealth of Nations*.[27] The framers understood that getting the fiscal house in order would be critical for the new state's power to act comprehensively on a number of fronts.

The new government would need to stabilize the monetary system and provide the country with the liquidity to achieve national objectives by establishing public credit, thus providing access to global capital markets. The fiscal power, after all, is the power to raise armies and navies and to build the infrastructures of sovereignty – the

---

[25] SARAH L. QUINN, AMERICAN BONDS: HOW CREDIT MARKETS SHAPED A NATION 23 (2019); see also EDWIN J. PERKINS, AMERICAN PUBLIC FINANCE AND FINANCIAL SERVICES 1700–1815 85–105 (1994); Charles W. Calomiris, *Institutional Failure, Monetary Scarcity, and the Depreciation of the Continental*, 48 J. ECON. HIST. 47, 47–68 (1988); Ben Baack, *Forging a Nation State: The Continental Congress and the Financing of the War of American Independence*, 54 ECON. HIST. REV. 639, 639–56 (2001).

[26] ALEXANDER HAMILTON, *No. 11 The Utility of the Union in Respect to Commercial Relations and a Navy*, IN THE FEDERALIST PAPERS (Alexander Hamilton et al., 2020) (originally published Nov. 23, 1787).

[27] SEAN WILENTZ, THE RISE OF AMERICAN DEMOCRACY: JEFFERSON TO LINCOLN 42–49 (2005).

"sinews of power," as the historian John Brewer puts it, and the lifeblood of the modern state.[28] Moreover, the government's power to create money out of debt, as Alexander Hamilton understood (but Adam Smith and David Hume did not) gave it enormous leverage to monetize the new nation's sovereignty and to create a circulating medium out of the state's status as a reliable debtor. This would require a different theory of money than the one Adam Smith articulated in *Wealth of Nations*.

Recall that for Adam Smith, money was a passive register of value, enabling trade that would merely be more onerous without it. Hamilton squarely rejected Smith's view that essentially read the state out of the cycle of money creation, treating the state as a dangerous predator that needed to be kept in check. In other words, rather than beginning with Adam Smith's and Thomas Jefferson's image of the nation as a household managing its resources through prudent husbandry and debt avoidance, Hamilton begins with a more sophisticated vision of the state's power to create money out of a cycle of debt and repayment. Hamilton, in other words, understood that it was only through debt that public money and a circulating medium could be created in the first place. Contrary to the deficit hawks and austerity advocates of his own day, Hamilton wanted to establish public credit by establishing the nation's status as a *reliable sovereign debtor state*. The new government would take an active role in money creation, treating money not only as Adam Smith's passive register of trade but also as an active system of value creation, the first step in mobilizing capital and enabling its productive circulation through society.[29]

In order to create a strong state, however, Federalists had to negotiate two competing theories of government. On the one hand, Federalists envisioned a strong centralized state modeled on America's European competitors. This state would be able to extract resources effectively from citizens and spend money on large nation-building projects at the discretion of Congress and the President. On the other hand, Anti-Federalists (later Republicans) argued that only a weaker central government in which states remained the primary political actors could avoid an onerous taxation regime and preserve liberty and local governance. The challenge for the Federalists was to thread this particular needle by crafting a government that

---

[28] John Brewer, The Sinews of Power: War, Money and the English State, 1688–1783 (Paperback ed., 1990) (1988).

[29] The literature on the financial position of the early United States is vast. For an excellent and accessible take interpreting the founding from the perspective of the Crisis of 2008, see William Hogeland, Founding Finance: How Debt, Speculation, Foreclosures, Protests, and Crackdowns Made Us a Nation (2012); see also Wilentz, The Rise of American Democracy, supra note 27, at 42–49. Economic historians provide invaluable insight into the unstable monetary situation that confronted the United States in its early years. See Charles W. Calomiris, Institutional Failure, Monetary Scarcity, and the Depreciation of the Continental, 48 J. Econ. Hist. 47, 47–68 (1988); Ben Baack, Forging a Nation State: The Continental Congress and the Financing of the War of American Independence, 54 Econ. Hist. Rev. 639–56 (2001); Douglass C. North and Barry R. Weingast, Constitutions and Commitment: The Evolution of Institutions Governing Public Choice in Seventeenth-Century England, 49 J. Econ. Hist. 803–32 (1989).

would compromise on the issue of slavery to ensure the cooperation of the Southern delegates while also engineering a system that would be strong enough to finance infrastructural nation-building.

After months of heated debate and political maneuvering, the final plan gave the Federalists most of what they wanted. While the Federalists prevailed at the Philadelphia Convention, however, the underlying political questions and states'-rights tension over the scope of federal power would not be resolved until after the Civil War, and even then would require a series of judicial and legislative interventions over the better part of the next century. Nevertheless, the initial result in 1787 was a government with much broader powers than the Anti-Federalists had wanted, but also one limited in important ways in its retention of the states' autonomy in managing local affairs. Important for the purposes of this study, the centralized power of the Constitution's new fiscal state gave the government strong "infrastructural powers" that would enable it to undertake large nationally unifying federal projects.[30]

Proponents of the laissez-faire story have to face an uncomfortable reality: The Articles of Confederation embody a decentralized laissez-faire model that the Constitution decidedly rejected. The Constitution, after all, announced its break with the decentralized model of the Articles of Confederation from its opening words. The Preamble speaks of "a more perfect union," which would "provide for the common defense" and "promote the general welfare."[31] Such language was given life the broad taxing and spending powers of Congress; the power to establish a post office and postal roads; the borrowing and coining of money; taxation; the power to raise armies and navies; and the power "[t]o make all Laws which shall be necessary and proper for carrying into Execution the foregoing Powers, and all other Powers vested by this Constitution in the Government of the United States, or in any Department or Officer thereof."[32] Article VI's Supremacy Clause clarified that federal law, not state law, would be the law of the land where state and federal law conflicted. Article VI also provided that "All debts contracted and engagements entered into, before the adoption of this Constitution, shall be as valid against the United States under this Constitution, as under the Confederation," which guaranteed that the new government would honor its outstanding war debts.

On their face, these were very broad powers; indeed, they represented a clear victory for Federalist nation-building through centralized government.[33] The

---

[30] Max Edling's *A Revolution in Favor of Government* has an extended discussion of the politics of the Constitutional Convention and ratification debate. See EDLING, *supra* note 22, Chapters 1–2. For a discussion of the "infrastructural power," see Michael Mann, *The Autonomous Power of the State: Its Origins, Mechanisms and Results*, 25 EUR. J. SOCIO. 185, 185–213 (1984).

[31] U.S. CONST., preamble; JAMES WILLARD HURST, LAW AND THE CONDITIONS OF FREEDOM IN THE NINETEENTH-CENTURY UNITED STATES 41–42 (1984) (1956).

[32] U.S. Const., art I, § 8.

[33] AKHIL REED AMAR, Chapter 3. Congressional Powers, *in* AMERICA'S CONSTITUTION: A BIOGRAPHY (Kindle ed. 2006).

Federalists had succeeded in getting much of what they wanted at the Convention: a broad state-building Constitution capable of exercising coordinated and centralized power on a continental and soon even a global scale. This would not be a laissez-faire Constitution that prevented the federal government from building its infrastructural state. Bare text, however, could not resolve the underlying political tensions that a compromised Constitution simply papered over. With a win in hand, Federalists soon set about laying the institutional framework for building the infrastructural nation in the 1790s. Section 2.2.2 explains how Alexander Hamilton's reforms of the 1790s laid the foundation for a future American infrastructure-financial state.

2.2.2 *Hamilton's Reforms, Political Economy, and the New Fiscal State*

It may be a surprise to modern readers that Alexander Hamilton does not appear in modern economic textbooks, effectively erased from economic history as a foundational thinker on par with Adam Smith.[34] As discussed in Chapter 1, the laissez-faire of Cold War liberalism re-imagined the Constitution as a defender of private rights against the state. Adam Smith typically holds a larger place in the imagination of latter-day economists than he did in that of the architects of early nationalism. To be sure, Adam Smith's writings were known and admired in the late eighteenth century. Hamilton, in fact, borrowed from Smith in his own writings, as did other figures of national importance, such as John Quincy Adams.[35] Yet, the assumption that America's "republic of liberty" followed the laissez-faire path that Smith advocated is historically misleading. For one thing, as discussed in Chapter 1, Adam Smith did not imagine an economy that would operate without the state. Alexander Hamilton's theories of public credit and manufactures might be less frequently cited by modern economic discourse, but they were at the core of the development of American state–led capitalism. In his economic writings, Hamilton, as the

---

[34] Christian Parenti's RADICAL HAMILTON: ECONOMIC LESSONS FROM A MISUNDERSTOOD FOUNDER (2020) is a recent attempt to correct this oversight.

[35] With respect to laissez-faire ideology, there has been a long debate about its influence on early American policy. For a careful side-by-side comparison of Hamilton's and Smith's writings, *see* Edward G. Bourne, *Alexander Hamilton and Adam Smith*, 8 Q. J. ECON. 328, 328–44 (1894). For John Quincy Adams and Adam Smith, *see* HOWE, WHAT HATH GOD WROUGHT, *supra* note 1, at 252. For Smith and the American founders, *see* SAMUEL FLEISCHACKER, ADAM SMITH'S RECEPTION AMONG THE AMERICAN FOUNDERS, 1776–1790, 59 WM. & MARY Q. 897, 897–924 (2002). *See* FRANK BOURGIN, THE GREAT CHALLENGE: THE MYTH OF LAISSEZ-FAIRE IN THE EARLY REPUBLIC (1989) for an argument that laissez-faire was not a driving force in the early United States. More recent appraisals have mapped important points of contact between Smith and American intellectuals but have emphasized that Americans did not take the same message from Smith as later economists did. Christopher W. Calvo, for example, not only notes the importance of laissez-faire for southern political economists in THE EMERGENCE OF CAPITALISM IN EARLY AMERICA (2020) but also explains that while Smith's ideas were well appreciated by Americans, they did not follow his prescriptions: "Smithian-inspired laissez-faire did not exercise ideological hegemony. In fact, the antebellum discourse demonstrates fundamental theoretical divisions between American thinkers and the larger Smithian tradition," 12; *see also* JEFF MADRICK, THE CASE FOR BIG GOVERNMENT (2010).

Secretary of the Treasury, maps out an alternative, state-centered theory of development sharply distinguishable from Smith's self-regulating invisible hand.

Hamilton's *First Report on Public Credit* (1790) and the *Report on the Subject of Manufactures* (1791) read like an architect's blueprint rather than the *a priori* deductive modeling that Smith inspired in the economics profession of the twentieth century. In comparing Smith's political economy to Hamilton's alternative model, Peter McNamara concludes that Hamilton's vision offers a more sophisticated theory of governance and statecraft to guide economics than does Adam Smith.[36] In a rebuke to Smith and his progeny, Hamilton rejects rational choice individualism and deductive methodologies. Recall that for Smith, we could work out economic laws in the first instance simply by allowing individuals pursue their own rational self-interest. By contrast, Hamilton places "passion and prejudice," "confidence," and "opinion" at the center of a pragmatic policy of *realpolitik*. As he wrote in a letter: "A great source of error in disquisitions of this nature is the judging of events by abstract calculations, which though geometrically true are false as they relate to the concerns of beings governed more by passion and prejudice than by an enlightened sense of their interests."[37] We should not rely on people's accurate sense of their own interests, in other words, because "[a] degree of illusion mixes itself in all the affairs of society." Pressed on all sides by the practical questions of statecraft, Hamilton largely rejected Smith's *a priori* style and embraced the perspective of a state-builder rather than an abstract theorist.

Hamilton's institution-building and pragmatic view is most clearly revealed in his policy solutions to a key issue facing the new nation: The massive debts incurred to wage the War of Independence. Hamilton's *First Report on Public Credit* (1790), written at Congress's request, answered the question of outstanding state war debt with a plan to centralize that debt in the federal government.[38] In his *Report on a National Bank* (1790), Hamilton patiently explained that a national bank with a sound currency could multiply capital by "circulat[ing] a far greater sum than the actual quantum of their capital in gold and silver … performing in every stage the office of money."[39] The Bank would increase the supply of a circulating medium, a

---

[36] Peter McNamara, Political Economy and Statesmanship: Smith, Hamilton, and the Foundation of the Commercial Republic 3 (1997): "I want to use the Smith-Hamilton comparison for a much broader purpose – as a contribution to the construction of a truly *political* economy that would supplement or, perhaps, replace mainstream neoclassical economics."

[37] From Alexander Hamilton to –, [Dec.–Mar. 1779–1780]," Founders Online, National Archives, https://founders.archives.gov/documents/Hamilton/01-02-02-0559-0002. (Original source: 2 The Papers of Alexander Hamilton, 1779–1781 236–251 (Harold C. Syrett, ed., 1961)).

[38] Larson, The Market Revolution in America, *supra* note 19, at 18–20; Frank Bourgin, *Alexander Hamilton: Credit and Finance*, in The Great Challenge, *supra* note 35; Thomas K. McCraw, The Founders and Finance: How Hamilton, Gallatin, and Other Immigrants Forged a New Economy 87–136 (2012).

[39] Alexander Hamilton, Final Version of the Second Report on the Further Provision Necessary for Establishing Public Credit (Report on a National Bank), Dec. 13, 1790, Founders Online, National Archives, https://founders.archives.gov/documents/

real problem in the early Republic and throughout the nineteenth century. But the government would have to deal with the outstanding state debts before it could consolidate a new fiscal regime. Hamilton's plan was for the new government to make a virtue out of necessity by transmuting state debts into a form of public money via a program of debt assumption. The program that Hamilton proposed was to increase the nation's access to public borrowing in order to create money from its sovereignty, which was an essential resource for the early American state. The use of public borrowing and sovereign debt to fund the functions of state, especially war, was a strategy well understood by Hamilton's time. As Hamilton argued, "[L]oans in time of public danger, especially from foreign war, are found an indispensable resource, even to the wealthiest of them."[40]

But Hamilton extended this insight in new directions. Building on the idea that debt is a necessary resource, Hamilton proposes a quasi-state credit theory of money in an era before the fiat currencies of the post-gold standard world, arguing that the market for public debt would be the source of both public and private money:

> But there is a consequence of this, less obvious, though not less true, in which every other citizen is interested. It is a well-known fact, that, in countries in which the national debt is properly funded, and an object of established confidence, it answers most of the purposes of money. Transfers of stock or public debt are there equivalent to payments in specie; or, in other words, stock, in the principal transactions of business, passes current as specie. The same thing would, in all probability, happen here under the like circumstances.[41]

The difference here between Smith's view of money as merely a technology that enables private trade and Hamilton's view that money was inherently public and government-centered could not be starker. Hamilton is arguing in essence that government debt is itself the source of money. Smith had viewed money as a convenience technology provided by governments to facilitate preexisting trade. Hamilton turns Smith's argument around: Rather than a sword of Damocles hanging over the head of a national household threatened with bankruptcy, a properly funded government debt is in fact the original source of public finance in the first place – not a threat so much as the fuel for future growth and expansion.

This view had important implications. Within bounds, fiscally responsible governments should leverage debt, making bets on future development to pay off past expenditures. But it is important to note that for Hamilton, there was an important caveat: Creditors would only lend in the future if the nation-state honored its moral

---

Hamilton/01-07-02-0229-0003. (Original source: 7 THE PAPERS OF ALEXANDER HAMILTON, SEP. 1790–JAN. 1791 305–42 (Harold C. Syrett, ed., 1963)).

[40] ALEXANDER HAMILTON, REPORT RELATIVE TO A PROVISION FOR THE SUPPORT OF PUBLIC CREDIT, Jan. 9, 1790, Founders Online, National Archives, https://founders.archives.gov/documents/Hamilton/01-06-02-0076-0002-0001. (Original source: 6 THE PAPERS OF ALEXANDER HAMILTON, DEC. 1789–AUG. 1790 65–110 (Harold C. Syrett, ed., 1962)).

[41] Id.

obligation to pay debts. Nevertheless, a pattern of reliable debt repayment would be the very foundation of the nation's creditworthiness. The government would need to be a good contracting partner with creditors, with a well-earned reputation for meeting its commitments. Thus, in Hamilton's view, the nation should always be in the process of retiring old debt; but likewise, it should always be accruing new debt to finance the future. Hamilton rejected the debt-phobia and balanced budget ethos of the Republican imaginary. In its place, he argued that debt should not be permanently extinguished once and for all. Aiming for a debt-free state might appear prudent to a Republican worried about financial ruin, but extinguishing debt once and for all could stymie growth and development, which in the future would rely on credit markets. While private debt might be perceived as a moral failing, as it was in the Republican ethos, government debt, if leveraged wisely, was a fiscal good and thus a public virtue. If for Adam Smith, the fiscal state was the problem, for Alexander Hamilton, it was the solution.[42]

In Hamilton's view, the government would work in tandem with creditors and financial institutions to create a *debtor state*, one that would borrow in order to finance future growth. The wealthy would buy government bonds and make their private capital available for public purposes. And, not coincidentally, wealthy elites would profit from the creation of debt-financed monetary expansion, strengthening their ties to the state. This would also serve as Hamilton's answer to Smith's concern about a predatory creditor class. Rather than allowing creditors and elites to prey upon the people, creditors would instead partner with the government to finance a growth model for the emerging market economy:

> To justify and preserve their confidence; to promote the increasing respectability of the American name; to answer the calls of justice; to restore landed property to its due value; to furnish new resources, both to agriculture and commerce; to cement more closely the union of the States; to add to their security against foreign attack; to establish public order on the basis of an upright and liberal policy;—these are the great and invaluable ends to be secured by a proper and adequate provision, at the present period, for the support of public credit.[43]

In order to fortify this partnership between the government and its creditors, the United States would need a stable monetary system. Hamilton's system of circulating public debt would provide this, but it would also help to fortify land prices which had fallen in the immediate post-revolutionary period, turning land into a liquid

---

[42] BRIAN BALOGH, A GOVERNMENT OUT OF SIGHT: THE MYSTERY OF NATIONAL AUTHORITY IN NINETEENTH-CENTURY AMERICA 79 (2009); Richard Sylla, *Political Economy of Financial Development: Canada and the United States in the Mirror of the Other, 1790–1840*, 7 ENTER. & SOC'Y 653, 657–59 (2006); RICHARD SYLLA, *Shaping the US Financial System, 1690–1913: The Dominant Role of Public Finance*, in THE STATE, THE FINANCIAL SYSTEM, AND ECONOMIC MODERNIZATION (Richard Sylla et al., eds., 1999).

[43] HAMILTON, REPORT RELATIVE TO A PROVISION FOR THE SUPPORT OF PUBLIC CREDIT PORT ON A NATIONAL BANK, *supra* note 40.

and fungible asset. Hamilton's debt assumption plan was, however, controversial. States such as Maryland, North Carolina, Pennsylvania, and Virginia had already paid off their wartime debts and little relished the prospect of subsidizing other states' debts. Hamilton's plan to pay the face value of Revolutionary War bonds would also reward speculators who had purchased those bonds at a discount from their original owners, who were often people of modest means. Not until Thomas Jefferson and James Madison managed to broker the so-called "dinner table bargain," which would relocate the nation's capital on the Potomac, away from New York's financial center in June 1790 was Hamilton able to win support for his proposal, for which Hamilton agree to a downward adjustment in Virginia's debt to secure agreement for his plan.[44]

Soon after this meeting, Congress passed several pieces of legislation known as the Compromise of 1790. The idea was that wealthy investors would purchase interest-bearing Treasury bonds, which the federal government would retire in part with a new proposed tax package, mostly on imported luxuries, including an excise on whiskey and new tariffs. One controversial issue was whether the government should have to pay the face, or "par," value of the bonds. After all, government bonds had been circulating at a steep discount for years. There was thus a basic fairness argument for not paying the par value of these instruments, as it would seem to reward speculators and to punish earlier holders of the paper who had sold them at a discount, often out of desperation. Nevertheless, in Hamilton's judgment, the debt had to be paid at its full value in order to honor the principle of contract law and creditworthiness.

But Hamilton's debt redemption plan would only work if there was a national bank that could serve as a proto-Federal Reserve, functioning as a financial firm of last resort in managing a stable circulating medium and maintain liquidity. After a bitter and protracted dispute, Congress reluctantly chartered the First Bank of the United States as a federal corporation on February 21, 1791. Hamilton modeled it on the Bank of England, arguing that such an institution was "a political machine of the greatest importance to the State."[45] The Bank would receive $10 million, 20 percent of that would be invested by the federal government itself. The Bank would then sell shares, which could be financed through a combination of gold and silver and government securities.[46]

Republican opponents of the Bank fulminated against the lack of constitutional authorization for such a vast undertaking, attacking what they saw as a corrupting consolidation of power in a centralized state: "Such a brazen repudiation of popular governance sparked howls of protest," John Lauritz observes, "as did the

---

[44] Max M. Edling, "*So Immense a Power in the Affairs of War*": *Alexander Hamilton and the Restoration of Public Credit*, 64 WM. & MARY Q. 287, 287–326 (2007); Jacob E. Cooke, *The Compromise of 1790*, 27 WM. & MARY Q. 523, 523–45 (1970).
[45] HAMILTON, REPORT ON A NATIONAL BANK, *supra* note 39.
[46] GORDON S. WOOD, EMPIRE OF LIBERTY: A HISTORY OF THE EARLY REPUBLIC, 1789–1815 98 (2009).

technical fact that the Constitution authorized neither banks nor corporations."[47] Undaunted, Hamilton replied to these objections with a theory of implied powers, setting the stage for the constitutionalized politics of internal improvements through the nineteenth century. Despite these constitutional controversies, the Bank, debt redemption, and the establishment of public credit laid the foundation for the state-building projects of the nineteenth century. By freeing up capital for both state and federal development projects, the Bank of the United States enabled the young country to enter the global credit markets at a crucial time in the new republic's industrial development, driven in no small part by the momentous advancement into the Western territories.

2.2.3 The Constitutional Battle over National Infrastructure

By conventional economic measures, Hamilton's plan and congressional policies were a success.[48] And the federal government soon invested in that class of public works most obviously authorized by the Constitution's clear language: the post office. During the congressional debates over the Postal Service Act, it became clear that the federalist Congress had ambitious plans for a new mail service as an early infrastructure of democracy.[49] Soon after Congress authorized The Postal Service Act in 1792, post offices multiplied across the country, forming the basis for the nation's early communication infrastructure. At the beginning of the decade, there were seventy-five post offices. By the end, that number increased more than ten-fold to 903. There were 21,000 miles of postal road by the end of the decade – more than a ten-fold increase over the number at the beginning of the period.[50] The post office became one of the most important and extensive federal infrastructure projects in modern times.[51]

Hamilton's success with the Bank, debt consolidation, and public credit, as well as the land ordinances, also helped ground the emerging liberal governance project. The light administrative footprint and financing through the impost tax, rather than a more heavy-handed models of tax collection, cloaked Federalism as a "government out of sight."[52] The young state had been active in creating "maps of legibility" from

---

[47] LARSON, THE MARKET REVOLUTION IN AMERICA, *supra* note 19, at 19.
[48] For a thorough discussion of the financial situation of the United States after the Revolutionary War, and Hamilton's plans to repair U.S. public finances, *see* RICHARD SYLLA, *Financial Foundations: Public Credit, the National Bank, and Securities Markets*, in FOUNDING CHOICES: AMERICAN ECONOMIC POLICY IN THE 1790S 59–88 (Douglas A. Irwin & Richard Sylla, eds., 2011).
[49] For the best modern history of the early postal service, *see* RICHARD R. JOHN, SPREADING THE NEWS: THE AMERICAN POSTAL SYSTEM FROM FRANKLIN TO MORSE (revised ed., 1995) (second printing 1998); *see also* Genevieve Lakier, *The Non-First Amendment Law of Freedom of Speech*, 134 HARV. L. REV. 2299, 2300–81, 2309–11 (2021).
[50] *See* MCCRAW, THE FOUNDERS AND FINANCE, *supra* note 38, at 132.
[51] *See* BALOGH, A GOVERNMENT OUT OF SIGHT, *supra* note 42, at 13.
[52] *Id.* at 69–72.

the beginning, with the Northwest Ordinance already laying out a legal framework for settling the "Territory of the United States North West of the River Ohio." Yet, as we have seen, the Federalist theory of state power faced concerted opposition. Republican opponents never tired of pointing out that the federal government's consolidation of power was a zero-sum game. It came at the expense of the federated states' autonomy and authority, and, in their view, undermined the democratic pillars upon which republican governance had in theory been predicated.

For decades after ratification, bitter partisan rivalries erupted over the interpretation of key constitutional provisions that would allow or frustrate the completion of massive federal internal improvement projects that the nation-builders envisioned. As Larson observes: "Internal improvements quickly emerged as a class of initiatives the federal government *might* undertake for the 'general welfare,' but for which authority was not clearly granted. In an atmosphere of bad faith and deepening partisan suspicion, Republicans in Congress crafted a 'strict construction' argument designed to limit national power almost regardless of the merits of the question."[53] Proponents of federal improvements looked to both explicit text and implied powers for authority to build lighthouses, dredge harbors, and cut canals across the eastern seaboard and into the western interior.[54] Narrow readings of constitutional text, on the other hand, were meant to keep power and ambition within bounds and to prevent an expansion of federal jurisdiction that would endanger the slaveholder's hegemony in the South.[55]

During the 1790s, for example, acrimony between Secretary of the Treasury Hamilton and Secretary of State Thomas Jefferson erupted over the Constitution's "necessary and proper" clause, sometimes referred to as its "elastic clause."[56] For the state-builders, this was authority enough for Congress to carry out an ambitious legislative agenda, including national infrastructure. Thomas Jefferson argued that this was a sort of verbal conjuring trick that would destroy the scheme of limited government laid out in the Constitution. As animus built between these close advisors to Washington, it began to undermine the nation's first presidential administration. In 1791, the first salvo came when Hamilton used the "necessary and proper" language in Article I, Section 8 ("the elastic clause"), to defend the First Bank of the United States, which was part of his wide-ranging reform plan to build a centralized fiscal state. Federalists began pushing readings of the Constitution

---

[53] Larson, Internal Improvement, supra note 6, at 39.
[54] See Adam S. Grace, From the Lighthouses: How the First Federal Internal Improvement Projects Created Precedent that Broadened the Commerce Clause, Shrunk the Takings Clause, and Affected Early Nineteenth Century Constitutional Debate, 68 ALB. L. REV. 97 (2004) for a discussion of the federalization of the light house system in the late eighteenth and early nineteenth centuries.
[55] See LARSON, THE MARKET REVOLUTION IN AMERICA, supra note 19, at 21.
[56] Article I, Section 8, allows Congress "to make all Laws which shall be necessary and proper for carrying into Execution the foregoing Powers, and all other Powers vested by this Constitution in the Government of the United States, or any Department or Officer thereof." U.S. CONST. art. I, § 8.

that relied on implied powers teased out from explicit constitutional text to support ambitious nation-building projects. After all, there was no explicit authorization in the Constitution to charter a federal corporation, and Congress had done that.

Nevertheless, for Republicans, the Bank epitomized the sort of corrupt elite institution that they had recently fought a war to escape. Hamilton disagreed with this argument and advocated for the Bank's constitutionality: "That every power vested in a government is in its nature sovereign, and includes, by force of the term, a right to employ all the means requisite and fairly applicable to the attainment of the ends of such power, and which are not precluded by restrictions and exceptions specified in the Constitution, or not immoral, or not contrary to the essential ends of political society."[57] This reading of the elastic clause – and the precedent it set – enraged Jefferson and Madison, who countered that when read in this way, there would be no limiting principle for federal power. John Marshall's Court did not actually settle the issue of the Bank's constitutionality until almost thirty years later, in *McCulloch v. Maryland*. Notably, the Court did so in language that echoed the long-deceased Hamilton: "Let the end be legitimate, let it be within the scope of the Constitution, and all means which are appropriate, which are plainly adapted to that end, which are not prohibited, but consistent with the letter and spirit of the Constitution, are constitutional."[58]

Congress authorized expenditures on post roads, surveys, light-houses, and other basic infrastructure in the 1790s.[59] Anti-Federalists may not have fully realized how much infrastructural power they were authorizing with Article I, Section 8's simple words: "To establish Post Offices and post Roads," but the expansive nature of this authority was not lost on Congress, which enacted the Postal Act of 1792, making the Postal Service a cornerstone of American development policy: "During the early decades of the Republic, the post office was one of the most important institutions in the economy; it moved the mail, lifeblood of commerce, and led a federal road-building program. This road building helped open the interior to settlement and investment and catalyzed the emerging capitalist environmental regime."[60]

But prominent Republicans were not so optimistic about this use of government power to build up the infrastructures of the emerging market state. Thomas Jefferson rightly wondered whether constitutional objections could be overcome by the semantic device of renaming every project a "post[al] road."[61] In addition, he worried that the post office – and really by extension, all large infrastructure projects – would become

---

[57] Alexander Hamilton, *Opinion as to the Constitutionality of the Bank of the United States*, in THE AVALON PROJECT: DOCUMENTS IN LAW, HISTORY AND DIPLOMACY, https://avalon.law.yale.edu/18th_century/bank-ah.asp.
[58] 17 U.S. 316, 421 (1819).
[59] Larson, *Internal Improvement, supra* note 6, at 45–46.
[60] PARENTI, RADICAL HAMILTON, *supra* note 34, at 234.
[61] Letter from Thomas Jefferson to James Madison (Mar. 6, 1796), Founders Online, National Archives, https://founders.archives.gov/documents/Jefferson/01-29-02-0004. (Original source: THE PAPERS OF THOMAS JEFFERSON, VOL. 29, 1 MAR. 1796–31 DEC. 1797 6–8 (Barbara B. Oberg, ed., 2002)).

a source of "boundless patronage," or in twentieth-century terms, "boondoggles." As he wrote to James Madison in 1796 while the latter was a congressional representative for Virginia: "Does the power to *establish* post roads, given you by Congress, mean that you shall *make* the roads, or only *select* from those already made, those on which there shall be a post? If the term be equivocal (& I really do not think it so), which is the safest construction? That which permits a majority of Congress to go to cutting down mountains & bridging of rivers...?"[62]

The legitimacy of massive internal investments in communication infrastructure, which had exploded in the 1790s, seemed for Jefferson to turn on what "establish" means. In a tortured bit of logic no less convoluted than the Federalists' claims of implied powers, Jefferson argues that the word "establish" in the phrase "[t]o establish Post Offices and post Roads" does not authorize the construction of such roads, but only includes the narrower power to classify already-existing roads as "postal roads." Although it is possible to dismiss these concerns as hairsplitting legal casuistry, in reality they reflected fundamental disagreements over the scope of federal power that continued well into the Jacksonian era (see Section 2.4) and of course continue into the present day.[63] They are, as they ever have been, debates about the meaning of American democracy as it is embodied in the core functions of the state. When congressional leaders debated the basic function and purpose for public expenditures on the postal roads and similar infrastructure, they were essentially debating what constitutes a public good – in essence what the "representative" value was for the nation. The rancorous partisan debates that continued into the nineteenth century reflected basic disagreements over the federal infrastructure power and whether and how that power could either nurture or destroy a fledgling democracy. Nevertheless, the Constitution's bare text could not (and cannot) resolve deep partisan divisions that lay at the heart of such arguments.

These were matters for political contestation that expressed themselves through sophisticated constitutional hermeneutics, generating principles that neither side was quite willing to respect when push came to shove.[64] For example, despite small-government Republicanism, Thomas Jefferson warmed to federal internal improvements as well as to other largescale federal initiatives, such as the Louisiana Purchase, finding adequate constitutional justification when the occasion warranted. When Andrew Jackson made war on the Bank of the United States, he invoked the same constitutional arguments that his Republican forebears had raised, but he was also willing to finance state banks (the "pet banks") when that suited political expediency. Moreover, as discussed below, President Jackson spent more on internal improvements than all other prior administrations combined. We must not lose sight of the intrinsically political nature of the constitutional discourse

---

[62] Mar. 6, 1796, Letter from Jefferson to Madison, *supra* note 61.
[63] *See* LARSON, THE MARKET REVOLUTION IN AMERICA, *supra* note 19, at 20–23.
[64] *See* BALOGH, A GOVERNMENT OUT OF SIGHT, *supra* note 42, at 92.

that has grown up around public investment in economy and society. Legal interpretation shapes politics, but the opposite is and has always been true.

2.2.4 *Jeffersonian Retrenchment?*

It is common to view Jefferson's presidency as a period of federal retrenchment, reflecting Republican principles of small government. Indeed, Jefferson reduced the federal government's administrative footprint and reduced taxes scaled back on some of the more ambitious centralized program of the Federalists.[65] Jeffersonian Republicans would, however, find it very difficult to maintain principled opposition to internal improvements and other state-building measures in the early decades of the nineteenth century. After all, when Jefferson took power, the demand for internal improvements were no less pressing than they had been during the Federalist period: "Petitions poured in to congressmen from their constituents, begging in traditional language for lighthouses, piers, and post roads, but increasingly asking as well for aid to turnpike and canal companies."[66] Goods needed to be shipped, and merchants and consumers alike would benefit from the systematic construction of trading networks. Yet, there was simply inadequate capital and expertise to achieve such objectives without the power of the federal government, most especially without the public credit and capacity to create a stable financial environment for foreign investment. Thus, despite Jefferson's agonizing over the appropriate constitutional authority to undertake large projects, "[n]evertheless, within a mere five years national roads and canals had assumed, along with a national university, a central role in Jefferson's policy."[67]

While the debate is still ongoing, the emerging consensus suggests that small-government principles did not prevent the gradual growth of administrative bureaucracy and expansive government action beginning the early nineteenth century.[68] As Jerry Mashaw writes: "The early years of Jefferson's first term were blessed with peace and prosperity, and Republican principles triumphed. Under Jefferson's leadership Congress substantially reduced the military establishment, abolished internal

---

[65] WILENTZ, THE RISE OF AMERICAN DEMOCRACY, *supra* note 27, at 101; EDLING, A HERCULES IN THE CRADLE, *supra* note 22, at 107.
[66] Larson, *Internal Improvement*, *supra* note 6, at 54.
[67] Joseph H. Harrison, Jr., "*Sic et Non*": *Thomas Jefferson and Internal Improvement*, 7 J. EARLY REPUBLIC 335, 340 (1987).
[68] *See*, for example, Jerry L. Mashaw, *Reluctant Nationalists: Federal Administration and Administrative Law in the Republican Era, 1801–1829*, 116 YALE L. J. 1636, 1735 (2007) ("To be sure, the Jeffersonian Republicans were reluctant nationalists. But, that is the irony of their state-building. They could starve national administration for funds and personnel, and they did. But in the end they could not avoid leaving a national administration that was larger in relation to the country's population than the one that they had inherited from those state-building Federalists who preceded them"); *see also* Jerry L. Mashaw, *Administration and 'The Democracy': Administrative Law from Jackson to Lincoln, 1829–1861*, YALE L. J. 117 (2008).

taxes, and made progress toward retiring the national debt. Resistance to new federal programs reinforced the domestic authority of the several states – as did the repeal of the Judiciary Act of 1801, which had expanded the federal judiciary."[69] This situation did not last long, as ambitions for western settlement and colonization, as well as the globalized European conflict which would lead America to war, created the need for federal infrastructural power to match the exigencies of the moment. Jefferson's skeptical attitude toward an expansive use of federal power, in other words, softened when he was faced with problems that only government power could effectively solve. This led to compromises of the Republican positions on taxation, banking, and the buildup of military forces: "When the practicalities of administration demanded that these principles be abandoned, Congress was determined to oversee administration in a more substantial and systematic way than it had during the Federalist period."[70] For example, the Embargo Act of 1807 closed American ports to export shipping as a response to privateers who had been harassing American vessels. The Embargo Act was designed to prevent America from being dragged into the wider conflict and granted the President broad authority to enforce the acts, which engendered legal challenges that were ultimately resolved in favor of the Act.

Jefferson's contemporaries also noted his expansive use of executive power when it was expedient. For example, in a letter to James A. Bayard, Alexander Hamilton wrote: "But it is not true as is alleged that he is an enemy to the power of the Executive, or that he is for confounding all the powers in the House of Rs. It is a fact which I have frequently mentioned that while we were in the administration together he was generally for a large construction of the Executive authority, & not backward to act upon it in cases which coincided with his views."[71] Recent historical consensus acknowledges that Jefferson, while not abandoning his Republican scruples, embraced the basic Federalist tenet that a strong state had to embrace important national infrastructure objectives.[72] The new congressional Republican majority also demonstrated its willingness to use national power to build infrastructure. For example, in 1802, Congress passed the Ohio Enabling Act, laying the foundation for Ohio's admission as a state, which Republicans hoped would neutralize Federalist control over the Northwest Territory. The Enabling Act was also the first congressional appropriation for internal improvements, creating a financing model in which 5 percent of the proceeds from the sale of federal lands would be dedicated

---

[69] Mashaw, *Reluctant Nationalists*, supra note 68, at 1640.
[70] Id. at 1643.
[71] Letter from Alexander Hamilton to James A. Bayard (Jan. 16, 1801), Founders Online, National Archives, https://founders.archives.gov/documents/Hamilton/01-25-02-0169. (Original source: 25 THE PAPERS OF ALEXANDER HAMILTON, JULY 1800–APR. 1802 319–24 (Harold C. Syrett, ed., 1977)).
[72] See BALOGH, A GOVERNMENT OUT OF SIGHT, supra note 42, at 117–18; Larson, *Internal Improvement*, supra note 6, 52–58.

to building a road connecting the Atlantic to Ohio. Congress also authorized the Cumberland Road in 1806, with construction on the road beginning in 1811 and finally being completed in 1837. Jefferson signed off on a $30,000 survey for the Cumberland Road on March 29, 1806, one of the most ambitious federal road-building projects undertaken before the twentieth century.[73]

Jefferson's Second Inaugural Address on March 4, 1805, offered a rapprochement to the internal improvers while maintaining the Republican ethos of sound household economics. In the Address, Jefferson takes credit for the reduction in internal taxes, while failing to acknowledge the fiscal stability that Federalist policies of the 1790s had enabled. Because the tax system was designed around import duties rather than onerous personal taxation, Jefferson argued, the nation could afford to build up its transportation system based on a financial surplus:

> These contributions enable us to support the current expenses of the government, to fulfil contracts with foreign nations, to extinguish the native right of soil within our limits, to extend those limits, and to apply such a surplus to our public debts, as places at a short day their final redemption, and that redemption once effected, the revenue thereby liberated may, by a just repartition among the states, and a corresponding amendment of the constitution, be applied, _in time of peace_, to rivers, canals, roads, arts, manufactures, education, and other great objects within each state.[74]

This passage captures an important and lasting difference between state-credit money ideas that Hamilton had developed and the deficit hawkery of the Republican – and later Democratic – imagination. The prudent Republican householder views money as part of the duty of husbandry: Jefferson speaks of state money as a finite resource that needs to be wisely managed. Jefferson envisions planning future growth based only on present abundance, paying off wartime debts and investing the surplus in domestic economic development. Like Hamilton, however, his rhetoric connects the financial and moral position of the United States as a responsible citizen that lives within its means and pays down its debts. Unlike Hamilton, though, Jefferson believed in a household model of state finance in which the responsible thing to do was to extinguish the debt and have the nation live within its means. As discussed in Section 2.2.1, however, it was not merely fiscal prudence that enabled the nation to invest in its infrastructure; it was, among other things, Hamilton's state-money reforms and the high rates of growth and expansion that generated the federal budget surpluses when Jefferson took office. Without Hamilton's fiscal centralization and public credit plan, there would arguably be no surplus for Jefferson to spend. In a profound historical irony, the funds Jefferson required to purchase the Louisiana Territory – the signature achievement of his administration, by his own admission –

---

[73] *See* Stephen Minicucci, *Internal Improvements and the Union, 1790–1860*, 18 STUD. AM. POL. DEV. 160, 163–64 (2004); HOWE, WHAT HATH GOD WROUGHT, *supra* note 1, at 212–13.

[74] President Thomas Jefferson, Second Inaugural Address (Mar. 4, 1805).

relied upon the foreign credit that Hamilton's fiscal vision procured. The same was true for the funds Madison needed to win the War of 1812.

2.2.5 *The Gallatin Plan*

With pressure mounting for federally financed transportation infrastructure, Henry Clay called for a report on internal improvements from Secretary of the Treasury Albert Gallatin, which Gallatin dutifully submitted to the Senate on April 4, 1808.[75] Gallatin's *Report of the Secretary of the Treasury on the Subject of Public Roads and Canals* reads like a monument to Enlightenment optimism and to the power of centralized authority to see like a state. Gallatin's ambitions were nothing less than to build a network of roads and canals along the Eastern Seaboard and into the interior that would materialize the dreams of the internal improvers dating back to the 1790s. Gallatin argued from the public interest in favor of federal involvement, beginning with transportation infrastructure based on the general public consensus of its pressing need: "The general utility of artificial roads and canals, is at this time so universally admitted, as hardly to require any additional proofs."[76] The report is written as an investment prospectus, laying out the cost of labor ("not considered a formidable obstacle"), touting logistical knowhow and banking on a general spirit of public improvement, which he was confident would override partisan wrangling. Gallatin's appeal to public-spiritedness was surely designed to allay Republican fears of logrolling, corruption, and "boondoggles."[77]

Echoing Adam Smith, Gallatin's prospectus frames transportation infrastructure as a technology of nation-building organized by a central fiscal authority whose goal was economic growth. Roads and canals are investments in national economy, he argued, and their existence depends on resources that only the national government possessed: "Good roads and canals, will shorten distances, facilitate commercial and personal intercourse, and unite by a still more intimate community of interests, the most remote quarters of the United States. No other single operation, within the power of government can more effectually tend to strengthen and perpetuate that union, which secures external independence, domestic peace, and internal liberty."[78] Individual corporate investments had found these large improvements

---

[75] For discussion of the Gallatin plan, its successes and failures, *see* Carter Goodrich, *The Gallatin Plan after One Hundred and Fifty Years*, 102 PROC. AM. PHIL. SOC'Y 436, 436–41 (1958); Carter Goodrich, *National Planning of Internal Improvements*, 63 POL. SCI. Q. 16, 16–44 (1948); Lawrence G Hines, *The Early 19th Century Internal Improvement Reports and the Philosophy of Public Investment*, 2 J. ECON. ISSUES 384, 384–92 (1968); John L. Larson, *Bind the Republic Together: The National Union and the Struggle for a System of Internal Improvements*, 74 J. AM. HIST. 363, 363–87 (1987).

[76] ALBERT GALLATIN, REPORT OF THE SECRETARY OF THE TREASURY ON THE SUBJECT OF PUBLIC ROADS AND CANALS 5 (1808).

[77] GALLATIN, REPORT, *supra* note 73, at 6.

[78] *Id.* at 7–8.

"unprofitable." Therefore, he concluded, "[t]he general government alone can remove these obstacles."[79]

The Gallatin report frames policy in terms of infrastructural nationalism, which it substantiates with surprising technical detail. It provides, for instance, a careful analysis of several proposed regional canal networks in terms of their fit and utility in an overall scheme of transportation infrastructure. Each canal system is broken down into the costs of completion and its utility either for trade or communication. Gallatin did extensive research to prepare his report, which offers data from extensive surveys that had been authorized by Congress in 1806. In this way, the report is a remarkably modern document, filled with calculations of cargo tonnage, detailed topographical analysis of specific projects, engineering specifications, very precise measurements as well as cost estimates and discussions of the work necessary to revive now abandoned or incomplete projects.

Gallatin's was a regional plan with nation-building ambitions and an eye to self-funding projects. The report proposes a $20 million plan to construct a national transportation network connecting the east coast to inland regions with several major goals in mind: "(1) Great canals, from north to south, along the Atlantic sea coast; (2) Communications between the Atlantic and western waters; (3) Communications between the Atlantic waters, and those of the great lakes, and river St. Lawrence; (4) Interior canals."[80] Gallatin writes of the Potomac project that "[a]t that place designated by the name of Great falls, the boats passing through a canal one mile in length, six feet deep, and twenty five feet wide, descend 76 feet by five locks, 100 feet long, and 12 feet wide each, and re-entering the river, follow its natural bed, eight miles and a half. Another canal of the same dimensions, and two miles and a half in length, brings them then through three locks and by a descent of 37 feet to tide water."[81] The Report provides detailed analyses of rock density and discusses the work that had already been completed: "The two lower locks of the Great falls, excavated out of the solid rock, have each a lift of 18 feet: the three upper locks of solid masonary [sic] are of unequal height, and have together a lift of forty feet."[82]

The great canals, which were estimated to cost $3 million, would link together the tidewater states in a commercial and military system whose value was an obvious boon to both nation-building and commerce: "It is unnecessary to add any comments on the utility of the work, in peace or war, for the transportation of merchandize, or the conveyance of persons."[83] Gallatin mentions the failure of various state corporate ventures to connect regions in the northeast that were undertaken in the 1790s. New Jersey, Delaware, and Maryland, for example, had chartered

---

[79] *Id.* at 7.
[80] *Id.* at 8.
[81] *Id.* at 31.
[82] *Id.* at 31.
[83] *Id.* at 10.

companies that had failed for lack of funds.[84] As Adam Smith had advocated in *Wealth of Nations*, Gallatin justifies each project in terms of the tonnage of human and mercantile cargo that it would move across its respective region. A Republican critic of Hamilton's fiscal state, worried about public debt, Gallatin was cautious in his financial engineering. He estimates that the twenty-two-mile canal linking Delaware and Maryland, for example, would when completed "greatly increase" the already 42,000 tons of passengers moving across the peninsula and would carry an estimated annual cargo of coal and other goods of 150,000 tons a year, including coal for Philadelphia. This canal alone would save the public $300,000 a year in carriage costs, which Gallatin calculates by taking the $2 difference between the land and canal carriage and multiplying it by the estimated total cargo per year and subtracting the tolls.[85]

A number of the state-subsidized corporate ventures in the 1790s had failed, or only been partially completed, disappointing high expectations. Thus, to the extent the planned projects would be built on prior corporate ventures, Gallatin's proposal was as much a bailout of a failed business model as it was a public–private partnership. The earlier ventures could not be completed or run profitably for financial and political reasons, each adding to the logistical challenges that inevitably doomed many projects. By recapitalizing these older projects with federal money and to turn them into self-liquidating infrastructure assets that would turn a profit, Gallatin borrowed from Adam Smith and forecasted an infrastructure model that would become common in America's future. In the report, he provided a detailed calculation of how much capital each project would need, how much would be needed to pay the remaining stockholders, and so on. After considering operations and upkeep, for example, the Delaware and Chesapeake canal could expect an annual net revenue stream revenue stream of $55,000 and would be financed with $650,000 of federal money. Part of the construction costs paid by the federal government could be recovered at 6 percent, yielding $55,000 in interest.

With Jeffersonian concerns in mind, Gallatin's version of "seeing like a state" would mean fiscal prudence and accountability, so to the extent possible, he advocated self-liquidating infrastructural projects, just as Adam Smith had counseled. Similarly, it meant accounting for property expended by corporate investors in prior projects – including individuals held in slavery by the state. When discussing a canal project in North Carolina, for example, Gallatin notes that "the capital expended is stated at 650,667 dollars, including sixty negroes and some tracts of land belonging to the company."[86] His passing comment on "sixty negroes" listed as capital reminds us that slave labor was deployed in state-directed infrastructure projects, a topic that is only recently receiving adequate attention as historians

[84] *Id.* at 12–14.
[85] *Id.* at 16.
[86] *Id.* at 27.

reveal how important slave labor was to "seeing like a state" in the antebellum United States.[87]

2.2.6 After Gallatin

Unfortunately for the state-builders, Gallatin was ahead of his time. Despite the depth of its analysis, the appeal to infrastructural nationalism and the obvious attractiveness to investors, no immediate action was taken on Gallatin's proposal. The British embargo of American trade culminating in the War of 1812 drained American coffers, bringing large federally financed projects to a grinding halt.[88] At the same time, however, the War was revealing the military and commercial necessity of a well-designed and federally funded transportation network.[89] Not surprisingly, internal improvements were taken up again after 1815 with renewed energy, even as a new party system was emerging in the wake of the American victory in 1815. During this "era of good feelings" in the years after the war, Whig politicians such as Henry Clay made the case for wider federal investment in infrastructure based on the idea of an "American System," which would have included a protective tariff, a national bank, and extensive federally financed internal improvements.[90]

John C. Calhoun introduced a bill in 1817 that would invest the surplus from the Second Bank of the United States in a novel type of infrastructure trust fund.[91] Styled "The Bonus Bill," the plan was essentially to revive the Gallatin Plan's vision of infrastructural nation-building through direct federal investment. Yet, to the disappointment of infrastructure nationalists, President Madison, who had signaled his support for the legislation, vetoed the Bonus Bill as one of his last acts as President in late 1817. Madison's veto message lays out the familiar constitutional objections to federally directed internal improvements. For those in the legacy of Jefferson, there was simply not enough explicit power in the Commerce, General Welfare, or

---

[87] Hall, Aaron, *Slaves of the State: Infrastructure and Governance through Slavery in the Antebellum South*, 106 J. AM. HIST. 19, 33 (2019); *see also* Aaron R. Hall, *Public Slaves and State Engineers: Modern Statecraft on Louisiana's Waterways, 1833–1861*, 85 J. S. HIST. 531, 531–76 (2019); RYAN A. QUINTANA, MAKING A SLAVE STATE: POLITICAL DEVELOPMENT IN EARLY SOUTH CAROLINA (2018); LARSON, THE MARKET REVOLUTION IN AMERICA, *supra* note 19, at 131; *see also* David Alff, *What Is Infrastructure Anyway*, BOSTON REVIEW, June 28, 2021: "Seldom acknowledged in these debates was the public standing of Indigenous Americans, for whom the establishment of settler-colonial transportation conduits entailed an influx of pioneers, land cessation, and removal. By making life more convenient for white Americans and inflicting harm on Indigenous tribes, public works underscored exclusion and starkly revealed which populations did and did not matter in the early American public."

[88] Joseph H. Harrison, Jr., *"Sic et Non": Thomas Jefferson and Internal Improvement*, 7 J. EARLY REPUBLIC 335, 343 (1987).

[89] DANIEL FELLER, PUBLIC LANDS IN JACKSONIAN POLITICS (1984) (see Chapter 2); FOREST HILL, ROADS, RAILS, AND WATERWAYS: THE ARMY ENGINEERS AND EARLY TRANSPORTATION 6 (1957).

[90] *See* Minicucci, *Internal Improvements*, *supra* note 70, at 164.

[91] The Debates and Proceedings in the Congress of the United States, 14th Congress, Second Session, 30 Annals of Cong. 855 (Feb. 1817).

Necessary and Proper Clauses to provide the legal grounds for such a broad assertion of federal jurisdiction. As Madison explained his veto decision:

> I am not unaware of the great importance of roads and canals and the improved navigation of water courses, and that a power in the National Legislature to provide for them might be exercised with signal advantage to the general prosperity. But seeing that such a power is not expressly given by the Constitution, and believing that it can not be deduced from any part of it without an inadmissible latitude of construction and a reliance on insufficient precedents; believing also that the permanent success of the Constitution depends on a definite partition of powers between the General and the State Governments, and that no adequate landmarks would be left by the constructive extension of the powers of Congress as proposed in the bill, I have no option but to withhold my signature from it, and to cherishing the hope that its beneficial objects may be attained by a resort for the necessary powers to the same wisdom and virtue in the nation which established the Constitution in its actual form and providently marked out in the instrument itself a safe and practicable mode of improving it as experience might suggest.[92]

When President Monroe similarly vetoed the Cumberland Road toll-collection bill in 1822, he renewed Madison's objections. His lengthy treatise, "Views of the President of the United States on the Subject of Internal Improvements," essentially reaffirmed a (softened) Jeffersonian view that there was no constitutional obstacle to funding internal improvement as long as the government did not attempt to maintain control over the infrastructure, one of the sticking points of federal jurisdiction animated in part by slaveholder fears of an ever-expanding federal power.[93] Tracking the growing state and local involvement with infrastructure (discussed in Chapter 4), Monroe made his argument based on the Tenth Amendment's reservation of police powers over the states and the proper investiture of sovereign power in the states over property and persons.

John Quincy Adams would seek to expand the federal government's role in transportation infrastructure. In his First Annual Message to Congress in 1825, Adams lays out a broad case for infrastructure in which the federal government would assert a truly national power of improvement:

> The great object of the institution of civil government is the improvement of the condition of those who are parties to the social compact, and no government, in whatever form constituted, can accomplish the lawful ends of its institution but in proportion as it improves the condition of those over whom it is established. Roads

---

[92] President James Madison, Veto Message on the Internal Improvements Bill (Mar. 3, 1817), https://millercenter.org/the-presidency/presidential-speeches/march-3-1817-veto-message-internal-improvements-bill.

[93] *See* President James Monroe, Views of the President of the United States on the Subject of Internal Improvements *in* 2 A COMPILATION OF THE MESSAGES AND PAPERS OF THE PRESIDENTS, 1789–1897 (Preamble, Document 20) (James D. Richardson, comp., Washington, DC: GPO, 1896–99), https://press-pubs.uchicago.edu/founders/documents/preambles20.html; Minicucci, *Internal Improvements*, *supra* note 70, at 164; HOWE, WHAT HATH GOD WROUGHT, *supra* note 1, at 212–13.

and canals, by multiplying and facilitating the communications and intercourse between distant regions and multitudes of men, are among the most important means of improvement. But moral, political, intellectual improvement are duties assigned by the Author of Our Existence to social no less than to individual man.[94]

This was one of the broadest statements of American developmentalism in the early nineteenth century and, as such, anticipates the developmental liberalism that would characterize the Progressive Era and continue until after the Second World War. But despite the fact that such a centralized infrastructure policy would remain controversial until the Civil War, the federal government remained active in internal improvements throughout the nineteenth century. For example, the Army Corps of Engineers continued to play an important role in federal infrastructure policy in the mid-nineteenth century. The General Survey Act of 1824 provided a total of $425,000 between 1824 and 1837 for surveys that assisted in the construction of the early railroad network.[95] Despite his veto of the Cumberland toll-road bill, for instance, President Monroe used his military authority under the executive power to direct the Army Corps of Engineers, established by Jefferson in 1802, to conduct surveys and complete smaller projects. After the General Survey Act, as the historian Forest Hill notes, "[t]he army engineers realized that they were in a strategic position to encourage internal improvements."[96]

And the Army Corps played a vital role in developing national infrastructure, a role that it continued to play in later periods of American history (for better or worse). The Army Corps increasingly lent its engineering expertise to improvement projects of "national importance" across the country. The federal government proved more than receptive to petitions requesting surveys for roads, canals, and railroads throughout the 1820s and into the 1830s.[97] In the 1820s, for instance, the Corps undertook a wide range of internal improvement projects, including, as Stephen Minicucci observes, "exploration and mapping of the country, improvement of navigation on the western rivers and lakes, and discovery of natural resources."[98]

2.2.7 Jacksonian Retrenchment?

Andrew Jackson ran his presidential campaign in 1828 against federal internal improvements, monopolies, the American System, and the recharter of the Bank of the United States. As with Jeffersonian Republicanism, Jackson was skeptical of

---

[94] President John Quincy Adams, First Annual Message to Congress (Dec. 6, 1825), https://millercenter.org/the-presidency/presidential-speeches/december-6-1825-first-annual-message.
[95] Minicucci, *Internal Improvements*, supra note 70, at 164; see also FOREST HILL, ROADS, RAILS, AND WATERWAYS, supra note 86; TODD SHALLAT, STRUCTURES IN THE STREAM: WATER, SCIENCE, AND THE RISE OF THE U.S. ARMY CORPS OF ENGINEERS (1994).
[96] *Id.* at 70.
[97] *Id.* at 69.
[98] *Id.* at 90.

a fiscal policy predicated on government debt, which he viewed through the lens of prudential morality, in which the nation is a household that needs to balance its budget. The expansive use of national power to finance and oversee a national internal improvement program ran up hard against his strict constructionist, anti-bank, pro-slavery, and populist views. So, it was no surprise when on May 27, 1830, he vetoed a plan to purchase $150,000 of stock in a Maysville turnpike project and other projects that he did not consider sufficiently national in character. Jackson's veto of the Mayville's Turnpike was a setback for infrastructural nationalism in the middle of the nineteenth century. Reflecting his anti-monopoly politics, and his open disdain for the corrupting influence of elite consolidation, Jackson echoed Republican concerns for national involvement with infrastructure going back to the 1790s. Like the famous veto of the charter of the Bank of the United States in 1832, the shift in policy reflected a skeptical anti-corporate politics and a concern about elite corruption and "consolidation." Singling out the method of federal stock subscriptions as particularly objectionable, Jackson's presidency was an abrupt departure from earlier policies reflected in the Gallatin plan.

Some have located the rise of American laissez-faire to the Jacksonian period. While there is some evidence to support this idea, it is misleading without further elaboration. There is little question that Jacksonian Democrats embraced small-government, anti-elite, and anti-corruption themes in their campaign rhetoric and policy. There is also little question that Jackson's rejection of the American System and his small-government ethos frustrated plans for greater direct federal involvement in infrastructure. The inability of the developmentalists to enact their sweeping infrastructure agenda during the internal improvements period meant that individual states would need to lead the effort to build transportation infrastructures. By the end of Jackson's presidency, states had moved into the infrastructure field, building roads, canals, and other transportation improvements, as we will see in Chapter 3.

Yet, importantly, Jacksonian policy altered the shape of federal policy in the field of infrastructure, rather than abandoning federal involvement altogether. Land sales, land grants, and state bank capitalizations during Jackson's administration laid the groundwork for continued building and expansion of transportation networks at the state level until the crisis of 1837 (discussed in Chapter 4): "In 1841, nine states (Ohio, Indiana, Illinois, Alabama, Missouri, Mississippi, Louisiana, Arkansas, and Michigan)—and, with three exceptions, all subsequent newly admitted states— were designated land grant states and guaranteed at least 500,000 acres of federal land to be auctioned to support transportation projects, including roads, railroads, bridges, canals, and improvement of water courses, that expedited the transportation of United States mail, military personnel, and military munitions."[99]

[99] Congressional Research Service, "Federal Grants to State and Local Governments: A Historical Perspective on Contemporary Issues" (Updated May 22, 2019), 14; John Bell Rae, *Federal Land Grants*

Curtailing Federalist policies allowed the states a greater role in regional and local development than the early infrastructural nationalists had intended, although even Gallatin's plan had envisioned coordination between state and federal governments to invest in corporate projects. Nevertheless, Jackson's administration spent more on infrastructure projects than all previous administrations combined.[100] What explains this seeming contradiction? What Jackson objected to was a particular kind of elite self-dealing that had excluded men like himself from the power and prominence he believed they deserved. In the final decades of the antebellum era, however, the federal government continued to fund projects, even when the political tensions ran high or when vital projects had been allowed to languish for decades. The Cumberland Road, for instance, had been approved in 1806 and in 1811, the government having signed a contract for the first ten miles of the road at $7,500 per mile. Yet, the last congressional appropriation for the road was not levied until 1838, bringing the total for the project to $7 million at its completion in 1841. In this and other ways, direct federal expenditures on infrastructure did not end with the Jacksonian retrenchment.[101]

Despite the decline of infrastructural nationalism under Jackson, federal spending on internal improvements tended to rise and fall over the course of the nineteenth century. During the 1840s and 1850s, for example, there was new infrastructure spending to improve rivers and harbors; lighthouses were built; and surveys were conducted and massive quantities of land appropriated for the transcontinental railroads.[102] Although Franklin Pierce, like his predecessors, vetoed several improvement bills, citing the familiar constitutional objections, Congress overturned his vetoes on river projects no fewer than five times in 1856.[103] The federal government never developed a coordinated, Gallatin-style plan in the nineteenth century; but there was an active federal presence through indirect methods of support. For example, "[t]he adoption of the land-grant policy made the Federal Government once more a major supporter of internal improvements, and even the states most firmly

---

in Aid of Canals, J. ECON. HIST., vol. 4, no. 2 (Nov. 1944): 167, 168; MAURICE G. BAXTER, HENRY CLAY AND THE AMERICAN SYSTEM (1995); CARTER GOODRICH, GOVERNMENT PROMOTION OF AMERICAN CANALS AND RAILROADS (1960); DANIEL FELLER, THE PUBLIC LANDS IN JACKSONIAN POLITICS (1984); *see also* MORTON GRODZINS, THE AMERICAN SYSTEM: A NEW VIEW OF GOVERNMENT IN THE UNITED STATES (1966), 35: "These debates did not prevent action. The national government, in the days of wagons, gave away 3.25 million acres for the support of wagon roads. When canal building boomed, it gave 4.5 million acres for this purpose to Illinois, Indiana, Michigan, Ohio, and Wisconsin; and 2.5 million acres to Alabama, Iowa, and Wisconsin to improve river navigation. It gave about 64 million acres to the states for flood control and to drain marshy lands. When steam road the rails, it gave grants for railroad construction;" *see also* Mashaw, *Reluctant Nationalists*, "Bureaucratizing Land," *supra* note 68, at 1696–1727; MATTHEW G. HANNAH, GOVERNMENTALITY AND THE MASTERY OF TERRITORY IN NINETEENTH-CENTURY AMERICA (2000).

[100] *See* Minicucci, *Internal Improvements, supra* note 70, at 163.
[101] *Id.* at 163.
[102] *Id.* at 167–68.
[103] Isaac Lippincott, *A History of River Improvement*, 22 J. of Pol. Econ. 630–60, 648 (1914).

committed against participation with their own money were quite willing to act as the transmitters of the largess from Washington."[104] Internal improvements continued to be popular in Congress in the antebellum era. Stephen Minicucci tabulates that "roll calls in Congress typically evinced modest majorities in favor of improvements. In 334 House roll calls relating to internal improvements between the 14th and 35th Congresses ... 54.5% of members cast a pro-improvement vote."[105] Federal spending on infrastructure before the Civil War was approximately $119.8 million, with $77.2 million of this directed to projects at the state level through various indirect mechanisms rather than under federal jurisdiction and control.[106]

2.3 CONCLUSION

In the first decades of the nineteenth century, the general public clamored for transportation infrastructure, as local economies and nascent market capitalism began to thrive and as travel increased with the advent of western migration. Public agitation for more reliable mail service, better roads to get perishables to market, more public bridges, public conveyances, and access to capital kept internal improvements at the fore of the congressional and presidential agenda through the first half of the century. Given the early aggressive Federalist push for bigger government, one could be forgiven for assuming that Jefferson would abandon the ambitious, state-centered Federalist agenda once he was in office. After all, the rise of a new Republican establishment in the early 1800s seemed to herald a new era in American infrastructural politics, one in which the federal government would reduce its role in the economy. However, while the issue of internal improvements remained a point of controversy until the Civil War, the federal government acted in many ways to subsidize and encourage internal improvements where that was feasible. Often that support was indirect (land grants, e.g., or federally sponsored surveys), but it is nevertheless clear that the federal government maintained an important position as a catalyst for development. However, because the federal government did not act decisively or quickly enough to keep up with demand for infrastructures, states moved into the field in the 1830s, a topic that Chapter 3 explores at length.

---

[104] Carter Goodrich, *The Revulsion against Internal Improvements*, 10 J. ECON. HIST. 145, 149 (1950).
[105] Minicucci, *Internal Improvements, supra* note 70, at 169–70.
[106] *Id.* at 161.

3

"A Wilderness of Turnpike Gates"

Roads and Public Authority in Antebellum America

3.1 INTRODUCTION

During the privatization craze of the 1980s, libertarians advocated toll roads as the cure for America's "crumbling infrastructure" problem. Turnpikes, after all, were some of the earliest public–private partnerships in American history. As Gerald Gunderson writes in "Privatization and the 19th-Century Turnpike,"[1] Americans invented an "ingenious" market mechanism for supplying its road deficit: the public–private partnership. In our current craze for public–private partnerships, it is natural that we look to the American turnpike experience for guidance. The turnpike experience in America offers a cautionary tale about the intrinsically public and political nature of transportation infrastructure. As libertarian commentator Timothy B. Lee concedes: "Roads are deeply intertwined with governments. They always have been and as far as I can see they always will be. This means that they'll never be truly private in the sense that other private companies like restaurants or shoe factories can be."[2] Chapter 3 illustrates Lee's insight and argues that highways and roads were a defining feature of "publicness" in the American antebellum experience. Turnpikes were organized as private businesses and charged tolls in order to recoup considerable investment and turn a profit. They were designed to be run as Adam Smith's self-liquidating infrastructure ventures. Turnpikes, however, could really not be operated as private businesses: They were inherently political undertakings that required the participation of legislatures, courts, investors, and the general public. Moreover, turnpikes were built in a field of political contestation in which Americans often resisted the privatization of customary public spaces.[3]

---

[1] Justin Yifu Lin, *An Economic Theory of Institutional Change: Induced and Imposed Change*, 9 CATO J. 191, 194 (1989).

[2] Megan McArdle & Timothy B. Lee, *The Mirage of Free-Market Roads*, ATL. (March 28, 2012), available at www.theatlantic.com/business/archive/2012/03/the-mirage-of-free-market-roads/255167/.

[3] Most of the scholarship studies local turnpike programs in individual states and provides the data upon which this chapter is based. For excellent economic history of the turnpikes, *see* especially Daniel B. Klein, *The Voluntary Provision of Public Goods? The Turnpike Companies of Early*

The "publicness" of highways in the antebellum era was not limited to roads provided directly by governments. Although turnpike franchisees had specified private rights to collect tolls and fees from travelers, they also had broad responsibilities to the public specified in their enabling statutes and enforced, albeit unevenly, by courts and legislatures. The private infrastructure franchise was subsidized and regulated by governments, reinforcing its deeply public nature. Although the publicness of transportation infrastructure was qualified by the property rights of the franchisees who operated them, publicness could also extend across the private franchise's operations when the interests of the general public clashed with the rights of the franchisee. Thus, legislatures were required to carefully balance the public's right of passage against the franchisee's right to collect fees and otherwise secure its investment. The legal and political environment of turnpikes qualifies a common view of the antebellum era that courts and legislatures adopted a pro-development jurisprudence that insulated enterprises from liability. This view, represented by Horwitz's *The Transformation of American Law*, suggests that American law lent institutional support to competitive enterprises during America's market revolution.[4] While it is true that law acted subsidized turnpikes and other ventures by insulating them from crushing liability in order to encourage development, it is also the case that courts and legislatures attempted to balance the business rights of the turnpikes against customary rights of free passage across the highway.

America 28 ECON. INQUIRY 788 (1990); Daniel B. Klein & John Majewski, *Economy, Community, and Law: The Turnpike Movement in New York, 1797–1845*, 26 L. & SOC'Y REV. 469, 469–512 (1992). *See also* ELLIS L. ARMSTRONG ET AL., A HISTORY OF PUBLIC WORKS IN THE UNITED STATES: 1776–1976 57–60 (1976); HIGHWAY RESEARCH BOARD, SPECIAL REPORT 83, LAW OF TURNPIKES AND TOLL BRIDGES: AN ANALYSIS 3–6 (1964). Other studies of turnpike programs in different states include: Jason M. Opal, *Enterprise and Emulation: The Moral Economy of Turnpikes in Early National New England*, 8 EARLY AM. STUD. 623, 623–45 (2010); Karl Raitz & Nancy O'Malley, *Local-Scale Turnpike Roads in Nineteenth-Century Kentucky*, 33 J. HIST. GEOGRAPHY 1, 1–23 (2007); Christopher T. Baer, Daniel B. Klein, & John Majewski, *From Trunk to Branch: Toll Roads in New York, 1800–1860*, 11 ESSAYS IN ECON. & BUS. HIST. 191 (1993); DANIEL P. JONES, COMMERCIAL PROGRESS VERSUS LOCAL RIGHTS: TURNPIKE BUILDING IN NORTHWESTERN RHODE ISLAND IN THE 1790S 21–32 (1991); Richard Deluca, *Competition V. Monopoly: Transportation and the Law in Nineteenth Century Connecticut*, 49 CONN. HIST. REV. 212, 212–27 (2010); John Joseph Wallis, *The Property Tax as a Coordinating Device: Financing Indiana's Mammoth Internal Improvement System, 1835–1842*, 40 EXP. ECON. HIST. 223–50 (2003); Alan D. Watson, *North Carolina and Internal Improvements, 1783–1861: The Case of Inland Navigation*, 74 N.C. HIST. REV. 37, 37–73 (1997); Gwilym R. Roberts, *The Struggle for Decent Transportation in Western Rutland County, 1820–1850*, 69 VT. HIST. 122, 122–32 (2001); Stanley J. Folmsbee, *The Turnpike Phase of Tennessee's Internal Improvement System of 1836–1838*, 3 J. S. HIST. ASS'N 453, 453–77 (1937); Emory L. Kemp & Janet K. Kemp, *A Thoroughfare through the Howling Wilderness: The Weston & Gauley Bridge Turnpike*, in ESSAYS ON THE HISTORY AND OF TRANSPORTATION AND TECHNOLOGY 45–90 (Robert J. Kapsch et al., eds., 2010); Robert F. Hunter, *The Turnpike Movement in Virginia, 1816–1860*, 69 VA. MAG. HIST. & BIOGRAPHY 278, 278–89 (1961); Henry Edmundson, *The Alleghany Turnpike, and 'Fotheringay' Plantation, 1805–1847: Planting and Trading in Montgomery County, Virginia*," 83 VA. MAG. HIST. & BIOGRAPHY 304, 304–20 (1975); Clinton J. Evans, *Private Turnpikes and Bridges*, 50 AM. L. REV. 527–35 (1916).

[4] MORTON J. HORWITZ, THE TRANSFORMATION OF AMERICAN LAW, 1780–1860 63–108 (1977).

3.2 ROADS, SPACE, AND LIBERAL GOVERNANCE

It is telling that John Locke's *Second Treatise on Civil Government* mentions roads as an example of our "tacit consent" to government regulation under an emerging liberal order:

> "[E]very man that hath any possession or enjoyment of any part of the domains of any government doth hereby give his tacit consent, and is far forth obliged to obedience to the laws of that government, during such enjoyment, as any one under it, whether his possession be of land to him and his heirs forever, or a lodging only for a week; or whether it be barely travelling freely on the highway; and, in effect, it reaches as far as the very being of any one within the territories of that government."[5]

Locke's jurisdictional account of the state's sovereignty is one that extends that sovereignty across every corner of the realm. His broad vision of public sovereignty over the "highway" anticipated the US experience over the course of nineteenth century. As Tennessee's highest court outlined succinctly in 1847: "The power to open roads is a prerogative of sovereignty; it has been delegated by the legislature to the county courts in this state, and is exercised by them, not as a judicial, but municipal, function."[6] While private roads were in broad use since colonial times, the highway nonetheless nearly defined *publicness* both in law and society. In *C. Knight* v. *Carrolton Railroad Company* (1854), the Louisiana Supreme Court affirmed that the precedent's application extended nearly to the front door of local habitations: "A street, or common way, between these habitations, for common use and convenience of all the neighbors or dwellers in these neighboring mansions, is an essential ingredient in the making of a town."[7] In other words, building and overseeing roads is one of the very objects that local sovereignty is designed for in the first place.

Legally speaking, "highway" had a much broader meaning in the nineteenth century than it does for us today. Joseph Angell and Thomas Durfee's influential *Law of Highways* (1857), for example, explained that turnpike roads, plank roads, railroads, bridges, ferries, and canals all fell within the definition of "highway" under common law. For this reason, Angell and Durfee stated categorically that "Highways are public roads, which every citizen has the right to use."[8] The Northwest Ordinance (1787), to cite another example, provided that "The navigable waters leading into the Mississippi and St. Lawrence, and the carrying places between the same, shall be common highways and forever free, as well to the inhabitants of the said territory

---

[5] JOHN LOCKE, TWO TREATISES OF GOVERNMENT, Section 119, Project Gutenberg E-Book, available at www.gutenberg.org/files/7370/7370-h/7370-h.htm. Thanks to Sharif Yousef for pointing me of this passage in Locke.
[6] *Franklin & C. Turnpike Co.* v. *Maury Cnty. Ct.*, 27 Tenn. 342, 354, 8 Hum. 342 (1847).
[7] 9 La. Ann. 284, 287 (Sup. Ct. 1854).
[8] JOSEPH K. ANGELL & THOMAS DURFEE, A TREATISE ON THE LAW OF HIGHWAYS 3 (1857).

as to the citizens of the United States, and those of any other States that may be admitted into the confederacy, without any tax, impost, or duty therefor." "Common highways and forever free" is a powerful phrase; it attests to Locke's republican vision of liberty and public power indissolubly linked together on the sovereign's transportation network.

That state and local authorities enjoyed broad jurisdiction to build transportation infrastructure in the nineteenth-century reflected Locke's broad vision of sovereignty. Antebellum law recognized the special legal status of the highway. Nineteenth-century statute books included separate headings for "Highways, Bridges, and Ferries," which established government responsibility and jurisdiction over transportation infrastructures.[9] In *De Jure Maris* (1670 [1787]), his influential treatise on riparian rights, the much-cited seventeenth-century jurist Matthew Hale offered a broad frame for the expansion of the public's interest and investment in the waterways and shorelines that abutted ferries, roads, turnpikes, bridges, and other transportation infrastructure. "The King, by ancient right of prerogative," he summarized the common law point, "hath had a certain interest in many fresh rivers, even where the sea doth not flow or re-flow, as well as in the salt or arms of the sea; and these are those which follow."[10] As early national infrastructure projects enabled routes of national expansion, publicness became even more deeply inscribed in roads and waterways, expanding territorial jurisdiction, even as it extended the authority of state and local governments across geographical space.

To be sure, an expansive legal definition of publicness, as with development policies generally, also hid bleaker realities. Free movement across American roads was not, after all, a right guaranteed to all people. Conveyance over America's transportation infrastructure was not available to enslaved or free black people during the antebellum era – anticipating a battle for the use of public infrastructures, which in fact continued into the twentieth century. Moreover, a broad legal notion of "publicness" meant little without the financial means to materialize those ambitions. These important caveats aside, a broad conception of publicness persisted in shaping the legal and political culture around transportation infrastructure, even for privately owned and managed turnpikes.[11] While frequently built with private capital and through entrepreneurial initiative, statutes, administrative bodies (such as Boards of Internal Improvement), and courts exerted legal control over the new transportation technologies as they

---

[9] WILLIAM J. NOVAK, THE PEOPLE'S WELFARE: LAW AND REGULATION IN NINETEENTH-CENTURY AMERICA 115–48 (1996).

[10] Cited in *Young v. Harrison*, 6 Ga. 130, 141 (1849).

[11] For an important analysis of law and public space, *see Public Ways: The Legal Construction of Public Space*, Chapter 4 in WILLIAM J. NOVAK, THE PEOPLE'S WELFARE: LAW AND REGULATION IN NINETEENTH-CENTURY AMERICA 115–48 (1996).

encompassed territories that spread across the eastern seaboard and westward into the nation's expanding interior.[12]

3.3 TURNPIKES: ECONOMICS AND POLITICS

From colonial times, road repair and maintenance were local affairs; they remained so throughout the nineteenth century. Towns appointed officers to maintain roads, and local authorities were empowered to levy a labor tax requiring all men over a certain age to perform a specified amount of road labor per year, or to find a substitute to do it for them.[13] Yet, compulsory maintenance was notoriously inefficient. Uncompensated workforces were inadequate to sustain the wear and tear of roads even before the nation's ebullient economy expanded traffic. In the absence of their capacity to build roads, or legislatures willingness to fund them, states increasingly relied on incorporated franchises to build new routes and to service or improve old ones.[14] Turnpike franchises were an attractive alternative to direct investment or raising state taxes for a number of reasons. First, they were familiar. The colonies themselves were not infrequently organized as proprietary corporate ventures. The colonial franchise model, after all, underpinned much of the nation's bridges and ferries. With the fickleness of public sentiment that attached to public works, Americans were comfortable with a model that coupled private capital with public power, though that seldom stood in the way of criticism for what they otherwise deemed to be alliances given to corruption and monopolistic abuses. Another reason often cited for this corporate form was for the way it spread risk and incentivized investment. By allowing consortiums to pool capital, manage liability, and control assets, individual investors could share in the profits of a range of chancy ventures, so offsetting the risk of any particular one.[15]

Each turnpike spanned a range of 15–50 miles and required a $1,500/mile investment to complete.[16] As Adam Smith understood, such extensive works would require state support. Despite better roadbuilding technologies through the early nineteenth century, the rise of the turnpikes was not, as in the case of railroads or

---

[12] William J. Novak, *The Public Utility Idea and the Origins of Modern Business Regulation*, in CORPORATIONS AND AMERICAN DEMOCRACY 139–76, 153 (Naomi R. Lamoreaux & William J. Novak, eds., 2017): "the reports, activities, and rulings of other various local and state turnpike commissioners, street and highway commissioners, canal commissioners, water commissioners, and the like pervaded the antebellum legal and political landscape."

[13] ARMSTRONG, HISTORY OF PUBLIC WORKS, supra note 3, at 57; Opal, *Enterprise and Emulation*, supra note 3, at 625–26.

[14] GEORGE ROGERS TAYLOR, THE TRANSPORTATION REVOLUTION, 1815–1860 17–18 (1951).

[15] For a good recent overview of corporations in American governance, *see* CORPORATIONS AND AMERICAN DEMOCRACY (Naomi R. Lamoreaux & William J. Novak, eds., 2017); *see also* Morton Horwitz, *Santa Clara Revisited: The Development of Corporate Theory*, 88 W. VA. L. REV. 173, 173–224 (1985); Pauline Maier, *The Revolutionary Origins of the American Corporation*, 50 WM. & MARY Q. 51, 51–84 (1993); William J. Novak, *The American Law of Association: The Legal-Political Construction of Civil Society*, 15 STUD. AM. POL. DEV. 163, 163–88 (2001).

[16] Klein & Majewski, *Economy, Community, and Law*, supra note 3, at 500.

canals, a result of new and better technologies. In the face of financial and logistical limitations, the "technology" that Americans turned to was the legal device of the infrastructure corporation itself, which allowed turnpike companies to raise capital to build and maintain roads where states lacked the capacity themselves. The corporate structure enabled capital financing that would, in principle at least, allow franchisees to realize a return on investment and would thus incentivize them to maintain roads and collect tolls. As with many improvements, the benefits of turnpikes were clear: Farmers and ranchers could move their goods to eastern markets; immigrant settlers could use turnpikes and plank roads on their trek out west. Trunk roads could connect inland regions to established roads and thus to the wider world. Turnpikes would also increase land values, values that could be realized by speculators. Moreover, The War of 1812 and the British embargo had revealed the full military importance of a transportation network to politicians and the broad public.

Turnpike building had been under way from the late eighteenth century. Albert Gallatin informed Congress in 1808 that fifty turnpike companies had been incorporated since 1803 in Connecticut alone and 39 roads totaling 770 miles had been constructed.[17] While some states provided little direct support to turnpike ventures (this was especially true in New England), others provided substantial aid through state-wide development programs, such as Pennsylvania, Maryland, and Virginia, with the latter creating the first turnpike statute in 1785.[18] The Connecticut legislature granted a franchise to build roads but expected towns to finance land purchases and bridge construction.[19] Kentucky sought to raise funds through a lottery in 1810.[20] The first turnpikes statutes contracted with companies to repair and upgrade existing roads. However, Pennsylvania created the first statewide initiative to build new roads when it chartered the Philadelphia-Lancaster Turnpike, which opened its sixty plus miles to traffic starting in 1794. Between that point and the end of the nineteenth century, companies operated over 1,500 turnpike ventures. Pennsylvania and New York, Massachusetts and Maine took the lead in turnpike construction in the Northeast. By the 1820s, Pennsylvania had invested over $1,000,000 in turnpikes ventures, an amount that had more than doubled by the 1840s. This was followed by substantial investments in other public–private transportation ventures such as bridges, railroads, canals, and other navigation enterprises.[21]

---

[17] FREDERIC J. WOOD, THE TURNPIKES OF NEW ENGLAND AND EVOLUTION OF THE SAME THROUGH ENGLAND, VIRGINIA, AND MARYLAND 32 (1919).
[18] Robert F. Hunter, *The Turnpike Movement in Virginia, 1816–1860*, 69 VA. MAG. HIST. BIOGRAPHY 278, 278–79 (1961); TAYLOR, *supra* note 14, at 22–24; JOHN LAURITZ, LARSON, THE MARKET REVOLUTION IN AMERICA: LIBERTY, AMBITION, AND THE ECLIPSE OF THE COMMON GOOD 54–55 (2010); WOOD, TURNPIKES OF NEW ENGLAND, *supra* note 17, at 7.
[19] JAMES WILLARD HURST, LAW AND THE CONDITIONS OF FREEDOM IN THE NINETEENTH-CENTURY UNITED STATES 30–49 (1984) (1956).
[20] Raitz & O'Malley, *Local-Scale Turnpike Roads*, *supra* note 3, at 6.
[21] LOUIS HARTZ, ECONOMIC THOUGHT AND DEMOCRATIC THOUGHT 83–85 (2014) (1968); Daniel B. Klein & Gordon J. Fielding, *Private Toll Roads: Learning from the Nineteenth Century*, 46 TRANSP. Q. 321, 321–41 (1992).

3.3 Turnpikes: Economics and Politics

But the most powerful support that states gave to the turnpike companies was in the form of generously granted corporate charters to build and operate turnpikes at a profit. Roads are intrinsically public forms, so the grant of corporate charter rights to partially privatize public spaces for profit was no small matter. Nevertheless, as George Sharswood noted in his 1908 edition of William Blackstone's *Commentaries*, Americans were adept at chartering "religious, literary, charitable, manufacturing, insuring, or money-lending associations, as well as railway, canal, bridge, and turnpike companies ... with which in number and variety no country so abounds as the United States."[22] Sharswood's observation is borne out by the large percentage of total incorporations in the early nineteenth century that were turnpike corporations. In New York, for example, 34 percent of all incorporations were for turnpike ventures. The number was 46 percent for Pennsylvania, 28 percent for Maryland, and 25 percent for New Jersey.[23] Where states demurred or were unable to finance turnpikes directly, private investors stepped in to fill the gap, pouring money into new turnpike ventures; prior to 1830, approximately 85 percent of the funding for turnpikes came from private sources.[24] The rise of the American corporation and the rise of American transportation infrastructure are part of the same story of American public–private development.[25]

The turnpikes were thus business ventures, yet another example of Adam Smith's self-liquidating infrastructure, expected, in theory at least, to pay their own way and possibly even realize a profit. Yet for the most part turnpikes turned out to be a financial disappointment. Compiling available data and noting exceptions, Daniel Klein concludes that "even the undiscounted total net payment of a turnpike was commonly negative. References to average yearly dividends usually put the figure at barely above zero."[26] To be sure, there were other ways to profit from the prospect of new transportation venture than direct profit. For example, purchasing land near a proposed turnpike route could produce a valuable real estate investment.[27] Nevertheless, turnpikes mostly failed to meet financial expectations and with few exceptions were turned over the states, becoming public roads. Economic historians have struggled to understand how, under these conditions, turnpikes could raise private investment money at all.

Why did investors finance new turnpike ventures with such a poor financial record? To begin with, Americans were desperate for adequate road infrastructure and states could simply not keep with the demand. Therefore, narrow investment rationality was probably not the primary motivation for buying turnpike stock;

---

[22] WILLIAM BLACKSTONE, COMMENTARIES ON THE LAWS OF ENGLAND, VOL 1 (1908) (1753), fn. 1, 468.
[23] Klein & Majewski, *Economy, Community, and Law*, supra note 3, at 470.
[24] Opal, *Enterprise and Emulation*, supra note 3, at 628.
[25] *See* Pauline Maier, *The Debate over Incorporations: Massachusetts in the Early Republic*, in MASSACHUSETTS AND THE NEW NATION 73–117 (Conrad E. Wright, ed., 1992).
[26] Klein, *Voluntary Provision of Public Goods?*, supra note 3, at 793–95.
[27] Opal, *Enterprise and Emulation*, supra note 3, at 629.

instead, business boosterism, civic engagement, and a desire for better local roads also encouraged an army of small investors to finance turnpikes, even facing the substantial risk they would not turn a profit. Companies advertised for stock subscriptions in the newspapers and turnpike enthusiasts tapped into strong regional rivalries to argue for more road development in their regions. Turnpike promoters also encouraged investors through solicitation in "town meetings, correspondence, person-to-person solicitation, and newspaper articles."[28] Daniel Klein has suggested that turnpike subscriptions were essentially a form of voluntary taxation that the public imposed on themselves to develop local road networks.[29] In any event, to the extent that turnpikes were designed to be self-liquidating infrastructure ventures on Adam Smith's model, they met with only limited success.

3.4 ROADS, LOCAL DEMOCRACY, AND REPUBLICANISM

It is worth considering why turnpikes were such a bad business investment in the first place. The answer to this question lies in infrastructure's public–private entanglements and its inherently political nature. So, although turnpikes were launched with mostly private capital, they were always publicly regulated – and their extensive public regulation and politically controversial nature were the very things that made them difficult to run as business ventures. Private businesses of course need to turn a profit; but public infrastructures are intended to be used by the wider public, and in the antebellum era, people had their own stubbornly customary notions about their rights to move freely across public space. Privatization schemes, however beneficial they could be in building roads where the states could not, had to contend with expectations and demands of increasingly vocal constituencies at the state and local levels. It is no surprise from this perspective that state legislatures were reluctant to allow toll rates that would permit turnpike owners to charge the necessary rates to compensate them for their outlays of capital. Nor were legislatures eager to enforce the turnpike's rights to charge rates in the first place when that would mean hauling members of the general public into court.

What Stanley J. Folmsbee writes of the Tennessee turnpike system in the 1830s can be generalized across the many turnpike ventures of the nineteenth century: "Among the causes of the poor showing on the part of the turnpike companies were the extravagant costs of construction ... and the failure of the legislature to protect the companies from the practice by which their customers evaded the payment of tolls by constructing short detours around toll gates."[30] The cost of building and

---

[28] Klein & Majewski, *Economy, Community, and Law*, supra note 3, at 500; Opal, *Enterprise and Emulation*, supra note 3, at 628–30.
[29] Klein, *Voluntary Provision of Public Goods?*, supra note 3, at 793–95; Wood, *Turnpikes of New England*, supra note 17, at 12.
[30] Stanley J. Folmsbee, *The Turnpike Phase of Tennessee's Internal Improvement System of 1836–1838*, 3 J. S. HIST. 453, 475 (1937).

maintaining the turnpike system, the inability to collect regular tolls from travelers, competition from railroads and canals, and the extensive publicness of the turnpikes led to low profits in an age of high expectations. The lack of financial success, in short, was due to the broadly political nature of the turnpike ventures, newer and better technologies such as canals and railroads, and the demands of the American people to move freely across public space.

An inherited culture of political republicanism, as well as anti-monopoly animus, also gave the general public ample reason to view turnpikes with skepticism. When the famous political essayist Thomas Paine wanted a metaphor for the obstacles faced by the radical republicanism that he envisioned for the emerging liberal order, he chose the turnpike gate: "The duty of man is not a wilderness of turnpike gates, through which he is to pass by tickets from one to the other."[31] This is Paine's rebuke to his nemesis, the arch-conservative Edmund Burke, whom he quotes prior to this passage supplying a list of the revered institutions – God, Parliament, king, magistrates, nobility, and priests – that Burke believed would act as a bulwark against revolutionary experiments. The turnpike gate for Paine is not just some stone and wood obstacle: It is a tangible example of the bureaucracy and tyranny that Europeans had to endure absent a true democracy. The turnpike gate was for Paine a spiritual condition; an example of natural law frustrated by undemocratic accretions of old-world institutions. The turnpike gate was to free movement across the democratic highway what corrupt old-world institutions were to radical republicanism: a check on progress across the "wilderness" of the new American nation. Paine's metaphor brilliantly condenses religious and secular imagery into a republican metaphor that would be readily understood by his readers, many of whom had their doubts about tollgates that were springing up everywhere in early America, demanding that they pay a fee to go about their customary business. The turnpike gate was an act of privatization of a public space, adding a layer of governance on top of the highway that Americans have often looked to as a basic right of free movement.

Although perhaps not as inclined as Paine to see in turnpikes a sinister metaphor of old-world corruption, Americans often voiced objections to turnpikes. Sometimes travelers would balk at paying a toll to traverse a road that was impassable because of bad weather conditions.[32] Members of the general public complained to their local representatives about the quality of roads and also objected to working off their road labor tax on the turnpikes. At times people resorted to direct democratic protest, as in this resolution from a Glocester, Rhode Island town hall meeting in 1798: "All persons living on the Turnpike Road in this town where Proprietors of said

---

[31] THOMAS PAINE, RIGHTS OF MAN (1971) (available in THE WRITINGS OF THOMAS PAINE, Vol. II (Moncure Daniel Conway, ed.), available at www.gutenberg.org/files/3742/3742-h/3742-h.htm).
[32] Walter K. Wood, *Henry Edmundson, the Alleghany Turnpike, and "Fotheringay" Plantation, 1805–1847: Planting and Trading in Montgomery County, Virginia*, 83 VA. MAG. HIST. & BIOGRAPHY 304, 313 (1975).

Turnpike are obligated to keep said Road in Repair [should] ... work out the Whole of their taxes on other roads." Many Glocester residents continued to be outraged by the new road, evading toll payment and sometimes turning to violence, prompting one commentator to remark that "[c]ollecting turnpike tolls from Rhode Island farmers was ... a hazardous occupation."[33] In response to the outrage, the turnpike company relaxed its toll-collection efforts, a policy of slack enforcement that seems to have been common elsewhere.[34] Americans were no strangers to these popular actions on the roads and in the backcountry. Road closures and popular actions to obstruct passage had occurred since the late eighteenth century during the "rural insurgencies" that attended the postrevolutionary economic transformations that imposed hardship on rural populations.[35]

There were also important questions of oversight raised by public money flowing into private hands. For example, a common complaint was that "company officers rather than the public authorities laid out the road; construction standards were vague and ... no upkeep enforcement was specified; exemptions were vague and did not cover all the cases thought to be appropriate; gate location was largely at the discretion of the company; there was no provision requiring that those petitioning the legislature for a charter give public notice of their intentions."[36] New York Governor DeWitt Clinton (1817–22), one of the most ardent supporters of development policies in nineteenth-century America, supported canals and turnpikes to open up western markets and settlement. But he advocated for greater public oversight so that turnpikes would be built in "in a manner most subservient to the public convenience." To achieve this, he advised that public officials be appointed to guarantee "[an] exact compliance from those companies with the intentions of government." Governor Clinton worried about inadequate legislative oversight because "no mode is prescribed to exact a compliance from the companies with the intentions of government."[37] Travel writer and businessman Elkanah Watson (1758–1842) was enthusiastic about turnpikes but expressed concerns that the public would be charged tolls even where the road was unpassable.[38] These concerns were widely shared by state governments, many of which created Boards of Internal Improvement to oversee turnpike and other local infrastructure development.[39]

Turnpike statutes thus had to carefully balance public rights in the "highway" against the private property rights of the franchisee. Legislatures could certainly not risk a laissez-faire approach to the turnpikes or treat them solely as private businesses.

---

[33] JONES, COMMERCIAL PROGRESS, *supra* note 3, at 27.
[34] *Id.* at 24–25.
[35] Terry Bouton, *A Road Closed: Rural Insurgency in Post-Independence Pennsylvania*, 87 J. AMER. HIST. 855, 855–87 (2000).
[36] Klein & Majewski, *Economy, Community, and Law*, *supra* note 3, at 485.
[37] Lynton K. Caldwell, *George Clinton – Democratic Administrator*, 32 N.Y. HIST. 134, 152 (1951).
[38] WOOD, TURNPIKES OF NEW ENGLAND, *supra* note 17, at 9.
[39] Raitz & O'Malley, *Local-Scale Turnpike Roads*, *supra* note 3, at 7–8.

They needed to regulate them and regulate them they did: by mandating what the turnpike company was required to do, how much it could make from its franchises, and requiring turnpikes to make their account books available for inspection by the government. Legislatures protected the franchisee's rights to collect tolls but at the same time imposed substantial public-regarding regulatory burdens on the turnpikes. The publicness of roads was also protected by standard provisions that stipulated that turnpikes would be turned over to public management when investors had recouped their investment. Public authorities, committees, or judges were appointed to ensure that roads were located where they were supposed to be. The number and distance between gates, toll rates, and toll exemptions were specified in the charter. However, the oversight of turnpikes was largely left in the hands of unpaid administrators who had little incentive to enforce the rights of the turnpike owners. And despite their benefits, Americans often resented the turnpikes. The political questions raised by turnpikes were serious and reflected important concerns about local democracy. As a result, as economic historian Daniel Klein notes: "[e]xtreme publicness marked the turnpikes."[40]

In one sense, of course, this publicness is no surprise. The highway was the very definition of public space for Americans. So, for example, travelers who needed to traverse private property because a road was obstructed could raise the defense of necessity against an aggrieved landowner suing for trespass: "Highways being established for public service, and for the use and benefit of the whole community, a due regard for the welfare of all requires, that when temporarily obstructed, the right of travel should not be interrupted."[41] Nevertheless, when we recall that turnpikes were businesses, the "extreme publicness" of turnpikes may at first appear strange. But that confusion vanishes when we recall that the turnpikes were severely limited in their ability to run their enterprises as private ventures. Because of the inherently public nature of roads under the law of highways, and the dicey politics surrounding tolls and privatization of customary public spaces, turnpike statutes created a form of limited license to operate roads at a profit; that license came with strong public oversight to protect the public and to quell potential protest against the deprivation of customary rights. The turnpike venture was a franchise, licensed and often partially financed by the state, and regulated in minute detail. This is true for other forms of franchised infrastructure as well, including canals, railroads, and ferries. The regulations that legislatures imposed were necessary to protect the public, to ensure that the franchisee actually built the road that they promised to build, and to protect customary rights. Section 3.5 explores the Ohio Turnpike Statute of 1840 to illustrate how much public oversight was built into the turnpike system. The statute reveals that legislatures had to walk a fine line between protecting the turnpike's expectation of return on investment, while being very solicitous of public concerns regarding the turnpike's privatization of public space.

---

[40] Klein, *Voluntary Provision of Public Goods?*, *supra* note 3, at 789.
[41] *Campbell v. Race*, 61 Mass. 408, 412 (Ma. Sup. Jud. Ct. 1851).

3.5 PUBLIC POWER AND PRIVATE RIGHTS: THE OHIO TURNPIKE STATUTE OF 1840

The Ohio turnpike charter statute from 1840 is typical of the level of public control over American turnpikes built into the regulatory framework of each state. The Ohio statute reveals the highly political nature of the turnpike companies and provides important insight into the regulatory ambitions of American states in the nineteenth century. The statute, as written, challenges the conventional view (such as Morton Horwitz's) that the law generally protected private infrastructure ventures at the expense of other interests that clashed with them. The Ohio statute reveals a legislature's attempt to balance the interests of the turnpike company against the interests of a broader public. Ohio's Chapter 127 ("Turnpikes") developed a strong regulatory approach to the turnpike companies that they authorized.[42] Some of the regulations were typical for any type of incorporation during the period, when companies were still created by special act of the legislature. For example, Chapter 127 specified the corporate and stock structure for any turnpike company, meetings, voting, bookkeeping, specifying the internal procedures and management for the company (Sections I–VI, XVII).

However, some legal provisions were specific to the turnpikes, such as public oversight by commissioners and an anti-fraud provision that disallowed the company from diverting turnpike funds to other purposes: "if any turnpike company shall, at any time, use their funds, or any part thereof, in any banking transaction or business, or shall issue or put in circulation, any bonds, bills or notes, calculated or intended to circulate as money or bank paper, or to pass as a circulating medium, or medium of exchange, or shall appropriate or use their funds for any other purpose" the turnpike would lose its charter (Section XXI).[43]

Once the company was chartered, it would be required "to lay out, locate, survey and make the turnpike road ... on the best route between the points or places designated in the special act by which such company may be incorporated" (Section VII). In order to accomplish this task, the turnpike company would need to acquire a lot of land, so the statute granted the turnpike company eminent domain powers to obtain the necessary rights of way and land that would be required to build the turnpike (Section VII). The exercise of eminent domain by state franchisees was a common practice, much lamented by anti-charter and anti-monopoly critics. However, the practice of granting eminent domain powers to corporations was generally upheld when challenged in court. As the New Hampshire court stated:

> The power to take private property for public use may be exercised by the government through the means of a private corporation. The fact that the members have

---

[42] 1840 Ohio Law Revised Statute, chapter 127.
[43] Section XXI reveals the deep connection between the early states' financial, banking, and transportation systems that will be taken up in Chapter 4.

a pecuniary interest, such as will give it in law the character of a private corporation, will not prevent the State from using it to accomplish a public object. In this State the legislature have exercised that right for sixty years in the case of turnpike roads, and of corporations created for the construction of locks and canals, and aqueducts, and the right can not now be drawn in question. So far as we are informed a different doctrine has not been held in any other jurisdiction.[44]

This power was well established by the time the New Hampshire court issued this decision in 1857. But this rule was not always the case. Prior to the early nineteenth century, infrastructure franchises could generally be built without fear of paying any damages to landowners where the government was simply taking land to build a road. The case that changed the approach to eminent domain payments for aggrieved landowners was *M'Clenachan* v. *Curwen* (1802). The plaintiff, a landowner in Chester, challenged the statute that created the first turnpike in Pennsylvania, running from Philadelphia to Lancaster. The plaintiff argued that the turnpike statute violated the Pennsylvania state constitution's takings clause, which required payments to landowners if their land was taken for public use, as was often the case when turnpikes were built.

Up to the time of *M'Clenachan* v. *Curwen*, neither the government nor the company it had chartered compensated owners when taking their land to build roads. The question that the court faced was whether the new postrevolutionary state constitutions had imposed that obligation on governments. The *M'Clenachan* court examined the history of roads since the time of the settlement by William Penn and found that the original grants of property had always contained a reservation of rights by the sovereign to take property to build public roads, which the court construed in this case as a type of tax that could be imposed on any landowner.[45] So, the landowner in *M'Clenachan* was not entitled to any payment, because he had purchased the land with the understanding that it could be taken by the government. After this case, American turnpike statutes began to include eminent domain clauses such as the one found in the Ohio statute.[46]

Little remarked in the classic accounts of nineteenth-century law is the apparently strange practice of allowing infrastructure ventures to enjoy eminent domain powers in the first place. Eminent domain, after all, is typically a power reserved to government. The US Constitution's Takings Clause provides that "private property [shall not] be taken for public use, without just compensation." State constitutions follow suit with their own takings clauses. That eminent domain was granted to

---

[44] In re Mt. Washington Road Co., 35 N.H. 134, 140 (Super. Ct. Judicature 1857).
[45] *McClenachan v. Curwen*, 6 Binn. 509, 511–16 (Sup. Ct. Pa. 1802).
[46] On the development of eminent domain in the nineteenth century, *see* HORWITZ, THE TRANSFORMATION OF AMERICAN LAW, *supra* note 4, at 63–67; Robert Brauneis, *The First Constitutional Tort: The Remedial Revolution in Nineteenth-Century State Just Compensation Law*, 52 VAND. L. REV. 55, 57 (1999); Scott M. Reznik, *Land Use Regulation and the Concept of Takings in Nineteenth Century America*, 40 UNIV. CHIC. L. REV. 854, 854–72 (1973).

chartered companies may seem like a remarkable abdication of the government's sovereign power. But allowing infrastructure companies the power of eminent domain speaks to the chartered companies as agents of government's infrastructural power and their quasi-public character. As Blackstone had already argued in his *Commentaries*, the fact that corporations were chartered to do public work meant that they also had public responsibilities, a point he made with reference to the corporation's delegated power of eminent domain in the United States: "The state, by virtue of its right of eminent domain, may take private property for public purposes upon making compensation. It may delegate this power to a private corporation, by reason of the benefit to accrue to the public from the use of the improvements to be constructed by the corporation. But such delegation of power to be used for private emolument as well as public benefit does not clothe the corporation with the inviolability or immunity of public officers performing public functions."[47]

The quasi-public nature of the "private" infrastructure company required courts and legislatures to balance the rights of the general public against the rights of the franchisee. So, for example, the legal system exercised some control over the award of excessive eminent domain awards granted by juries. In *Clarksville & Hopkinsville Turnpike v. T.W. Atkinson* (1853),[48] the Tennessee Supreme Court overturned as "unreasonable and excessive," a jury award of $420 to an aggrieved landowner whose land was taken for turnpike construction. On the other hand, legislatures felt that they needed to protect the general public from incautious or negligent construction attendant upon the exercise of eminent domain by the turnpike. The Ohio statute therefore qualifies the franchisee's general right of eminent domain in a long paragraph that specifies the turnpike's obligations to minimize damage to adjoining landowners, a major issue in many infrastructure ventures, including canals and railroads.

Further attesting to the added protection that adjacent property owners enjoyed in the nineteenth century, the Ohio legislature provided a method for calculating damages in the event that the landowner and company could not agree. Damages would be determined by arbitration conducted "by three disinterested freeholders, one to be chosen by such owner or owners, one by such company or their agent, and the third by the other two" (Section VII). This provision represents a compromise between the interests of the turnpike and the interests of landowners. Forbidding jury awards favored the turnpike owners, because juries were wont to side with the aggrieved property owners. "Disinterested freeholders," on the other hand, reminds us of a jury of our peers, in this case a democratic check on the power of the public–private turnpike venture.

Further, allowing the turnpike owners and the landowner each to have a say in who the decision-makers would be is also a gesture toward local democratic empowerment. There were other measures to protect the public. Thus, although a turnpike

---

[47] Blackstone, *Commentaries*, *supra* note 22.
[48] Clarksville & Hopkinsville Tpk. Co. v. Atkinson, 1 Sneed (TN) 426, 429, 33 Tenn. 426, 429 (1853).

company could remove materials from private property required to build a "firm, even, secure and substantial road," the Ohio statute required the turnpike to give notice to the landowner, as well as provide the landowner with other rights to seek arbitration for damages (Section VIII). The statute provided the precise width of the road (sixty feet), as well specifying its material composition ("stone, gravel or wood or other convenient materials") (Section IX). The turnpike company could open the road for travel only after "three judicious disinterested freeholders" examined the road to determine that it met the charter specifications (Section X). Each of these provisions speaks to the control that legislatures attempted to exert over the turnpike companies as the latter built up the early American road system in a field of democratic contention.

Tolls, like taxes, are not popular; it is thus no surprise that legislatures were reluctant to authorize tolls that would be adequate both for road upkeep and for the corporate franchisee to turn a profit. Legislatures, for example, did not often grant increases in the roll rates over time.[49] Whatever the merits of a particular turnpike proposal in the abstract, after all, the average American was accustomed to traversing the public highway and would have very good reasons to be skeptical of enclosures around customary public spaces. Turnpike statutes thus included toll exemptions that represented another political compromise between the turnpike company and often discontented local citizenry who resented paying the toll collector to go to church or deliver goods to market. The Ohio statute, for example, includes a list of toll exemptions that were common in the turnpike laws since the late eighteenth century. Toll exemptions allowed passage free of charge for travelers who were using the turnpike for a list of specified reasons.

While these varied across statutes, Ohio's exemption for various kinds of civic and religious travel from the payment of tolls was standard: "That all persons going to and from public worship on the sabbath, funerals, militia musters, jurymen going to and from court, the troops and armies of the United States and of this state, and all persons conveying the public mails of the United States, may pass on any such turnpike road free from toll" (Section XI). Here is a Massachusetts statute from 1802: "any person who shall be passing with his horse or carriage to or from public worship, or with his horse or team to or from any mill, or with his horse, team, or cattle to or from his ordinary labor on his farm, or on the common or ordinary business of family concern within the same towns; or any person passing on military duty."[50] Another turnpike statute included "public worship; a funeral; a grist-mill for the grinding of grain for family use; a blacksmith's shop to which he usually resorts; a poll or town meeting to vote; a physician or midwife; jury duty or to give witness

---

[49] Klein & Majewski, *Economy, Community, and Law*, supra note 3, at 499: "Very rarely were toll rates increased. To what extent companies even petitioned for increases we do not know, but it appears to have been little."

[50] "An Act Establishing the Norfolk and Bristol Turnpike Corporation," 1801 Mass. Acts 374 (Chapter 69), archived online at https://archives.lib.state.ma.us/handle/2452/105488.

in court; military service; and no toll shall be taken at a gate from anyone residing within one mile of the gate."[51] The list of toll concessions demonstrates their political and social character and reflect either common intuitions about fairness or various sorts of customary rights that people had expected from the public roads they had used since colonial times.

The toll statutes were riddled with such exemptions; they generally provided weak protections for the rights of the turnpike franchise to collect a toll. Mechanisms for actual enforcement of the franchisee's rights were even weaker than they appear on paper. The nature of the toll exemptions also suggest that people understood transportation infrastructure as an important part of their common-law and republican heritage of customary rights. The exemption for travel to religious service and funerals, for example, speaks volumes about the importance of free travel for important communal activities and suggests that Americans did not expect to pay tolls on their way to socially important events of a sacred or ceremonial nature. The exemptions in the New York statute for the grinding of family grain or the "blacksmith shop to which he usually resorts" tell us that there were notions of customary rights at play, rights that many imagine having disappeared in the modernizing wave of the antebellum market revolution. The exemption for voting or attending a town meeting tells us that Americans resented having to pay a toll in order to vote. Taken together, the exemptions suggest that far from being irrational rejection of corporate privilege based on resentment, passage across "the highway" was a customary right that Americans expected to continue to enjoy without having to pay a non-customary fee.

Despite the generous exemptions, Americans nevertheless tried to cheat the system by faking exemptions and otherwise dodging the toll collector. Toll evasion and "shunpiking," for example, turned out to be major concerns for the antebellum turnpike franchises. The term shunpiking itself refers to a variety of workarounds that Americans developed to avoid paying a toll. Americans could also be quite inventive in this regard, so much so that the word shunpike itself has a long afterlife in the American experience; it is still in use today to describe driving across an alternative route around a toll road. Shunpiking could include devices as simple as toll evasion by simply not paying the toll collector to more elaborate schemes to build alternative routes around the toll road.[52] Reports indicate that while it was a widespread problem, it was neither cost-effective nor politically feasible to punish or adequately deter shunpikers.[53] Lax enforcement further reinforces the very public nature of the turnpikes and the prescribed limits of the franchisee's right to collect tolls.

Legislators were aware of this problem and provided penalties for shunpiking, as in the 1840 Ohio statute "That if any person or persons using any such a turnpike

---

[51] Klein & Majewski, *Economy, Community, and Law, supra* note 3, at 494–95.
[52] DANIEL WALKER HOWE, WHAT HATH GOD WROUGHT: THAT TRANSFORMATION OF AMERICA, 1815–1848 213–14 (2007).
[53] Klein & Majewski, *Economy, Community, and Law, supra* note 3, at 497.

road shall, with intent to defraud any such turnpike toll, &c. company or to evade the payment of toll, pass through any private gate or bars, or along any other ground near any turnpike gate which shall be erected in pursuance of this act.... shall, for every such offense, forfeit and pay to the president, directors and company, owning such a turnpike road, the sum of five dollars" plus the cost of the suit (Section XII). This would appear to offer strong protection to the franchise. As always, however, it is important to read statutes closely. Notice that the legislature qualified its prohibition in Section XII with an important caveat: One needs to have specifically intended to defraud the turnpike company in not paying the toll. Showing that a person specifically intended anything is always a difficult legal hurdle. Showing that a violator specifically intended to defraud a turnpike company would have involved concrete evidence that that person deliberately avoided the toll gate, rather than merely inadvertently failing to pay the toll (for example, by going around the toll road via an alternative route where the turnpike company claimed a right to payment). The higher bar for intent would allow Americans to escape fines by claiming that they did not intend to defraud the turnpike company at all; they had merely neglected to pay for some other reason.

In some cases, people took matters into their own hands in order to avoid paying a toll. Sometimes there was even violent conflict and property damage surrounding the turnpikes. The problem was common enough in England that William Blackstone, a supporter and investor in turnpikes, mentioned the "malicious destruction of turnpike gates and toll bars" as one of his offenses against the public peace in his *Commentaries*.[54] The problem of "malicious destruction" persisted in America. Evidence that travelers defaced posted toll signage is indicated by the Ohio statute's $20 penalty, plus costs, for "any person wilfully defacing or destroying any guide board, mile post or stone, or painted list of rates..." (Section XV). The mention of the "painted list of rates" suggests that members of the public took the initiative to provide themselves and members of their community with an illegal discount by painting lower toll rates over the listed rates, another act of everyday popular rebellion against the turnpike's authority to collect tolls. But travelers were also protected from abusive practices by toll collectors so that "if any toll gatherer on any turnpike road shall unreasonably detain any passenger after the toll has been paid or offered to be paid, or shall demand or receive greater toll than shall be allowed by law on such road" the toll collector would be liable for a $20 fine (Section XVII).

In some cases, a member of the public destroyed a turnpike gate because they believed that the turnpike gate was built on a public highway. In *Wales* v. *Stetson* (1806), the Massachusetts court was prepared to allow the company to levy a fine for the gate's destruction and for avoiding the toll if the company could show that it had not built the gate improperly across a public road. The legal answer to this question could be found in the language of the corporate grant, which did not allow

---

[54] *Dean v. State*, 13 Md. App. 654, 670 fn. 6 (1971) (citing Blackstone).

the company to build on the "old highway" as it had done. Therefore, the gate was a public nuisance and could be removed without penalty.[55] Tucked into Section XII on penalties for toll evasion, moreover, is a provision that "nothing in this act shall be so construed as to prevent persons using any such road, between the gates, for common purposes." This provision on "common purposes" ensured that people could move on the turnpike free of charge if, for example, they happened to live between two gates and wanted to travel on the road. Statutes also provided for fines against overzealous toll collectors.

However, in some early New York cases, judges seemed skeptical of litigious plaintiffs who pressed their claims of harassment too far against turnpike companies. They would not allow turnpike companies to be fined for minor disputes or to allow the general public to exploit statutory loopholes. The plaintiff in *Conklin v. Elting* (1807), for example, was a farmer who "had been in the practice for many years of going to his wood-lots, to make posts and rails for the use of his farm; and a road had long been open between his dwelling-house and the same woodland; part of which road is included in the turnpike." This customary travel entitled him to a toll exemption under the New York statute for those "going to or from [their] common business." The toll collector nevertheless detained the plaintiff for ten minutes, and he sued under the statute's provision for the $25 fine. The court denied the fine because the plaintiff was exempt from the toll and therefore was not within the meaning of the provision on fines, which only applied to paying travelers.[56] The New York legislature clarified that the statute's penalty against wrongful toll collection also applied to those travelling freely. Thus, in *Skinner v. Anderson* (1852), the New York court noted the change in statutory language and held in favor of a clergyman who was forced to pay a toll despite the fact that he was on his way to preach a sermon.[57]

In addition to provisions protecting the public against wrongful toll collection, it is not clear how vigorously local authorities would have enforced fines against toll evasion. For example, in one case of alleged toll evasion in New York, the Monterey, Cooper's Plains, Painted Post, and Corning Plank Road Company brought the defendant, a person named in the caption as "Faulkner," before a justice of the peace to enforce the $25 penalty for purportedly attempting to move past the gate with his "span of horses" by paying the toll with a bank note. Although the reported decision does not tell us why this tender of payment was rejected, it is possible that the toll collector believed the note was counterfeit. Also, it is important to keep in mind that in an era of wildcat banking, with hundreds of local banks scattered across the country each issuing its own currency, tenders of local bank notes would often be viewed with a measure of skepticism. Whatever the case, the court of appeals

---

[55] *Wales v. Stetson*, 2 Mass. 143, 146 (Ma. Sup. Jud. Ct. 1806).
[56] *Conklin v. Elting*, 2 Johns 410, 411–13 (N.Y. Sup. Ct. 1807). The Supreme Court of New York came up with the same result under in *Norval v. Cornell*, 16 Johns 73, 74 (N.Y. Sup. Ct. 1819).
[57] *Skinner v. Anderson*, 12 Barb. 648, 650–52 (N.Y. Sup. Ct. 1852).

sided with the defendant: simply attempting to pay a toll with a bank note did not meet New York's statutory definition of "forcibly or fraudulently pass[ing] any gate" that would violate its statute.[58]

Courts also sided with the broad public in cases where they had to decide how far the turnpike's private rights extended. These cases arose in a variety of circumstances where the court was required to decide whether the turnpike qualified as a public highway. When they were called upon to do so, judges typically held that turnpikes were public highways despite their hybrid public–private character. The Massachusetts case of *Commonwealth v. George Wilkinson* (1834) lays out the standard approach to turnpikes:

> We think, that a turnpike road is a public highway, established by public authority for public use, and is to be regarded as a public easement, and not as private property. The only difference between this and a common highway is, that instead of being made at the public expense in the first instance, it is authorized and laid out by public authority, and made at the expense of individuals in the first instance; and the cost of construction and maintenance, is reimbursed by a toll, levied by public authority for the purpose. Every traveller has the same right to use it, paying the toll established by law, as he would have to use any other public highway.[59]

This Massachusetts decision is far from unique. Many courts reached the same results, often relying on the law of public highways to do so.[60] These courts were also following the lead of the legislature when they decided that the turnpike roads

---

[58] The Monterey, Cooper's Plains, Painted Post & Corning Plank Road Co. v. Faulkner, 21 Barb. 212, 213 (N.Y. Sup. Ct. 1855).

[59] *Commonwealth v. Wilkinson*, 33 Mass 175, 177, 16 Pick. 175 (1834).

[60] See, for example, *Pickard v. Howe*, 53 Mass. 198, 208, 12 Metcalf 198 (1846) (turnpike a public highway); *Lexington & O.R. Co. v. Applegate*, 38 Ky. 289, 8 Dana 289, 295–96 (1839) (same); *Huntingdon Cambria & Ind. Turnpike Co. v. Brown*, 2 Pen. & W. 462 (1831) ("Our turnpike roads are public highways, and it is the franchise of the citizen to use them, free of every restriction that is not explicitly imposed by the legislature"); Wadsworth v. Smith, 2 Fairf. 278, 282 (1834) ("All the books, which we have been able to consult, consider toll as a common charge, which it is the prerogative of the government alone to impose and regulate"); *Chagrin Falls & C. Plank Road Co. v. Cane*, 2 Ohio St. 419, 426 (1853) ("The public had acquired, and we are bound to suppose, had paid for, to the satisfaction of the owners, a perpetual *easement* in the land covered by the road, which gave the right to all persons to pass and repass over it at pleasure, either on foot or by any mode of conveyance they might see fit to employ and also the right to improve it, for that purpose, in any manner that might be thought, by the legislature, most conducive to the end in view, and would best subserve the interests and convenience of the public at large); *In re Mt. Washington Road Co.*, 35 N.H. 134, 140 (1857) ("[turnpikes] being open to all travelers, are public highways; and the circumstance that a toll is paid for the use of them does not deprive them of their public character"); *but see* Buncombe Turnpike Co. v. John Baxter, 32 N.C. 222, 10 Ired. 222, 222–23 (1849) (turnpike not a public road for purposes of a statute exemption citizens from "working 'on roads without the limits of that town'") and Nolensville Turnpike Co v. Baker, 23 Tenn. 315, 318 (1843) ("We are of opinion that the turnpike at the gate is, in the language of the charter, on the ground occupied by the old road, and consequently its existence as a public road is not preserved by that provision of the charter, but that it is abolished by the construction of the turnpike.")

should be treated as public highways. The turnpike statutes were carefully crafted to protect the public's interest in good roads, providing precise specifications for the road and imposing clear obligations on the contractor. States delegated only that power necessary to construct the desired road with as little possibility for broader aggrandizement of police powers.

Other courts use the law of highways to protect the legislative police power and public regulation. In *Joshua Gilmore* v. *Amos Holt* (1826), for example, a party sued a field driver for trespass. The driver had been appointed by town authorities to impound stray cattle wandering around "at large."[61] If Holt had recovered the cattle on a publicly owned road, there would have been no dispute. In this case, however, Holt had impounded the cattle as they were "going at large within the town of Andover" in a space that happened to be owned by the Essex Turnpike company. Joshua Gilmore, the owner of the impounded cattle, claimed that since this was not a public highway, Amos Holt had no right to collect his livestock and impound them (leading to penalties that Gilmore would have to pay on pain of forfeiting his valuable livestock). The court flatly rejected Gilmore's position: "And we think a turnpike road passing through a town is as much a highway, for the purposes of the act, as a road laid out by authority of the Court of Sessions or of the town. The mischief is the same. Towns cannot prevent droves of cattle from passing over any roads within their territory; but they have a right by law to require that they shall be watched, in order to prevent them from breaking into inclosures and doing damage."[62]

Sometimes turnpike companies complained that they were being asked to do more than their charters required. This was the case with *Commonwealth* v. *Worcester Turnpike Corporation* (1825), for example, where the defendant argued that the town of Roxbury, Massachusetts, was asking it to maintain part of a road that they claimed was the town's responsibility to maintain.[63] That part of the road, they asserted, was "an ancient road" and a "public highway" that was the government's duty to oversee. Chief Judge Isaac Parker, a Federalist appointee to the Massachusetts Supreme Judicial Court, rejected this claim and held that since the company had been collecting tolls on this road, they had to maintain it: "They surely cannot, by neglecting their duty, exempt themselves from the penalty prescribed by law for this very neglect. [A]fter they have undertaken to erect their gates and to receive toll, they are liable to the charge of keeping the road in repair."[64]

---

[61] 21 Mass. 258, 4 Pick. 258 (1826); *see also* Pickard v. Howe, 53 Mass. 198, 208, 12 Metcalf 198 (1846) (another stray cattle case that cites *Gilmore* v. *Holt* to reach the same result).

[62] *Gilmore* v. *Holt*, 21 Mass. 258, 4 Pick. 258, 276 (1826). Twenty years later, a Massachusetts court applied the same reasoning, citing *Gilmore: Pickard* v. *Howe*, 53 Mass. 198, 12 Metcalf 198, 208 (1846): "No objection arises as to the place where the cattle were taken up; a turnpike road being a highway within the meaning of the statute restraining cattle from going at large."

[63] *Commonwealth* v. *Worcester Turnpike Corp.*, 3 Pick. 327 (Mass. 1825).

[64] *Worcester Turnpike Corp.*, 3 Pick. at 330.

Courts were also quick to remind turnpike corporations of their public obligations when the occasion warranted. Since the companies were creatures of explicit grant, members of the public could challenge actions of the turnpike company by arguing that they exceeded the bounds of their authority as specifically granted in the charter. Because the infrastructure companies were created by statute, deciding questions of public and private would often involve parsing legislative intent and by tracing corporate grants back to their original language. *The People v. The Kingston and Middleton Turnpike Road Company* (1840) nicely illustrates the quasi-public nature of the turnpike corporation and by extension, all infrastructure ventures in the antebellum era. The State of Pennsylvania filed a writ of quo warranto against the Kingston and Middletown Turnpike Road Company alleging that they had "usurp[ed] the liberties, privileges and franchises of being a body politic and corporate."[65] The quo warranto writ is a common law form designed to challenge the actions of a public official, with a history dating back to the early use of franchises by the English to do public work such as keeping the peace.

The *Kingston* plaintiff used the quo warranto writ to argue that the Middleton Turnpike Company had not kept its end of the bargain when it promised to construct a road within the precise parameters laid down by the legislature in the turnpike statute. The Pennsylvania attorney general made thirty specific complaints in the pleadings indicating where the franchisee had failed to maintain the road according to the statutory specifications. The state's lawyer further argued that the Middleton Turnpike's failure to do what it had promised to do amounted to a forfeiture of its right to collect tolls under the doctrines of *misuser and nonuser*; this was another common law form of action (related to quo warranto) where a charter right could be forfeit upon non-completion of a duty. The court reasoned that since forfeiture of a right was disfavored, "slight departures are overlooked."[66] Thus the court would not deprive the Middleton Turnpike of its public franchise for minor violations. Nevertheless, the court ruled against the company on most of the issues presented, holding that there needed to be a trial on whether the company had substantially performed its duties.

Because the quo warranto writ is only available to compel actions by public officials, the *Kingston* court had to answer the question whether the turnpike company qualified as "public." In answering this question in the affirmative, the *Kingston* court recognized that the turnpike company was performing a public service, and it was reluctant to punish it by requiring the company to forfeit its corporate franchise, which is one possible result of a successful quo warranto action. Nevertheless, the company still had duties to the public that it was required to discharge. The court frames its discussion by imagining the corporation as a tool of economic development, but one that was more than just an opportunity for private business to reap

---

[65] *People v. Kingston & M. Turnpike Road Co.*, 23. Wend. 193 (N.Y. 1840).
[66] *People v. Kingston & M. Turnpike Road Co.*, 23. Wend. 193, 211 (N.Y. 1840).

a profit. The turnpike corporation had an obligation that flowed to the public; the dereliction of this duty to "live up to the fundamental law of their being" as public–private tools of government had led the public to regard the turnpike with such distrust and suspicion:

> Under proper regulations, they are often eminently useful instruments in the hands of citizens to promote valuable and meritorious enterprizes, public and private; and at an early day, and even at this time, none more so than those instituted to construct our public thoroughfares, or less gainful to the corporators. But their usefulness as well as public favor depend upon an honest and faithful fulfilment of the duties they have assumed. It is the neglect of these, the failure to live up to the fundamental law of their being, that has mainly contributed to the doubt as to the wisdom of their creation, and the disfavor with which they are now regarded by many. Their own as well as the public interests will be best consulted by holding them to a strict accountability. The terms and conditions of their grant being settled and accepted, they ought not to be allowed to act beyond its scope and end, nor come short of it. Within this line of duty, their acts should be liberally expounded, and indulgently regarded both by the courts and the public.[67]

The *Kingston* court's encomium to the value of corporations for infrastructure appeared in many decisions of nineteenth-century courts. Together, they map out a "public benefits" theory of corporate infrastructure (discussed in Chapter 4) through which courts viewed such ventures as "quasi-public" or as simply provided general benefits to the public at large. Such statements remind us of Horwitz's argument that common law courts evolved a pro-development jurisprudence that advantaged new enterprises over older ones.

However, the *Kingston* court carefully qualifies its praise by reminding the company that it has duties and that neglecting those duties placed the turnpikes in "disfavor" with many members of the public. Thus, to the extent that courts developed a pro-development jurisprudence, we need to qualify that by noting that antebellum courts did not share our sharp distinctions between public and private, nor did they view corporations as merely tools of private profit. Judges developed a pro-development jurisprudence by ruling against incumbent franchises, but they remained solicitous of the rights of specific litigants who challenged franchises when they overstepped their charter rights or when those rights clashed with the rights of the general public.

Where later city and state development plans increased responsibilities of turnpike companies laid out in their charters, courts had to decide whether to respect the terms of the original grant or to allow the planned development with increased responsibilities to the franchisee. For example, *In re Kensington Dist. Division* (1830), a Pennsylvania statute authorized surveyors to enter any property in order to lay the foundations for a town plan.[68] The statute also changed the road grading and other

---

[67] *People v. Kingston & M. Turnpike Road Co.*, 23. Wend. 193 209 (N.Y. 1840).
[68] In re Kensington Dist. Division, 2 Rawle 445 (Pa. 1830).

specifications in ways that departed from the original corporate grant of 1801. These departures from the original charter terms increased the obligations of the turnpike franchise, thus increasing their expenses. Now the company would have to spend more money on what was likely already a low-profit venture. The Germantown and Perkiomen Turnpike Road challenged the state's authority to alter the terms of their original grant. This is precisely the type of litigation that boomed in the early nineteenth century as rapid growth and new building clashed with the vested rights of older corporate grants.

The question is one that often recurred in nineteenth-century law: Could the legislature change the favorable terms of the original deal they had used to lure new investors to build infrastructure now that those terms had become inconvenient to their new development plans? Older ventures of course argued that changing the rules in the middle of the game was fundamentally unfair, which makes an intuitive kind of sense. However, the legal theory under which the lawyer proceeded in *Kensington* was one that courts were increasingly loathe to accept. Essentially, the turnpike lawyer argued that his client's enterprise enjoyed certain rights that had vested at the time of the original grant and could not now be changed. Under this vested rights theory, the idea is that the government's police power to regulate in the public good – its right, for example, to charter new companies and build new infrastructure – did not include the power to change the value of their franchise rights by imposing new costs and responsibilities. This vested rights argument was a vestige of eighteenth-century notions of property and one that the Supreme Court would squarely reject in the *Charles River Bridge* case in 1837 (discussed in Chapter 4).

The court in *Kensington* rejected plaintiff's vested rights theory, which holds that once a party's rights have become fixed in a contract or grant, the state's police power cannot nullify that right. Even before the definitive statement in *Charles River Bridge* (1837), American courts did not adopt a strong vested rights approach to these sorts of police power questions, which arose frequently in the expansive growth of the early nineteenth century. The Kensington court treated the legislative police power as a flexible, pragmatic, and utilitarian one: "The intention of the legislature was, to give all the authority necessary to the commissioners, to lay out the town in the manner most convenient and useful to the inhabitants of the district; and in furtherance of this object, so highly beneficial to the citizens, they have vested in the surveyors full and plenary authority, liable to be reviewed and corrected in the manner therein prescribed."[69] The Pennsylvania court reasoned that this was essentially a takings claim and that such claims could be raised in the usual manner under the relevant state law. Only a true taking could be compensated, not merely an impairment of a contract right.

What the Kensington court was denying, of course, was the sort of regulatory takings claims that would come to fruition in the twentieth century in *Pennsylvania*

---

[69] In re Kensington Dist. Div., 2 Rawle 445, 447 (Pa. 1830).

Coal v. Mahon (1922) and subsequent jurisprudence. Here, we see the court acting as an agent of development, as Horwitz describes, but development could also mean ruling against franchisees and in favor of a broadly defined public interest. The public interest could be served by a privately owned fee-generating franchise closely following the legislature's directives.

3.6 CONCLUSION

As in Locke's formulation, a strong sense of public authority permeated the management and governance of road networks in the antebellum United States, including turnpikes. The ambivalence around turnpikes attests to the deeply political nature of roads and other public infrastructure in the liberal order. Turnpikes, despite serving as an example of private infrastructure for contemporary observers, were nevertheless treated as quasi-public instrumentalities of the states in the antebellum era. On the one hand, legal doctrines that embraced a pro-development approach seem to favor the entrepreneur and an environment of competition among infrastructure franchises. This has led to narratives about the privatization of American law in the antebellum era during the market revolution. As historians note, however, the line was never clearly drawn between public and private in the nineteenth century. We should remember that courts were often solicitous of traditional rights and prerogatives even as they cleared the way for public–private partnerships. Moreover, despite the fact that much of the money raised for turnpikes was private, the resulting enterprises were established under the auspices of state regulation. Because they were sometimes politically unpopular, legislatures had to ensure that local democracy was protected even if that meant ruling against the interests of turnpike companies.

4

The Panic of 1837 and the Infrastructure Crash

"They have not much taste for cathedrals and palaces, but 'the useful magnificence of roads and bridges' excites their admiration."

Benjamin R. Curtis, *North American Review*, January, 1844

"The system of public works exercises an influence more powerful upon the morals, and in some respects, upon the interests of the people, than the government itself."

Report of the Select Committee, February 4, 1854, Pennsylvania Senate Journal, 328–37

4.1 INTRODUCTION

Between 1815 and 1860 the population of the U.S. nearly quadrupled, increasing from 8.4 million to more than 31.5 million in a little more than two generations.[1] Americans migrated into cities in the northeast to take new jobs in factories working raw materials into the consumer goods of the market revolution. As they did, infrastructure building boomed: railroads, canals, roads, ferries, and steamboats expanded across the eastern United States and westward into new settlements. Some of the expansion was boosted by new technologies, such as the steamboat and railroad; the first commercially viable railroads, for example, were open to traffic in the late 1820s. Maryland chartered the Baltimore and Ohio Railroad Company (B&O) in 1827 and it opened to traffic in 1830. By the 1830s states had chartered hundreds of railroad companies; by 1860 there were over thirty thousand miles of railroad stretching across the United States.

Canal-building technologies also improved dramatically in the antebellum era. When New York completed the Erie Canal in 1825, its success inspired other states to emulate the model, which fed the infrastructure building boom in the 1830s. Several states had infrastructure development programs, including Pennsylvania,

---

[1] U.S. DEP'T OF COMMERCE, BUREAU OF THE CENSUS, HISTORICAL STATISTICS OF THE UNITED STATES: COLONIAL TIMES TO 1970 8 (Bicentennial ed. 1975) (series A-1 and A-2). These data are available on the Internet Archive at https://archive.org/details/HistoricalStatisticsOfThe UnitedStatesColonialTimesTo1970/mode/2up.

Indiana, Illinois, and Michigan.[2] The improved roads, canals and railroads, and federal postal network built during the nineteenth century facilitated the growth of markets and the movement of populations from isolated rural regions to the newly industrializing cities – just the sort of commercial expansion through infrastructure that Adam Smith had imagined in *Wealth of Nations*.[3]

The national government continued to provide important aid in the form of land grants, support by the Army Corps of Engineers and federally-sponsored surveys, capitalization of state banks, and direct investment such as the Cumberland Road. Throughout the nineteenth century, the post office network expanded, representing one of the most extensive infrastructure work of the period.[4] Nevertheless, as we saw in Chapter 2, the federal government was slow to meet the demand for internal improvements because of congressional infighting and conflicting visions of federal power and constitutional authority. In the 1820s and 1830s, state governments acted decisively (and in many cases recklessly) in the face of federal paralysis to build their own transportation and communication networks. States had a major advantage over the national government.

Because they possessed legal and political sovereignty, states could create the institutional blueprints for development by legislative fiat, capitalizing on their unique charter powers to establish a financial-infrastructure complex whose reach extended to global capital markets. States exercised their charter powers liberally during the century, granting hundreds of new charters for railroads, canals, banks, and turnpikes.[5] By one calculation, American states chartered 22,419 corporations between 1790 and 1860.[6] As William Novak observes in *The People's Welfare*: "The

---

[2] For a nicely detailed account of some of the state internal improvement programs of the era, see Chapter 6, *State Initiatives Again* in JOHN LAURITZ LARSON, INTERNAL IMPROVEMENT: NATIONAL PUBLIC WORKS AND THE PROMISE OF POPULAR GOVERNMENT IN THE EARLY UNITED STATES (2001). *See also* LOUIS HARTZ, ECONOMIC POLICY AND DEMOCRATIC THOUGHT: PENNSYLVANIA, 1776–1860 (reprinted 2014) (1948).

[3] A useful overview of the tradition of public works can be found in AMERICAN PUBLIC WORKS ASSOCIATION, HISTORY OF PUBLIC WORKS IN THE UNITED STATES, 1776–1976 (1976). For a classic account of infrastructure development in the period, see GEORGE ROGERS TAYLOR, THE TRANSPORTATION REVOLUTION, 1815–1860 352–83 (1951), especially Chapter XVI, *The Role of Government*. *See also* CAROL SHERIFF, THE ARTIFICIAL RIVER: THE ERIE CANAL AND THE PARADOX OF PROGRESS, 1817–1862 (1996). FOREST G. HILL, ROADS, RAILS & WATERWAYS: THE ARMY ENGINEERS AND EARLY TRANSPORTATION (1957).

[4] The U.S. postal service was an important federal driver of American development policy in the nineteenth century: "[T]he presence of a post office is indicative of a much broader state presence and functionality, for example, via legal services and regulation, access to land, and security of other forms of property rights, which are prerequisites for most innovative activity. Also important was the fact that, already by the 1830s, the post office was a modern bureaucratized institution." Daron Acemoglu, Jacob Moscona, & James A. Robinson, *State Capacity and American Technology: Evidence from the Nineteenth Century*, 106 AM. ECON. REV. 61, 62 (2016).

[5] OSCAR HANDLIN & MARY FLUG HANDLIN, COMMONWEALTH: A STUDY OF THE ROLE OF GOVERNMENT IN THE AMERICAN ECONOMY: MASSACHUSETTS, 1774–1861 51 (revised ed., 1987) (1947).

[6] Richard A. Sylla & Robert E. Wright, *Corporation Formation in the Antebellum United States in Comparative Context*, 55 BUS. HIST. 653, 654 (2013).

extensive public works projects of the early republic, accompanied by the redefinition of public rights in roads, rivers, and harbors, marked the emergence of a nascent American state and the power of the well-regulated society. By the Civil War, legislators and courts successfully secured formal public authority and control over the nation's most important communication and transportation thoroughfares."[7]

As Adam Smith predicted, governments would take the lead in infrastructure investments. Despite the pressing need and available legal authority, however, state governments were simply not in the position to finance ambitious public works from their tax bases. While they did tax, they also used the legal powers that Novak chronicles to underwrite a form of infrastructure financing that Smith recognized, even as he warned against the excesses of sovereign debt.[8] Financial data from the Tenth U.S. Census of 1880 tells us that beginning in the 1820s, but accelerating quickly in the next decade, states incurred large debts to finance banks, canals, railroads, and turnpikes.[9] States were able to capitalize these ventures by exercising their unique legal powers to create markets for investment where none existed before. Improvements were organized as self-liquidating projects: they were for-profit investments meant to pay their own way.

Moreover, infrastructure promised to underwrite the political dream of a world without taxes. After all, if infrastructure could be debt financed with little up-front cost and creditors paid from the proceeds, then unpopular property taxes might be avoided altogether. But the debt-fueled infrastructure plan was precarious. Investors gambled that these investments would pay dividends over a long period providing a continuous stream of revenue. For their part, states nurtured the dream of taxless financing by laying the legal and financial foundations required to launch infrastructure ventures. In turn, they were able to tap into European capital markets, selling bonds to foreign investors backed by their reputations as reliable debtors. It soon became clear, however, that the debt-fueled infrastructure plan involved a massive gamble, underwritten by American self-confidence in boundless growth.

In only a few years, millions of foreign dollars flowed into American states, feeding an infrastructure building mania that lasted into the next decade. Since few possessed the gold to settle bills in specie directly, bills of exchange and other financial instruments circulated in an expanding transatlantic trading system. Unsurprisingly, the debt-fueled infrastructure boom of the 1830s precipitated a financial panic in 1837, when nervous British bankers begin to constrict the flow of credit to the states. Although the flow of credit resumed soon after the Panic, there was soon a wave

---

[7] WILLIAM J. NOVAK, THE PEOPLE'S WELFARE: LAW AND REGULATION IN NINETEENTH-CENTURY AMERICA 146 (1996).

[8] For a helpful, if polemical, overview of sovereign debt theory, see JEROME E. ROOS, WHY NOT DEFAULT?: THE POLITICAL ECONOMY OF SOVEREIGN DEBT (2019).

[9] U.S. DEP'T OF THE INTERIOR, CENSUS BUREAU, REPORT ON THE VALUATION, TAXATION, AND PUBLIC INDEBTEDNESS IN THE UNITED STATES, AS RETURNED AT THE TENTH CENSUS (JUNE 1, 1880) (1884), www.census.gov/library/publications/1884/dec/vol-07-valuation-taxation.html.

of sovereign debt defaults and several outright repudiations in eight states and the Florida territory in 1841–1842.[10] Americans assessed the subsequent economic depression through a republican and moral framework. States had abused the public trust; reckless debt-financed investments enabled what many saw as a corrupt channeling of public funds into private hands by unaccountable elites. In the aftermath, states scrambled to pay creditors and forestall default or outright repudiation of their obligations to pay on the bonds, proposing tax hikes and seeking federal bailouts. The popular tax-revolts that followed spurred a process of legal transformation that forever altered the political economy of infrastructure in the United States.

Beginning in the 1840s, states redesigned the legal and financial framework for infrastructure investment by amending their existing constitutions or writing new ones. These amendments capped the amount of debt that states could incur, required public referenda before debt could be issued, and required that governments only borrow for "public purposes." Ultimately, this legal transformation constricted the range of action for states; at the same time the new restrictions wound up shifting infrastructure investment to the local level, where cities stepped in to fill the gap created by the new limitations on state action. The shift from state to city was in part due to the way state constitutional amendments were worded: they specifically targeted the evils of overleveraged debt and corruption at the state level. Cities were not mentioned in the constitutional amendments. Therefore, infrastructure building and finance moved to the local level.

For several decades, state courts were left to sort out the appropriate scope of public action in the infrastructure field by deciding whether governments were taxing for a truly "public purpose" when they invested in for-profit infrastructure ventures. Courts sided with the government, often against aggrieved taxpayers who were challenging local infrastructure investment based on language in the new constitutional provisions. State courts quickly neutralized the new limitations by giving government wide latitude in deciding what counted as a legitimate "public purpose." "Public" was what the government said it was as a matter of policy. State and local governments also found other ways around these provisions, and cities expanded local infrastructure provision that their residents began to expect. After the Civil

---

[10] My understanding of the financial aspects of infrastructure investment, bond markets and legal reform is heavily indebted to institutional economists. See, for example, D. Roderick Kiewiet & Kristin Szkaly, *Constitutional Limitations on Borrowing: An Analysis of State Bond Indebtedness*, 12 J. L. ECON., & ORG. 62, 62–97 (1996); John Joseph Wallis, *Constitutions, Corporations, and Corruption: American States and Constitutional Change, 1842 to 1852*, 65 J. ECON. HIST. 211, 211–56 (2005); William B. English, *Understanding the Costs of Sovereign Debt Default: American State Debts in the 1840s*, 86 AM. ECON. REV. 259, 259–75 (1996); John Joseph Wallis & Barry R. Weingast, *Dysfunctional or Optimal Institutions? State Debt Limitations, the Structure of State and Local Governments, and the Finance of American Infrastructure*, in FISCAL CHALLENGES: AN INTERDISCIPLINARY APPROACH TO BUDGET POLICY 331, 331–65 (Elizabeth Garrett et al., eds., 2008); John A. Dove & Andrew Young, *US State Constitutional Entrenchment and Default in the Nineteenth Century*, 15 J. INST'L ECON. 963–82 (2019); John Joseph Wallis, *What Caused the Crisis of 1839?* (Nat'l Bureau of Econ. Rsch, Historical Working Paper No. 0133, 2001).

War, courts and legal authorities increasingly sided with laissez-faire theories that challenged local government's infrastructural powers, a topic taken up in Chapter 5.

4.2 A PRO-DEVELOPMENT LEGAL MODEL

States were well-suited to enter the development game by virtue of their unique position *as* governments. After all, they could create the legal frameworks for infrastructure development through state legislatures and courts. Public authority was inscribed in the Federal and state constitutions, which envisioned active governments working toward the common good. The U.S. Constitution empowered state and local governments to manage their own internal affairs. The 10th Amendment, for example, lays out the basic framework for that power: "The powers not delegated to the United States by the Constitution, nor prohibited by it to the States, are reserved to the States respectively, or to the people." State constitutions likewise include police power clauses that enabled governments to regulate for the health, safety, morals, and general welfare of the population. Some state constitutions, in fact, specifically included internal improvements clauses to make the legal authority to build infrastructure abundantly clear. Michigan's constitution of 1835 for example lays out a pro-development model that contemplates state involvement in infrastructure investment.

> Internal improvement shall be encouraged by the government of this state; and it shall be the duty of the legislature, as soon as may be, to make provision by law for ascertaining the proper objects of improvement, in relation to roads, canals and navigable waters; and it shall also be their duty to provide by law for an equal, systematic, economical application of the funds which may be appropriated to these objects.[11]

States also passed hundreds of ordinary laws enabling infrastructure building for roads, bridges, ferries, and other forms of development.[12] A pragmatic and utilitarian understanding of "useful works" allowed states to subsidize "industrial, agricultural, commercial, and communication systems," as well as education and public works.[13] Pennsylvania, Georgia, California, and Massachusetts, for example, used legal and political authority and corporate charter powers to build transportation, financial, and commercial infrastructures.[14] The broad scope of government action

---

[11] MICH. CONST. of 1835, art. 12, § 3 (1835) (available online at www.legislature.mi.gov/documents/historical/miconstitution1835.htm.)
[12] *See* Novak, *The People's Welfare, supra* note 7, at Chapters 3–4.
[13] HANDLIN & HANDLIN, COMMONWEALTH, *supra* note 5, at 52.
[14] Historians from the 1940s through the 1960s mapped the developmental initiatives at the state level in the pre-New Deal era. See, for example HANDLIN & HANDLIN, COMMONWEALTH, *supra* note 5, at 51; *see also* MILTON S. HEATH, CONSTRUCTIVE LIBERALISM: THE ROLE OF THE STATE IN ECONOMIC DEVELOPMENT IN GEORGIA TO 1860 (1954); BRAY HAMMOND, BANKS AND POLITICS IN AMERICA FROM THE REVOLUTION TO THE CIVIL WAR (1985); G. HERBERTON EVANS, JR., BUSINESS INCORPORATIONS IN THE UNITED STATES, 1800–1943 (1948); JOHN WILLIAM CADMAN, JR., THE CORPORATION IN NEW JERSEY: BUSINESS AND POLITICS,

contemplated by the state constitution and in the many state policies and actions that shaped economic and social life in early nineteenth century Massachusetts. Massachusetts, for example, supported the development of internal improvements through lotteries and the granting of exclusive franchises for various forms of transportation where financing could not be raised through direct taxation.[15]

Early American states, however, did not limit themselves to assisting what we would classify as public works infrastructure; they also extended aid to paper mills, glasshouses, fisheries, and other commodity production crucial to emergent industries.[16] Moreover, early American states retained wide regulatory jurisdiction over the marketplace, specifying, sometimes in minute detail, quality standards for a variety of goods and empowering inspectors to ensure the quality of diverse commodities and markets, although of course with varying degrees of success and with a limited administrative capacity. For example, there were extensive marketplace regulations for a wide variety of commodities such as shoes, nails, livestock, and foodstuffs; laws in the 1780s set quality standards for among other things "lumber, flaxseed, butter, pot and pearl ash, beef and pork, pickled and dried fish, tobacco, butter, onions, and lime."[17]

Therefore, it was not a radical break from the past when states began expanding their presence in the development field in the 1830s. But new building faced an old problem: some existing infrastructure ventures enjoyed monopoly privileges granted by legislatures in an earlier era. Courts were initially protective of private rights that states had given to infrastructure companies, sometimes stretching back into the eighteenth century. These enterprises had vested interests and they sued to block new development that would challenge their revenue streams. One issue that arose was around "retroactive" laws where legislatures created a new law that disrupted private rights that some party had enjoyed under the earlier legal regime. The U.S. Constitution, for example, embodies a suspicion of retroactive laws in the *ex post facto* clause. Early state courts tended to be protective of entrenched property interests, and private rights more generally, against legislative power. So for example in *Dash v. Van Kleeck* (1811) the Supreme Court of New York used the occasion of a prison escape to weigh in on the illegitimacy of retroactive laws as matter of general

1791–1875 (1949); EDWARD CHASE KIRKLAND, MEN, CITIES, AND TRANSPORTATION: A STUDY IN NEW ENGLAND HISTORY, 1820–1900 (1948).
[15] HANDLIN & HANDLIN, COMMONWEALTH, *supra* note 6, at 69–70.
[16] *Id.* at 71–73.
[17] *Id.* at 65. The Massachusetts Supreme Judicial Court, that state's court of last resort, would note that such subsidies were particularly necessary at an earlier stage of development. *See Lowell v. City of Boston*, 111 Mass 454, 464 (Sup. Jud. Ct. 1873) ("That mills for the sawing of lumber for purposes of building, grinding grain for food, and the manufacture of material for clothing, may be of such necessity to a community, especially in the early settlement of a country, as to make their establishment a provision for a public service, we do not question. It is doubtless within the power of the Legislature to declare the existence of a public exigency for the establishment of a mill, for which the right of eminent domain may properly be exercised.").

legality (although not of constitutional law, since the federal Constitution did not apply to state criminal proceedings at the time).[18]

Another line of cases dealt with the question of whether a charter creates a public or a private corporation, a distinction that was not clear at the time and one that occasioned much debate in the nineteenth century. The Supreme Court, under Chief Justice John Marshall initially sided with the vested interests, holding for example in *Dartmouth College* v. *Woodward* (1819) that the Contracts Clause of the U.S. Constitution prevented the State of Vermont from altering the terms of Dartmouth College's corporate charter, which it had received from King George III.[19] By the 1830s, however, the United States Supreme Court reversed course and opened the way for new state-led infrastructure ventures. In one of the most famous cases, *Charles River Bridge* v. *Warren Bridge* (1837), Justice Taney's Supreme Court held that the Warren Bridge company could build its bridge, despite the fact that the Charles River Bridge enjoyed a local monopoly granted by a charter in the seventeenth century. Thus, the Court held, companies with older charter grants could not effectively veto future development that competed with their established rights. State and federal law thereafter opened the legal field for state and local investments in new infrastructure ventures.[20]

4.3 TAXLESS FINANCE AND DEBT REPUDIATION AND THE CRISIS OF INFRASTRUCTURE INVESTMENT

It was clear, then, that states had adequate legal authority for direct investments in infrastructure. Moreover, a general spirit of optimism about business conditions, and strong credit with foreign lenders, encouraged states to satisfy their constituencies' desires for improvements. As the federal government assessed the development environment of the 1830s almost half a century later: "With an improved credit abroad; with an ardent desire at home to push improvements even beyond the wants of population; with manufacturing and commercial industries rapidly increasing, and apparent prosperity on all hands; it is not surprising that ... credit to an immense amount was thus created, and that the entire country felt the stimulating effects of these expenditures."[21]

---

[18] 7 Johns. 477 (N.Y. Sup. Ct. 1811). For a discussion of this issue under New York law see Laura Inglis, *Substantive Due Process: Continuation of Vested Rights?* 52 AM. J. LEGAL HIST. 459 (2012); *see also* MORTON J. HORWITZ, THE TRANSFORMATION OF AMERICAN LAW, 1780–1860, 109, 111 (1977): "Previous state concessions to private interests thus had come to represent obstacles to continued growth, and for the first time state efforts to encourage economic growth began to diverge from private efforts to preserve existing legal expectations." The natural law theorists of the twentieth century would highlight these vested rights cases to support their claims that American law had always taken a Lockean approach to protecting property and contract rights.

[19] 17 U.S. 518 (1819).

[20] HORWITZ, TRANSFORMATION OF AMERICAN LAW, *supra* note 18, at 63–139.

[21] CENSUS BUREAU, REPORT ON THE VALUATION, TAXATION, AND PUBLIC INDEBTEDNESS IN THE UNITED STATES, *supra* note 9, at 524.

Financing the public good was very expensive. Projects such as the Erie Canal, for example, required massive up-front capital to build and a lot of money to expand. This was also true of canals more generally, and it was also true of railroads and the banks that made infrastructure investments possible.[22] States were well-positioned to spur infrastructure investment because they controlled important sovereign resources: the exclusive power to charter corporations and the power to borrow on public credit. States also enjoyed the power to charter banks or infrastructure ventures with financial strings attached; so for example they could require banks to lend money or to issue stocks and bonds directly to infrastructure ventures. Andrew Jackson's successful war on the Bank of the United States, and subsequent expansion of state banking, also provided a crucial opportunity for states to enter the development field.

States subsidized infrastructure both indirectly and directly. Indirectly, they could offer a variety of incentives to reduce building costs. Many states exempted railroads from taxation, for instance, or otherwise limited their tax liability.[23] They frequently granted canals, railroads and turnpikes the power of eminent domain (sometimes to the chagrin of outraged property owners).[24] State courts "subsidized" development in their own way by altering longstanding doctrines to weaken property rights, reduce damages to adjacent landowners and otherwise broaden the scope of public action.[25] State legislatures developed several ways of directly capitalizing infrastructure ventures. First, they could levy *ad valorem* taxes on property owners who stood to benefit from infrastructure. The second option, though innovative, ultimately proved itself to be untenable: Governments could create ambitious public works programs through what economic historians call "taxless finance."[26] The most common form of taxless finance was for states to sell their own bonds and then use the proceeds to purchase an interest in a railroad, canal, turnpike, or bank. In another iteration, they simply traded the state bonds for corporate bonds, allowing the company to capitalize its operations by selling state bonds to the public directly. Finally, states could guarantee the bonds of the company, making the enterprise an attractive investment.[27]

As John A. Dove explains: "The rationale [for taxless finance] was that an investment or improvement would create a dividend or revenue stream to cover servicing and repayment. In the best case, the dividends/revenue could actually reduce future

---

[22] Warren E. Weber, *Early State Banks in the United States: How Many Were There and When Did They Exist?* 30 FED. RESERVE BANK MINNEAPOLIS, Q. REV. 28, 28–40 (September 2006).
[23] TAYLOR, THE TRANSPORTATION REVOLUTION, *supra* note 3, at 89.
[24] *Id.* at 89; SHERIFF, THE ARTIFICIAL RIVER, *supra* note 3, at 80–81; CARTER GOODRICH, GOVERNMENT PROMOTION OF AMERICAN CANALS AND RAILROADS, 1800–1890, 51–120 (1960).
[25] HORWITZ, TRANSFORMATION OF AMERICAN LAW, *supra* note 18, at 109–39.
[26] Joseph Wallis & Barry R. Weingast, *Dysfunctional or Optimal Institutions?*, *supra* note 10, at 331–64; Wallis, *Constitutions, Corporations, and Corruption*, *supra* note 10, at 211–56.
[27] B. U. RATCHFORD, AMERICAN STATE DEBTS 89 (1941).

tax burdens."[28] It is worth noting that the taxless finance options were only open to states in the first place because they had established good track records of debt repayment (on much smaller dollar amounts) after 1815, which secured the confidence of British and European bankers and investing publics. European capital markets were eager for investment opportunities, particularly in a geographically expanding nation, where development seemed all but guaranteed for decades to come. Taxless financing, however, was risky: if the infrastructure project failed to produce adequate revenues (as many did), taxpayers were on the hook for payments to creditors – an unhappy outcome that fomented the democratic agitation for legal reforms after the Panic of 1837.

Taxless financing also had other short- and long-term consequences. First, in the short term, taxless finance provided enormous sums of money to build infrastructure without taxing the public up front. (As detailed in the following text, the numbers involved were truly staggering.) This resulted in a large number of successful infrastructure projects that probably would not have been built otherwise. Second, taxless finance also provided short-term political benefits to states, because they were able to advance commercial interests in response to demands of constituents for better infrastructure. Notably, taxless finance through global bond markets also required states to promote their reputations abroad as reliable debtors. In order to sell Pennsylvania railroad bonds in London, government enterprises had to assure foreign buyers that they would receive payments on the bonds in the future. Thus, intangibles such as reputation, character, and credit were crucial to the taxless finance revolution of mid-century.[29]

The third factor was at least as consequential as the first two: taxless finance allowed states to hide the true long-term costs and investment risks of building behind a web of complicated financial details that few could understand, much less track. Opaque financial structures also provided ample opportunity for self-dealing and fraud. Given the transatlantic financial markets, the opacity may have been inevitable. Prior to the telegraph, information moved slowly through the transatlantic economy; business was conducted at large distances with imperfect information about prices and economic conditions in faraway lands. Global finance also required middlemen and brokers, who were not always competent or trustworthy to manage complex financial dealings. Transatlantic trade largely existed in a bubble of trust, credit, and reputation: "In 1836 bill brokerage – the

---

[28] Dove & Young, US State Constitutional Entrenchment, supra note 10, at 10.
[29] See JESSICA M. LEPLER, THE MANY PANICS OF 1837: PEOPLE, POLITICS, AND THE CREATION OF A TRANSATLANTIC FINANCIAL CRISIS (2013). For a good contemporary analysis of bond politics in the United States, see SARAH L. QUINN, AMERICAN BONDS: HOW CREDIT MARKETS SHAPED A NATION (2019); see also A. M. MILLHOUSE, MUNICIPAL BONDS: A CENTURY OF EXPERIENCE (1936); Bessie C. Randolph, Foreign Bondholders and the Repudiated Debts of the Southern States, 25 AM. J. INT'L L. 63–82 (1931).

business of buying and selling bills – was a massive transatlantic enterprise in its own right, much larger than it had been a decade or two earlier. It was a trade that involved delicate calculations about the odds that a promise to pay would eventually be honored."[30]

Each node in the network – commercial houses, banks, legislatures, infrastructure companies, and public confidence – depended on the strength of every other, which increased their vulnerability to economic fluctuations, faulty or incomplete information, and mismanagement. In hindsight, the 1880 census observed an additional risk: "At that time the money-lenders of Europe were not so familiar with the difference in value existing between the securities of different states, and the promptitude with which the national obligations had been paid made it thereafter less difficult to negotiate state loans."[31] States, in short, used their legal monopoly to develop a new financial-infrastructure complex that connected banks, legislatures, and corporations into a new system of political economy tied to transatlantic trade and global finance. So, while taxless finance expanded the infrastructural power of the states, it did so at the cost of entangling them in a web of globalized finance that they could not fully control. In the span of a few years, state governments incurred enormous debt to finance the building boom, as millions of debt-financed dollars were poured into railroads, canals, and other improvement projects. While state governments acted as investors of last resort, their expanded role caused them to absorb massive financial risks in the process. According to the 1880 census tally, American states had incurred debt in the amount of $174,306,994 in 1838. Economic historians have brought that figure into greater focus: "Total borrowing by the states approached a level nearly twice as high as the debt of the federal government at its peak in the half-century between 1790–1840."[32] For context, the state debts of 1840 were roughly 15% of GDP, which would be approximately $3.15 trillion in today's economy.[33] To give just one example of the debts that some states incurred, Indiana issued $10,000,000 in bonds in 1836, which promised to pay 5% interest. This would have required the state to pay $500,000 a year – ten times its annual budget – to service the debt.[34]

---

[30] Alasdair Roberts, America's First Great Depression: Economic Crisis and Political Disorder After the Panic of 1837 31 (2012).

[31] Census Bureau, Report on the Valuation, Taxation, and Public Indebtedness in the United States, *supra* note 9, at 524.

[32] John J. Wallis, John J., Richard Sylla, & Arthur Grinath, *Sovereign Debt and Repudiation: The Emerging-Market Debt Crisis in the U.S. States, 1839–1843* 1 (Nat'l Bureau of Econ. Rsch, Historical Working Paper No. 10753, 2004), www.nber.org/papers/w10753.

[33] Federal Reserve System Board of Governors, St. Louis Fed, State and Local Governments; Debt Securities and Loans; Liability, Level (updated June 9, 2022), https://fred.stlouisfed.org/series/SLGSDODNS.

[34] John Joseph Wallis, *The Other Foundings: Federalism and the Constitutional Structure of American Government*, in Founding Choices: American Economic Policy in the 1790s 199 (Douglas A. Irwin & Richard Sylla, eds., 2010).

States	1820 to 1825	1825 to 1830	1830 to 1835	1835 to 1838	Total
Alabama	$100,000		$2,200,000	$8,500,000	$10,800,000
Arkansas				3,000,000	3,000,000
Illinois			600,000	11,000,000	11,000,000
Indiana			1,890,000	10,000,000	11,890,000
Kentucky				7,369,000	7,369,000
Louisiana	1,800,000		7,335,000	14,000,000	23,135,000
Maine			554,976		554,976
Maryland	57,947	$576,680	4,210,311	6,648,033	11,492,980
Massachusetts				4,290,000	4,290,000
Michigan				5,340,000	5,340,000
Mississippi			2,000,000	5,000,000	7,000,000
Missouri				2,500,000	2,500,000
New York	6,872,781	1,624,000	2,204,979	12,229,288	22,931,048
Ohio		4,400,000	1,701,000		6,101,000
Pennsylvania	1,680,000	6,300,000	16,130,003	3,166,787	27,276,790
South Carolina	1,250,000	310,000		4,000,000	5,560,000
Tennessee			500,000	6,648,000	7,148,000
Virginia	1,030,000	469,000	686,500	4,132,700	6,318,200
Total	12,790,728	13,679,689	40,012,769	107,823,808	174,306,994

Source 1880 Census: Volume 7, "History of State Debts," 523.

Even prior to the Panic 1837, the rate at which states were taking on debt was unsustainable. The impending financial crisis was already set in motion by events in the years prior to the Panic. Warnings echoed loudly from disparate quarters that the situation was precarious and unsustainable. Andrew Biddle, for one, President Jackson's long-time rival, would blame Jackson's veto of the Second Bank of the United States for unleashing the financial chaos of the late 1830s. Jackson's veto of 1832 had led to proliferating state banks across the United States, which flooded the states with "soft" currency, money issued in great quantities without the backing of adequate gold reserves. As part of Jackson's war against the Second Bank of the United States, he issued an executive order to deposit treasury funds into so-called "pet banks" in 1833. (The so-called pet banks were state banks often run by allies of President Jackson, which received special favor in the form of federal deposits). Jackson's attack on the Bank drew fire from Congress, and on March 28, 1834, it ultimately led to his censure along party lines for failing to disclose documents pertinent to the Bank veto (a censure that was expunged a few years later when Democrats again controlled the Senate).[35] Nevertheless,

---

[35] UNITED STATES SENATE, SENATE CENSURES PRESIDENT, Mar. 28, 1834, www.senate.gov/about/origins-foundations/parties-leadership/censure-president-jackson.htm.

the Deposit and Distribution Act of 1836 moved $30M of surplus funds from land sales and tariff revenue to the state banks.

The proliferation of state banks led, among other things, to a rapid expansion of circulating cash, and to rampant land speculation, especially in the West. President Jackson responded to the economic turmoil for which his own policies were partially responsible with hard-money policies designed to fortify the financial system. On July 11, 1836, Jackson issued his Species Circular, which, after August 15, 1836, required that payment for public lands be tendered in gold or silver. His order was in response to depreciating bank-issued paper currencies that were increasingly exchanged for land purchases. The Specie Circular stirred controversy even among Jackson's own party; Democrats split between hard and soft money positions, and the issue would continue to be divisive for much of the century. Yet, Jackson's Circular had the unintended effect of restricting the supply of circulating money, sparking a downturn in western investments.

The complex nature of international finance only made matters worse. A year before the Panic, British and European financiers worried about the general health of their American investments. The Bank of England and other large creditors were particularly concerned that gold was draining from their reserves faster than it could be replenished. Creditors decided in 1836 to raise their discount rates on American bills of exchange. A "discount rate" is a way of measuring the present value of some financial instrument against some expected future payoff on that instrument. In effect, the Bank of England would now demand payments in gold closer to the face value of financial instruments. In other words, banks were proposing that they receive more actual gold to pay off the value of the debt that they held. This is in effect a way of raising the rates that their American debtors had to pay on their outstanding financial obligations. One consequence of this was that more ready gold would be required to do business, causing a potential disruption to the flow of cheap credit that fueled expansionary infrastructure building in American states.

While the Bank of England made their decision behind closed doors, news gradually spread through the merchant houses that were extending credit in the complex transatlantic economy. Even the *threat* of reducing the availability of credit was enough to send shock waves through the business community. As one merchant house lamented: "This decision places all houses in jeopardy that do business with American dealers in British merchandise."[36] Information moved slowly back and forth across the Atlantic, injecting more financial speculation and projections into calculations based on information arriving weeks in arrears of facts on the ground. By the end of 1836, the potential for a financial catastrophe loomed on the horizon. The British sought assurances that states would raise

---

[36] LEPLER, MANY PANICS, *supra* note 29, at 55.

taxes to cover their obligations or that the federal government would arrange a bailout of mounting state debts.[37] For a brief period, state and federal policy makers restored confidence, and following the short-lived Panic of 1837, British credit resumed.

When creditors again lost their resolve in 1839, Massachusetts Senator Daniel Webster was dispatched to Britain to calm jittery investors and to ensure them of the full faith and credit of the United States' political institutions.[38] Famed as a silver-tongued orator, Webster's endorsement was a full-throated appeal to national character: it "would be an open violation of public faith, which would be followed by the penalty of dishonor and disgrace" he intoned with moral gravitas; "a penalty no state would be likely to incur."[39] Given the particular intricacies of America's representative government, British creditors could be forgiven if they imagined US senators to speak for the federal and state governments. Credit flowed again between 1837 and 1841.

The "disgrace" that Webster dismissed as unlikely nevertheless arrived in July of 1841 when Michigan stopped paying on its debt. Between 1841 and 1842, Florida, Louisiana, Maryland, Illinois, Arkansas, Michigan, Pennsylvania, Mississippi, and Indiana either defaulted or repudiated their debts entirely.[40] "The problem was straightforward," in Alasdair Roberts's assessment. "In the 1830s, many American states borrowed heavily from British investors to finance canals, railroads, banks, and other projects. The states could not repay these loans when the economy collapsed unless they established new taxes, which they refused to do. And so many states defaulted."[41] The economic depression that followed was one of the worst economic downturns in American history, causing severe distress across the country for several years.

Senator Thomas Hart Benton of Missouri, a hard-money partisan whose nickname was "Old Bullion," conveyed the pervading despair that gripped the nation: "The goods are worn out; the paper money has returned to the place from whence it came; the operation is over, and nothing remains of the transactions but the $170,000,000 of debt, its devouring interest, and the banks, canals, and

---

[37] ROBERTS, AMERICA'S FIRST GREAT DEPRESSION, *supra* note 30, at 51–52.
[38] The trip was apparently not solely official. Webster worked behind the scenes to sell 15,000 acres of prime real estate, including land positioned near a new canal. ROBERTS, AMERICA'S FIRST GREAT DEPRESSION, *supra* note 30, at 52.
[39] Quoted in ROBERTS, AMERICA'S FIRST GREAT DEPRESSION, *supra* note 30, at 52; *see also* JONATHAN A. RODDEN, HAMILTON'S PARADOX: THE PROMISE AND PERIL OF FISCAL FEDERALISM 55–72 (2006).
[40] John A. Dove, *Credible Commitments and Constitutional Constraints: State Debt Repudiation and Default in Nineteenth Century America*, 23 CONST. POL. ECON. 66, 77 (2012); William B. English, *Understanding the Costs of Sovereign Default*, *supra* note 10; REGINALD C. MCGRANE, FOREIGN BONDHOLDERS AND AMERICAN STATE DEBTS (2000) (1935) offers a much-cited account of the issue of state debts in the nineteenth century.
[41] ROBERTS, AMERICA'S FIRST GREAT DEPRESSION, *supra* note 30, at 49.

roads which represent it. The whole of these banks have failed once, and most of them twice, in two years; the greater part of the roads and canals are unfinished, and of those finished several are unproductive."[42] He continued in the same speech, alluding to the now devalued American securities: "In Europe, although backed by the credit of the states, they rate from one-half to three-fourths of their nominal value."[43]

During the late 1830s, states petitioned Congress for a federal bailout. With crisis in the air, President Tyler spoke to Congress on March 25, 1842, reminding foreign debtors that they had incurred debt contracts with individual states, not the federal government. But Tyler nevertheless reassured creditors that states would be responsible debtors: "nor will I doubt but that, in view of that honorable conduct which has evermore governed the States and the people of the Union, they will each and all resort to every legitimate expedient before they will forego a faithful compliance with their obligations."[44] President Tyler's message to creditors was clear: No federal bailout would be forthcoming.[45] The British responded with outrage and mockery at the defaults and repudiations, mercilessly excoriating their American debtors, with terms such as "injustice," "turpitude," "impunity," and "ruin" describing the disaster caused by American fecklessness.[46] In 1845, the London *Literary Gazette* published a satirical poem mocking American debt repudiators, sung to the tune of Yankee Doodle:

> Yankee Doodle borrows cash,
> Yankee Doodle spends it,
> And then he snaps his fingers at
> The jolly flat who lends it.
> Ask him when he means to pay,
> He shews no hesitation,
> But says he'll take the shortest way,
> And that's repudiation![47]

---

[42] CENSUS BUREAU, REPORT ON THE VALUATION, TAXATION, AND PUBLIC INDEBTEDNESS IN THE UNITED STATES, *supra* note 9, at 527.

[43] *Id.*

[44] Zachary Tyler, U.S. President, Message Regarding Finances and Fiscal Policy (Mar. 25, 1842), https://millercenter.org/the-presidency/presidential-speeches/march-25-1842-message-regarding-finances-and-fiscal-policy.

[45] C. Randall Henning & Martin Kessler, *Fiscal Federalism: US History for Architects of Europe's Fiscal Union* (Peterson Inst. Int'l Econ., Working Paper Series WP12-1, 2012), at 1, 6–7.
For an extended discussion of the bailout question, see ROBERTS, AMERICA'S FIRST GREAT DEPRESSION, *supra* note 30, at 73–84.

[46] Quoted by ROBERTS, AMERICA'S FIRST GREAT DEPRESSION, *supra* note 30, at 65.

[47] Cecil Harbottle, *A New Song to an Old Tune*, LITERARY GAZETTE, London, Jan. 18, 1845, at 45, https://ia802305.us.archive.org/11/items/sim_literary-gazette_1845-01-18_1461/sim_literary-gazette_1845-01-18_1461.pdf; see also ROBERTS, AMERICA'S FIRST GREAT DEPRESSION, *supra* note 30, at 65 (quoting this passage).

As painful as it was to be painted as repudiators, many Americans had to agree with the underlying verdict. Future Supreme Court justice Benjamin R. Curtis published an influential analysis of the debt crisis in the *North American Review* in 1844. The 1880 U.S. Census quotes his essay extensively in its postmortem of the crisis that sunk the nation into a protracted depression. Not mincing words, Curtis characterized the investment boom as "reckless" and "rash:" "Some, who in former times would have found occupation suited to their daring tempers in the field, embarked their recklessness in commerce; others, whose rashness under ordinary circumstances would have been soon checked by disaster or prevented from showing itself by want of means, found that their energy and love of adventure had made them loaders."[48] And many shared Curtis's sense of the reckless course that the states had embarked on in the speculative boom years. In the end, the credit of the American states was ruined.[49]

4.4 LAW REFORMS AND THE RISE OF PUBLIC PURPOSE LIMITS ON STATE INVESTMENT

The Panic of 1837 and its aftermath revealed the troubling entanglements between financial, legal, and material infrastructures. It also revealed the quandaries that can result from mixing public money with private enterprises without adequate limitation and oversight. These problems were not lost on state legislatures, which made several important legal reforms in response to the infrastructure crash. The first was to create general incorporation laws, which made it much easier to start companies without the special permission of the legislatures. On this reform, some states had taken the early lead. New York had revised its own constitution in 1821 to allow freer incorporation. Easier incorporation guarded against the insider dealing and special privileges that a broader public had long complained of.[50]

By mid-century, however, many policy makers were in agreement that the fiscal order of the states needed to be reformed. In the decade before the Civil War, nineteen of the thirty-four states revised or wrote new constitutions that dramatically enduringly altered infrastructure policy in the United States. The process of constitutional revision continued into the twentieth century, and some version of these revisions continue to exist in all but five current state constitutions. Each state modified its constitution in response to the financial crisis as it developed under different circumstances, so the specific language and provisions vary.[51] Michigan,

---

[48] CENSUS BUREAU, REPORT ON THE VALUATION, TAXATION, AND PUBLIC INDEBTEDNESS IN THE UNITED STATES, *supra* note 9, at 525.
[49] ROBERTS, AMERICA'S FIRST GREAT DEPRESSION, *supra* note 30, at 50; GOODRICH, GOVERNMENT PROMOTION, *supra* note 24, at 122–65.
[50] Michael Les Benedict, *Laissez-Faire and Liberty: A Re-Evaluation of the Meaning and Origins of Laissez-Faire Constitutionalism*, 3 L. HIST. REV. 293, 314–23 (1985).
[51] For a comprehensive overview of the many revisions of state constitutions in the period under consideration here, see G. ALAN TARR, UNDERSTANDING STATE CONSTITUTIONS (1998), especially

for example, revised its constitution in 1850, barring the state from carrying out improvements altogether: "The state shall not be a party to, nor interested in, any work or internal improvement, nor engaged in carrying on any such work, except in the improvement of or aiding in the improvement of the public wagon roads and in the expenditure of grants to the state of land or other property."[52]

While the reforms varied, there were four general types of debt provisions: (1) requirement of a referendum to approve debt; (2) requirements that debt be approved by a supermajority of the legislature; (3) restrictions on issuing guaranteed debt; (4) provisions that pegged guaranteed state debt to some other revenue source.[53] Rhode Island, Pennsylvania, New Jersey, and New York, for example included "credit clauses" that prevented states or their subdivisions from giving or loaning credit to "any individual, association or corporation."[54] Iowa's constitution of 1846 is worth examining in greater detail, because it contains many of the elements common in debt limitation provisions of the period:

> The General Assembly shall not in any manner create any debt or debts, liability or liabilities, which shall singly or in the aggregate, with any previous debts or liabilities, exceed the sum of one hundred thousand dollars, except in case of war, to repel invasion, or suppress insurrection; unless the same shall be authorized by some law for some single object, or work to be distinctly specified therein, which law shall provide ways and means, exclusive of loans, for the payment of the interest of such debt or liability as it falls due, and also to pay and discharge the principal of such debt or liability within twenty years from the time of the contracting hereof, and shall be irrepealable until the principal and the interest thereon shall be paid and discharged; but no such law shall take effect until at a general election it shall have been submitted to the people, and have received a majority of all the votes cast for and against it at such election, and all money raised by authority of such law, shall be applied only to the specific object therein stated, or to the payment of the debt thereby created, and such law shall be published in at least one newspaper in each judicial district, if one is published therein, throughout the State, for three months preceding the election at which it is submitted to the people.[55]

Each of these provisions is designed to disentangle, democratize, and make more transparent the public and private dimensions of state infrastructure investment.

Chapter 4, *Nineteenth-Century State Constitutionalism*, id. at 94–135; *see also* Carter Goodrich, *The Revulsion against Internal Improvements*, 10 J. ECON. HIST. 145, 145–169 (1950).

[52] MICH. CONST. of 1850, art. 14, § 9 (1850) (available online at www.legislature.mi.gov/documents/historical/miconstitution1850.htm); *see also* Michael Gallagher & Madeline Kasper, *The Internal Improvements Clause*, 3 READING CONST. 1, 1–15 (2018).

[53] Kiewiet & Szakaly, *Constitutional Limitations on Borrowing*, *supra* note 10, at 65; ROBERTS, AMERICA'S FIRST GREAT DEPRESSION, *supra* note 30, at 71–86.

[54] David A. Pinsky, *State Constitutional Limitations on Public Industrial Financing: An Historical and Economic Approach*, 111 UNIV. PA. L. REV. 265, 265–327 (1963).

[55] IOWA CONST. of 1846, art. 8, § 1 (1846). This constitution is available online at http://publications.iowa.gov/17470/1/1846IA%20const.pdf.

Notwithstanding their highly technical language, the new constitutional provisions embedded longstanding republican norms of good governance in the fiscal operations of state and local governments. Chief among Iowa's safeguards is the absolute cap on general indebtedness of $100,000, except in specified emergencies. This is the precursor of balanced budget amendments and debt caps that are common in state constitutions today.[56] In some state constitutions, the nineteenth century figures still remain, placing untenable restrictions on state indebtedness in the twenty-first century.

If you read further into the text, however, the language provides for an important exception to that general rule "for some single object" with dedicated revenues ("ways and means") and a plan to pay off the debt within twenty years, without the option of repudiation ("shall be irrepealable"). Such clauses commit governments in advance to specific projects that they could reasonably finance. Furthermore, Iowa's constitution democratizes infrastructure finance by requiring a referendum supported by a majority. Building on democratic principles, the constitution requires public notice of the law "published in at least one newspaper in each judicial district," further reinforcing the democratic and anti-corruption principles and mandate for transparency that spurred the initial revisions.

Despite their variety, a common theme runs through the respective constitutional reforms: they were each designed to prevent irresponsible borrowing, financial manipulation, self-dealing, and other forms of corruption.[57] As we saw in Chapter 1, concerns about government debt shaped republican debate since the eighteenth century, and these concerns continue to influence policy around financial governance in our own time. The basic idea behind the state constitutional amendments and broader legal reform was self-evident: Governments should only incur debt or tax the people for the public good. The Illinois constitution provides the standard

---

[56] For a collection of contemporary debt limits, see RONALD K. SNELL, STATE CONSTITUTIONAL AND STATUTORY REQUIREMENTS FOR BALANCED BUDGETS: APPENDIX TO STATE BALANCED BUDGET REQUIREMENTS: PROVISIONS AND PRACTICE (National Conference of State Legislatures, updated Mar. 2004), www.ncsl.org/research/fiscal-policy/state-constitutional-and-statutory-requirements-fo.aspx; see also NATIONAL CONFERENCE OF STATE LEGISLATURES, NCSL FISCAL BRIEF: STATE BALANCED BUDGET PROVISIONS" (Oct. 2010), www.ncsl.org/documents/fiscal/StateBalancedBudgetProvisions2010.pdf.

[57] I rely heavily on the literature concerning debt defaults and constitutional revision. See for example, Nadav Shoked, *Debt Limits' End*, 102 IOWA L. REV. 1239, 1239–98 (2017); Richard Briffault, *The Disfavored Constitution: State Fiscal Limits and State Constitutional Law*, 34 RUTGERS L. J. 907, 907–57 (2003); Kiewiet & Szakaly, *Constitutional Limitations on Borrowing*, supra note 10, at 62–97; Note, *Legal Limitations on Public Inducements to Industrial Location*, 59 COLUM. L. REV. 618, 618–47 (1959); A. JAMES HEINS, CONSTITUTIONAL RESTRICTIONS AGAINST STATE DEBT (1963); John Joseph Wallis, *State Constitutional Reform and the Structure of Government Finance in the Nineteenth Century*, in PUBLIC CHOICE INTERPRETATIONS OF AMERICAN HISTORY 33–52 (Jac C. Heckelman et al. eds., 2000); Richard C. Schragger, *Democracy and Debt*, 121 YALE L. J. 860–86 (2012); Stewart E. Sterk & Elizabeth S. Goldman, *Controlling Legislative Shortsightedness: The Effectiveness of Constitutional Debt Limitations*, 1991 WIS. L. REV. 1301, 1301–68 (1991).

template: "Public funds, property or credit shall be used only for public purposes."[58] Such provisions reflected a republican concern about fairness and transparency, but it also embodied widespread anti-elite and anti-monopoly sentiments increasingly common in a rapidly democratizing age.

Despite the broad remit of public power that William Novak rightly identifies in nineteenth-century law, state reforms hoped to redefine what counted as "public," separating *publicness* from mere government action and reasserting republican and democratic elements into state infrastructure politics. The reforms frankly acknowledged that "public–private partnerships" required vigilant public oversight of government officials, whose incentives to align investment with public interests were at best imperfect. Although rarely discussed with reference to the Panic of 1837 and its aftermath, the constitutional reforms remapped the legal terrain of *public* and *private* in the United States. In principle, at least, the reforms would make more difficult for states to borrow huge sums, while invoking the promise of taxless investment as political cover. In practice, however, the reforms created other problems.

If the reforms were designed to make *state finances* more transparent and responsible, for example, in practice this was achieved only by making *municipal finances* more complicated and riskier. The debt limitations only applied to states after all; municipalities were free to enter the financial markets to build, modernize, and extend their own infrastructures to service rapidly growing urban populations. Governments quickly developed workarounds to stay within the letter of constitutional law, while still incurring debts for public work at the local level. In the decades ahead, states passed laws authorizing municipal aid, much of it for railroads, as well as for streets, sewers, water systems, and other modern urban amenities.[59] Several decades after the crash of the 1840s, cities themselves were deep in debt for local improvements: an aggregation of over $200M by 1850 and nearly $850M by 1880.[60]

The constitutional reforms also had the effect of empowering courts to arbitrate the legitimate bounds of public authority in the years to come. "Public purpose," for example, is a malleable term without an obvious or fixed meaning. When was aid to an infrastructure company really for a "public purpose" and when was it a short-sighted cash grab by corrupt governments?[61] The answer that state courts provided, ironically, was that it was up to the legislature to decide the thorny questions of *publicness* as a matter of policy. Deference to state legislatures, of course, was precisely the open-ended authority that the reformers meant to prevent. Judicial deference to the legislature was made clear in one of the first cases that tested the power of cities to invest for a public purpose: *Sharpless* v. *Mayor of Philadelphia* (1853). In *Sharpless*,

---

[58] ILL. CONST. art. VIII, § 1(a).
[59] John A. Dove, *Financial Markets, Fiscal Constraints, and Municipal Debt: Lessons and Evidence from the Panic of 1873*, 10 J. INST'L. ECON. 71, 75 (2014).
[60] *Id.*
[61] Joseph Lesser & Vigdor D. Bernstein, *The Evolution of Public Purpose, General Welfare, and American Federalism*, 19 URB. LAW. 603, 603–43 (1987).

the Pennsylvania Assembly authorized Philadelphia to purchase shares in several railroad companies. Property owners and taxpayers sued to enjoin the city from purchasing the stock on state constitutional grounds, claiming that the investment would "add another million of dollars to the already heavy debt of the city, impair the public credit thereof, and greatly augment the taxes of the people."[62]

Plaintiffs' arguments reflect the embittered experiences of the debt crisis of the 1840s. With that experience at the fore, Chief Justice Jeremiah S. Black unsurprisingly acknowledged the potential problems with public investments in infrastructure, noting their potential to cause a "startling calamity."[63] But Justice Black quickly pivoted away from such pragmatic concerns of policy: The court could not simply weigh costs and benefits because, as an institution, the court was bound to interpret and apply the law, not to veto investment decisions made by elected representatives. Constitutional interpretation, he reasoned, was a "strictly ... a judicial question."[64] The state constitution had vested legislative power in the Assembly and therefore it fell to the Assembly to make difficult policy decisions: "To me," Justice Black reasoned, "it is plain that the General Assembly may exercise all powers which are properly legislative, and which are not taken away by our own, or by the federal constitution, as it is that the people have all the rights which are expressly reserved."[65] The narrow legal question was whether the railroad investment scheme violated either the state or federal constitutions. With this principle in hand, Chief Justice Black dispensed with most of plaintiffs' arguments, which were based on what they claimed was the foolish and ill-advised policy of debt-backed investments to corporate ventures.

Justice Black could not, however, so easily dismiss the most serious claim the defendants put forward: By imposing a tax to invest in railroads, the Assembly simply used public money for a private purpose, a clear violation of the state constitution. Justice Black's response echoed that of other nineteenth-century courts. Railroads, he stated, are "public highways," notwithstanding the fact that corporations are formed to manage them as self-liquidating private ventures:

> A railroad is a public highway for the public benefit, and the right of a corporation to exact a uniform, reasonable, stipulated toll from those who pass over it, does not make its main use a private one. The public has an interest in such a road, when it belongs to a corporation, as clearly as they would have if it were free, or as if the tolls were payable to the state, because travel and transportation are cheapened by it to a degree far exceeding all the tolls and charges of every kind, and this advantage the public has over and above those of rapidity, comfort, convenience, increase of trade, opening of markets, and other means of rewarding labor and promoting wealth.[66]

[62] 21 Pa. 147, 158 (1853).
[63] Id. 159.
[64] Id. 159.
[65] Id. 161.
[66] Id. 169.

This is an example of what I will call the "public benefit theory" of government investment. When the question arose whether a government was improperly channeling money into private hands, courts were often given to extolling the utility and general importance of even for-profit infrastructures to the general public. American infrastructure development, many courts observed, was broadly beneficial, and that was no less true because corporations were privately benefiting from doing that work. After all it was evident to everyone that infrastructure was necessary to the business of everyday life and that reality was only amplified by the general nineteenth-century spirit of improvement. Applying this public benefit theory, the *Sharpless* court would seem to be simply rubber-stamping the government's investment decisions without much judicial oversight. But if that was a problem, it was already implied in how states had amended their constitutions. Justice Black could find no language in the state constitution that forbade cities from investing in a for-profit railroad; likewise, there was nothing preventing states from authorizing a local-government workaround.

For several decades after *Sharpe*, state courts were similarly forgiving in their reading of public purpose requirements. Another taxpayer challenge in Illinois five years after *Sharpe*, for instance, pursues the same logic. The constitutional language at issue in *Prettyman v. Supervisors of Tazewell County* provided that "the credit of the State shall not be given to, or in aid of, any individual, association, or corporation."[67] Judge Pinkney A. Walker made short interpretive work of the taxpayer challenge, noting that "[t]he credit of the State alone is mentioned; counties and cities are not named. It is a familiar rule of construction, that the express mention of one thing, implies the intention to exclude others."[68] By clever lawyering, government officials were able to circumvent precisely the sort of unrestrained *publicness* that the constitutional revisions were intended to curb. Other state courts were similarly disposed to dismiss challenges to local government debt-financed infrastructure schemes.[69] The prominent jurist Theodore Sedgwick summarized the state of the legal field in his magisterial 1857 *Treatise* on constitutional law, concluding that "[i]t is now the settled doctrine throughout the several States, that the business

---

[67] *Prettyman v. Supervisors of Tazewell County*, 19 Ill. 406, 411 (1858).
[68] 19 Ill. at 411.
[69] *Commissioners of Leavenworth County v. Miller*, 7 Kan. 479, 497 (1871) ("we would say that the constitution means just what it says. It says the *state* shall never be a party in carrying on any works of internal improvement, and it means the *state*, and not *Leavenworth county*; and to hold that this restriction upon the state is also a restriction upon counties, cities, etc., is to put words in the constitution which its framers omitted, and to overturn a well-settled rule of constitutional and statutory construction"); *Gelpcke v. City of Dubuque*, 68 U.S. 175 (1863) (upholding Dubuque's railroad investment on state constitutional grounds); *Pattison v. Supervisors*, 13 Cal. 175, 185 (1859) ("The convention did not consider that an inhibition upon the State to construct internal improvements, in her capacity as such, by means of loans, prohibited her from authorizing other agencies to construct them by such mean"); *Clark v. City of Janesville*, 10 Wis. 136 (1859) (Wisconsin state constitution did not prevent "cities, counties and towns" from incurring debt for infrastructure development).

and purposes of railroads, canals, public highways, turnpikes, bridges, and other such public means for travel and for the transport of goods, are a public use within the meaning of the Constitution."[70] Sedgwick collected cases from across the states involving waterworks, gas companies, sewers, and other types of infrastructure that qualified as "public" when challenged.[71]

4.5 CONCLUSION

The decades after the Civil War saw a rapid expansion of public power and state subsidy to infrastructures. For a time, courts continued to broaden the domain of publicness and the legal space for public infrastructure investments. As discussed in Chapter 5, in the case of *Munn v. Illinois* (1876), for example, the Supreme Court ratified broad power of states to regulate private property for the public good.[72] At the same time, a judicial countermovement attempted to reign in expansive public governance in the Progressive era. What amounted to "public purpose" garnered renewed attention, as conservative courts began to scrutinize the use of public money for private ventures. Critics of expansive publicness were especially concerned with way that governments used their taxing powers to finance development. Judge Thomas Cooley, an influential jurist and judge of the Michigan Supreme Court, signaled a major change in the prevailing attitude toward infrastructure subsidies. When he was still a Michigan judge, Cooley penned a decision in *People ex. rel. Detroit & Howell Railroad v. Salem* (1870), which signaled the reversal of the prevailing view that for-profit infrastructure was in essence "public."[73] Judge Cooley struck down the public investment scheme in a suit brought by taxpayers: "I have said that railroads are often spoken of as a species of public highway ... But their

---

[70] THEODORE SEDGWICK, A TREATISE ON THE RULES WHICH GOVERN THE INTERPRETATION AND CONSTRUCTION OF STATUTORY AND CONSTITUTIONAL LAW 446 (1874).

[71] *Id.* at 446.

[72] *Munn v. Illinois*, 94 U.S. 113, 125 (1876); *see* Harry N. Scheiber, *Road to Munn: Eminent Domain and the Concept of Public Purpose in the State Courts*, 5 PERSP. AM. HIST. 329, 329–402 (1971); Molly Selvin, *This Tender and Delicate Business: The Public Trust Doctrine in American Law and Economic Policy*, WIS. L. REV. 1403–42 (1980).

[73] *People ex. Rel. Detroit & Howell Railroad v. Salem*, 20 Mich. 452 (1870); *see also Bay City v. State Treasurer*, 23 Mich. 499, 504 (1871) for a sense of Cooley's historical understanding of what had gone wrong with the earlier internal improvement investments: "Our state had once before had a bitter experience of the evils of the government connecting itself with works of internal improvement. In a time of inflation and imagined prosperity, the state had contracted a large debt for the construction of a system of railroads, and the people were oppressed with heavy taxation in consequence. Moreover, for a portion of this debt they had not received what they bargained for, and they did not recognize their legal or moral obligation to pay it. The good name and fame of the state suffered in consequence. The result of it all was that a settled conviction fastened itself upon the minds of our people, that works of internal improvement should be private enterprises; that it was not within the proper province of government to connect itself with their construction or management, and that an imperative state policy demanded that no more burdens should be imposed upon the people by state authority for any such purpose."

resemblance to the highways which belong to the public ... is rather fanciful than otherwise .... They are not, when in private hands, the *people's highways;* but they are private property, whose owners make it their business to transport persons and merchandise in their own carriages, over their own land, for such pecuniary compensation as may be stipulated."[74]

This judicial about-face threatened to shake the foundation of the period's infrastructure policy. The problem of "pecuniary compensation" had not, after all, impeded earlier courts from classifying railroads, canals, and turnpikes as "public." As we have seen, American courts were accustomed to declaring that for-profit infrastructure ventures were essentially public by the simple fact government created them with their police powers for the public good and that they had obvious benefits for everyone; they had recourse to the ancient law of highways and other common law doctrines when they needed to for legal support. By the 1870s, however, government infrastructure policy faced a more hostile judiciary than ever before. Conservative legal authorities were increasingly vocal in checking the unrestrained publicness asserted by Progressive-era infrastructure policies. Cooley's own *Treatise on The Constitutional Limitations Which Rest upon the Legislative Power of the States of the American Union* (1868) signaled the new direction: "Everything that may be done under the name of taxation is not necessarily a tax; and it may happen that an oppressive burden imposed by the government, when it comes to be carefully scrutinized, will prove, instead of a tax, to be an unlawful confiscation of property, unwarranted by any principle of constitutional government."[75] The U.S. Supreme Court ratified the view that not all purposes were *public* just because the government labeled it as such in *Savings and Loan Association v. City of Topeka* (1875).[76] Expanding on that decision, legal reformers scoured nineteenth-century case law for precedents that could fortify the challenge to the expansive publicness of the Progressive fiscal order. Jurists, politicians, economists, and policymakers developed the enduring arguments of laissez-faire legalism that is often mistakenly associated with the antebellum era.[77] In the process, legal culture sharpened liberalism's division between public and private spheres.

Debt-financed investment at the state level spurred the antebellum era's infrastructure revolution. The dream of taxless finance, however, inspired reckless investments that led to a crash and precipitated a far-reaching legal revolution in state and local finances that influences modern economic theory. Legal scholars have noted the decline in these constitutional prohibitions in certain states, as politicians found

---

[74] 20 Mich. at 478.
[75] Thomas Cooley, A Treatise on the Constitutional Limitations Which Rest Upon the Legislative Power of the States of the American Union 486 (2d ed., 1871) (1868).
[76] 87 U.S. 655 (1875).
[77] *See,* for example, Christopher G. Tiedeman, A Treatise on the Limitations of Police Power in the United States: Considered from both a Civil and Criminal Standpoint (2015) (1886).

4.5 Conclusion

end-runs around state constitutions and their checks on public borrowing: special purpose districts, special funds, accounting legerdemain, and other means, to name a few.[78] Nevertheless, the complicated field of state and local infrastructure policy is a direct descendent of the Panic of 1837.

As we turn to the Progressive Era, we will see how the increasingly specialized and technical nature of infrastructures began to alter the national and global landscape. Communication, water, gas and electric, sewage, and waste systems have expanded and complicated infrastructure layout and financing. In a real sense, bureaucracy itself became a form of infrastructure, and this sense of management as infrastructure would reshape the emerging infrastructural state. Necessitated by emerging technologies, the diversification of urban infrastructure – "roads, highways, bridges, ferries, streets, sidewalks, pavements, wharfs, levees, drains, water-works, gas-works" among others – required teams of specialists to manage the interface of complex systems.[79] Professionals across fields such as engineering, law, urban planning, and economics, as well as good-government reformers worked to ensure that corrupt urban political machines would have less sway over handing out infrastructure contracts. And as market principles and laissez-faire legalism cast a wide net over the general culture, public utilities theory carved out space for nonmarket logics based on sophisticated new conceptions of the "public good."

---

[78] C. Robert Morris, Jr., *Evading Debt Limitations with Public Building Authorities: The Costly Subversion of State Constitutions*, 68 YALE L. J. 234–68 (1958); Brian Edward Wheeler, *Oklahoma Constitutional Law: In re Oklahoma Capitol Improvement Authority: The Eulogy for Oklahoma Constitutional Debt Limitations*, 53 OKLA. L. REV. 319–343 (2000); Joshua G. Urquhart, *Disfavored Constitution, Passive Virtues? Linking State Constitutional Fiscal Limitations and Permissive Taxpayer Standing Doctrines*, 81 FORDHAM L. REV., 1263, 1263–1314 (2012); see also ALBERTA M. SBRAGLIA'S DEBT WISH: ENTREPRENEURIAL CITIES, U.S. FEDERALISM, AND ECONOMIC DEVELOPMENT (1996), 102: "Local governments in the twentieth century faced the task of investing within a complex framework of limitations constructed by state government, state courts, and the Supreme Court. Their response was to develop mechanisms – legal, financial, and organizational – that would allow them to circumvent these limitations. Given that these restrictions were intended to restrain local borrowing, local officials who wished to borrow at higher levels than those permitted had to find ways to honor the letter of the law while violating its spirit."
[79] *Leavenworth Cty. Com'rs v. Miller*, 7 Kan. 479, 493–94 (1871).

5

"The Ground under Our Feet"

The Birth of Public Utilities

5.1 INTRODUCTION: INNOVATION, REFORM, AND REACTION

The Tenth Census (1880), "Railroads, Steam Craft, Canals, Telegraphs, and Telephones," reports 86,782 miles of railroads operating with net earnings per mile of $2,623. The largest category of transported railroad goods at the time was coal, at approximately 89 million tons, suggesting the growing importance of coal for the economy as well as links between energy and transportation infrastructures. Railroads were also large employers, with the 1880 Census reporting that 418,957 people working for railroads in a variety of occupations. The report indicates that steamboats and canals were still important, although losing out to larger railroad networks. Communication networks also began expanding after the Civil War: There were 110,000 miles of telegraph wire and several dozen companies, although Western Union had the largest revenues from messages sent of any telegraph company at the time. There were 32,734 miles of telephone wires laid by 1880.[1]

As Adam Smith already predicted in the eighteenth century, infrastructure at this scale would require government support and investment. Since Alexander Hamilton's time American government acted in many ways to build up the infrastructures of the market state. Government action was often "out of sight," but governments at every level had always subsidized development by directly or indirectly benefiting infrastructure expansion. Nevertheless, after the Civil War, the federal, state, and city governments assumed a much more active role in the economy than they had before.[2] "Publicness" expanded across infrastructure networks such as railroads, which had always been treated for legal purpose as "highways," despite their private ownership

---

[1] DEP'T OF THE INTERIOR, COMPENDIUM OF THE TENTH CENSUS 1312, 1323 (revised ed., June 1, 1880), www2.census.gov/library/publications/decennial/1880/1880-compendium/1880b_p1-01.pdf.

[2] RICHARD FRANKLIN BENSEL, YANKEE LEVIATHAN: THE ORIGINS OF CENTRAL STATE AUTHORITY IN AMERICA, 1859–1877 ix (1990); *see also* MORTON KELLER, REGULATING A NEW SOCIETY: PUBLIC POLICY AND SOCIAL CHANGE IN AMERICA, 1900–1933 (1994); THEDA SKOCPOL, PROTECTING SOLDIERS AND MOTHERS: THE POLITICAL ORIGINS OF SOCIAL POLICY IN THE UNITED STATES (1995).

structure. Infrastructure technologies such as telegraphy, railroads, gas, electricity, water, and sanitation assumed greater importance for the modern world, and they were more dependent on government action than ever before.

Governments used every tool in their toolbox to encourage infrastructure development: subsidies, taxation, direct investment, land grants, and debt financing through bonds. As local governments moved into the infrastructure field, they also needed to arrange rights of way, permits, and charters to authorize new buildings. As Harry Scheiber writes, at the center of new development in the late nineteenth century were a variety of legal innovations: "First, the state judges engaged in doctrinal innovation across a broad front to establish the parameters of the great trinity of governmental powers, namely taxation, eminent domain, and the police power. Second, they regularly advanced the common law in ways that either impelled or constrained rights of contract, in both respects greatly enlarging the overall formative influence of public authority on the workings of the private marketplace."[3]

As state and local governments moved into the infrastructure field, they also revolutionized public finance and set the stage for infrastructure politics in the twentieth century. Governments at every level broadened their fiscal footprints to accommodate new infrastructure development after the Civil War. As A. M. Hillhouse noted in 1936, "[t]he rise of the metropolis necessitated enormous expenditures. Municipal water supply, streets, sewage disposal, traffic, playgrounds, school systems, government machinery and a multitude of other things grew out of urban concentration."[4] Large infrastructure projects meant more land, money, and other resources appropriated for public purposes. In practice this meant more taxation and higher levels of government indebtedness. As a result, between 1870 and 1932, state and local per capita indebtedness increased nearly fourfold.[5]

Recall that state governments had imposed limitations on state borrowing for infrastructure after the crisis of the late 1830s and 1840s. Governments were not supposed to direct public money into private hands, but this legal principle was in inevitable conflict with the public–private model of infrastructure development. In any event, state governments created numerous workarounds, most notably by allowing cities to tax and spend instead of states doing it themselves. Local governments expanded their tax bases and entered the bond market to finance new infrastructure and general

---

[3] Harry N. Scheiber, *Law and the Imperatives of Progress: Private Rights and Public Values in American Legal History*, 24 NOMOS 303, 304 (1982); Frank M. Loewenberg, *Federal Relief Programs in the 19th Century: A Reassessment*, 19 J. SOCIO. SOC. WELFARE 121–36 (1992). For the international exchange of political ideas and movements that characterized Progressivism, see DANIEL T. RODGERS, ATLANTIC CROSSINGS: SOCIAL POLITICS IN A PROGRESSIVE AGE (1998). Keller's REGULATING A NEW SOCIETY, *supra* note 2, provides good coverage of the legal and regulatory revolution that reshaped American life in the decades after the Civil War.
[4] ALBERT M. HILLHOUSE, MUNICIPAL BONDS: A CENTURY OF EXPERIENCE 37 (1936).
[5] *Id.* 36.

business development.[6] When taxpayers challenged these expenditures on state constitutional grounds, state courts upheld taxation on the grounds that what counted as "public purpose" was a policy question that should be left for the legislature to decide. However, as publicness expanded, conservative judges in the 1870s began to uphold taxpayer and other challenges to government largesse to private ventures.

Finally, the Civil War fundamentally changed the balance of power between federal and state governments. The 14th Amendment seemed to promise a new era of expanded rights for black Americans and other groups against discriminatory state power. However, courts interpreted the Civil War amendments narrowly when it came to the promise of civil rights and used the new amendments to expand protections for business property and to challenge the new expansive social and infrastructural state. As public power spread like a web over economic life, conservative jurists such as Ernst Freund, Christopher Tiedemann, Thomas Cooley, and others asked whether there were any limits at all on government power to advance what legislatures called "the public good." Their views would inform laissez-faire legalism from its rise after the Civil War until its demise in the 1930s.

During the height of laissez-faire legalism, conservative judges would take a much closer look at public–private partnerships, scrutinizing broad claims of *publicness* that legislatures used to justify government investment in fee-generating infrastructure franchises and other businesses. What were the proper boundaries between public and private? Legislatures were surely committed to expansive interpretations of their police powers, but could the Constitution or common law supply any limits? For the first time in American history, laissez-faire doctrines gained real purchase in law and policy, and courts expanded private rights for corporations in the process hardening the divide between *public* and *private* that we have come to imagine as a timeless feature of American life. Nevertheless, the period of laissez-faire legalism had only a short lifespan, especially with regards to publicly subsidized infrastructure development. The story of infrastructure into the twentieth century is the story of publicly subsidized and regulated infrastructures.

5.2 THE 14TH AMENDMENT: A LEGAL REVOLUTION

The post-war Constitutional amendments altered the legal landscape for infrastructure in sometimes unpredictable ways. The 13th Amendment provided that "Neither slavery nor involuntary servitude, except as a punishment for crime whereof the party shall have been duly convicted, shall exist within the United States, or any place subject to their jurisdiction." This abolished chattel slavery but left the way open for convict labor in the years to come. The 15th Amendment held that "race, color, or

---

[6] For a discussion of road development and tax reform, see R. Rudy Higgens-Evenson, *Financing a Second Era of Internal Improvements: Transportation and Tax Reform, 1890–1929*, 26 Soc. Sci. Hist. 623–51 (2002); *see also* Eric H. Monkkonen, The Local State: Public Money and American Cities (1995) for a discussion of the expansion of local government debt after the Civil War.

previous condition of servitude" could not be used as means to deprive black men of the right to vote, but left open many questions of voting rights, which are still being litigated today. The 14th Amendment, however, proved to be the most important of these amendments for infrastructure and state investment. Section 1 reads:

> All persons born or naturalized in the United States, and subject to the jurisdiction thereof, are citizens of the United States and of the state wherein they reside. No state shall make or enforce any law which shall abridge the privileges or immunities of citizens of the United States; nor shall any state deprive any person of life, liberty, or property, without due process of law; nor deny to any person within its jurisdiction the equal protection of the laws.

The Due Process, Equal Protection, and Privileges and Immunities clauses, which promised to extend federal legal protection to "persons" and "citizens" from arbitrary treatment of state governments. But what did these provisions mean? Early Supreme Court decisions interpreting the 14th Amendment reinforced state police powers against the new federal regime, dampening hopes that the Due Process, Privileges and Immunities, and Equal Protection clauses might be used to extend rights to women, African Americans and other groups lobbying for greater legal protections and broader concepts of citizenship. At the same time, courts reinforced the regulatory powers of state and local governments over infrastructure and social life. The 14th Amendment was read in ways that favored new forms of corporate property rights under the Due Process and Equal Protection clauses. Most notably, the rise of substantive Due Process affected the legal regime around government infrastructure regulation for several decades by creating new ways that courts could scrutinize government investment in infrastructure. Old ideas about laissez-faire that had circulated since Adam Smith's time found a temporary home in state and federal courts.

5.2.1 Slaughterhouse Cases (1873)

The first major decision interpreting the Civil War Amendments was *The Slaughterhouse Cases* (1873), which involved an 1869 Louisiana state law that created a corporation that would enjoy an exclusive right to maintain a slaughterhouse in New Orleans and "prohibiting all other persons from building, keeping, or having slaughterhouses, landings for cattle, and yards for cattle intended for sale or slaughter, within those limits." The law further required that "all cattle and other animals intended for sale or slaughter in that district, should be brought to the yards and slaughterhouses of the corporation, and authorizing the corporation to exact certain prescribed fees for the use of its wharves and for each animal landed."[7] Plaintiffs were independent butchers who did not want to practice their trade in the specified slaughterhouse. They sued the Crescent City Livestock Landing and

---

[7] 83 U.S. 36, 36 (1872).

Slaughter-House Company, arguing that the state-granted monopoly effectively deprived them of their "unrestricted" right to pursue their calling.

Justice Miller reasoned that the monopoly did not prevent the butchers from conducting their business: They simply had to pursue their calling in a specified location and pay a reasonable fee. The legislature had the authority to regulate trade within its jurisdiction under its police powers. Quoting *Gibbons v. Ogden* (1824), Justice Miller starts with a standard caveat that despite being difficult to define, the police power is broad and includes: "Inspection laws, quarantine laws, health laws of every description, as well as laws for regulating the internal commerce of a State, and those which respect turnpike roads, ferries, &c., are component parts."[8] It certainly included the power to create a corporation for the purposes of public health.

But the plaintiffs did not limit themselves to arguing against the monopoly. They invoked the 13th and 14th Amendments, claiming that the monopoly "create[d] an involuntary servitude," abridged their privileges and immunities as citizens of the United States, deprived them of property without due process, and denied them the equal protection of the laws. Basically, their argument was that they had a right to practice their trade wherever they wanted, not only in the location chosen by the government. These were novel claims that tested the boundaries and possibilities of the recent amendments, which the plaintiffs hoped would protect their rights and liberties against state governments. After all, the Civil War had fundamentally altered the balance of power between the state and federal governments and seemed to promise an expansion of citizenship rights. But Justice Miller declined the opportunity to extend the 13th and 14th Amendments as far as many had hoped. Justice Miller left open the possibility that the protections of the 14th Amendment could apply outside the context of race and slavery. Nevertheless, he reasoned, the Civil War Amendments were aimed at the evil of slavery, and not designed to provide more general citizenship rights. The 14th Amendment speaks of the "privileges and immunities of citizens of *the United States*" (emphasis in original), which did not include the right to pursue a trade.[9]

Justice Field's dissent is notable because it helped lay the foundation for a more laissez-faire view of government regulation, one that became substantive due process and fundamental rights jurisprudence. For Field, the question presented could not be answered by reference to the state's police power. After all, the 14th Amendment had created the category of "citizens of the United States" and clarified that those citizens had fundamental rights that could not be abridged by the states: "The fundamental rights, privileges, and immunities which belong to him as a free man and a free citizen now belong to him as a citizen of the United States, and are not dependent upon his citizenship of any State." But what were these fundamental rights? The Constitution's text, after all, does not specify the content of "rights,

---

[8] 83 U.S. at 36.
[9] For the litigation history and legal reasoning of the *Slaughterhouse Cases* see RONALD M. LABBÉ & JONATHAN LURLE, THE SLAUGHTERHOUSE CASES: REGULATION, RECONSTRUCTION, AND THE FOURTEENTH AMENDMENT (2003).

privileges, and immunities of citizenship." Justice Field reaches into the canon of classical economic theory to find an answer. He quotes Adam Smith on the "inviolable" right of property in one's own labor.[10] The right to pursue a business, for Field and for many others in the burgeoning laissez-faire movement, was one of the most fundamental rights of all, and one that was protected by the new 14th Amendment against increasingly expansive public action. This theory of economic rights helped plant the seeds that would come to fruition in *Lochner* v. *New York* (1905).

5.2.2 Munn v. Illinois (1877)

The Slaughterhouse Cases held that the new amendments would not protect the right to pursue a trade as a fundamental federal right. By the same token, they held that local police powers were alive and well even after the Constitution was amended to extend federal jurisdiction over the states. In the 1870s, local governments would use these police powers to expand the regulatory reach of the infrastructural state. One of the major initiatives involved railroad regulation. After the Civil War, American farmers faced a series of challenges. The cost of moving agricultural products from the mid-west to eastern markets was rising, due in part to railroad monopolies and grain elevators that could charge high rates to move and store farm products. Soon after the war ended, a farmer and Bureau of Agriculture clerk Oliver Hudson Kelley and others created the National Grange of the Order of Patrons of Husbandry, a civic group that advocated for the interests and improvement of farmers. The organization was broken up into local chapters called "granges," which eventually boasted nearly 800,000 members across the country. These groups formed a very powerful lobby in several midwestern states, including Illinois, Wisconsin, Iowa, and Minnesota, where states passed laws regulating key commercial infrastructure: railroads and grain elevators. These were dubbed "The Granger Laws" and they imposed extensive regulations on railroads and storage companies – laws that anticipated the regulatory state that would emerge in the decades to come.

Railroad and storage companies challenged the Illinois version of these regulations, which imposed a number of requirements on railroad companies and warehouses including, but not limited to: recordkeeping, the right to examine books and records, licensing requirements, and a maximum storage charge. In *Munn* v. *Illinois* (1877), the Supreme Court heard a challenge to the Illinois law, which plaintiffs framed in terms of the 14th Amendment, now adding Article I, Section 8's

---

[10] "'The property which every man has in his own labor,' says Adam Smith, 'as it is the original foundation of all other property, so it is the most sacred and inviolable. The patrimony of the poor man lies in the strength and dexterity of his own hands; and to hinder him from employing this strength and dexterity in what manner he thinks proper, without injury to his neighbor, is a plain violation of this most sacred property. It is a manifest encroachment upon the just liberty both of the workman and of those who might be disposed to employ him. As it hinders the one from working at what he thinks proper, so it hinders the others from employing whom they think proper.'" 83 U.S. at 110–11 n.39.

Commerce Clause. Munn was one of a series of cases dubbed the Granger Railroad Cases where the Court was asked to resolve the growing dispute between railroad companies and the states that were actively regulating them.[11]

The question was whether the 14th Amendment's Due Process Clause protected the companies against "taking" their property via regulation. The Court thus began with the text of the 14th Amendment's Due Process clause, which does not allow the state to *"deprive* any person of life, liberty, or property, without due process of law" (emphasis added). Was there a sense in which Illinois had "deprived" the railroad companies of "life, liberty, or property"? In answering this question in the negative, Chief Justice Waite restated the traditional view that the police power "authorize[s] the establishment of laws requiring each citizen to so conduct himself, and so use his own property, as not unnecessarily to injure another." He calls this "the very essence of government," which is expressed in the old common law maxim: *sic utere tuo ut alienum non laedas* (use your property in such a way that it does not injure others). In the License Cases (1847), the Court reminds us, Chief Justice Taney had called this "the power to govern men and things."

According to Chief Justice Waite, the 14th Amendment had not fundamentally altered the state's power to regulate in the public good, a power that extended to the price regulation at issue in the case. The state could, as it always had, regulate "ferries, common carriers, hackmen, bakers, millers, wharfingers, innkeepers, &c., and, in so doing, to fix a maximum of charge to be made for services rendered, accommodations furnished, and articles sold."[12] Strikingly, Justice Waite finds support for this proposition in ancient legal principles expressed in the pages of Lord Hale's *De Portibus Maris* (circa 1670) and *De Jure Maris* (circa 1667).[13] One example from Lord Hale – a wharf that others must use "because there is no other wharf in that port" – implicates Adam Smith's intuitions about natural monopoly. Where shippers are forced to use a particular private wharf to move goods, the wharf may not take "arbitrary and excessive duties for cranage, wharfage, pesage, &c.... but the duties must be reasonable and moderate, though settled by the king's license or charter." In other words, if someone owns a port facility that goods must pass through to enter the commercial market, the "king's license or charter" entitled him to set a reasonable rate for the service. And so it was, *mutatis mutandis*, for the sovereign state of Illinois.

---

[11] See, for example, *Chicago, Burlington & Quincy R. R. v. Iowa*, 94 U.S. 155 (1877); *Peik v. Chicago & Nw. Ry. Co.*, 94 U.S. 164 (1877); *Chicago, Milwaukee & St. Paul R. R. v. Ackley*, 94 U.S. 179 (1877); *Winona & St. Peter R. R. v. Blake*, 94 U.S. 180 (1877); *Stone v. Wisconsin*, 94 U.S. 181 (1877). For a good overview of the railroad rate controversy, see RICHARD C. CORTNER'S THE IRON HORSE AND THE CONSTITUTION: THE RAILROADS AND THE FOURTEENTH AMENDMENT (1993).

[12] Munn v. Illinois, 94 U.S. 113, 125 (1876).

[13] For an extended discussion of the common-law regulatory powers upheld in *Munn v. Illinois*, see Harry N. Scheiber, *The Road to Munn: Eminent Domain and the Concept of Public Purpose in the State Courts*, 5 PERSP. AM. HIST., 329, 329–402 (1971); *see also* Charles Fairman, *The So-Called Granger Cases, Lord Hale and Justice Bradley*, 5 STAN. L. REV. 587–679 (1953).

From these and similar examples, Justice Waite concludes that the police power extends to any monopoly that the public was required to use to conduct business:

> There is no doubt that the general principle is favored, both in law and justice, that every man may fix what price he pleases upon his own property, or the use of it, but if for a particular purpose the public have a right to resort to his premises and make use of them, and he have a monopoly in them for that purpose, if he will take the benefit of that monopoly, he must, as an equivalent, perform the duty attached to it on reasonable terms.[14]

The question thus became whether the warehouses were facilities that people are essentially required to use to engage in commerce. In answering this question in the affirmative, Justice Waite uses the warehouse lawyers' own arguments against them, quoting at length from the plaintiffs' description of the importance of their clients' warehouses to commerce from West to East: "Thus, it is apparent that all the elevating facilities through which these vast productions 'of seven or eight great States of the West' must pass on the way 'to four or five of the States on the seashore' may be a 'virtual' monopoly." If the warehouses were really as important as their lawyers claimed, then there was no reason why they should not be regulated under the same police power that covered "the common carrier, or the miller, or the ferryman, or the innkeeper, or the wharfinger, or the baker, or the cartman, or the hackney-coachman...."[15]

Justice Waite reasoned that state rate regulation was just as permissible now as similar regulations had been under common law: Sovereignty then and now implies the power to govern in the public interest. The 14th Amendment had not changed that. However, the Court notably rejects the plaintiff's claim under the Commerce Clause, reasoning (implausibly) that the warehouses "may become connected with interstate commerce, but not necessarily so."[16] The Supreme Court would revisit the Commerce Clause issue for networked infrastructures in the 1880s. By then, it would be impossible to ignore the networked future of transportation and communication infrastructures.

The dissent by Justice Field in *Munn* echoes his dissent in the *Slaughterhouse Cases* and indicates the more conservative jurisprudence that was already emerging in the 1870s, one that would reshape legal and political culture in the decades to come: "The principle upon which the opinion of the majority proceeds is, in my judgment, subversive of the rights of private property, heretofore believed to be protected by constitutional guaranties against legislative interference..."[17] Field's dissent reflects a more skeptical view of legislative power to declare something

---

[14] 94 U.S. at 127–28. On the monopoly point, see Charles K. Burdick, *The Origin of the Peculiar Duties of Public Service Companies*, 11 COLUM. L. REV., 743, 746–47 (1911) ("It would seem a reasonable conclusion from these cases that virtual monopoly or a monopolistic tendency is a necessary condition precedent to the exercise of police power in the way of regulating rates").

[15] 94 U.S. at 131–32.

[16] *Id.* at 135.

[17] *Id.* at 137.

"public" by fiat: "There is no magic in the language, though used by a constitutional convention, which can change a private business into a public one or alter the character of the building in which the business is transacted…One might as well attempt to change the nature of colors by giving them a new designation."[18] Surely declarations of publicness could not be taken at face value, because if they were then the legislature could simply assert a price-setting power over anything by declaring it public. This was certainly closer to what nineteenth century courts were doing when they declared that the legislature could decide for itself what counted as public. Nevertheless, at some point government action over the economic value of an investment would be a taking.

Justice Field approached the public–private question faced by countless prior courts with a much more skeptical stance toward regulation and taxation, and his analysis is informed by economic reasoning. When the state set a price cap on warehouse rates, it essentially reduced the financial value of the plaintiff's business. Absent the regulation, the warehouse could charge what customers were willing to pay. With the regulation, customers paid less than they would otherwise be required to. The power to regulate prices thus raised an important question: Could the legislature of Illinois reduce the value of a warehouse business to zero, for example, by requiring that the warehouse charge no fee at all? Justice Field saw this as a very real implication of the majority's reasoning: surely the Due Process clause must protect more than the bare title to a valueless property? For example, what if a government regulation utterly destroyed the profitable use of a property by forbidding its commercial use altogether: "There is, indeed, no protection of any value under the constitutional provision which does not extend to the use and income of the property, as well as to its title and possession."[19] Justice Field would have provided much stronger protections for the right of business owners to set their own rates according to their own dictates, absent a nuisance that the legislature could regulate under the police power. Justice Field's view would for a time command center stage as laissez-faire theories were for the first time in American history becoming a powerful, albeit short-lived, force shaping law and policy.

5.2.3 *Laissez Faire and Substantive Due Process under the 14th Amendment*

As I have been arguing throughout this book, liberal governance in the United States had always used public power to build up infrastructures, often through public–private

---

[18] Id. at 138. Justice Bradley had made a similar observation the same year about a federal land grant requiring a railroad to provide free transportation for the federal government even where the federal land grant stipulated that it would be "free from all toll or other charge for the transportation of property or troops:" "But where, as in the laws under review, the railroad is referred to throughout in its character as a road, as a permanent structure, and designated and required to be a 'public highway,' it cannot, without doing violence to language and disregarding the long established usage of legislative expression…be extended to embrace the rolling stock or other personal property of the railroad company." *Lake Superior & Mississippi R. R. Co. v. U.S.*, 92 U.S. 442, 455 (1876).

[19] 94 U.S. at 143.

entanglements. Governments funneled public money into infrastructure ventures in pursuit of what many considered to be the public benefits of development. This trend only accelerated in the late nineteenth century and has only continued ever since. Nevertheless, expansive government and a seemingly boundless sense of public power – even for the purposes of development – have always had their detractors: for example, anti-monopoly and anti-elite attacks on corporate privilege, constitutional objections to federal infrastructure initiatives, complaints about government corruption, and so on. After the Civil War, however, detractors were able to frame their objections with new theories of laissez faire, which gained real purchase in American law for the first time. As Sidney Fine writes in *Laissez Faire and the General Welfare State*: "In the period between Appomattox and the accession of Theodore Roosevelt to the presidency in 1901, laissez faire was championed in America as it never was before and has never been since."[20] For a time, laissez-faire and private economic rights more generally would become important sources of limitation on regulatory power and would form the basis of a new counter-theory of liberal government that would inform conservative legalism in the later twentieth century.

Conservative legalists found justification for limited government in American history, the common law and through novel interpretations of the Civil War amendments. The 14th Amendment proved important to their general claim that the Constitution protected what we would now call "economic rights:" the right to contract, to own property, and to be free from government control of private transactions. These rights as they saw it were under threat by expansive social legislation, labor movements, and other radical challenges to the capitalist order. Christopher Tiedeman's *A Treatise on the Limitations of Police Power in the United States* (1886), for example, offers up a story of an increasingly radical American present that should be sharply distinguished from its more authentic laissez-faire past:

> [T]he sphere of governmental activity was [in the past] confined within the smallest limits by the popularization of the so-called *laissez-faire* doctrine, which denies to government the power to do more than to provide for the public order and personal security by the prevention and punishment of crimes and trespasses….[T]he political pendulum is again swinging in the opposite direction, and the doctrine of governmental inactivity in economical matters is attacked daily with increasing vehemence…Socialism, Communism, and Anarchism are rampant throughout the civilized world.[21]

---

[20] Sidney Fine, Laissez Faire and the General Welfare State: A Study of Conflict in American Thought 1865–1901 (1956). We would now qualify Fine's "never since" language. Fine published his book in 1956. Since that time, neoliberal policies and a free-market consensus have championed versions of laissez faire in various forms, even if largely failing to live up to these ideas in practice; see Brian Balogh, Government out of Sight: The Mystery of National Authority in Nineteenth-Century America 309–15 (2009). This issue will be taken up in the Conclusion.

[21] Christopher Tiedeman, A Treatise on the Limitations of Police Power in the United States: Considered from both a Civil and Criminal Standpoint vi (1886).

The treatise writers (and many others) saw the expansive publicness of their own time as a radical innovation that violated the American tradition of liberty and small government. Furthermore, they viewed the 14th Amendment as codifying an American tradition of liberty and fairness embodied in the idea of a neutral state – one that would not favor one class over another or allow legislative capture to distort the workings of the baseline market economy. At the same time, they drew upon American traditions of republicanism to confine the powers of legislatures, which they saw as open to corruption by radical and corrupt interest groups.

The conservatives worried that Progressivism was acting contrary to American traditions of liberty when it extended public power in dangerous ways, most especially into the heart of the worker–owner relationship and into the system of private property more generally. As a general descriptive matter, it is important to point out that their view of American laissez-faire before the Civil War is mistaken, as this book has been chronicling. But perhaps it is better to view this historical narrative not so much as a mistake, but rather as an enduring mythology with a deep imprint on American political culture. It is enough to point out for now that laissez-faire theories often came with a specific historical narrative about the American legal tradition, one that was generally shared by later Progressive and liberal thinkers, even as they worked to justify the New Deal Order (this topic is explored in full in Chapter 6).

Thomas Cooley's *Treatise on the Constitutional Limitations Which Rest upon the Legislative Power of the States of the American Union* (1868), Ernst Freund's *The Police Power, Public Power and Constitutional Rights* (1904), and other important treatises found limits to the police power. Even the conservatives, however, had to concede that American law had allowed legislatures broad regulatory authority. Nevertheless, they worked to cabin expansive police powers by arguing that that power had limits drawn by the Constitution and by common law.[22] One way to

---

[22] Since the time of *Lochner*, there has been a spirited debate over the nature and limits of substantive due process. Howard Gillman's The Constitution Besieged: The Rise & Demise of Lochner Era Police Powers Jurisprudence (1993) provides a good starting place for those looking for an overview of the issues that were at stake. Herbert Hovenkamp's *The Political Economy of Substantive Due Process*, 40 Stan. L. Rev. 379–447 (1988), offers important insights into the intellectual history at work in substantive due process, albeit one that partakes of the myth of antebellum laissez faire that has been far too common in legal and political history. See also Michael Les Benedict, *Laissez-Faire and Liberty: A Re-Evaluation of the Meaning and Origins of Laissez-Faire Constitutionalism*, 3 L. & Hist. Rev. 293 (1985) (discussing how laissez-faire constitutionalism fits with an Anglo-American suspicion of special legislation and monopolies); Charles W. McCurdy, *Justice Field and the Jurisprudence of Government-Business Relations: Some Parameters of Laissez-Faire Constitutionalism*, 61 J. Am. Hist. 970 (1975) (laying out the standard view of substantive due process as a continuation of Jacksonian democracy and the policing of interest group conflict); Christopher T. Wonnell, *Economic Due Process and the Preservation of Competition*, 11 Hastings Const. L. Q. 91–134 (providing an economic defense of *Lochner* and substantive due process) (1983). The afterlife of *Lochner* and substantive due process and theories of the private economy is taken up in Chapter 6.

read substantive due process is as an expression of long-held Jeffersonian animus toward special privileges and class legislation.[23] The 14th Amendment suggested that it protected a limited class of political rights derived from the Due Process and Equal Protection clauses. Unlike procedural Due Process – which promises basic fair treatment before the law – the substantive variety protects certain fundamental rights against government regulation.

Moreover, the 14th Amendment's Equal Protection clause embodied a commitment to nondiscriminatory treatment by the government. Taking these ideas seriously also created the obligation for courts to ensure that government was not captured by the sorts of factions that worried the early Republicans and Jacksonian Democrats. These included the rights of property and contract and generally the right to reap the fruits of your own labor without unjust confiscation by government. Needless to say, this commitment to a demarcated realm of "noncoercive" transactions in the abstract did not always extend its full protections to racial minorities, to women or to other vulnerable groups.[24]

5.3 THE REVIVAL OF "PUBLIC PURPOSE" LIMITS ON TAXATION

One way that laissez-faire legalism gained traction in the state courts in the 1870s was through attacks on government taxing power. Following the constitutional limits laid out in Chapter 4, local governments began spending more money than ever before to build up hard infrastructures. This raised important questions about the scope of the government's power to act in the public interest when that was in conflict with private rights. In an era of rising local government expenditures, it is no surprise that important challenges to local investment decisions came in the area of taxation. Recall that American law had always treated infrastructure ventures as public, or at least, "quasi-public," when it came to justifying investment and legal regulation. This was accomplished in a variety of ways, including through the ancient law of the highway, which allowed states classify as "public" railroads, canals, and turnpikes. But the crisis of the 1830s and 1840s changed things as states attempted to reign in abuses by reducing their power to invest for anything other than a "public purpose." On their face, these reforms were designed to prevent corruption, mismanagement, and waste. But it was never clear what counted as a "public purpose" in the first place. When courts were called upon to decide what *public* meant, they generally held that the legislature could decide that as a matter of policy, despite the fact that the constitutional amendments were meant to shackle legislative discretion.

The basic legal issue was whether government taxes to fund various development projects were genuinely being spent for a public purpose, as state law required.

---

[23] Hovenkamp, *The Political Economy of Substantive Due Process, supra* note 22, at 394–98.
[24] *Id.*

More than a decade after *Sharpless* had declared that public purpose was defined however the legislature wanted, Judge Thomas Cooley signaled a new judicial countertrend concerning public–private partnerships funded with tax money. The case where Cooley announced the new approach, *People ex rel. Detroit & Howell Railroad v. Salem Township Board* (1870), was decided two years after he had published *Constitutional Limitations*.[25] The *Salem* case involved a local bond issue, supported by tax revenue, to aid in the construction of a railroad. The state raised the familiar argument that the railroad was a public highway that it was allowed to subsidize with tax dollars. Judge Cooley balked at that argument, rejecting the social benefit theory that had guided earlier courts in determining what counted as "public:"

> The road, when constructed, is nevertheless to be exclusively private property, owned, controlled, and operated by a private corporation for the benefit of its own members... Primarily, therefore, the money, when raised, is to benefit a private corporation; to add to its funds and improve its property; and the benefit to the public is to be secondary and incidental, like that which springs from the building of a grist-mill, the establishment of a factory, the opening of a public inn, or from any other private enterprise which accommodates a local want and tends to increase local values.[26]

As we have seen, the fact that railroads were propriety ventures had not stopped earlier courts from deciding that they were functionally "public." Courts in the antebellum era had held fast to a social benefit theory of public–private infrastructure (i.e., the general public needed railroads and canals, so they were therefore a public benefit when it came to government action). However, Judge Cooley was announcing a new principle of law that departed from the prior view: his extensive discussion of *publicness* over many pages includes only a handful of legal citations.

Nevertheless, Cooley's reasoning in *Salem* captured an emerging conservative mood, which suggested that some limit needed to be drawn around the power of the government to tax and spend to subsidize development. Courts are now beginning to abandon the antebellum public benefits theory in favor of something akin to a narrower view of the government's basic purpose under modern capitalism. We now see the view that the government should be neutral and that courts should be on guard against legislative capture by interest groups. *Salem*'s distinction between primary and secondary benefits is also telling for another reason: it reveals an emergent distinction, reflected in neoclassical economics, between primary, firm-driven production and trade and the secondary benefits of that activity to the general public.

---

[25] 20 Mich. 452 (1870). For a good overview of the public purpose doctrine, see Joseph Lesser & Vigdor D. Bernstein, *The Evolution of Public Purpose, General Welfare, and American Federalism*, 19 URBAN LAW. 603, 603–43 (1987).

[26] 20 Mich. at 477.

5.3 The Revival of "Public Purpose" Limits on Taxation

This is Adam Smith's idea in a nutshell: firms exist in a private marketplace and we need to be on guard against distortion by government subsidy and regulation. It also fits with republican concerns about class legislation and legislative capture. The distinction now begins to emerge between enterprises that were truly public (because they were not private businesses), and those that were truly private, because they produced commodities for sale in the marketplace or where benefits from the business flowed into private hands. Courts across the country began scrutinizing public expenditures more closely to determine whether governments were actually spending tax money on public goods.[27]

Recognizably laissez-faire rationales also begin to bolster Judge Cooley's common-law approach. Chief Judge John Appleton of the Maine Supreme Court, for example, was a proponent of a new laissez-faire legalism that would ripen into substantive due process between the 1870s and the 1930s. Like Cooley, Judge Appleton roundly rejected the antebellum era's social benefit theory of public subsidy. When he was called upon to judge the validity of a loan to help relocate a saw-mill and box factory as part of a business development plan, he struck down the scheme and took the opportunity to elaborate an emergent economic theory of enterprise capitalism: "Capital naturally seeks the best investment, or its owners do. Those who by industry and economy have become capitalists are more likely to invest it well than those

---

[27] See, for example, *Hansen v. Vernon*, 27 Iowa 28, 33–34 (1869) (Judge Dillon overturning a railroad subsidy and criticizing earlier courts, including *Sharpless*, for allowing them: "A most unfortunate mistake it was: counties and cities throughout the State, acting under the sanction of that decision, incurred debts amounting to several millions of dollars, and, in many cases, exceeding the[i]r [sic] ability to pay. Disaster, the child of extravagance and debt, and dishonor, the unbidden companion of bankruptcy, are the bitter but legitimate consequences of that decision, 'and the end is not yet.' In every other State in which a similar decision was made, similar consequences have ensued."); *See also Lowell v. Boston*, 110 Mass. 454, 472 (1873) (bonds issued to aid property owners in repairing fire damage struck down because "[t]here is no public use or public service declared in the statute now under consideration, and we are of opinion that none can be found in the purposes of its provisions"); *Taylor v. Ross Cty. Com'rs*, 23 Ohio St. 22, 28 (1872) ("The act entitled an act to authorize counties, cities, incorporated villages, and townships, to build railroads, and to lease and to operate the same... is repugnant to the above-cited prohibitory clause of the constitution of Ohio, and is therefore unconstitutional and void"); *Whiting v. Sheboygan and Fon du Lac R.R. Co.*, 25 Wis. 167, 187 (1870) (striking down tax subsidy to railroad subsidy on the ground that it was a private company: "The property in the road having, by the creation of the corporation and the franchises granted to it, been converted into private property, devoted exclusively to the gains and emolument of the individual stockholders, the incidental benefits accruing to the public by reason of the investment, can no more sustain a tax than the like incidental benefits arising to the public from the employment of the capital or labor of the citizens in any other business or enterprise of a purely private character"); *Curtis Adm'r v. Whipple*, 24 Wis. 350, 356 (1869) (distinguishing impermissible tax to support a private school from a tax to support a public school: "The state normal schools are public, not private, schools, and the grounds, buildings, fixtures and apparatus belong to the public, and not to private individuals or corporations. Hence, if taxes have been levied and collected to aid in the construction of buildings or the purchase of grounds, it was not taxation for merely private purposes, as is the case here"); *Weeks v. Milwaukee*, 10 Wis. 242 (1860) (special tax exemption granted to build a hotel struck down where it required other taxpayers to make up the shortfall caused by the tax exemption).

who, having gained none, have none to lose. The sagacity shown in the acquisition of capital, is best fitted to control its use and disposition."[28] Judge Appleton further elaborates this claim with a critique of taxation that was rarely echoed in the "laissez-faire" nineteenth-century courts: "The wealth of the country is lessened by the time spent in assessing and collecting taxes, and by the taxes collected, if unproductively expended."[29] Government should be neutral with regard to economic activity, letting enterprises rise or fall on their own merits.

Not all courts were as explicitly laissez-faire in their reasoning, but they nevertheless began to narrow the scope of publicness where taxation for infrastructure was concerned. These courts focused their attention of the plain language of state law. In *Taylor v. Ross County Commissioners* (1872), the Supreme Court of Ohio was called upon to decide whether an approved tax to aid several railroads violated the state constitution's anti-aid provision.[30] Chief Justice White was not willing to accept the traditional view that railroads were categorically public highways and held that the tax in favor of the railroads violated the state constitution. A decade after *Taylor*, the Ohio Supreme Court again invalidated a complicated railroad aid scheme on the grounds that the state constitution "forbids the union of public and private capital or credit in any enterprise whatever."[31] Rulings such as these, however, did not end investment in infrastructure, and courts continued to rule on public–private entanglements throughout the late nineteenth century and into the twentieth century.

When faced with the tax question, the US Supreme Court adopted Judge Cooley's theory that tax subsidies could not flow to truly private enterprises. The leading case here is *Savings and Loan Association v. City of Topeka* (1874), which was a challenge to a local bond issue to support the King Wrought-Iron Bridge Manufacturing and Iron-Works Company, of Topeka, Kansas. Plaintiffs challenged this on the grounds that the subsidy was not for a truly public purpose. Justice Miller upheld the tax challenge and roundly rejected the nineteenth-century social benefit theory:

---

[28] *Allen v. Inhabitants of Jay*, 50 Me. 124, 128–29 (1872).
[29] 50 Me. 124, 129.
[30] 23 Ohio St. 22 (1872).
[31] *Wyscaver v. Adkins*, 37 Ohio St. 80, 96 (1881) (quoting *Walker v. Cincinnati*, 21 Ohio 14, 37 (1871)). The full quote from *Walker v. Cincinnati* explains that the "mischief" that the Ohio anti-aid provision intended to remedy was the mixing of public and private investment: "Take, for instance, that which relates to *the mischief* to be provided against. Pray what was the mischief? It was the mixing up the municipal funds with private funds and private enterprises, in subscriptions to the stock, and loans of money and credit to private corporations and associations, for the construction of railroads, turnpikes, and canals. Look at the proceedings of the constitutional convention, and there you will find the formidable array of private corporations to which such aid had been given. There was *the mischief*, and this 6th section was the *remedy*." *Walker v. Cincinnati*, 21 Ohio at 37; *see also Garland v. Bd. of Revenue of Montgomery Cty.*, 87 Ala. 223, 227 (1889) (invalidating under the state anti-aid clause a tax to build a railroad bridge).

5.3 The Revival of "Public Purpose" Limits on Taxation

If it be said that a benefit results to the local public of a town by establishing manufactures, the same may be said of any other business or pursuit which employs capital or labor. The merchant, the mechanic, the innkeeper, the banker, the builder, the steamboat owner are equally promoters of the public good, and equally deserving the aid of the citizens by forced contributions. No line can be drawn in favor of the manufacturer which would not open the coffers of the public treasury to the importunities of two-thirds of the businessmen of the city or town.[32]

The turn away from the earlier social benefit theory of economic development seemed to sharpen the distinction between *public* and *private* that had not been well developed in the antebellum era. Whatever "private" meant, it had not prevented government subsidies to infrastructure ventures in the nineteenth century. Now, however, truly commercial ventures, such as manufacturing, could in theory no longer receive the kind of direct subsidies that they did before. So, for example, in *Parkersburg* v. *Brown* (1883) the Supreme Court pointed to *Savings and Loans Association* v. *Topeka* to strike down municipal bonds that were issued to support manufacturing businesses.[33] Manufacturing businesses were truly private ventures, notwithstanding any claimed public benefit. Courts developed this principle in a number of cases across several decades, most famously perhaps in *Lochner* v. *New York* (1905), which struck down a maximum hour law on the grounds of freedom of contract.[34]

Returning to substantive due process, we can see that for several decades, courts took a dim view of tax-subsidized economic development. However, public purpose – the close relative of substantive Due Process – was revived only for a short period before it eventually evolved into a more forgiving "reasonableness" standard for development subsidy and regulation under the 14th Amendment.[35] Courts eventually made their peace with the infrastructural state, which reflected a new realism

---

[32] *Citizens' Savings & Loan Ass'n* v. *City of Topeka*, 87 U.S. 655, 665 (1874).
[33] 106 U.S. 487, 500 (1883).
[34] 198 U.S. 45 (1905); *see also Allgeyer* v. *Louisiana*, 165 U.S. 578 (1897) (law requiring residents to use an an-state insurer violated the 14th Amendment's protection of liberty of contract).
[35] See, for example, *Chicago, Milwaukee, and St. Paul Ry. Co.* v. *Minn. ex. rel R. R. Warehouse Comm'n*, 134 U.S. 418, 456 (1890) ("The supreme court authoritatively declares that it is the expressed intention of the legislature of Minnesota, by the statute, that the rates recommended and published by the commission, if it proceeds in the manner pointed out by the act, are not simply advisory, nor merely *prima facie* equal and reasonable, but final and conclusive as to what are equal and reasonable charges; that the law neither contemplates nor allows any issue to be made or inquiry to be had as to their equality or reasonableness in fact."); *Stone* v. *Farmers' Loan and Trust Co.*, 116 U.S 307, 329–30 (1886) (the fact that a railroad is chartered by the state "implies authority to charge a reasonable sum for the carriage. In this way the corporation was put in the same position a natural person would occupy if engaged in the same or like business. Its rights and privileges in its business of transportation are just what those of a natural person would be under like circumstances; no more, no less. The natural person would be subject to legislative control as to the amount of his charges. So must the corporation be").

about the role of the state in the economy culminating in the New Deal (a topic explored in Chapter 6). Moreover, in terms of real-world policy, governments at every level continued to subsidize and regulate infrastructures during the entire "*Lochner* era."[36] The adoption of a "reasonableness" standard recognized the importance of government-subsidized and regulated infrastructures to modern life. The real domain of substantive due process was not to be found in its policing of the public–private divide in general, as has often been supposed. Rather, courts seemed more concerned with "class legislation" and redistribution, which led them to strike down some protective legislation, for example, early consumer law, worker protections, and so on.

In other words, the judicial hostility to state-subsidized, public–private development was important, but short-lived. Despite cases such as *Parkersburg*, for example, the Supreme Court turned out to be forgiving in its approach to public investment in infrastructure, even when plaintiffs challenged tax-funded investment schemes under the 14th Amendment's Due Process clause. Examples of bonds or taxes for infrastructure that were upheld in the years after *Topeka* include irrigation in California, energy and water subsidies in Maine, agricultural business development plans in North Dakota, and a tax-supported railroad tunnel in Colorado.[37] The Supreme Court was especially reluctant to declare some subsidy "private" where the state courts themselves had already upheld the expenditure under state law. Of course, this was the very same public benefits theory that state courts had developed even after the constitutional revisions of the mid-nineteenth century. The 14th Amendment's due process clause turned out to be little help to aggrieved taxpayers in the decades after *Topeka* who

---

[36] Benedict, *Laissez-Faire and Liberty*, supra note 22, at 293, 302 (1985): "On the state level government was more active, and in more active violation of laissez-faire economic tenets. Local authorities in many areas continued to promote transportation development with tax abatements, debt guarantees, and public subscriptions to stock issues. At the same time, many states passed stiff new regulations to govern the conduct of their transportation enterprises."

[37] *Milheim v. Moffat Tunnel Improvement Dist.*, 262 U.S. 710, 717–19 (1923) (tax-supported railroad tunnel could not be challenged under Due Process clause where state legislature and courts had found it to be public); *Green v. Frazier*, 253 U.S. 233, 242 (1920) (taxation to support a state-wide development plan was not purely private: "In many instances states and municipalities have in late years seen fit to enter upon projects to promote the public welfare which in the past have been considered entirely within the domain of private enterprise"); *Jones v. City of Portland*, 245 U.S. 217, 224 (1917) (taxing for "wood, coal and fuel yards" was a legitimate public purpose: "The authority to furnish light and water by means of municipally owned plants has long been sanctioned as the accomplishment of a public purpose justifying taxation with a view to making provision for their establishment and operation. ...We see no reason why the state may not, if it sees fit to do so, authorize a municipality to furnish heat by such means as are necessary and such systems as are proper for its distribution"); *Fallbrook Irrigation Dist. v. Bradley*, 164 U.S. 112, 160 (1896) (Money appropriated for massive irrigation project in California truly public because "in a state like California, which confessedly embraces millions of acres of arid lands, an act of the legislature providing for their irrigation might well be regarded as an act devoting the water to a public use, and therefore as a valid exercise of the legislative power").

argued that their money was being taken improperly when government levied it for a public purpose.[38]

5.4 BOOTH'S *LAW OF RAILWAYS* (1911): BALANCING PUBLIC AND PRIVATE RIGHTS

If we turn to the local level, we see that cities often addressed their transportation infrastructure needs by chartering more companies to run trams, railways, horse-drawn carriages, and other services. The competitive franchise was the most common model in the nineteenth century, and franchises were routinely (and often improvidently) granted for an array of basic infrastructural services such as gas, water, sanitation, transportation, etc. Transportation was provided by an array of competing enterprises that presented new legal challenges. Despite these challenges, however, nobody could deny the importance of the new street railways as a major driver of development, urban growth, and suburbanization. As Chief Judge Adams of the Iowa supreme court observed:

> But street railroads certainly are coming to be regarded as of great importance, if not indispensable. The tendency of modern cities is to spread over large areas for the purpose of securing better light and air. This is made possible principally by the cheap and easy mode of transit which street railroads furnish. They are not simply a present convenience, but they anticipate and promote the growth of cities. They create, to some extent, their own patronage, by the promotion of the growth and the distribution of the population. Without question, they are of sufficient importance to call for very careful consideration, both by legislatures in the enactments of statutes concerning them, and of courts in construing the same.[39]

Henry J. Booth's *Treatise on the Law of Street Railways* (1911[1892]) nicely illustrates the balancing approach that courts developed when faced with complicated entanglements of private power and public interest. Booth's *Treatise*, first published in 1892 and revised several times thereafter, analyzed thousands of common-law cases with the goal of constructing a workable legal framework to sort out private rights from public power. Like the other treatises, Booth's is exhaustive: Spanning

---

[38] See, for example, *Carmichael v. S. Coal & Coke Co.*, 301 U.S. 495, 509 (1937) (tax on company for unemployment benefits not unconstitutional: "This Court has repeatedly held that inequalities which result from a singling out of one particular class for taxation or exemption, infringe no constitutional limitation"); *Helvering v. Davis*, 301 U.S. 619 (1937) (upholding the Social Security employer tax and noting that "[t]he conception of the spending power advocated by Hamilton and strongly reinforced by Story has prevailed over that of Madison, which has not been lacking in adherents"); *Cochran v. La. Bd. of Educ.*, 281 U.S. 370, 375 (1930) (where a tax was levied to purchase school books "we cannot doubt that the taxing power of the state is exerted for a public purpose"); *Nicchia v. New York*, 254 U.S. 228, 231 (1920) (licensing tax "does not amount to the taking of one man's property and giving it to another, nor does it deprive dog owners of liberty without due process of law").
[39] *Des Moines St. R. R. Co. v. Des Moines Broad Gauge St. R.R. Co.*, 33 N.W. 610, 613 (Iowa 1887).

over a thousand pages, the *Treatise* delves into a vast body of cases to survey the judicial approach to local railway disputes in the later nineteenth century. As Booth chronicles, state courts also struck a pragmatic compromise when it came to public–private entanglements. At the local level, the law needed to balance the police power of legislatures – and the rights of the general public – carefully against the private rights of infrastructure companies.

Booth begins his treatise with a familiar assertion that "[e]xcept as restrained by the constitution, the legislative power is untrammeled and supreme."[40] Again, it is the legislature that ultimately draws lines between public and private:

> The grant of the right to maintain in the public highway permanent tracks not necessary to its use in the ordinary mode of travel and to propel cars thereon and to demand toll is in derogation of common right; hence its source can be found only in the sovereign power of the state, which, acting through the legislature, has unquestioned power to authorize the construction and operation of railways, to be operated by either animal or mechanical power, across or along any of the public highways, either within or without the limits of municipal corporations.[41]

Public power flowed from the legislature to cities, whose power "is not subject to judicial control, unless its action is ultra vires [exceeding its proper authority], fraudulent, or in violation of contract rights."[42] Booth returns to the law of highways current since Locke's time as the correct legal norm; but as Booth recognizes that general principal would not help sort out all the conflicts that could occur in densely-packed cities between private property owners, the general public and city governments.

Some of those conflicts were between franchise owners and the general public. Courts upheld broad public power in the streets, echoing the strong police powers William Novak identified as the *salus populi* tradition: "The public has a right of free passage over every part of the street, and no traveler thereon, whether by public or private conveyance or otherwise, has a right superior to that of any other traveler, except in pursuance of a lawful franchise granted in the exercise of sovereign authority."[43] In other words, the franchise could only assert those narrow rights granted in their contracts – otherwise, jurisdiction over the streets vested with government in trust for the general public. The government could also specify levels of service and other details of operation in the public interest, but governments were not allowed to delegate away police powers of the city.[44] However, government control over franchises had to strike a balance between public and private rights.

---

[40] Henry Judson Booth, A Treatise on the Law of Street Railways: Embracing Urban, Suburban and Interurban Surface, Subsurface and Elevated Roads, Whether Operated by Cable or Steam Motor 6 (2019)(1911).
[41] Booth, Law of Street Railways, *supra* note 40, at 5.
[42] *Id.* at 26.
[43] *Id.* at 17.
[44] *Id.* at 21.

5.4 Balancing Public and Private Rights

On the one hand, contractors had valuable legal rights that the government could not override at will. So, for example, the grant of a streetcar franchise was a contract, which meant that the city could not violate the contract terms without consequence. And as Booth notes, franchisees frequently sued to enforce these contract rights. So where the city of Springfield, Missouri, had given the Springfield railroad the "right to construct, maintain, and operate a street railroad on certain designated streets and the public square for twenty years," the city could not "destroy its usefulness" with an iron fence blocking passage.[45] Nor could the City of Asheville, North Carolina "arbitrarily...declare its contract with the defendant [railway company] at an end."[46] By the same token, streetcar franchises were able to negotiate favorable tax treatment for themselves under their charter, which the legislature could not abrogate.[47]

On the other hand, those contract rights only went so far. Thus when a franchisee argued that it was only responsible for obligations explicitly spelled out in the contract, the Supreme Court of Kansas reminded the company that "[i]t is well settled that grants of this class are not to be extended by construction beyond the plain terms in which they are conferred, but should be construed strictly against the corporation, or those claiming under the grant, and in favor of the public."[48] Moreover, despite the contractual nature of the franchise, the government could authorize competing franchises without violating anything like "vested rights." The central legal point was based in franchise law: An infrastructure venture such as a railway is still a creature of the state because its power derives from a government charter. In spite of protecting the rights of railway ventures, Booth explains, the franchise had only so much power as was delegated to it by the government that gave it life.[49]

But the fact that local railways were incorporated at the state level also meant that they could sometimes prevail in conflicts with local governments. In *City of Clinton v. Cedar Rapids & M.R.R. Co.* (1868), Iowa Judge F. Dillon made it clear that the law of the public highway meant that even local infrastructure franchises were creatures of the state and could not simply be blocked by local ordinances:

> The State, by its legislature, must, in the nature of things, be deemed to have control over its highways and its means of communication. It cannot be doubted, that it is competent for the legislature to pass a law to the effect that any highway in the country, and any street in a city, may be used by any railroad company without the consent of the adjoining proprietors in the case of the highway, and without the consent of the city in the case of the street... [W]here the fee of the street is in the public or in the city corporation in trust for the public—for the city holds the fee not for itself or its inhabitant alone, but for the general public, equally and

---

[45] Springfield Ry. Co. v. Springfield, 58 Mo. 674, 676 (1885).
[46] Asheville St. Ry. Co. v. City of Asheville, 109 N.C. 688, 14 S. E. Rep. 316, 316 (1892).
[47] BOOTH, LAW OF STREET RAILWAYS, *supra* note 40, at 9.
[48] City of Wyandotte v. Corrigan, 10. P. 99, 101 (Kan. 1886).
[49] BOOTH, LAW OF STREET RAILWAYS, *supra* note 40, at 9–10.

as well–the legislature may authorize the street to be used by a railroad company without the consent of the city and without compensation to the city.[50]

In other words, private corporate infrastructure licensed by the state is never fully private and cannot simply be enjoined as local nuisances, absent special legislation. They were in an important sense public spaces under the law of the highway. Also, because cities are municipal corporations and creatures of the states that create them, there were limits on their powers. Because delegations of power were anchored in law, courts had to determine whether the charter exceeded the delegated police power. Had cities given away too much public power to private contractors in the rush to provide citizens with infrastructure? They also had to adjudicate conflicting claims of infrastructure ventures to determine whose charter rights should prevail, as well as determining whether the government's actions were truly public in character.[51]

However, if the franchisee was using its delegated power in the prescribed way, its rights were protected. So, for example, a city could grant easements and rights-of-way to a franchisee, which would survive attack in the courts. These could include grants in perpetuity, which courts would protect under property rights theories. If a corporate franchise was not limited in duration, a court would generally not

---

[50] City of Clinton v. Cedar Rapids & Mo. River R.R. Co., 24 Iowa 455, 477 (1868).

[51] See, for example, *Henderson v. Ogden City Ry. Co.*, 26 P. 286 (Utah 1891) ("We are of the opinion that the city council of Ogden City, in the exercise of a reasonable discretion, may grant the right to lay down railway tracks in its streets"); *Canal & Claiborne St. R. R. Co. v. Crescent City R. R. Co.*, 6 So. 849, Syll. 1 (La. 1889) ("The city government of New Orleans, by delegated power from the legislature, has the paramount control and regulation of the streets of the city, and can grant the use of a street railway already constructed to another, which she has authorized to be operated"); *Christopher & Tenth St. R. R. Co. v. Cent. Crosstown R. R. Co.*, 67 Barb. 315, 316 (1875) ("the rights conferred upon the plaintiff, by its charter, were not exclusive, and did not prevent the legislature from conferring authority to fix the terminus of the defendant's road at the North river, at the point designated"); *Des Moines St. R.R. Co. v. Des Moines Broad Gauge St. R. R. Co.*, 33 N.W. 610, 614 (Iowa 1887) (thirty-year exclusive franchise was "reasonable; and our holding is that, under our statute which empowers cities to authorize or forbid the laying down of a street-railroad track, a city council may make a reasonable provision by contract for present and future street-railroad service, and may secure the company contracted with against the impairment of its profits for a limited time, and against interference with its extension during the time, if a larger and better or more immediate service can be thus obtained"); *Glaessner v. Anheuser-Busch Brewing Ass'n*, 13 S.W. 707, 708–9 (Mo. Sup. Ct. 1890) (city could not devote part of a public street for the use of a private corporation, such as Anheuser-Busch); *Fanning v. Osborne*, 102 N. Y. 441, 447 (1886) ("The right to construct and operate a street railway is a franchise which must have its source in the sovereign power. The legislative power over the subject is also subject to the limitation that the franchise must be granted for public, and not for private purposes, or at least public considerations must enter into every valid grant of a right to appropriate a public street for railroad uses"); *Mikesell v. Durkee*, 9 P. 278, 280 (Kan. 1886) ("We think it may be laid down, broadly and upon general principles, that no city has any right or authority to give permission to any individual or corporation to construct or operate a purely private railroad upon any of the public streets of the city; and that all the statutes which have reference to railroad companies or others constructing or operating railroads through or upon the public streets of a city simply have reference to such railroad companies or others as perform the duties of common or public carriers, and to such railroads as are public or *quasi* public in their character.")

read a limitation into the grant. However, property owners who objected to new infrastructures presented many challenges to new infrastructures and a number of state constitutions and other laws required the government to obtain consent from abutting landowners to the development of a transportation venture or new route. Property owners could effectively block new developments and could not have their objections overcome by an exercise of eminent domain, for example.[52] The issue of consent also generated litigation around the question of who had standing to object, with the interests of owners trumping those of renters and others who did not have actual fee simple ownership of the abutting property.[53] Due process requirements of notice protected the potential interests of those whose consent could not be obtained in a timely manner.[54] Some jurisdictions developed home rule arrangements that required local control over infrastructure.

The question of how much power and control the legislature may abdicate to infrastructure ventures has been a persistent feature of the American model since the nineteenth century. It shows up today in periodic enthusiasm for infrastructure privatization and the arguments of opponents who point to the potential loss of democratic control that those arrangements may entail. The awkward balancing of rights that Booth identifies more accurately reflects the messiness of public–private governance in the United States at the turn of the century than either expansive Progressivism, which accepted few limits on public governance, or conservativism's absolute limits derived from common law or the Constitution. As Booth chronicles, turn-of-the-century American courts attempted to ensure continued public control over a dispersed franchise system as it intersected with a variety of public and private interests.

5.5 THE COMMERCE CLAUSE AND THE RISE OF REGULATED INDUSTRIES

Unlike local streetcars, gas, and water systems, however, communication and transportation infrastructures were linked together into regional, national, and even global networks. While Justice Field's holding in *Munn* upheld the state's power to regulate in the public interest, that theory only made sense because the regulated warehouses were wholly located within one state – already a tenuous holding when we recall that railroads, telegraphs, and other infrastructures were increasingly part of networked systems, with increasing congressional involvement. Individual state regulations may have made sense for local infrastructures and smaller systems of the nineteenth century; after *Munn*, however, courts had to rule on state regulatory

---

[52] BOOTH, LAW OF STREET RAILWAYS, *supra* note 40, at 33; DANIEL T. ROGERS, ATLANTIC CROSSINGS: SOCIAL POLITICS IN A PROGRESSIVE AGE 153 (1998).
[53] BOOTH, LAW OF STREET RAILWAYS, *supra* note 40, at 36.
[54] *Id.* at 38.

power over expansive infrastructure networks that crisscrossed jurisdictions. When they did, they recognized the growing trend toward federal regulation of networked infrastructure. With respect to networked infrastructure, American law began to transfer the police power recognized in *Munn* to Congress under the Commerce Clause as well as to state regulatory agencies.

5.5.1 Telegraphs

Telegraphs provide a good example of new infrastructure networks that were spreading across the country after the Civil War. By the 1850s, the telegraph system in the United States was in disarray, and there were a number of contentious legal issues that had to be sorted out.[55] By the 1860s, the telegraph industry was entering a period of consolidation, with Western Union as one of the last remaining telegraph firms, and effectively a monopoly. Like other large industries, it received special legal and political benefits, including the right to run telegraph lines over public lands. States have regulated telegraph companies since their beginning in the 1840s, granting rights of way, authorizing penalties for damaging lines, regulating the disclosure of business information contained in messages and even creating rules for how companies received and sent messages. There was a general trend from *authorizing* telegraph operations to *regulating* them.[56]

It is important to note, however, that even when states *authorized* telegraphs, they also *regulated* them, following a pattern common to other nineteenth-century infrastructures. New York's 1848 telegraph statute, for example, used customary police powers and the law of the highway to extend its own sovereign authority across the telegraph network, permitting construction "along and upon any of the public roads and highways, or across any of the waters within the limits of this state, by the erection of the necessary fixtures ... provided the same shall not be so constructed as to incommode the public use of said roads or highways, or injuriously interrupt the navigation of said waters...."[57] Another provision of the same act conferred the power of eminent domain to telegraph companies, just as states had done for canals, turnpikes, and railroads. However, lest we conclude that all regulation simply favored companies over the general public, individual states also used their power to protect the broad public from unfair treatment, legislating against discriminatory pricing and other monopolistic practices. The legislative concern for discriminatory treatment of the general public was a central feature of later public utility regulation, which built on these early efforts at the state level to legislate in the public good.

---

[55] Tomas Nonnenmacher, *State Promotion and Regulation of the Telegraph Industry, 1845–1860*, 61 J. ECON. HIST. 19, 19–46 (2001).
[56] *Id.* at 29–31.
[57] Telegraph Act of 1848, Act of Apr. 12, 1848, ch. 265, 1848 N.Y. Laws 392.

The problem with a state-by-state approach was that the new infrastructure systems were truly national, and sometimes international, in scope. Regulations designed for more localized nineteenth-century infrastructures would become obstacles to running twentieth-century networked systems. The networked future of communication infrastructure became clear with the completion of the first intercontinental telegraph line in 1861. The Civil War revealed the importance of the rapid flow of information across geographical space, and the federal government began to envision telegraphy as a node in a system or network to forward basic purposes of statecraft. Large corporate providers certainly understood this: As Western Union grew into the first national telecommunications firm, it was inevitable that it would begin to lobby for greater federal involvement to fend off state-level regulation. Congress broadened federal jurisdiction throughout the 1860s and in 1866 passed a statute "to aid in the construction of telegraph lines, and to secure to the government the use of the same for postal, military, and other purposes." Congress passed this law under the Commerce Clause and the Postal Clause of Article I of the Constitution.

The law was tested in *Pensacola Telegraph Company* v. *Western Union Telegraph Company* (1877) when Florida granted the exclusive right to use telegraph lines to the Pensacola Telegraph company and Western Union asserted authority to string lines in that same territory under the federal statute. Chief Justice Waite had no trouble finding authority under the Commerce and Postal Clauses for Congressional action:

> [The telegraph] is not only important to the people, but to the government. By means of it the heads of the departments in Washington are kept in close communication with all their various agencies at home and abroad, and can know at almost any hour, by inquiry, what is transpiring any where that affects the interest they have in charge. Under such circumstances, it cannot for a moment be doubted that this powerful agency of commerce and intercommunication comes within the controlling power of Congress, certainly as against hostile state legislation.[58]

The postal and commerce clauses were "not confined to the instrumentalities of commerce, or the postal service known or in use when the Constitution was adopted..., They extend from the horse with its rider to the stage coach, from the sailing vessel to the steamboat, from the coach and the steamboat to the railroad, and from the railroad to the telegraph, as these new agencies are successively brought into use to meet the demands of increasing population and wealth."[59] As Thomas Jefferson had rightly feared (from his Republican perspective), the postal clause would be used to expand federal jurisdiction over state and local government. The federal government would only extend its jurisdiction over telecommunications throughout the twentieth century.

---

[58] *Pensacola Tel. Co. v. W. Union Tel. Co.* 96 U.S. 1, 10 (1877).
[59] 96 U.S. 1, 21 (1877).

5.5.2 Railroads

The trend toward federal regulation of networked infrastructures is also reflected in the regulatory fate of railroads. In 1862, Congress passed an aid package to the Union Pacific Railroad, invoking "postal, military, and other purposes" in its enabling act.[60] Railroads were rapidly becoming the largest networked infrastructure in the country. Yet they were still being regulated and taxed on a piecemeal basis from state to state. Recall that *Munn* had implausibly held that Illinois could regulate railroad and warehouse rates despite the fact that railroads were increasingly part of an interstate system of networked commercial infrastructure. This argument was taken up again in *Wabash, St. Louis & Pacific Railway Company* v. *Illinois* (1886). Following *Munn*, the piecemeal regulatory system was becoming increasingly unmanageable in the emergent world of networked infrastructure systems. The Illinois law at issue in *Wabash* was a regulation against discriminatory pricing, which was common in state statutes. Here the Supreme Court squarely faces the issue that it dodged in *Munn*: Could Illinois regulate transshipments that moved through the state to other locations?

Justice Miller admits that prior case law, including his own decision in *Munn*, had essentially gotten this question wrong when it missed the interstate dimension of networked transportation infrastructure. The Commerce Clause after all was designed to extend federal jurisdiction over the national flow of goods across state lines:

> And it would be a very feeble and almost useless provision, but poorly adapted to secure the entire freedom of commerce among the states which was deemed essential to a more perfect union by the framers of the Constitution, if, at every stage of the transportation of goods and chattels through the country, the state within whose limits a part of this transportation must be done could impose regulations concerning the price, compensation, or taxation, or any other restrictive regulation interfering with and seriously embarrassing this commerce.[61]

Justice Miller's point about patchwork state laws "seriously embarrassing…commerce" as it moved across wide territories was certainly sound and reflected trends toward broader regulation of integrated networks in the twentieth century. However, there was a wrinkle in Justice Miller's reasoning that the Dissent was quick to point out: Congress had not yet regulated railroads under its Commerce power. In other words, it was one thing to say that a federal statute trumped state law on the same issue. This was implied by the Constitution's Supremacy Clause. It was another thing to strike down a state law where Congress might (or might not) choose at some

---

[60] "An Act to Aid in the Construction of a Railroad from the Missouri River to the Pacific Ocean, and to Secure to the Government the Use of the Same for Postal, Military, and Other Purposes." Act of July 2, 1864, 38 Cong. chapter 216, 13 Stat. 365.
[61] Wabash, St. Louis & Pac. Ry Co. v. Ill., 118 U.S. 557, 573 (1886).

later date to regulate in that area: "No one disputes that Congress might, if it saw fit, under its power to regulate commerce among the several states, regulate the matter under consideration; but it has not done so."[62] Until Congress chose to regulate railroad rates, the power to do so remained vested with the states under their police powers.

Justice Gray's dissent offers a familiar defense of local *police* and the law of the highway for its claim that regulatory power over the railroads was vested in Illinois:

> The highways in a state are the highways of the state. Convenient ways and means of intercommunication are the first evidence of the civilization of a people. The highways of a country are not of private, but of public, institution and regulation. In modern times, it is true, government is in the habit, in some countries, of letting out the construction of important highways, requiring a large expenditure of capital, to agents, generally corporate bodies created for the purpose, and giving to them the right of taxing those who travel or transport goods thereon as a means of obtaining compensation for their outlay. But a superintending power over the highways, and the charges imposed upon the public for their use, always remains in the government. This is not only its indefeasible right, but is necessary for the protection of the people against extortion and abuse. These positions we deem to be incontrovertible. Indeed, they are adjudged law in the decisions of this Court. Railroads and railroad corporations are in this category.[63]

These words harken back to the eighteenth century, to the era of internal improvements, the law of turnpikes and the broad sense of publicness that shaped nineteenth-century legal and political culture. Justice Gray's framing of infrastructure as "the first evidence of a civilization of a people" echoes Adam Smith's comments on the same topic a century earlier: Infrastructure is the material precondition for an advanced society. Justice Gray's comment that highways are public things properly located under the jurisdiction of the sovereign is one that John Locke could have agreed with, as did countless antebellum courts.

But increasingly the question was: Which sovereign, state, or federal? The law of the highway at the state level provided what seemed more and more to be an archaic answer to a very modern question of how to regulate network infrastructures. Instead, the law of public utility would step in to regulate the new world of networked infrastructures, with massive railroad corporations providing of the most compelling rationale to do so. Nevertheless, the modern regulatory regime – of which public utility is but one prominent example – was built on the foundation of older common law concepts such as police power, law of the highway, common carrier, the law of public callings and *Munn*'s own "affected with a public interest."

---

[62] 118 U.S. at 581. This principle was eventually codified as the "dormant Commerce Clause." For an overview of the dormant commerce clause, see Martin H. Redish & Shane V. Nugent, *The Dormant Commerce Clause and the Constitutional Balance of Federalism*, 1987 DUKE L. J. 569, 569–617 (1987).
[63] 118 U.S. at 586.

Congress codified and expanded the idea of "affected with public interest" when it created the Interstate Commerce Commission (ICC) in 1887. The ICC was the first federal regulatory agency, and it took as its task the setting of railroad rates, ensuring nondiscriminatory pricing and curbing abuses in the industry.[64] The law was on its face intended to make interstate infrastructures more democratic and represented an ambitious extension of the Federal government's infrastructural power:

> It shall be unlawful for any common carrier subject to the provisions of this part to make, give, or cause any undue or unreasonable preference or advantage to any particular person, company, firm, corporation, association, locality, port, port district, gateway, transit point, region, district, territory, or any particular description of traffic, in any respect whatsoever; or to subject any particular person, company, firm, corporation, association, locality, port, port district, gateway, transit point, region, district, territory, or any particular description of traffic to any undue or unreasonable prejudice or disadvantage in any respect whatsoever.[65]

Congress followed up the Interstate Commerce Act with other legislation such as the Hepburn Act (1906), the Manns-Elkins Act (1910), the Valuation Act (1913), and other laws in the twentieth century that extended jurisdiction over common carriers.[66] As William Novak writes: "[I]n many ways, the modern American administrative and regulatory state was built directly on the legal foundation laid by the expanding conception of the essentially public services provided by corporations in the dominant sectors of the American economy: for example, transportation, communications, energy supply, water supply, and the shipping and storage of agricultural product."[67] Later economists and other critics would look with a skeptical eye at the ICC and federal regulatory legislation, arguing that such consolidation only led to capture of the agencies by the very parties they were supposed to be regulating. Already beginning in the mid-twentieth century, economists would challenge the rationale and design of public utility regulation. During the years of deregulation beginning in the 1970s, Progressive and New Deal price-setting and other authority would be further challenged and ultimately scaled back. Nevertheless, as an historical matter, the ICC and related regulation represented a move forward toward the twentieth-century regime of regulated infrastructures under an expanded police power.

---

[64] Mark H. Rose, et al., The Best Transportation System in the World: Railroads, Trucks, Airlines, and American Public Policy in the Twentieth Century (2006).

[65] Interstate Commerce Act of 1887, Pub. L. 49–104, 24 Stat. 379 (enacted Feb. 4, 1887) (eff. Apr. 7, 1887) (codified at 49 U.S.C.A. § 1 *et seq.*).

[66] Hepburn Act of 1906, Pub. L. 59–337, 34 Stat. 584 (eff. Jun. 29, 1906).

[67] William J. Novak, *The Public Utility Idea and the Origins of Modern Business Regulation*, in Corporations and American Democracy 139 (Naomi R. Lamoreux & William J. Novak, eds., 2017).

5.6 "AFFECTED WITH A PUBLIC INTEREST:" PUBLIC UTILITY AND THE NEW ORDER

Infrastructure innovations in the late nineteenth century changed the way Americans lived their everyday lives. Frank Sprague's Electric Railway & Motor Company started producing its innovative electric trolley in the late 1880s with designs that formed the basis for modern light rail systems. The first mass transit systems were built in the 1890s and changed the shape of rapidly growing cities, with downtown business cores linked to expanding suburbs. Alexander Graham Bell patented the telephone in 1876 and telephony spread slowly across the United States into the twentieth century. Thomas Edison's patent for the light bulb was approved in 1879, spurring the gradual electrification of cities. The new technologies required more energy than ever before, and governments and corporations created "networks of power" to link infrastructures into networked systems for delivering resources to firms, consumers, and the state.[68] Infrastructure was becoming so implicated in modern life by the later nineteenth century that its provision could not wholly be left to the whims of a competitive market. Certain services would be taken for granted; their abundant supply at an affordable price would become embedded in American ideas of citizenship and good government. These taken-for-granted goods and services would form the basis for our modern idea of "infrastructure."

A new generation of reformers argued for expanding the jurisdiction of public utility over larger areas of economic and social life. At the same time, public utility infrastructure would become foundational for twentieth-century liberal justifications for regulating the economy. The idea of public interest would be integrated into the modern American state and would be a powerful normative idea until it came under sustained attack later in the twentieth century.[69] *Munn*'s holding that

---

[68] There have been a number of excellent historical studies of specific infrastructures and systems in the period. For the rise of modern energy infrastructure, see CHRISTOPHER F. JONES, ROUTES OF POWER: ENERGY AND MODERN AMERICA (2014); THOMAS P. HUGHES, NETWORKS OF POWER: ELECTRIFICATION IN WESTERN SOCIETY, 1880–1930 (1983). DAVID E. NYE'S ELECTRIFYING AMERICA: SOCIAL MEANINGS OF A NEW TECHNOLOGY, 1880–1940 (1990) provides a comprehensive account in the social history of technology. For modern mass transit, see BRIAN J. CUDAHY, CASH, TOKENS AND TRANSFERS: A HISTORY OF URBAN MASS TRANSIT IN NORTH AMERICA (1990); *see also* Zachary M. Schrag, 'The Bus Is Young and Honest': Transportation Politics, Technical Choice, and the Motorization of Manhattan Surface Transit, 1919–1936, 41 TECH. & CULTURE 51, 51–79 (2000). For the rise of telecommunications, see RICHARD R. JOHN, NETWORK NATION: INVENTING AMERICAN TELECOMMUNICATIONS (2010); MARK H. ROSE, CITIES OF LIGHT AND HEAT: DOMESTICATING GAS AND ELECTRICITY IN URBAN AMERICA (1995); Michael R. Fein describes the new regime for New York roads in PAVING THE WAY: NEW YORK ROAD BUILDING AND THE AMERICAN STATE, 1880–1956 (2008).

[69] For a recent overview of public utilities history and economics, see David E. McNabb, *Public Utilities: Essential Services, Critical Infrastructure*, in PUBLIC UTILITIES, SECOND EDITION: OLD PROBLEMS, NEW CHALLENGES 3–18 (2016); MARTIN G. GLAESER'S PUBLIC UTILITIES IN AMERICAN CAPITALISM (1957) is an invaluable resource for the development of public utilities through the middle of the twentieth century.

businesses "affected with a public interest" were proper subjects of regulation would form the basis for much twentieth-century business regulation.

The public utility concept was already built into classical liberal theory. Recall that Adam Smith had already provided that natural monopolies were exempt from the general rule of competition. By the later nineteenth century, *natural monopoly* and *public utility* would emerge as a middle ground between laissez-faire capitalism and socialism – although there were many socialists who made publicly owned infrastructures into a plank in their own reform programs.[70] Edmund J. James, the director of the recently established Wharton School, reflects the emerging reform consensus when he writes in *The Relation of the Modern Municipality to the Gas Supply* (1886):

> A very superficial consideration of the case will…be sufficient to convince anyone that an ample supply of and strong gas at low prices has become an absolute necessity of every modern city. Our notion of what is indispensable to our lives changes from time to time. But we may almost measure the progress of civilization itself by the increase in the number of those things which have become absolutely necessary to our daily existence and comfort… It has become as necessary to our artificial mode of living as bread and water.[71]

Edmund James was not alone in thinking about the new infrastructures as "indispensable," an idea that was rapidly becoming a consensus view. A highly influential political economist, Richard Ely, was a key figure in the development of Progressive public utility politics. His writings mapped new theories of public utility, and reconceptualized infrastructures such as energy and transportation as "the ground beneath our feet." In "Problems of To-Day" Ely made the case for turning the "gas supply, street-car service, highways and streets, electric lighting… telegraphs and telephones…, lighthouses, ferries" into public utilities.[72] This idea was further elaborated into a political theory of the public good that promised democratic control over infrastructures.[73] The idea of public utility was at the center of an emergent understanding of government regulatory responsibility over an ever-expanding domain of economic life.[74] By expanding public control over infrastructure, Progressive-era reforms laid the groundwork for modern public–interest liberalism.

Chartered corporate ventures had provided the lion's share of antebellum infrastructures. When cities needed more water services or street lighting, for example, they chartered another company to provide that service. But there were many problems with this system. For one thing, the corporate ventures often had inadequate

---

[70] Adam Plaiss, *From Natural Monopoly to Public Utility: Technological Determinism and the Political Economy of Infrastructure in Progressive-Era America*, 57 TECH. & CULTURE 806, 811 (2016).
[71] Edmund J. James, *The Relation of the Modern Municipality to the Gas Supply*, 1 PUBL'N AM. ECON. ASS'N 7, 10 (1886)
[72] Quoted in Plaiss, *From Natural Monopoly*, supra note 70, at 812.
[73] *Id.* at 811.
[74] Novak, *The Public Utility Idea and the Origins of Modern Business Regulation*, supra note 67, at 155.

incentives to invest in expensive capital upgrades and were sometimes content to squeeze as much as they could out of the contract in the short-term (a problem Adam Smith had already identified in the late eighteenth century). To take just the example of water provision, competing franchises faced a number of challenges that they could not overcome:

> Until the 1850s most cities relied upon private firms, but in most cases the private efforts failed technically and economically, especially in the largest cities. Few private entrepreneurs or corporations had the capital, the condemnation power, the concern for public health, or the economic will to build and maintain water supply systems that would serve the entire public. Concerned about profits, few private companies proved to be willing to serve poorer people from whom they could expect meager revenues.[75]

Overlapping water franchises also led to health and safety issues that could not be profitably addressed by corporate providers. For example, before the creation of municipal fire departments and modern public utility infrastructure, private water companies often did not supply adequate water pressure for use in fighting fires, arguing that it was too expensive to upgrade existing pipes to allow greater water flow. Government inefficiency in the antebellum era also created another problem: There were no permanent city and state bureaucracies, so management generally changed with electoral cycles.[76]

Likewise, the competing franchise system also led to a great deal of corruption, as political machines handed out lucrative service contracts to well-connected constituents.[77] Richard Ely called these "the evils of municipal politics" that plagued the prevailing public–private infrastructure model and that reformers would need to fight against.[78] While political machines held on to their patronage empires for as long as they could, professionalism and good government politics largely succeeded in transforming urban infrastructure from a scattered and ad hoc affair toward a liberal-technocratic regime of infrastructure governance. Planning and coordination shaped the material practices of infrastructure, as cities strove to free themselves from entanglements with political machines and their pay-to-play corrupt contracting practices.[79]

---

[75] Stanley K. Schultz & Clay McShane, *To Engineer the Metropolis: Sewers, Sanitation, and City Planning in Late-Nineteenth-Century America*, 65 J. AM. HIST. 389, 391–92 (1978).

[76] *Id.* at 391.

[77] For an excellent discussion of the possibility for corruption in public utility administration, see Werner Troesken, *Regime Change and Corruption: A History of Public Utility Regulation*, in CORRUPTION AND REFORM: LESSONS FROM AMERICA'S ECONOMIC HISTORY 259–81 (Edward L. Glaeser & Claudia Goldin, eds., 2006).

[78] RICHARD T. ELY, AN INTRODUCTION TO POLITICAL ECONOMY 71 (1901).

[79] See Rodgers, Atlantic Crossings, *supra* note 3 (especially Chapters 4 and 5); Alexandra W. Lough, *Editor's Introduction: The Politics of Urban Reform in the Gilded Age and Progressive Era, 1870–1920*, 75 AM. J. ECON. SOCIO. 8, 8–22 (2016); Jon A. Peterson, *The Birth of Organized City Planning in the United States, 1909–1910*, 75 J. AM. PLAN. ASS'N 123, 123–33 (2009); Samuel P. Hays, *The Politics of Reform in Municipal Government in the Progressive Era*, 55 PAC. NW. Q. 157, 157–69 (1964).

Innovations in technology and medicine, for example, the germ theory of disease, encouraged reformers and planners to view problems of illness, fire prevention, water, and sanitation as part of an integrated approach to urban infrastructure management. Public health concerns led cities to adopt integrated water and sewage systems; by the turn of the twentieth century, sewers were an essential feature of urban and town infrastructures throughout the country.[80] Trolleys, telephones, gas, and electric systems are capital-intensive and technologically sophisticated; they cannot be operated without expertise; and infrastructure technologies began to press their own arguments in favor of professionalized policymaking: "the new technology necessitated a permanent bureaucracy to acquire land, oversee construction, administer on a day-by-day basis, and to plan for long-term needs. The public works could be built most efficiently by technological and managerial experts who could survey the topography, choose appropriate construction materials, and draw readily upon the experiences of their counterparts in other cities."[81]

The argument for public utilities was essentially that certain services should be decommodified, or at least removed from the domain of open market competition, and reimagined as publicly available services, which were an entitlement of all people at a reasonable price. Classical economics, anti-monopoly animus, and the pragmatics of networks converged on a simple idea: it does not make sense to have competing providers of fixed networks, considering that only one set of pipes or wires are necessary or practical to distribute services to particular locations. To be sure, cities experimented with competing overlapping franchises even for network services. For a period cities granted multiple franchises for gas and electric service, for example, but this turned out to be "ruinous and short-lived" and the trend was toward consolidation of networked infrastructure.[82] It was abundantly clear by the early twentieth century, as Ely wrote, that "free competition is impossible in the case of electric lighting, gas, water, and elevated railway services," and that some form of public regulation or outright government ownership was inevitable in the future.[83] Despite the powerful reform trends to break up monopolies in the Progressive era, increasingly it became obvious that certain infrastructure monopolies were a necessary evil. The crucial thing would be to regulate them in what came to be called the public interest.

It is important to note that the public utility argument was not just an economic one: It also implied a blueprint for the common good built on a foundation of technological progress. Progressive reformers used a moral vocabulary to argue for

---

[80] Schultz & McShane, *To Engineer the Metropolis, supra* note 75, at 395.
[81] *Id.* at 397; *see also* James E. Rauch, *Bureaucracy, Infrastructure, and Economic Growth: Evidence from U.S. Cities During the Progressive Era*, 85 AM. ECON. REV. 968–79 (1995).
[82] Robert L. Swartwout, *Current Utility Regulatory Practice from a Historical Perspective*, 32 NAT. RES. J. 289, 298–300 (1992).
[83] ELY, POLITICAL ECONOMY, *supra* note 78, at 72; ALFRED E. KAHN, THE ECONOMICS OF REGULATION: PRINCIPLES AND INSTITUTIONS, VOL I: ECONOMIC PRINCIPLES (1970).

infrastructure's utopian possibilities, mapping the "intimate relationship between technology and the social, economic, and governmental structure of cities."[84] Reform discourse was a mixture of practical and utopian themes and framed infrastructure as the key to broader social, economic, and political democracy. When they imagined the cities of the future, Progressives envisioned cleaner, safer, more rational, and more planned geographies than the ones they saw when they looked around them in 1900. When Colonel George E. Waring, Jr., an influential sanitation reformer, imagined New York City a hundred years in the future, he predicted a more rational, humane, and better-governed world: "The people have learned what good government is, and they will not give it up for long under any administration."[85]

This brave new world would be pioneered by government acting in the common good. Leading up to the First World War, states created state commissions to regulate the pricing and service levels of a mixture of public and private utilities. Indeed, the Progressive era was an age of innovation in management and public bureaucracy: new agencies and commissions were formed at the state, county, and city level to oversee infrastructures, making their management more technocratic, which also had the effect of reifying them into systems that could be manipulated by expert knowledge. This had the effect of removing public infrastructures from complete capture by local politics. Likewise, the new clout of experts and engineers in city planning tended to diminish the power of urban machines as decisions about health-related infrastructures such as water and sewage were made based on the general public welfare, rather than on patronage of well-connected contractors.[86]

The newly minted state commissions, which had their own problems of corruption and capture, were vested with broad legal authority to ensure fair rates to consumers and a "reasonable" rate of return on investment to the company.[87] While

---

[84] Schultz & McShane, *To Engineer the Metropolis, supra* note 75, at 389.
[85] COLONEL GEORGE E. WARING, *New York, A.D. 1997 – A Prophecy, in* ALBERT SHAW, LIFE OF COL. GEO. E. WARING, JR. THE GREAT APOSTLE OF CLEANLINESS 36–42 (1899).
[86] Schultz & McShane, *To Engineer the Metropolis, supra* note 75, at 395–96.
[87] Martin G. Glaeser lays out the following categories of regulated entities under the state commission system: "The scope of state regulation under the commission system varies in different states. In its most developed form it applies to the following industries: (1) common carriers by rail, highway, and water...; (2) telephone, telegraph, and cable companies; (3) utilities supplying water, electric light and power, electric railway and bus service..., natural and artificial gas service, heating and refrigerating services." GLAESER, PUBLIC UTILITIES, *supra* note 69, at 115; Bruce W. Dearstyne, *Regulation in the Progressive Era: The New York Public Service Commission*, 58 N.Y. HIST. 330–47 (July 1977). For the debate over whether cities or states should control utilities, see David Nord, *The Experts Versus the Experts: Conflicting Philosophies of Municipal Utility Regulation in the Progressive Era*, 58 WIS. MAG. HIST. 219–36 (1975). For water systems see Letty Anderson, *Hard Choices: Supplying Water to New England Towns*, 15 J. INTERDISC. HIST. 211–34 (1984); Scott E. Masten, *Public Utility Ownership in Nineteenth-Century America: the 'Aberrant' Case of Water*, 27 J. L., ECON., AND ORG. 604–54 (2011); David Cutler & Grant Miller, *Water, Water Everywhere:*

the problem of calculating reasonable rates continues to be a vexing one for regulators and economists, it nevertheless supplies the guiding principle for public utility pricing.[88] The idea of a reasonable rate, however, was by no means a Progressive innovation. Instead, it finds its roots in older ideas of a just price, free from coercion, which can be traced back to classical and medieval notions mediated through the common law.[89]

Many socialists and Progressives argued passionately that public ownership was the only way to secure democratic control over the new infrastructures. For them, the basic purpose of public utility for the common good could be served in no other way. Political economists continue to debate whether only publicly owned infrastructures can serve the public interest or whether regulated private monopolies can serve the same purpose. Whatever the merits of these ideas, the future of utility infrastructure was a mixture of public and private models. Crucially, in practice, "public" has not always necessarily meant "publicly owned." This fact was abundantly clear when antebellum legislatures and courts provided that even profit-making companies could be acting in the public good when they built infrastructures. It continued to be the case in the Progressive era and beyond. Today we are accustomed to roads, highways, bridges, etc. as quintessential infrastructures, which are typically managed in trust by government for the broader public. However, we are also accustomed to other utilities – for example, power & communication – providing infrastructural services as regulated private entities.[90] But whatever the ownership structure, utilities are subject to regulation by government entities at the local, state, and federal levels. And whether public or private, American law has supplied ample justification from within its own tradition to support subsidy and regulation.

Municipal Finance and Water Supply in American Cities, in GLAESER & GOLDIN, CORRUPTION AND REFORM, *supra* note 77, at 153–88; Mansel Griffiths Blackford, *Businessmen and the Regulation of Railroads and Public Utilities in California During the Progressive Era*, 44 BUS. HIST. REV. 307–19 (1970).

[88] Novak, *The Public Utility Idea and the Origins of Modern Business Regulation*, *supra* note 67, at 168 ("Millions of pages and barrels of ink would be spent debating such extraordinarily complex things as the best means of calculating a rate of return, the nature of a 'reasonable' versus an 'unreasonable' rate, and the comparative interests of corporations, shareholders, and the public at large"); *see also* Swartwout, *Current Utility Regulatory Practice*, *supra* note 82 (providing an historical overview of reasonableness); McNabb, *Public Utilities*, *supra* note 69, at 17 ("Utilities are supposed to provide a common benefit to each class of users, but users do not always enjoy equal benefit from the products of the utility. Moreover, homeowners are often charged a higher rate for the service than are industrial users, for example. Despite this legally sanctioned price discrimination, prices charged by utilities to all their customers must be seen as 'reasonable' by regulators and the general public.").

[89] William Boyd, *Just Price, Public Utility, and the Lost History of Economic Regulation in America*, 35 YALE J. REG. 721 (2018); see also Gustavus Robinson, *The Public Utility Concept in American Law,"* 41 HARV. L. REV. 277–308 (1928).

[90] TROESKEN, *Regime Change and Corruption*, *supra* note 77, at 260–63.

5.7 CONCLUSION

The victories of public purpose and substantive due process with respect to development subsidies and economic regulation had a fairly short shelf life in American law. Laissez-faire doctrines persisted into the 1930s, but even by then their scope was drastically reduced as America moved into the developmental New Deal state. Nevertheless, laissez-faire was prominent enough that several generations of liberal lawyers and economists would dedicate their careers to dismantling its conceptual foundations (a topic taken up in Chapter 6). After their defeat in the courts in the late 1930s, however, one was more likely to encounter laissez-faire arguments as part of a general theory of American exceptionalism, offered as just-so stories about "the way things have always been." With respect to real-world law and policy, however, the conservative treatise writers, public purpose, and substantive due process were fighting a losing game. The infrastructural-regulatory state was built around the pragmatic rationale of development and public utility. On the whole, it has been difficult to defeat arguments in favor of development and utility on the grounds of constitutional principle.

The 14th Amendment certainly lent new weight to corporate property rights. However, infrastructure was creating its own public demand in ways that could not be cabined by calls to protect private economic power of entrepreneurs and owners. Instead, American law and political culture eventually made peace with the idea of regulated infrastructure monopolies. This would be the case until the crisis years of the 1970s and the deregulation of the Reagan revolution that followed. Moreover, as I have been arguing throughout the book, "public" and "private" were not clearly demarcated in nineteenth-century legal and political culture, despite the fact that the division between the two as readily identifiable separate spheres has been a feature of liberal political and economic theory since the late nineteenth century. In any event, whatever theory said, in practice, courts and legislatures could not so readily separate regulable public action from nonregulated spheres of private autonomy and ownership.

The Progressive infrastructure regime laid the groundwork for modern politics of privatization and government in the public good. Tax revolts, fiscal politics, environmental, labor, and a host of other issues around infrastructure are now perennial features of American political debate. Despite these controversies, American law has, for better or worse, continued to be pro-development. With few exceptions, especially in the area of labor law, which was tilted strongly in favor of employers, law at the turn of the twentieth century was moving swiftly in the direction of more government action over economic matters and not less. But more public regulation did not necessarily mean direct government ownership of infrastructure enterprises. In practice, despite the passionate arguments against private monopolies, many forms of infrastructure would continue to be provided by private firms through the twentieth century. Other forms of twentieth-century infrastructure would be provided by competitive firms using integrated public systems (e.g., highways), which in turn supported a private transportation systems (e.g., trucks and automobiles). Although the public utility idea largely succeeded, the idea that only government-owned infrastructure could really work in the public interest did not become the prevailing model in practice. The "affected with public interest" standard did not disappear in the laissez-faire era only to be replaced during the New Deal. Rather, the roots of broader infrastructure regulation in the twentieth century were built around the Progressive idea of public utility.

6

The Death of Laissez-Faire and the Rise of Infrastructure in the Cold War

"[t]he conception of the spending power advocated by Hamilton and strongly reinforced by Story has prevailed over that of Madison, which has not been lacking in adherents"

Justice Cardozo, *Helvering v. Davis*, 301 U.S. 619 (1937)

"Praise the Lord and pass the infrastructure"

General Alfred Gruenther, 1952

6.1 INTRODUCTION

American government in the twentieth century grew larger and more involved in building and regulating the market state than even Alexander Hamilton could have dreamed. After the Depression, the federal government embarked on the largest spending program in American history, inaugurating an era of government spending in which taxes, budgets, and public works have continued to shape political discourse and policy to the present. The rise of the administrative state, while built out of earlier regulatory efforts, charted a new course in law and politics. The primary actors in formulating policy and managing the New Deal's public works programs understood quite well that they were living in a pivotal historical moment in which the relationship between citizen and state would be forever altered. The key actors used newly available tools of public relations and propaganda to sell the New Deal to the public and to quell critics who claimed that New Deal programs were "boondoggles" that simply wasted taxpayer money on frivolous projects – a style of fiscal conservatism that is an antecedent to our contemporary politics of budget austerity and deep skepticism of government and pork barrel politics.[1]

Nevertheless, in the decades following the New Deal, historians such as Richard Hofstadter and Arthur Schlesinger wrote generally positive assessments, reflecting an emerging liberal consensus around the New Deal.[2] As Jason Scott Smith puts it

---

[1] For a good overview of "boondoggles," *see* JASON SCOTT SMITH, BUILDING NEW DEAL LIBERALISM: THE POLITICAL ECONOMY OF PUBLIC WORKS, 1933–1956 135–59 (2006).

[2] Some classic contemporary accounts of the New Deal include CARL N. DEGLER, OUT OF OUR PAST: THE FORCES THAT SHAPED THE MODERN AMERICA (1959); RICHARD HOFSTADTER, THE AGE OF REFORM: FROM BRYAN TO F.D.R (2011) (1955); ARTHUR M. SCHLESINGER, JR.,

in a recent reappraisal of the New Deal, the basic consensus view is as follows: "Dr. New Deal made a bold attempt to end widespread unemployment and place the nation on a course toward recovery. Although the temporary programs he did set up did not accomplish these goals, they provided much-needed welfare for the jobless; when the European conflict erupted, Dr. Win-the-War took over, effectively ending the Depression while his predecessor's short-lived remedies were quietly phased out."[3]

The consensus view, in other, words, while lauding the accomplishments of the New Deal, emphasized the New Deal programs as temporary emergency measures. On this view, the New Deal was essentially a large employment project designed to get a suffering nation back to work, an effort whose short-term success is still being debated.[4] However, the New Left critics in the 1960s saw the New Deal as at best a missed opportunity, a badly flawed and incomplete project that failed to advance the goals of a just society.[5] At worst, perhaps the New Deal was really an instrument for corporate liberalism to consolidate its ideological and institutional hegemony in mid-century America, leading to the rise of the military industrial complex that

---

THE AGE OF ROOSEVELT: THE COMING OF THE NEW DEAL (1958); ARTHUR M. SCHLESINGER JR., THE AGE OF ROOSEVELT: THE POLITICS OF UPHEAVAL (1960); *see also* ALAN BRINKLEY, THE END OF REFORM: NEW DEAL LIBERALISM IN RECESSION AND WAR (1995); John W. Jeffries, *The "New" New Deal: FDR and American Liberalism, 1937–1945*, 105 POL. SCI. Q. 397, 397–418 (1990); John J. Coleman, *State Formation and the Decline of Political Parties: American Parties in the Fiscal State*, 8 STUD. AM. POL. DEV. 195, 195–230 (1994). GAIL RADFORD'S THE RISE OF THE PUBLIC AUTHORITY: STATEBUILDING AND ECONOMIC DEVELOPMENT IN TWENTIETH-CENTURY AMERICA (2013) provides valuable historical coverage of the quasi-public agencies that perform so much infrastructure management in the United States since the Progressive Era. ALBERTA M. SBRAGLIA'S DEBT WISH: ENTREPRENEURIAL CITIES, U.S. FEDERALISM, AND ECONOMIC DEVELOPMENT (1996) provides invaluable analysis of the public–private entanglements in American infrastructure history, focusing on the many ways that local government has overcome limitations placed on debt-financed infrastructure development in the modern world: "Public power has mobilized private money for public purposes. Over time, such investment has become disconnected from the normal political and administrative processes of local policy making." *Id.*, at 1.

[3] SMITH, BUILDING NEW DEAL LIBERALISM, *supra* note 1, at 9.
[4] Economists continue to debate the overall success of the New Deal, using a variety of data to reconstruct how effective government spending was in alleviating the short-term crisis of the Great Depression. *See*, for example, Price Fisher, *How Successful Was the New Deal? The Microeconomic Impact of New Deal Spending and Lending Policies in the 1930s*, 55 J. ECON. LITERATURE 1435, 1435–85 (2017); John Joseph Wallis, *Lessons from the Politics Economy of the New Deal*, 26 OXFORD REV. ECON. POL'Y 442, 448 (2010). ("Relief policies were not directed at promoting economic recovery, but providing assistance to those harmed by the depression. Economists often ignore the political and social value of relief, preferring to focus solely on whether a programme aided or retarded the process of recovery and growth. This is a particularly myopic perspective when thinking about an economic catastrophe such as the Great Depression.")
[5] WILLIAM E. LEUCHTENBURG, FRANKLIN D. ROOSEVELT AND THE NEW DEAL, 1932–1940 (1963); NEW DEAL THOUGHT (Howard Zinn, ed., 1966); PAUL K. CONKLIN, FDR AND THE ORIGINS OF THE WELFARE STATE (1967).

President Eisenhower warned of when he left office in 1961. Beginning the 1960s, economists and historians noted the cozy relationships between regulated industries and regulators and advanced theories of "regulatory capture."[6] Others developed a New Left line of argument that points to the racial and other inequities built into New Deal programs.[7] In many ways, we are still untangling the legacy of the New Deal today.[8]

Recently, historians have emphasized the positive long-term legacy of the New Deal in terms of American infrastructure, whose afterlife has been far longer than was previously understood.[9] The New Deal represented the largest federal investment in infrastructure in American history. The Civil Works Administration alone employed over four million in 1933–34, who worked on thousands of projects across the country: schools, airports, highways and roads, land reclamation, public buildings, and many other types of projects.[10] The more optimistic view points to the infrastructural achievements of mid-century liberalism, such as the national highway system, local, regional, and national airports, schools, water systems, and a host of basic infrastructures that are still in use today. Robert D. Leighninger, Jr.'s, *Long-Range Public Investment: The Forgotten Legacy of the New Deal*, for example, offers a positive assessment of the New Deal, emphasizing its continuing beneficial effects in the present: "The New Deal, in a very short period of time, contributed a tremendous amount to the nation's public life in the form of physical and cultural infrastructure. That investment paid dividends for many decades thereafter and in many

---

[6] *See*, for example, Thomas Merrill, *Capture Theory and the Courts: 1967–1983*, 72 CHICAGO-KENT L. REV. 1039, 1039–1117 (1997); Barton J. Bernstein, *The Conservative Achievements of Liberal Reform, in* TOWARDS A NEW PAST: DISSENTING ESSAYS IN AMERICAN HISTORY 263–88 (Barton J. Bernstein, ed., 1968); *see also* GABRIEL KOLKO, THE TRIUMPH OF CONSERVATISM: A REINTERPRETATION OF AMERICAN HISTORY, 1900–1916 (1963); GABRIEL KOLKO, RAILROADS AND REGULATION, 1877–1916 (1965); PAUL J. QUIRK, INDUSTRY INFLUENCE IN FEDERAL REGULATORY AGENCIES (1981).

[7] *See*, for example, MICHAEL K. BROWN, RACE, MONEY, AND THE AMERICAN WELFARE STATE (1999); HARVARD SITKOFF, A NEW DEAL FOR BLACKS: THE EMERGENCE OF CIVIL RIGHTS AS A NATIONAL ISSUE (2008) (1978); NANCY L. GRANT, TVA AND BLACK AMERICANS: PLANNING FOR THE STATUS QUO (1990).

[8] PAUL SABIN'S PUBLIC CITIZENS: THE ATTACK ON BIG GOVERNMENT AND THE REMAKING OF AMERICAN LIBERALISM (2021) makes an important point about the critique of the New Deal in the 1960s and 1970s: whatever its merits, in the end, the left-wing attack on big government helped to fuel the rise of neoliberalism.

[9] SMITH, BUILDING NEW DEAL LIBERALISM, *supra* note 1, at 9–10.

[10] BONNIE FOX SCHWARTZ, THE CIVIL WORKS ADMINISTRATION, 1933–1934: THE BUSINESS OF EMERGENCY EMPLOYMENT IN THE NEW DEAL 182–85 (2014) (1984). Ray C. Fair, *U.S. Infrastructure: 1929–2019* (Cowles Foundation Discussion Paper No. 2187, July 31, 2019), available at https://papers.ssrn.com/sol3/papers.cfm?abstract_id=3432670; Christopher Jones & David Reinecke. *Infrastructure and Democracy*, 33 ISSUES SCI. & TECH. (2017), https://issues.org/infrastructure-and-democracy/; John Joseph Wallis, *The Birth of the Old Federalism: Financing the New Deal, 1932–1940*, 44 J. ECON. HIST. 139, 139–59 (1984).

cases is still paying back."[11] Today, it is common for the New Deal and its infrastructures to figure as a tangible example of government acting in the public good.[12]

This chapter explains new fractures within liberalism (and a new consensus) about the legal and constitutional basis for state regulation and investment in the economy. Section 6.2 "A New Realism: Public, Private, and the State" picks up where Chapter 5 left off and explains the continuing power of a small-state view of American constitutional history. The scale of the Great Depression and the obvious need for federal intervention mooted laissez-faire arguments that harkened back to an imagined world of Jeffersonian yeoman farmers and sturdy individualists. Nevertheless, the continuing vitality of laissez-faire sparked debates in law, economics, and public policy about the proper role of government that in important ways continue to the present. The myth of a laissez-faire nineteenth century continues to be useful for a variety of purposes: It can serve as inspiration for conservatives seeking a return to a simpler past and as a cautionary tale for Progressives who want more state involvement in the economy: "Oddly, both conservatives and progressives agree on one thing: nineteenth-century Americans embraced the free market and the principles of *laissez-faire*."[13]

Section 6.2 explains the decline of laissez-faire's legitimacy among new institutional economists and legal thinkers, who challenged neoclassical theories of markets as self-sustaining systems. Richard Ely, Thorstein Veblen, and other allies of Progressive politics developed institutional accounts of modern capitalism that mapped its complex socio-political machinery. Throughout the Progressive Era, legal and economic thinkers saw laissez-faire as a serious obstacle to the political economy of regulated capitalism that they envisioned. These "legal realists" mounted a concerted opposition to the small-state Lockean tradition that had gained prominence since the late nineteenth century, along with the neoclassical and marginal economics that many read as a defense of existing inequalities. Realists argued that private rights, for example, property and contract, were not pre-political and natural,

---

[11] ROBERT D. LEIGHNINGER JR., LONG-RANGE PUBLIC INVESTMENT: THE FORGOTTEN LEGACY OF THE NEW DEAL 218 (2007); NICK TAYLOR, AMERICAN MADE: THE ENDURING LEGACY OF THE WPA: WHEN FDR PUT THE NATION TO WORK (2008); M. Houston Johnson V, *Laying Foundations: New Deal Public Works and Aviation Infrastructure*, 30 J. POL'Y HIST. 695, 695–726 (2018); *see also* David Plotke, *The Endurance of New Deal Liberalism*, 10 STUD. AM. POL. DEV. 415, 415–20 (1996); Howard Markel, *Infrastructure*, 95 MILBANK Q. 5, 5–10 (2017); Kian Goh, *Planning the Green New Deal: Climate Justice and the Politics of Sites and Scales*, 86 J. AM. PLAN. ASS'N 188, 188–95 (2020). Eric Rauchway's WHY THE NEW DEAL MATTERS (2021) emphasizes the positive legacy of the New Deal, which seems closer to an emerging consensus of the modern Democratic party (*see*, for example, President Biden's 2021 infrastructure bill and the Green New Deal).

[12] *See*, for example, Matt Blitz, *When America's Infrastructure Saved Democracy*, POPULAR MECHANICS, Jan. 23, 2017, www.popularmechanics.com/technology/infrastructure/a24692/fdr-new-deal-wpa-infrastructure/; Zachary D. Carter, *Wrestling with the New Deal*, AM. PROSPECT, May 28, 2021.

[13] BRIAN BALOGH, A GOVERNMENT OUT OF SIGHT: THE MYSTERY OF AUTHORITY IN NINETEENTH CENTURY AMERICA 2 (2012).

as Lockean theorists had insisted. Instead, governments were always involved in setting the rules of the game in advance through law and policy.

Categories such as public and private, for example, were not written in stone, they were practical dimensions of governance rather than metaphysical features of reality. Realism therefore suggested a functional problem to the public/private approach that had so troubled courts in the *Lochner* era. Realists argued that public power creates the institutional framework for private rights, an insight which they took as justification for government regulation of capitalism. The insights of the legal realists were gradually domesticated into a general "legal process theory," which answered criticisms of the administrative state with technocratic vision of neutral agency expertise governing in the public good. Their position on the legitimacy of regulation was treated as common sense among liberal technocrats of the new order, although this was by no means universal even at the time and came under great pressure in the post-1960s period. The expansion of the New Deal regulatory and fiscal machinery generated new challenges, and the administrative state was controversial from its inception.[14] Those debates were resolved in favor of a state-centered model of economic and social developmentalism, until the New Deal order itself entered a crisis period in the 1970s.

Section 6.3 "Modernization Takes Flight in the Cold War" locates the rise of infrastructure as a common term within modernization theory and development economics, which provide the post–Second World War with a western-centered model of capitalist growth. Modernization theory drew on social science, economics, and political theory to map society and economy as reciprocal systems that were amenable to policy intervention. Development economists, for example, such as Walt Whitman Rostow included infrastructure under the label "social overhead capital" as an item that was necessary for any advanced society. "Infrastructure" begins to circulate in American discourse in the early 1950s as a novel concept among staffers at the World Bank and later in Congressional debates over the Marshall Plan. It first takes on a narrow meaning of military facilities and the resources that supported those facilities. From there, it becomes a portable concept that development economists could use to predict the "take off" or stagnation of emerging societies measured by rates of growth, GDP, social stability, and technological advance. We see our contemporary sense of infrastructure crystallize in the 1950s and 1960s as the material precondition for a flourishing modern capitalist democracy.

---

[14] Anne M. Kornhauser's DEBATING THE AMERICAN STATE: LIBERAL ANXIETIES AND THE NEW LEVIATHAN, 1930–1970 (2015) presents an excellent account of the controversy surrounding the New Deal administrative state; *see also* KENNETH FINEGOLD & THEDA SKOCPOL, STATE AND PARTY IN AMERICA'S NEW DEAL (1995); Karen Orren & Stephen Skowronek, *Regimes and Regime Building in American Government: A Review of Literature on the 1940s*, 113 POL. SCI. Q. 689, 689–702 (1998); KIMBERLY J. MORGAN & ANDREA LOUISE CAMPBELL, THE DELEGATED WELFARE STATE: MEDICARE, MARKETS, AND THE GOVERNANCE OF SOCIAL POLICY (2011).

6.2 A NEW REALISM: PUBLIC, PRIVATE, AND THE STATE

We sometimes imagine state-centered liberalism arising fully formed in the New Deal, but the regulatory liberalism of the twentieth century had deep roots in the Progressive Era.[15] Progressive reformers had already solidified the permanent role of the technocratic class, with governments at every level already extensively involved in regulating economic life, despite continued resistance by the Supreme Court. As liberal governance had moved leftward throughout into the late nineteenth century, conservatives, such as Herbert Spencer, offered laissez-faire and competition as powerful counterarguments to the socialist trend within liberal societies.[16] Conservatives drew on the liberal tradition to place the interests of property above that of labor. The problem was that the liberal tradition was not as hostile to the regulation of property as its conservative defenders often suggested. John Stuart Mill's *On Socialism* (1869), to take one example, showed that utilitarian liberalism was open to the possibility that more government regulation would be necessary in a world of deepening inequality and agitation for reform:

> However irrefutable the arguments in favor of the laws of property may appear to those to whom they have the double prestige of immemorial custom and of personal interest, nothing is more natural than that a working man who has begun to speculate on politics, should regard them in a very different light. Having, after long struggles, attained in some countries, and nearly attained in others, the point at which for them, at least, there is no further progress to make in the department of purely political rights, is it possible that the less fortunate classes among the "adult males" should not ask themselves whether progress ought to stop there? Notwithstanding all that has been done, and all that seems likely to be done, in the extension of franchises, a few are born to great riches, and the many to a penury, made only more grating by contrast.[17]

While Mill was never a socialist, he understood that the demands of the propertyless classes in western countries after the democratic reforms of the nineteenth century could not go unanswered. Nevertheless, laissez-faire and anti-regulatory ideas continued to provide a powerful counterargument to social democracy among economists and legal elites. As J.M. Keynes suggested in 1926, laissez-faire "ideas accorded with the practical notions of conservatives and of lawyers. They furnished a satisfactory intellectual foundation to the rights of property and to the liberty of the individual in possession to do what he liked with himself and with his own. This was one of the contributions of the eighteenth century to the air we still breathe."[18]

---

[15] Kimberley S. Johnson, Governing the American State: Congress and the New Federalism, 1877–1929 (2007).

[16] Pierre Dardot & Christian Laval, The New Way of the World: On Neoliberal Society 1–47 (Gregory Elliott trans. 2013).

[17] J. S. Mill, On Socialism 14–15 (2009) (1869).

[18] J. M. Keynes, *The End of Laissez Faire* (1926), available at www.panarchy.org/keynes/laissezfaire.1926.html.

A Lockean-liberal constitutional tradition provided one way to highlight the American creed of the negative state that had been under attack since the 1870s. Princeton political scientist Edward Samuel Corwin, for example, had made the case since the Progressive Era that American constitutional law was primarily animated by natural law principles derived from John Locke, which suggested a Constitution designed to protect private rights such as property and liberty.[19] Proponents of the natural law Constitution could point to the lack of a federal police power and protection of property and contract and other elements that fit neatly within a Lockean liberal framework. Roscoe Pound, eminent jurist, dean of the Harvard Law School, and ambivalent Progressive, developed similar natural law themes in the 1920s. His *The Spirit of the Common Law* (1921), for example, characterizes the common law as a domain of "abstract individualism ... and judicial decision in the last century."[20] The case-by-case methodology of courts was ideally suited to preserve an authentically American legal culture.

Pound explains that many factors including Puritanism, laissez-faire economic thinking, the frontier spirit, the Reformation, etc. reflected an anti-statism that was built into America's cultural and political foundations. The center of Pound's narrative is the property-holding individual whose rights were protected from encroachment by the Constitution and common law: "What is peculiar to Anglo-American legal thinking, and above all to American legal thinking, is an ultra-individualism, an uncompromising insistence upon individual interests and individual property as the focal point of jurisprudence."[21] Pound's account builds on the widely influential A.V. Dicey's *Law and Public Opinion in England* (1905), which concluded that "the American Declaration of Independence ... embod[ied] that faith in laissez faire which was in practice the most potent and vital principle of Benthamite reform."[22] These views were attractive to lawyers, who continued to develop accounts of the Constitution built around a stark opposition between public power and private rights, and a legal framework designed to limit government

---

[19] *See*, for example, Edward S. Corwin, *The Basic Doctrine of American Constitutional Law*, 12 MICHIGAN L. REV. 247, 255 (1914) ("We are now prepared to consider the underlying doctrine of American Constitutional Law, a doctrine without which indeed it is inconceivable that there would have been any Constitutional Law. This is the Doctrine of Vested Rights, which-to state it in its most rigorous form-setting out with the assumption that the property right is fundamental, treats any law impairing vested rights, whatever its intention, as a bill of pains and penalties, and so, void"); EDWARD S. CORWIN, THE "HIGHER LAW" BACKGROUND OF AMERICAN CONSTITUTIONAL LAW 365–409 (1928); Edward S. Corwin, *The Doctrine of Due Process of Law Before the Civil War*, 24 HARV. L. REV. 366, 366–85 (1911).

[20] ROSCOE POUND, THE SPIRIT OF THE COMMON LAW 35 (2015).

[21] POUND, THE SPIRIT OF THE COMMON LAW, *supra* note 20, at 37; "In Pound's view, natural law derived from reason was the best tool that the early Americans could have used to reform the English law without losing its essential spirit of liberty. Natural law allowed Americans to accept part of traditional law, and thus not begin purely from scratch but to test all of traditional law by reason." *Id.*

[22] ALBERT VENN DICEY, LECTURES ON THE RELATION BETWEEN LAW AND PUBLIC OPINION IN ENGLAND DURING THE NINETEENTH CENTURY (2008) (1905) (ebook, loc. 2038).

power. Robert McCloskey, writing in the 1957, summed up the traditional view of the Supreme Court's role in American democracy as a check on the state: "It possesses the power of declaring the law, and in that is found the safeguard which keeps the whole mighty fabric of government from rushing to destruction. This negative power, the power of resistance, is the only safety of popular government ... In other words, the essential business of the Supreme Court is to say 'no' to government."[23]

The legal profession was particularly vocal in warning against the dangers of an unaccountable bureaucracy. In an address before the Maryland State Bar Association, John Lord O'Brian, a prominent attorney, raised alarm at the "The Menace of Administrative Law" (1920), which threatened property rights and due process: "It was inevitable that during the war ... democracy should submit itself to the exercise of autocratic powers in the hands of Federal administrators ... The food regulation; the fuel control; the war taxation; the operation of the railroads; the adjustment of claims against the government on informal contracts, brought into existence a new bureaucracy which fixed standards, disposed of property rights and in the field of revenue interpreted the laws of Congress solely through the mouthpiece of administrative official."[24] The experience of the first red scare and the use of executive power to quash dissent during the First World War leant additional weight to these concerns. Roscoe Pound, Felix Frankfurter, Ernst Freund, and other important writers had been working through the implications of the administrative state since the 1920s.[25] Their central concerns were that decision-making by bureaucrats violated due process of law and private property and was a radical departure from the court-centered legal decision-making that lawyers were accustomed to navigating.[26]

Reformers in the 1920s and 1930s needed arguments that legitimated public action, particularly when it came to claims about constitutional protections for

---

[23] ESSAYS IN CONSTITUTIONAL LAW 6 (Robert G. McCloskey ed., Knopf 1957) (internal quotation marks omitted). For helpful overviews of Cold War constitutionalism, see Herman Belz, *Changing Concepts of Constitutionalism in the Era of World War II and the Cold War*, 59 J. AM. HIST. 640, 640–69 (1972); *see also* Asli Bâli & Aziz Rana, *Constitutionalism and the American Imperial Imagination*, 85 UNIV. CHICAGO L. REV, 257, 257–92 (2018).

[24] John L. O'Brian, *The Menace of Administrative Law (1920)*, 23 BUFF. L. REV. 65, 65–72 (1974).

[25] *See*, for example, Roscoe Pound, *The Growth of Administrative Justice*, 2 WISC. L. REV. 321, 321–39 (1924); GERARD C. HENDERSON, THE FEDERAL TRADE COMMISSION: A STUDY IN ADMINISTRATIVE LAW AND PROCEDURE (1924); JOHN DICKINSON, ADMINISTRATIVE JUSTICE AND THE SUPREMACY OF LAW IN THE UNITED STATES (1927); Felix Frankfurter, *The Task of Administrative Law*, 75 PENN. L. REV. 614, 614–21 (1927); Ellis W. Hawley, *The New Deal State and the Anti-Bureaucratic Tradition*, in THE NEW DEAL AND ITS LEGACY: CRITIQUE AND REAPPRAISAL 77–92 (Robert Eden ed., 1989).

[26] Nicholas S. Zeppos, *The Legal Profession and the Development of Administrative Law*, 72 CHICAGO-KENT L. REV. 1119, 1119–57 (1997); *see also* RONEN SHAMIR, MANAGING LEGAL UNCERTAINTY: ELITE LAWYERS IN THE NEW DEAL (1995); JEROLD S. AUERBACH, UNEQUAL JUSTICE: LAWYERS AND SOCIAL CHANGE IN MODERN AMERICA (1976).

property rights that they saw as an obstacle to the regulated world they envisioned. One of the most important areas of contest would be over the field of economics, which had been embroiled in controversy since the late nineteenth century. As Oliver Wendell Holmes, Jr., had predicted in 1897 in his overview of new legal developments "the man of the future is the man of statistics and the master of economics."[27] The "marginal revolution" in economics began in the second half of the nineteenth century in the writings of Alfred Marshall, William Stanley Jevons, Carl Menger, Léon Walras, and others.[28] Marxists had argued that capitalists appropriated the value produced by workers to accumulate private wealth while impoverishing the laboring classes. Marginalism supplied an elegant answer to the socialist critique of exploitation that was implied by the labor theory of value. Classical and later Marxist theory had insisted that value was an objective factor of production – reflecting how much capital had been invested, the cost of labor and materials, etc. Thus, firms made pricing decisions based on these factors of past investment and cost. The marginalists turned this thinking on its head by showing that resources are distributed across the system of production and distribution based on the contribution of each factor to the end product. Marginalism shifted the frame away from an objective theory of value toward a theory centered on consumer preference and rational choice.

The "margin" in marginalism refers to the idea that consumers make choices incrementally, basing decisions on how much value the person can obtain from a particular transaction under particular circumstances. So, for example, a consumer might pay $5 for a mocha latte at Starbucks but would not purchase a second one for $5. However, they might buy the second one if it were priced at $2.50, which reflects the diminishing marginal utility of a second latte to that individual. In other words, pricing is based on a consumer's willingness to pay, not solely on factors of production that are internal to the firm. That same analysis can be applied to every factor of production and consumption. A decision "at the margins" just means that the decision is affected by factors (e.g., already having one cup of coffee) that move the cost along a curve that eventually drops to (or near) zero for further units under conditions of perfect competitive efficiency. One potential implication of this idea was that preexisting property allocations are generally efficient because they reflect the natural process of calculation made by rational actors who, if left to their own devices, generate something like an

---

[27] Oliver Wendell Holmes, *The Path of the Law* 10 HARV. L. REV. 457, 469 (1897).
[28] *See, for example,* WILLIAM STANLEY JEVONS, THEORY OF POLITICAL ECONOMY (1871); JOHN BATES CLARK, THE DISTRIBUTION OF WEALTH: A THEORY OF WAGES, INTERESTS AND PROFITS (1899); CARL MENGER, PRINCIPLES OF ECONOMICS (1871); LÉON WALRAS, ELEMENTS OF PURE ECONOMICS (1954); BARBARA H. FRIED, THE PROGRESSIVE ASSAULT ON LAISSEZ FAIRE: ROBERT HALE AND THE FIRST LAW AND ECONOMICS MOVEMENT (1998); Herbert Hovenkamp, *The Marginalist Revolution in Legal Thought*, 46 VAND. L. REV. 305, 305–59 (1993); Herbert Hovenkamp, *Regulation and the Marginalist Revolution*, 71 FLORIDA L. REV. 455, 455–514 (2019).

equilibrium across well-functioning markets.[29] Labor and capital each receive their fair share of the social product under conditions of perfect competition, which could imply that government meddling in the process would only distort the market. Across the twentieth century, marginalism cemented the "market" as an independent force with its own dynamics rooted in the natural process of production and exchange.[30]

Many at the time saw conservative implications in the new economics.[31] Some criticized marginalist theories as painting too rosy a picture of choice, rationality, and markets, a debate that continues to the present. Institutional economists countered marginalism's growing influence by dismantling the neoclassical idea of the market as a feature of the natural order. Within the new political economy, the market was a social and political construct that rested on man-made infrastructures of laws, institutions, and culture. In 1898, Thorstein Veblen asked "Why Is Economics Not an Evolutionary Science?" He answered the question in his usual scathing manner, by pointing to the lack of interest among economists in new fields such as anthropology and psychology, and for not having a well-developed theory of society: "The active material in which the economic process goes on is the human material of the industrial community," not the idealized and abstract person of economics.[32] The political economy of the future would require a better understanding of market society's actually existing machinery before it could manipulate the levers of power and policy in the complex world of the twentieth-century capitalism. A study of institutions would show that market societies are embedded in social and cultural structures, an insight that would be confirmed by a growing body of social science research.

Legal realists, a loosely affiliated group of American jurists, approached the laissez-faire problem with a clinical attitude toward received wisdom. They chipped

---

[29] This was certainly how many Progressives understood the neoclassical position at the time. Herbert Hovenkamp, however, argues that marginalism was not as committed to the market as an independent force as many have argued that it was. He points to marginalism's relative indifference to the public–private divide and to its theory of pricing, which he argues actually paved the way for government regulation rather than socialism: "Regulation under marginalist principles did not lead to a large increase in public business ownership, as socialism threatened. To a significant extent, however, it deprived private firms of the power to make their own economic decisions about market entry, price, and other central features of private property. Regulation became public ownership in disguise. Every element of private firm behavior within an agency's jurisdiction became subject to government review under a public interest standard." Hovenkamp, *Regulation and the Marginalist Revolution*, supra note 28, at 459.

[30] For overviews of the debates around marginalism, *see*, for example, Jens van't Klooster, *Marginalism and Scope in the Early Methodenstreit*, 44 J. HIST. ECON. THOUGHT 105, 105–24 (2022); *see also* FRIED, THE PROGRESSIVE ASSAULT ON LAISSEZ FAIRE, supra note 28.

[31] *See* SIDNEY FINE, LAISSEZ FAIRE AND THE GENERAL WELFARE STATE: A STUDY OF CONFLICT IN AMERICAN THOUGHT, 1865–1901 198–251 (1956).

[32] Thorstein Veblen, *Why Is Economics Not an Evolutionary Science?*, 12 Q. J. ECON. 373, 384, 387 (1898).

away at the temple's foundations and attacked laissez-faire theories at their intellectual center: the notion of preexisting private rights. Wesley Newcomb Hohfeld, a law professor who taught at Stanford and Yale, fired early salvos against the notion that rights are foundational rather than relative.[33] Hohfeld broke apart rights into analytical categories and showed that, for example, a property right was only meaningful because it could be enforced against someone else who might have a competing claim. One of the important consequences of his approach was that it was no longer possible to speak in general of rights of property, as if those rights floated in a vacuum. Rights, he suggests, are embedded in relational structures. Your right to enjoy your property, after all, was predicated at all times on the existence of a legally enforceable restraint upon someone else's power to trespass. This implied that rights were relative and contextual, not absolute grounds of an independently existing private economy (a view that some marginalists eventually came to recognize). Rights were just conventional ways that law and society distributed access to resources, a point that utilitarians had been making since the eighteenth century.[34] If this was the case, then Hohfeld's argument had a radical subtext, which others quickly realized: It meant that social policy could alter preexisting rights without violating anything like Lockean natural law.

Property rights were a point of contention between laissez-faire and Progressive reformers since the late nineteenth century. The political economists had argued that property rights formed the bedrock for liberal capitalist democracy. Many critics pointed to the conservative implications of that position since practically speaking few people had any property at all, except for selling their own labor power. Robert Lee Hale, a key figure in the new realism, understood property rights to be one of the most important conceptual foundations of the classical liberal model his cohort were attacking. The classical argument was that the realm of private transactions was voluntary and largely non-coercive. When people engaged in Adam Smith's "truck and barter," they were doing so based on a principle of free exchange between relative equals. The state, by contrast, was the realm of coercion and power

---

[33] Wesley Newcomb Hohfeld, *Some Fundamental Legal Conceptions as Applied in Judicial Reasoning*, 23 YALE L. J. 16, 16–59 (1913); Wesley Newcomb Hohfeld, *Fundamental Legal Conceptions as Applied in Judicial Reasoning*, 26 YALE L. J. 710–70 (1917). For the overlap between legal realism and institutional economics, see Neil Duxbury, *Robert Hale and the Economy of Legal Force*, 53 MOD. L. REV. 421 (1990).

[34] *See*, for example, J.S. MILL, PRINCIPLES OF POLITICAL ECONOMY (1848) ("When the 'sacredness of property' is talked of, it should always be remembered, that any such sacredness does not belong in the same degree to landed property. No man made the land. It is the original inheritance of the whole species. Its appropriation is wholly a question of general expediency.... The claim of the landowners to the land is altogether subordinate to the general policy of the state. The principle of property gives them no right to the land, but only a right to compensation for whatever portion of their interest in the land it may be the policy of the state to deprive them of"); Frederick G. Whelan, *Property as Artifice: Hume and Blackstone*, 22 NOMOS 101, 101–29 (1980); FRIED, THE PROGRESSIVE ASSAULT ON LAISSEZ FAIRE, *supra* note 28, at 71–107.

whose primary purpose was to police violence and fraud. Defenders of a new regulatory liberalism would need to attack this formulation head on, because they wanted government control to even the playing field. Hale does this by extending Hohfeld's basic insight that rights were contextual.

For example, take the assumption of non-coercive exchange of labor for money. For Hale, this assumption was imprecise and contained a buried premise: that only coercion by the state really counted as coercion. But Hale demanded clear definitions of premises, which meant that we would need to know what counted as "coercion" and "force" in the first place if we were going to mark a distinction between legitimate and illegitimate state action. This after all had been such an important point of contention between Progressives and conservatives for decades. If we stand by the laissez-faire and marginalist assumptions that private law was the realm of free exchange, then we really have no grounds for criticizing unfair labor conditions, since it is always possible to say (as many people did) that a worker can just find another job if he or she does not like the terms of a labor contract. Therefore, the question of uncoerced consent would need to addressed head on.

Hale's "Coercion and Distribution in a Supposedly Non-coercive State" (1923) develops Hohfeld's point that government is an active force that does a lot more coercing that classical liberalism recognized: "What is the government doing when it 'protects a property right'? Passively, it is abstaining from interference with the owner when he deals with the thing owned; actively, it is forcing the non-owner to desist from handling it, unless the owner consents."[35] Government created the field of power relations in which property rights had actual force in the world. Hale was arguing the case that socialists had been making since the nineteenth century, that the system of property and wages was shot through with coercion from the beginning and thus that we could not treat "private" domains of property and contract as a neutral baseline.[36] J. M. Keynes put the point this way a few years later:

> Let us clear from the ground the metaphysical or general principles upon which, from time to time, *laissez-faire* has been founded. It is *not* true that individuals possess a prescriptive "natural liberty" in their economic activities. There is *no* "compact" conferring perpetual rights on those who Have or on those who Acquire. ….
> It is *not* a correct deduction from the principles of economics that enlightened self-interest always operates in the public interest. Nor is it true that self-interest generally *is* enlightened; more often individuals acting separately to promote their own ends are too ignorant or too weak to attain even these. Experience does *not* show

---

[35] Robert L. Hale, *Coercion and Distribution in a Supposedly Non-Coercive State*, 38 POL. SCI. Q. 470, 471 (1923); for an overview of realism, see MORTON HORWITZ, THE TRANSFORMATION OF AMERICAN LAW, 1870–1960: THE CRISIS OF LEGAL ORTHODOXY (1992) (especially Chapters 5 and 6); *see also* FRIED, THE PROGRESSIVE ASSAULT ON LAISSEZ FAIRE, *supra* note 28.

[36] *See*, for example, LEONARD HOBHOUSE ET AL., PROPERTY, ITS DUTIES AND RIGHTS: HISTORICALLY, PHILOSOPHICALLY, AND RELIGIOUSLY REGARDED (1915); BRUCE A. ACKERMAN, RECONSTRUCTING AMERICAN LAW 6–22 (1984).

that individuals, when they make up a social unit, are always less clear-sighted than when they act separately.[37]

If power relations exist even within private transactions, such as labor and consumer contracts, then the distinction between interference and non-interference that earlier liberals had insisted upon begins to lose its force: "We have to discriminate between what Bentham ... used to term *Agenda* and *Non-Agenda*, and to do this without Bentham's prior presumption that interference is, at the same time, 'generally needless' and 'generally pernicious.'"[38] The government was "intervening" all the time, and not only in the obvious cases, as when it assisted strikebreakers or enjoined picketers but also by establishing the ordinary legal rules that governed the entire process of production and exchange.[39] If this was true, then in theory, the government could correct preexisting inequities with the levers of ordinary policy. The realists dismantled the conceptual foundations of standalone private rights and found at their center policy choices and a network of preexisting social relationships, inequality, and power differentials.

After the Crash of 1929, the question of the government role in the economy took on a new urgency as the alphabet soup of New Deal agencies and programs built up an administrative state whose constitutional foundations were unsettled. As the first legal realists and liberals took power after the Depression, they began to govern through the new administrative agencies. The classical liberal distinction between "agenda" and "non-agenda" would be all but erased for several decades, as the New Deal state propped up the business economy, invested in infrastructure, and created new legal regimes in labor law, consumer law, banking regulations, etc. By the middle of the 1930s, FDR's new agencies commanded a large role in society, and the federal bureaucracy expanded its reach: "By the end of the 1930s, the bureaucrats were in charge. In expanding the federal government's field of play in the preceding decades, Congress and the White House had created dozens of agencies, departments, bureaus, and commissions to handle this new and staggering workload."[40] The new administrative state was big government with a vengeance, and critics of

---

[37] Keynes, *The End of Laissez Faire, supra* note 18.
[38] *Id.* 18.
[39] Some important texts in realism include Robert L. Hale, *Law Making by Unofficial Minorities*, 20 COLUM L. REV. 451, 451–56 (1920); Morris Cohen, *Property and Sovereignty*, 13 CORNELL L. Q. 8, 8–30 (1927); JOHN R. COMMONS, THE LEGAL FOUNDATIONS OF CAPITALISM (1924); Louis L. Jaffe, *Law Making by Private Groups*, 51 HARV L. REV. 201, 201–253 (1937); John Dewey, *The Historic Background of Corporate Legal Personality*, 35 YALE L. J. 655, 655–73 (1926); Robert Lee Hale, *Bargaining, Duress and Economic Liberty*, 43 COLUM L. REV. 603, 603–28 (1943); HORWITZ, THE TRANSFORMATION OF AMERICAN LAW, *supra* note 35, at 145–244.
[40] JOANNA GRISINGER, THE UNWIELDY AMERICAN STATE: ADMINISTRATIVE POLITICS SINCE THE NEW DEAL 1 (2012). The administrative state has remained controversial since the New Deal, and many have attempted to square largescale bureaucratic governance with American constitutional and democratic norms. *See*, for example, Susan E. Dudley, *Milestones in the Evolution of the Administrative State*, 150 DAEDALUS 33, 33–48 (2021); CASS SUNSTEIN & ADRIAN VERMEULE, LAW AND LEVIATHAN: REDEEMING THE ADMINISTRATIVE STATE (2020); ADRIAN VERMEULE, LAW'S

the agencies had voiced concerns about bureaucratic government since the 1920s, worried that the new agencies created too much regulatory power over business, threatened the rule of law, and undermined property interests.[41]

The Supreme Court settled some of the larger questions but left many unresolved. Laissez-faire theory and *Lochner's* constitutional right of business to be free from certain kinds of restraints fell in *West Coast Hotel v. Parrish* (1937), removing legal obstacles to New Deal labor regulation.[42] In *Helvering v. Davis* (1937), Justice Cardozo settled question of whether there were constitutional limits to the spending power of Congress: "[t]he conception of the spending power advocated by Hamilton and strongly reinforced by Story has prevailed over that of Madison, which has not been lacking in adherents"[43] Substantive due process limits on taxation and regulation largely disappeared in the 1930s, and in case after case, the Supreme Court upheld the Commerce power against the many challenges to the New Deal social legislation:

> The power of Congress over interstate commerce is complete in itself, may be exercised to its utmost extent, and acknowledges no limitations other than are prescribed in the Constitution. Congress, following its own conception of public policy concerning the restrictions which may appropriately be imposed on interstate commerce, is free to exclude from the commerce articles whose use in the states for which they are destined it may conceive to be injurious to the public health, morals or welfare, even though the state has not sought to regulate their use….It is no objection to the assertion of the power to regulate interstate commerce that its exercise is attended by the same incidents which attend the exercise of the police power of the states.[44]

State-centered regulation and administrative governance would begin to define "the public interest." James M. Landis's *The Administrative Process* (1938) made the case that administrative agencies would better work to ensure fair and efficient administration in many cases than courts could.[45] This would require neutral agency expertise and professional management to strike a careful balance among the interests of different groups. The Administrative Procedure Act of 1946, which provided some

---

ABNEGATION: FROM LAW'S EMPIRE TO THE ADMINISTRATIVE STATE (2016); Morton J. Horwitz, THE TRANSFORMATION OF AMERICAN LAW, 1870–1960: THE CRISIS OF LEGAL ORTHODOXY (1992) provides a valuable account of the shift in legal theory that created space for public-facing legal liberalism of the New Deal and Civil Rights era. *See* HORWITZ, THE TRANSFORMATION OF AMERICAN LAW, *supra* note 35.

[41] Joseph Postell, *The Anti-New Deal Progressive: Roscoe Pound's Alternative Administrative State*, 74 REV. POL. 53, 53–85 (2012); Mark Tushnet, *Administrative Law in the 1930s: The Supreme Court's Accommodation of Progressive Legal Theory*, 60 DUKE L. J. 1565, 1565–1637 (2011); KIM PHILLIPS-FEIN, INVISIBLE HANDS: THE BUSINESSMEN'S CRUSADE AGAINST THE NEW DEAL (2009).

[42] *West Coast Hotel v. Parrish*, 300 U.S. 379 (1937).

[43] *Helvering v. Davis*, 301 U.S. 619 (1937).

[44] *United States v. Darby*, 312 U.S. 100 (1941).

[45] JAMES M. LANDIS, THE ADMINISTRATIVE PROCESS (1938).

of the accountability and oversight that many had complained of since the 1920s, represented a compromise with business interests, creating an administrative order still being debated today.[46]

Economic planning had been on the agenda since the end of the Second World War. As Benjamin Hartz states in his Foreword to Louis Hartz's famous Cold War treatise *The Liberal Tradition in America* (1955): "Almost all of the great issues of our time, not excluding world peace, are closely related to governmental regulation of economic affairs."[47] That phrase – regulation of economic affairs – seems almost anodyne today and more likely to conjure an image of bureaucrat in a gray flannel suit tabulating data on agriculture yields. Nevertheless, in the context of the Red Scare and the early Cold War, the idea of economic planning could still be controversial. While liberals advanced the constructive role of the state, they also struck American notes of self-reliance, democracy, and capitalism, discovering a home-grown developmentalism that had deep roots in the supposed "laissez faire" days of the nineteenth century. The key for understanding the continuities between past and present would be government-managed economic growth toward the ends of liberal capitalist democracy – which in practice could mean imposing this on "underdeveloped" countries by military force if need be to contain the Communist threat.

Cold War liberalism would need to domesticate state planning by showing that it enjoyed an unimpeachably American pedigree. Harry N. Scheiber, an historian who wrote important development studies himself, situates his colleagues' new interest in American development history in the context of nation-building and economic growth: "Intrigued by the problems of the underdeveloped countries of our own time, historians and economists have given considerable attention in recent years to nineteenth-century American economic growth."[48] Carter Goodrich was an important figure in the new economic history and wrote important works on state-financed canal building in the nineteenth century. Goodrich, writing in 1948, captures the uneasy position that many found themselves in as they attempted to inoculate economic planning against charges that it was a foreign imposition on American laissez-faire capitalism:

> Economic planning, it is now recognized, is by no means a new thing in American history. To be sure the term came into general currency only with the first Soviet five year plan and with the activities of the New Deal, and there is of course no American precedent for total planning of a national economy in the Russian sense. But, by the more inclusive definition under which the term has been used to refer to certain of the New Deal measures, the advocacy and practice of economic

[46] George B. Shepherd, *Fierce Compromise: The Administrative Procedure Act Emerges from New Deal Politics*, 90 Nw. U. L. Rev. 1557, 1557 (1996).
[47] Louis Hartz, The Liberal Tradition in America: An Interpretation of American Political Thought Since the Revolution, vii (1955).
[48] Harry N. Scheiber, *Review of American Canals and Railroads, 1800–1890 by Carter Goodrich, Julius Rubin, H. Jerome Cranmer and Harvey H. Segal*, 75 Pol. Sci. Q. 608, 608–10 (1960).

planning have long been significant parts of the American tradition. For the present purpose the term may be taken to mean the adoption by government or community of deliberate and concerted policies which are designed to promote economic expansion or prosperity and in which positive action to provide favorable conditions for economic activity is emphasized more strongly than negative regulation or the correction of abuses. In this broad sense our record shows many cases of economic planning.[49]

We are now a long way from Adam Smith and a timeless American laissez-faire. The mention of "total planning," Russia, and the "Soviet five year plan" unmistakably locates Goodrich in his Cold War moment. What we see here is the creation of a counter-myth that insulates the new state-centered liberalism from charges that it was really just foreign-born socialism in disguise. Goodrich strikes a reassuring tone for readers worried that the new liberalism would be the first perilous step, in Friedrich von Hayek's phrase, down a road to serfdom.[50]

Internal improvements and state development policies of the nineteenth century provided important counterevidence to the story of an exceptionally American revolution against government. Goodrich's *The Government and the Economy, 1783–1861* (1967) makes the point clearly, with reference to "social overhead capital" (discussed below) and infrastructure: "If American governments helped to provide what in many of the developing countries is called the 'infrastructure,' they did so in the belief that individuals and corporate enterprise would be eager to build the superstructure upon it."[51] American infrastructure, subsidized by government, created the template for the flourishing capitalist democracy that followed. The fact that Goodrich could cite an American story located far in the past, based on American federalism, also avoided the negative valences of "total planning," and provided historical precedent for American-led ambitions to remake the post-War world.[52]

The key to understanding this new liberalism was that the developmental state that it endorsed promised to contribute to economic growth and political stability, while also acting as an agent of social progress. By 1952, Robert Lee Hale, only thirty years before an insurgent thinker of the new order, argued confidently in *Freedom through Law: Public Control of Private Governing Power* that laissez-faire was a dead letter in the modern world. Hale summed up the realist and institutionalist outlook that he and many others had developed across law and public policy for several generations. On the one hand, as Hale could not fail to acknowledge, the state was capable of great evil: "'Statism' is often singled out as the prime enemy of individual liberty. Unrestricted power can, indeed, crush liberty." On the other hand, despite this real danger, the state supplied the basic framework for a society governed by

---

[49] Carter Goodrich, *National Planning of Internal Improvements*, 63 POL. SCI. Q. 16, 16 (1948).
[50] FRIEDREICH A. HAYEK, THE ROAD TO SERFDOM (1944).
[51] THE GOVERNMENT AND THE ECONOMY, 1783–1861 xvi, xxxiii (Carter Goodrich ed., 1967).
[52] Michael Brenes & Daniel Steinmetz-Jenkins, *Legacies of Cold War Liberalism*, DISSENT 116, 116–24 (2021).

the rule of law: "But in our revolt against statism we must not forget that while the state is capable of destroying our liberties it is also essential to their very existence."[53] This is a very different view from the Lockean model of classical liberalism based in a small government primarily concerned with private rights and non-intervention. And indeed, many noted the sharp contrast between classical liberal theory on the one hand and the institutional realities of managed capitalism on the other hand.[54] It is also a more moderate view than Hale and his cohort developed a generation before. The model of government regulation Hale maps out in the book's pages was now simply a codification of twenty years of established precedent. From the realist and institutionalist point of view, it was therefore possible to treat the legal questions as largely settled. The state as envisioned by the new liberalism would be a crucial vector for development and regulation of post-war capitalism. Engineers, lawyers, economists, and other experts would become the default custodians of that new system.

6.3 "PRAISE THE LORD AND PASS THE INFRASTRUCTURE": MODERNIZATION TAKES FLIGHT IN THE COLD WAR

By the 1950s, the Supreme Court had legitimated the New Deal, public trust in government was near historic highs and there was widespread faith in technology and expertise.[55] Keynesian economic policy would in theory manage business cycles and create regimes of full employment and rising prosperity. Good institutional design would keep forces in balance under a theory of "countervailing power," with government, unions, consumer groups, etc. acting on behalf of a public that otherwise lacked organization.[56] Reforms of the public utility industry sought to break up monopolies that controlled much of the nation's energy infrastructure.[57] New Deal infrastructure achievements inspired confidence in modern technological progress, and American successes were touted as anti-communist tonic. As Supreme Court Justice William O. Douglas explained to an audience of Tennessee politicians:

---

[53] ROBERT L. HALE, FREEDOM THROUGH LAW: PUBLIC CONTROL OF PRIVATE GOVERNING POWER 4 (1952).
[54] Kurt L. Hanslowe, *Regulation by Visible Public and Invisible Private Government: Of Theory and Practice*, 40 TEX. L. REV. 88, 88–135 (1961).
[55] *Trust in Government: 1958–2015*, in PEW RESEARCH CENTER, BEYOND DISTRUST: HOW AMERICANS VIEW THEIR GOVERNMENT (Nov. 23, 2015).
[56] JOHN KENNETH GALBRAITH, AMERICAN CAPITALISM: THE CONCEPT OF COUNTERVAILING POWER 108–153 (1952).
[57] *See*, for example, MARTIN G. GLAESER, PUBLIC UTILITIES AND AMERICAN CAPITALISM (1957); William M. Emmons III, *Franklin D. Roosevelt, Electric Utilities, and the Power of Competition*, 53 J. ECON. HIST. 880, 880–907 (1993); PHILIP J. FUNIGIELLO, TOWARD A NATIONAL POWER POLICY: THE NEW DEAL AND THE ELECTRIC UTILITY INDUSTRY, 1933–1941 (1973); Nidhi Thakar, *The Urge to Merge: A Look at the Repeal of the Public Utility Holding Company Act of 1935*, 12 LEWIS & CLARK L. REV. 903, 903–42 (2008).

"[t]he TVA [Tennessee Valley Authority] can be … utilized as one of the major influences to turn back the tide of communism which today threatens to engulf Asia."[58] The Council of Economic Advisors (CEA), formed in 1946, advised Presidents since Harry Truman on managing the business cycle and accelerating economic growth.[59] By the 1950s, the "economy" entered the modern political lexicon, where it began to mean the totality of factors that form a system within a particular geographical area, one for which growth measured by GDP was a key barometer of success.[60] Only economic growth could deliver on the democratic promise of broad-based prosperity while also containing the threat of Communism.

The situation in Europe, however, as well as twenty years of New Deal regulation and investment, showed that economic growth can malfunction in many ways and was sometimes dependent on government action. In their work, economic historians had reminded readers that early-stage capitalist economies required government action to produce desired market outcomes. One way to capture the layered and dependent nature of capitalist enterprise was through the idea of "social overhead capital." Social overhead capital, like infrastructure, acknowledges that massive upfront public investment is needed in order to jump start the private economy of production, consumption, and distribution. Economic history provided good evidence that this had been the case in the United States and the recent experience with the Marshall Plan only confirmed historical precedent. In the 1950s, social overhead capital begins to circulate among staffers at the World Bank as a concept that supported their view of investment in large public projects with money supplied by American bankers.[61] Unlike earlier economic theory, the World Bank does not treat big engineering projects merely as an overhead cost to be paid in order to launch economic growth. Infrastructure projects are viewed instead as potential investment opportunities that can pay dividends. There is another related shift at

---

[58] David Ekbladh, "Mr. TVA": Grass-Roots Development, David Lilienthal, and the Rise and Fall of the Tennessee Valley Authority as a Symbol for U.S. Overseas Development, 1933–1973, 26 DIPLOMATIC HIST. 335, 335 (2002): (quoting Justice William O. Douglas); David Ekbladh, Meeting the Challenge from Totalitarianism: The Tennessee Valley Authority as a Global Model for Liberal Development, 1933–1945, 32 INT'L HIST. REV. 47, 47–67 (2010).

[59] ROBERT M. COLLINS, MORE: THE POLITICS OF ECONOMIC GROWTH IN POSTWAR AMERICA 17–39 (2000); Charles L. Shultze, The CEA: An Inside Voice for Mainstream Economics, 10 J. ECON. PERSP. 23, 23–39 (1996); Bradford De Long, Keynesianism, Pennsylvania Avenue Style: Some Economic Consequences of the Employment Act of 1946, 10 J. ECON. PERSP. 41–53 (1996).

[60] Timothy Mitchell, Rethinking Economy, 39 GEOFORUM 1116, 1116–21 (2008); see also MEG JACOBS, POCKETBOOK POLITICS: ECONOMIC CITIZENSHIP IN TWENTIETH-CENTURY AMERICA (2005); ROBERT J. GORDON, THE RISE AND FALL OF AMERICAN GROWTH: THE U.S. STANDARD OF LIVING SINCE THE CIVIL WAR (2017).

[61] William J. Rankin, Infrastructure and the International Governance of Economic Development, 1950–1965, in INTERNATIONALIZATION OF INFRASTRUCTURES 61, 64–65 (Jean-François Auger et al., eds.) (2009). The related term "social capital" had been in circulation in one form or another since the early twentieth century, if not before. See JAMES FARR, SOCIAL CAPITAL: A CONCEPTUAL HISTORY, 32 POL. THEORY 6, 22 (2004).

work here. Infrastructure is a commercial prospect, not just as a cost to be paid, and government is now figured as a business that co-manages important ventures with the private sector: "The difference was not the nature of the state, but simply the role of government: if the solution to industrializing 'backward' areas was to treat entire countries or regions as one large business, the World Bank positioned itself (and its recipient governments) as top management; private enterprise would be responsible for day-to-day operations. Social overhead capital was thus a way of marrying the central-planning focus of economists … with a post-Keynesian division between public and private."[62] The important political distinction between public and private was subordinated to the function that different assets played within economic development models.[63] A realism about the public/private, state/economy divide implied a view of government as a guiding force in the development of emerging capitalism.

Infrastructure entered this environment as an important development concept, making its way into English usage through British interactions with the French army during First World War.[64] NATO's Common Infrastructure Programme was launched in 1949, and it defined infrastructure as a "generic term" referring to various military installations and supporting structures.[65] Infrastructure begins to circulate in high-level planning circles in the late 1940s, where it justifies an ecological view of investment, with American dollars sent overseas with the purpose of rebuilding or remaking societies into modern liberal democracies fashioned in America's image. However, infrastructure was slow to catch on as an all-purpose planning concept, and some expressed skepticism at this novel word without a clear definition. In a full-page cover story on the ongoing reconstruction of Europe, the *New York Times* included a two-paragraph item of interest titled "Use of 'Infrastructure' is Baffling to Acheson":

> Secretary of State Dean Acheson expressed puzzlement tonight over the word 'infrastructure,' a favorite bureaucratic morsel in the language of European defense. The word is used to describe the facilities and installations, such as roads, communications and headquarters buildings, that must accompany the construction of

---

[62] Rankin, *Infrastructure and the International Governance of Economic Development, supra* note 61, at 65; ALBERT HIRSCHMAN, THE STRATEGY OF ECONOMIC DEVELOPMENT (1958); John Adler, *The Fiscal and Monetary Implementation of Development Programs*, 42 AM. ECON. REV. 584, 584–600 (1952).

[63] Rankin, *Infrastructure and the International Governance of Economic Development, supra* note 61, at 67 ("Privatized infrastructure is relatively common; private public works are a logical impossibility").

[64] HENRY PETROSKI, THE ROAD TAKEN: THE HISTORY AND FUTURE OF AMERICA'S INFRASTRUCTURE 13 (2017); William H. Batt, *Infrastructure: Etymology and Import*, 110 J. PRO. ISSUES ENG'G 1, 1–6 (1984); David Alff, *What Is Infrastructure, Anyway?* BOSTON REV., June 28, 2021, available at https://bostonreview.net/articles/what-is-infrastructure-anyway/.

[65] Ashley Carse, *How a Humble French Engineering Term Shaped the Modern World*, in INFRASTRUCTURES AND SOCIAL COMPLEXITY: A COMPANION 31 (Atsuro Marito et al., eds., 2017).

airfields or naval bases ... 'One thing I can't explain to you is how these facilities came to be called by the name 'infrastructure.' But despite this heavy handicap, good progress was made on this issue, too.[66]

When Representative Walter Henry Judd of Minnesota was concerned during debates over the Marshall Plan about local cost sharing, he calls attention to the term: "seems to me that those possibilities should be stimulated so far as they reasonably can be, and that they, taken in connection with so-called infrastructure, that is, expenditures for fields and things of that character..."[67] Several years later, however, General Alfred Gruenther, Chief of Staff, Supreme Headquarters Allied Powers Europe, boasted of his success with ongoing reconstruction efforts in Europe and seemed to embrace the concept: "At the NATO Lisbon Council meeting in 1952 ... I suggested the motto be: 'Praise the Lord and pass the infrastructure.' I don't think this did more than create an atmosphere. But we got our infrastructure."[68] Infrastructure was the largest single budget item, with nearly 40 percent of the early grant funds to rebuild Europe earmarked for infrastructure projects.[69]

Throughout the 1950s, politicians felt the need to offer further definitions of this new term, typically in defense of some spending proposal. When Rhode Island Senator Theodore Francis Green spoke to the Senate Committee on Foreign Relations in 1951, he suggested that the term might not be widely understood and took the trouble to define it:

> One of the most imposing problems to be faced in building the defenses of Western Europe was described by General Gruenther as the "infrastructure" problem. This is a French word used to describe what we might call the "overhead" part of an operation. For example, military planning in Europe, development of the "infrastructure" would mean broadly the development of the facilities absolutely essential to combat operations, such as airfields for fighter aircraft, communications facilities, depots for storage of various types of military equipment, and so forth.[70]

---

[66] *Use of 'Infrastructure' is Baffling to Acheson*, N.Y. TIMES, March 1, 1952, at 3.
[67] 97 Cong. Rec. H13008 (Oct. 11, 1951) (statement of Rep. Walter Henry Judd); 98 Cong. Rec. H5651, H5668 (May 21, 1952); 98 Cong. Rec. H8480 (June 28, 1952); 99 Cong. Rec. S4853 (May 13, 1953) (the infrastructure program "will include a wide range of projects such as airfields, telecommunications, naval bases and port facilities, pipelines and radar installations. The military authorities of NATO now have a financial planning figure to which they can work for over 3 years. In addition, an improved system is ready to be put into operation to insure closer financial supervision over the expenditure of common infrastructure funds."); 99 Cong. Rec. S4857 (infrastructure aid will be a "stabilizing factor"). For other uses of the term in the early 1950s, 18 Fed. Reg. 6523–6554, 6546 (Oct. 14, 1953).
[68] C. L. Sulzberger, *Foreign Affairs: The Generals: II – Gen. Gruenther Shifts Priorities*, N.Y. TIMES, June 20, 1956, at 30.
[69] CURT TARNOFF, CONG. RSCH. SERV., 7-5700/RF5079, THE MARSHALL PLAN: DESIGN, ACCOMPLISHMENTS, AND SIGNIFICANCE 12 (Jan. 18, 2018), 12; *see also* Jack Raymond, *Bonn Rebuffs U.S. on Aid Now to Cut Dollar Outflow*, N.Y. TIMES, Nov. 23, 1960, at 1; *U.S. NATO Share Down, Bonn's Up*, N.Y. TIMES, March 1, 1961, at 12.
[70] UNITED STATES SENATE, COMMITTEE ON FOREIGN RELATIONS, UNITED STATES FOREIGN AID PROGRAMS IN EUROPE: REPORT OF THE SUBCOMMITTEE OF THE COMMITTEE ON

6.3 Modernization Takes Flight in the Cold War

Infrastructure continued to require explanation in Congress for several years through the mid-1950s. Representative Everett McKinley Dirksen, an Illinois Republican, spoke at great length in August 1954 about the proposed military aid package to Europe, which included items classified as "infrastructure":

> That is a good mouth-filling word which ought to frighten even a Senator. But, to break it down, "infra" means "under," so the infrastructure means the understructure. In the case of an automobile, it would be the undercarriage; so this is the undercarriage for the military-assistance program in Europe. What does it embrace? Airfields. First, in the primary line; and, secondly, further back, for a second periphery, if that becomes necessary. That means fuel. That means equipment. That means installations and all the other things which are necessary for an effective and quickly functioning military structure.[71]

Representative Dirksen's definition captures something important about infrastructure's function within public policy: It acknowledges that systems have primary and secondary functions, centers, and peripheries. If you want to build up Western European military defense, that will obviously mean money for rebuilding airfields. However, airfields are only useful if they are supported by adequate fuel and equipment. If you want a car to drive, you need a chassis to hold it together. If you buy the metaphor, then it follows that if you want an effective reconstruction effort, that will involve a substantial amount of (costly) logistical support that will be part of that larger objective. If you want to convince skeptical politicians to loosen the purse strings, they need to grasp the extensive (and expensive) precursors that are truly involved in a government-led social engineering project as massive as the Marshall Plan. The abstraction of infrastructure as a catch-all term is a useful rhetorical tool to justify large financial investments in the sort of complex projects that modern states undertake. Yet, skeptics noted the fact that infrastructure conceived in this way tended to widen the financial commitment of the United States. The journalist Arthur Krock, for example, included "infrastructure" in his list of economic "gobbledygook" words which he defined as a "N.A.T.O term designed to make sure that the United States will foot the entire bill."[72]

Infrastructure turned out to be an indispensable concept to convince Congressmen of the need for more financing to support economic development and military defense in the post-War order. It was so useful, in fact, that members of Congress began to wield "infrastructure" in debates over funding for domestic projects, sometimes in terms that echo the internal improvement debates of the nineteenth century.

Foreign Relations on United States Economic and Military Assistance to Free Europe, Senate Doc. No. 56, at 18 (1951), *referenced at* 97 Cong. Rec. S9843 (Aug. 13, 1951); *see also* Peter A. Shulman, *What Infrastructure Really Means*, Atl. (July 13, 2021).

[71] 100 Cong. Rec. S14496 (1954).
[72] Arthur Krock, *In the Nation: Bringing the Political Lexicon up to Date among the Administrators at the Capitol*, N.Y. Times, Sep. 27, 1951, at 30.

For example, in August of 1951, Michigan Republican Senator Homer S. Ferguson advocated for funding the St. Lawrence Seaway to improve transportation between the Midwest and Canada. The proposed Senate bill cites "the national interest" as the basis for constructing the waterway and provides the important caveat that the seaway will be financed on a "self-liquidating basis," with the proposed financing in the form of bonds "amortized by toll charges over a 50-year period or less."[73] Senators were particularly concerned about the self-liquidation issue, but they also wondered whether the St. Lawrence Seaway was essential for the national interest. Senator Ferguson defended the project on the grounds that America's infrastructure provided important advantages for national commerce:

> Development of infrastructure, or the underlying foundation of an economy for either peace or war, has long plagued the buildup of defense in Europe. The United States has infrastructure—in our great transportation network, in our communications system, in our fuel and power developments. The St. Lawrence Seaway would be an addition to this infrastructure of almost incalculable value and significance through the increased capacity which it would give our national transportation system.[74]

Military and civilian officials had also supported the plan, Ferguson noted, for its potential for military preparedness. This argument was hard to defeat in 1951, even though some Senators seemed doubtful whether there was really a defense rationale for a waterway in the northern Midwest. Ultimately, Senator Smith of New Jersey, a port state that had every reason to oppose competing infrastructure in the Midwest, supported the plan, which had been endorsed by President Eisenhower on national security grounds. Citing military purposes for civilian infrastructure became a common method of gaining approval for large projects. Two of the largest infrastructure investments of Eisenhower's administration – the St. Lawrence Seaway and the interstate highway system – were justified in part with appeals to their utility for military defense.

The bureaucratic register of the term – which made it seem ridiculous to earlier critics – is precisely what made infrastructure an indispensable keyword for modern economic governance, and eventually placed infrastructure into modern democratic politics and culture. One of infrastructure's virtues is that it binds together military and commercial development projects into a common managerial and logistical framework. It acknowledges the complexity and dependency of engineering technologies on ecologies of public and private investment. This feature of infrastructure, however, further blurs the lines between public and private since

---

[73] 100 Cong. Rec. S332 (Jan. 18. 1954).

[74] *Id.*; 110 Cong. Rec. S6940–7041, S6964, 6965 (Apr. 6, 1964) (Statement of Senator Ernest Gruening) ("The cost of restoring the previously existing infrastructure alone will come close to half a billion dollars ... Much of the infrastructure of Alaska – including highways, airports, railways and port facilities – is damaged").

infrastructure is a material link binding together a mutually reinforcing system of government and business. Blurred lines are a natural consequence of using infrastructure as a development concept in a networked world of public–private actors who are each viewed functionally, as contributing to an overall project of growth. Another casualty of the new political economy of capitalism was the public/private distinction that American law had struggled with since after the Civil War.[75]

When viewed in this way, infrastructure places great pressure on the normative categories of public and private, which begin to seem less relevant to economics, despite the fact that they are still relevant as legal and political concepts. However, if your goal is rebuilding or launching a self-sustaining economy, infrastructure carries a good deal of persuasive force. Once you concede the value of some objective – such as military defense or trade – it is difficult to argue that you should not include funding for the supporting structure that it depends on. One of the crucial questions will then be how to define a "supporting structure." What sorts of activities were "economic," and which were merely "social"? Did the difference matter? From a developmental perspective, they begin to seem like the same problem.

The sociologists Max Weber, Talcott Parsons, and other theorists provided the foundations for a more comprehensive view of economy and society that optimistic mid-century government planners needed.[76] Modernization theory provided a framework for measuring progress toward the goal of a well-functioning capitalist democracy, linking culture and economics into mutually reinforcing systems. Unlike many intellectuals who worried about alienation and other darker themes in the 1950s and 1960s, modernization theorists were optimistic and modeled development through certain well-defined stages on the path to capitalist modernity whose endpoint they took as a given.[77] W.W. Rostow's *The Stages of Economic*

---

[75] HORWITZ, THE TRANSFORMATION OF AMERICAN LAW, *supra* note 35, at 193–212; *see also* MORTON GRODZINS, THE AMERICAN SYSTEM: A NEW VIEW OF GOVERNMENT IN THE UNITED STATES 236–52 (Transaction Books 1984).

[76] For modernization theory, see MICHAEL LATHAM, MODERNIZATION AS IDEOLOGY: AMERICAN SOCIAL SCIENCE AND "NATION BUILDING" IN THE KENNEDY ERA (2000); ARTURO ESCOBAR, ENCOUNTERING DEVELOPMENT: THE MAKING AND UNMAKING OF THE THIRD WORLD (1995); NILS GILMAN, MANDARINS OF THE FUTURE: MODERNIZATION THEORY IN COLD WAR AMERICA (2003); Joyce Appleby, *Modernization Theory and the Formation of Modern Social Theories in England and America*, 20 COMPAR. STUD. SOC'Y HIST. 259, 260 (1978) ("The strength of modernization theory lies in the underlying commitment to account for the totality of changes involved in the creation of a modern nation. Where liberal social theory and classical economics encouraged scholars to analyze change from the perspective of the isolated individual – his wants, his nature, and his means – the pioneers of sociology began with society and recognized in the patterned behavior of men and women the presence of structures which, though intangible, were nonetheless objects to be studied scientifically"); H. W. ARNDT, ECONOMIC DEVELOPMENT: THE HISTORY OF AN IDEA (1987); Albert O. Hirschman, *The Rise and Decline of Development Economics*, in THE THEORY AND EXPERIENCE OF ECONOMIC DEVELOPMENT: ESSAYS IN HONOR OF SIR W. ARTHUR LEWIS 372–90 (Mark Gersovitz et al., eds., 1982).

[77] Dorothy Ross, *Whatever Happened to the Social in American Social Thought, Part 2*, 19 MOD. INTEL. HIST. 268, 270–71 (2022).

Growth: A Non-Communist Manifesto (1960), for example, provided the template for "take off," the unified process that catalyzed "traditional," peasant societies to become "high mass consumption societies."[78] Rostow's analysis of development revealed the importance of "social overhead capital" to the formation of modern societies, which includes "railways, ports and roads."[79] Rostow explained that social overhead capital was treated differently for societies in early stages of development because they lack the pool of capital needed for big projects. Early-stage infrastructure projects do not yield immediate profits, they are "lumpy" (i.e., they are not useful in small increments, only in completed networks) and "the profits from social overhead capital often return to the community as a whole – through indirect chains of causation – rather than directly to the initiating entrepreneurs."[80] For these reasons, governments would need to take responsibility for early-stage infrastructures.

For Rostow, as for other Cold War economic historians, the American antebellum example was instructive: "[E]ven in so highly capitalist a transitional society as the United States between 1815 and 1840, state and local governments played a major role in initiating build-up of social overhead capital. The Eerie Canal was built by the New York state legislature; and the great American continental railway networks were built with enormous federal subsidies in the form of land grants."[81] America had many advantages in the race for growth, including the sort of "vigorous, independent" and "enterprising" culture that supported rapid takeoff into capitalist modernity.[82] For the "underdeveloped" societies trapped in an earlier stage of the universal cycle that theorists identified, planning and government investment would be particularly important. Rostow's contribution was to turn a static conception of "overhead capital" into a more dynamic model that highlighted the fact that infrastructure must precede production of goods and services, serving as a precondition of them, a point that was already suggested in Adam Smith's concept of public works. From the planning point of view, emerging economies had persistent infrastructure problems that delayed their takeoff into capitalist modernity. They did not have well-established road networks or adequate communications. They had cultural drawbacks of "peasant" societies, which did not produce the entrepreneurial orientation that would launch them on their path to capitalist modernity.[83]

We can understand infrastructure's new comprehensive direction by considering the Congressional debate surrounding the Special United Nations Fund for

---

[78] Walt Whitman Rostow, The Stages of Economic Growth: A Non-Communist Manifesto 4–16 (3d ed. 1990).
[79] Id. at 17–18.
[80] Id. at 25.
[81] Id. at 25.
[82] Id. at 98.
[83] Latham, *Modernization as Ideology, supra* note 76, at 69–108.

Economic Development (SUNFED, est. 1958). SUNFED was one of the many Cold War initiatives to win global position against the Soviet Union by aiding "underdeveloped" economies through international aid. Democratic Senator Hubert Humphrey laid out the basic rationale for international development: "This desire to develop the 'infrastructure' is a new idea politically but a very widely recognized idea among economists. Former plans have been geared to economies already possessing a strong infrastructure."[84] Development economics encouraged Congressmen to view infrastructure as part of an institutional ecosystem of public and private investment. This potentially widened infrastructure's conceptual scope quite drastically:

> This additional financing should be directed toward providing the underdeveloped countries with what is called the economic-social "infrastructure," on which the apparatus of production proper is based. The "infrastructure" may be defined as the set of basic facilities needed for effective production, such as a minimum of roads, power stations, schools, hospitals, housing, and Government buildings. Experience has shown that it is only when this basis has been established that production can be developed smoothly and that private initiative can play its full part.[85]

We have now returned to this book's starting point. This is Adam Smith's argument about public works in a nutshell: Economic growth would be impossible without infrastructure. To begin with, the report directs us to the main purpose of financing infrastructure, which is providing support for the "apparatus of production." "Schools, hospitals, housing, and Government buildings" are not at first glance like airfields and factories. Yet, these are all necessary supporting facilities to achieve a modern standard of living, which would nurture self-sustaining market systems built around norms of western production and technology. But how much support does the baseline apparatus of production need before it becomes self-sustaining? The phrase "economic-social 'infrastructure'" suggests an answer to that question: Engineering an economic takeoff would require more than just factories and airfields. It would require an ambitious project of remaking entire societies and cultures in the image of the modern West.

Subtly redefining infrastructure as "schools, hospitals, housing, and Government buildings" suggests the ideological issue that lurks at the heart of the modern infrastructure politics. Is infrastructure really just the airfields that appear in the NATO planning documents or does it mean something much more comprehensive than that? It turned out that modernization could require much

---

[84] 102 Cong. Rec. S11321–11514, S11377 (June 29, 1956); *see also* Ronald A. Manzer, *The United Nations Special Fund*, 18 INT'L ORG. 766–89 (1964).
[85] 102 Cong. Rec. S11321–11514, 11378 (June 29, 1956).

more ambitious investment than merely building industrial capacity or roads. The plasticity of infrastructure implied that "economic" aid would potentially need to consider the entire social system that supplies the supporting framework for modern capitalist democracy. The SUNFED Report addresses this issue by waving it away; since social and hard infrastructures were both just as necessary for development, they were both "infrastructure" and therefore by definition worthy of support:

> Distinctions, which are theoretical rather than practical, are normally made between the various types of infrastructure investments; some are social because they provide for the education, health, and welfare of the population; others are economic because they tend more directly to promote the economic development of a region. Some investment projects are self-liquidating in the sense that they yield a profit to the investor of sufficient size and over a sufficiently short period to be financed by commercial loans or by private capital; others relate to projects which, although non-self-liquidating, nevertheless constitute an indispensable part of the infrastructure. This category includes roads, schools, hospitals, and other facilities which add to the nation's productive potential, but which are not usually operated in such a way as to yield a profit within a reasonably short period.[86]

This small dispute over definitions suggests a larger tension between social liberalism and fiscal conservatism, which can be obscured by the term infrastructure. Those who want to support social infrastructure and those that want to include only the hard installations (e.g., roads and airfields) that directly contribute to growth will disagree on how much to include in the infrastructure category, because once something is tagged as "infrastructure," financial support for that thing becomes a necessity. The SUNFED report struggles to fit both into the same model of development: "From the general economic point of view, all 'infrastructure' investments, whether social or economic, provided that they are not unnecessarily large and that they are integrated in a coherent development program, are directly or indirectly self-liquidating, since they all contribute to the short-term or long-term development of the economy."[87] As long as the aid was intended to "attain the maximum rise in national income," it should be counted as infrastructure.[88] In a sense, then, social infrastructure is at least as important to modernize developing societies as hard infrastructures. Nevertheless, it should be noted that in practice, a more conservative definition of infrastructure prevailed when it came to loans to the developing world.[89]

---

[86] Id.
[87] Id.
[88] Id.
[89] Howard Stein, Beyond the World Bank Agenda: An Institutional Approach to Development 10–11 (2008).

In the 1960s, infrastructure appears in the press without any need for scare quotes or definition, suggesting that it was beginning to acquire its contemporary meaning.[90] America's own history continued to provide a homegrown example of state-led infrastructure investment that could provide a template for the developing world. Chester Bliss Bowles, then Ambassador to India, wrote a review essay on development for the *New York Times* in 1964 in which he highlights the struggles of Asian, Latin American, and African countries to achieve the takeoff into capitalist modernity predicted by development theory. Very much a Cold War liberal, Bowles first congratulates postcolonial leaders for leaving behind their youthful flirtations with communism to pursue the hard work of practical statecraft needed for takeoff into capitalist modernity. Then he lays out the central case for state-led infrastructure development. American history supplied the very material he needed to argue his case:

> We may start with an obvious fact: In any developing nation, government must play a central and critically important role. Only through government planning, government capital and government supervision can many of the basic tools be provided which are required to start things moving ... For instance, the so-called infrastructure — the roads, rail transport, schools, power and the communications networks — are in large measure a governmental responsibility.
>
> Even in the United States, where private enterprise has played such a vital role, government has often been forced to carry a heavy share of the burden in these areas. One of the first acts of our new national Congress in the seventeen-nineties was to provide federal subsidies to expand our merchant marine. In the eighteen-thirties the Eerie Canal, the first effective transportation link between the East Coast and the fast-developing new West, was built with public funds — borrowed in large measure from England. Thirty years later the privately owned and managed American railroads were given massive Federal grants of public land to finance the unprecedented program of railroad construction...

Bowles then reminds readers that the same kind of development model had been in place in the United States since the Second World War, when "the ... Government promptly took over the planning, control and much of the

---

[90] See, for example, 108 Cong. Rec. H23546–23720, H23681 (Oct. 13, 1962) ("the United States should help build up the infrastructure of the Indonesian economy-transport, light industry, and so forth-which in turn will provide the basis for heavy capital investment in the future); *Who's Who in Capital's Farm Power Infrastructure*, N.Y. TIMES, Apr. 5, 1970, at 57; *Complacency Worries Singapore*, N.Y. TIMES, Jan. 19, 1970, at 66 ("a recent book on the third world referred to the growth of 'broken-backed states' – countries with good infrastructures from their colonial governments, but which were slowly grinding to a halt economically"); C.L. Sulzberger, *Foreign Affairs: Paradise Losing*, N.Y. TIMES, Oct. 13, 1967, at 38 ("Both possess the infrastructure of modernity: good communications, spending cities, fine universities, hospitals, resorts"); *Excerpts from McNamara's Final Report to Congress on Nation's Defense Posture*, N.Y. TIMES, Feb. 2, 1968, at 16 ("in a related effort, we believe progress is beginning to be made in ferreting out the hidden Vietcong infrastructure").

management of the economy." Governments at every level were still subsidizing infrastructure, including housing, education, scientific research, and agriculture. And he added a dig at conservative critics of government ownership: "Many American business leaders who shudder at the very thought of government owned and managed enterprises are now among the most enthusiastic recipients of government subsidies."[91]

Nevertheless, conservative critics took issue with this sort of argument, as they continue to do today. In 1964, Republican Representative Thomas Curtis of Missouri took another approach, suggesting the conservative critique of debt-financed growth that would soon dominate American politics. Keynesian advocates of government spending, whom Curtis calls "neo-Federalists," had been arguing for decades that federal debt was not a problem because it created wealth and because government was in the best position to manage the business cycle. But surely deficit spending had limits that had to be observed. Curtis, a prominent supporter of the Civil Rights Movement, criticized international development aid at length and asked whether infrastructure was what critics had always feared: bureaucratic "gobbledygook" designed to expand the reach of government at the expense of the for-profit sector:

> It was to the effect that private money would not be spent to build infrastructure— infrastructure being the Government gobbledygook word for schools, roads, communications, sewers, and other community facilities…Private enterprise builds roads, schools, sewers, communication systems all over the world, whatever it needs, including new communities, lock, stock, and barrel, in order to implement its basic economic purpose. Who built the infrastructure in Venezuela, roads, railroads, communications, yes, educational facilities, including the school buildings, in order to extract the oil and now the iron deposits?[92]

Deficits had become a major issue in American politics since the 1950s, and Curtis was expressing a growing consensus within the Republican party around debt and deficits. Infrastructure spending was near its historical highpoint, and the Federal government was increasing its spending to fight the War on Poverty. More generally, between Representative Curtis and Chester Bliss Bowles, we can see two competing visions of infrastructure and development come into view. On the one hand, the confident vision of developmentalism in Bowles's essay that stretches back in time to the state-building aspirations of internal improvements in the nineteenth century that the economic historians of the 1950s and 1960s cited as precedent. This is infrastructure development as progress, with society and economics functioning within a mutually reinforcing frame. On the other hand,

---

[91] Chester Bowles, *The Developing Nations' Greatest Need: The Developing Nations*, N.Y. TIMES, Apr. 12, 1964, at SM15.
[92] 110 Cong. Rec., H8813 (Apr. 22, 1064) (Remarks of Sen. Thomas B. Curtis).

we have Curtis's dismissal of the "Government gobbledygook" of infrastructure, whose artificiality its critics can dismiss as just a code word for big government at its worst. This is fiscal conservativism and an alternative vision of how debt, deficits, and taxation act as hard limits to the infrastructural ambitions of modernization. It is also a reassertion of the priority of business capital and private initiative in building up the infrastructure of market society.

6.4 CONCLUSION

The 1960s was the high point for both federal infrastructure spending and for modernization theory's optimistic view of human progress. The Vietnam War, the Civil Rights movement, the women's and environmental movements challenged the premises of a generalized "public good" administered by neutral experts. New Deal infrastructures represent the hubristic monumentalism of the modernist vision, and now big government looked to many on the left and on the right as an obstacle to their very different visions of democracy. The many uncounted costs of development, industrialism, and consumerism became evident through a burgeoning environmentalist movement. Ernst Schumacher's bestselling *Small Is Beautiful: Economics as if People Mattered* (1973), which is still in print, critiqued the growth model that had shaped policy for several decades, offering an ecological people-centered vision in its place.[93] Critics of modernization theory and development aid argued that modernization imposed a western-centered, neocolonialist debt regime on the third world.[94]

The term public interest that had guided mid-century government and law was criticized as vague and elusive: "Public interest ... has come to mean some criterion or desideratum by which public policy may be measured, some goal which policy ought ideally to pursue and attain. But just whose standard it is to be remains the problem."[95] The case for governing in the public good, as conceived by the New Dealers, was also badly weakened by economists who had been arguing for decades against the inefficiencies of the regulatory state.[96] In the late 1970s, price

---

[93] ERNST F. SCHUMACHER, SMALL IS BEAUTIFUL: ECONOMICS AS IF PEOPLE MATTERED (1973).
[94] *See*, for example, WILLIAM EASTERLY, THE ELUSIVE QUEST FOR GROWTH: ECONOMISTS' ADVENTURES AND MISADVENTURES IN THE TROPICS 36 (2001) ("Many times over the past fifty years, we economists thought we had found the right answer to economic growth. It started with foreign aid to fill the gap between 'necessary' investment and saving. Even after some of us abandoned the rigidity of the 'necessary' investment idea, we still thought investment in machines was the key to growth. Supplementing this idea was the notion that education was a form of accumulating 'human machinery' that would bring growth"); see also Arturo Escobar, *Encountering Development*, supra note 76.
[95] Frank J. Sorauf, *The Conceptual Muddle*, 5 NOMOS: AM. SOC'Y POL. LEGAL PHIL. 183 (1962).
[96] *See* Sam Peltzman et al., *Economic Theory of Regulation after a Decade of Deregulation*, 1989 BROOKINGS PAPERS ON ECON. ACTIVITY: MICROECONOMICS 1, 1–59 (1989) (providing a still-useful overview of the economic critique of regulation from the 1960s through the 1980s).

controls and cartel protections began to loosen, and deregulation remade airlines, trucking, and telecommunications.[97] Economists and politicians sought to reduce regulatory burdens on businesses, for example by requiring cost–benefit analysis anchored in Chicago-school equilibrium theories for proposed regulations to determine whether they were in the aggregate benefit of society. In American intellectual circles, laissez-faire and negative liberty enjoyed a revival, and refurbished narratives about the priority of the private economy as a facilitator growth revitalized market politics and burnished the prestige of the private sector By the 1980s, state-centered liberalism was in decline across the western world, ushering in an era now described as "neoliberal." The federal government withdrew from its commitments to investing in state and local infrastructures in the late 1970s. And it was at that moment that infrastructure had a revival as a major theme in American politics.[98]

---

[97] Susan E. Dudley, *Improving Regulatory Accountability: Lessons from the Past and Prospects for the Future*, 65 CASE W. RSRV. L. REV. 1027, 1027–57 (2015); Andrew Downer Crain, *Ford, Carter, and Deregulation in the 1970s*, 5 J. TELECOMMUN. HIGH TECHNOL. LAW 413 (2007).

[98] Ross, *Whatever Happened to the Social in American Social Thought*, supra note 77, at 270–71.

Conclusion

"Our Crumbling Infrastructure"

On June 8, 1982, Ronald Reagan delivered a speech to the British Parliament that highlighted key themes of the late Cold War, including the Berlin Wall, tensions between East and West, and laid out the American-led strategy of containment in spreading "the global campaign for democracy now gathering force:" "The objective I propose is quite simple to state: to foster the infrastructure of democracy – the system of a free press, unions, political parties, universities – which allows a people to choose their own way, to develop their own culture, to reconcile their own differences through peaceful means.... It is time that we committed ourselves as a nation – in both the public and private sectors – to assisting democratic development."[1] These were the sweeping themes that Cold War developmental theory had emphasized since the 1950s in arguments about the historical path toward liberal capitalist democracy. As this book has been chronicling, Reagan's rhetoric has deeper roots in a developmental imagination that links together civil society, political liberalism, capitalism, and a normative vision of democracy.

In the world of practical policy discourse, however, a new sense of national decline and a desire for repair and renewal emerges in infrastructure debates around the same time as Ronald Reagan's speech. Across the twentieth century, federal infrastructure spending peaked in the 1960s, then leveled off and then declined in the 1970s.[2] The drop off in federal investment meant that more building and upkeep fell to cities and states, placing great strain on budgets.[3] New Deal infrastructures built

---

[1] Ronald Reagan, "Address to Members of the British Parliament," June 8, 2022, *Ronald Reagan Presidential Library & Museum*, www.reaganlibrary.gov/archives/speech/address-members-british-parliament.

[2] Ray C. Fair, *U.S. Infrastructure: 1929–2019*, July 31, 2019, COWLES FOUNDATION DISCUSSION PAPER NO. 2187, July 2019, Available at SSRN: https://ssrn.com/abstract=3432670 or http://dx.doi.org/10.2139/ssrn.3432670.

[3] PETER K. EISINGER, THE RISE OF THE ENTREPRENEURIAL STATE: STATE AND LOCAL DEVELOPMENT POLICY IN THE UNITED STATES 68–9 (1988): "Combined with rising inflation and a sluggish economy, these diverse factors converged to brake the growth of federal aid to state governments, a trend that had scarcely wavered since the depression. The process was accelerated during the first Reagan administration, so that by 1983 the real value of intergovernmental dollars had fallen by 25 percent, the number of aid programs had declined to 405, and federal grants fallen from 17 percent of all federal outlays to 11.4 percent..."

fifty years before were nearing the end of their useful life just at the moment when state and local governments were tasked with doing more with less federal aid. In Ray C. Fair's recent assessment: "[T]he infrastructure results combined with the results for the government budget deficit suggest that the United States became less future oriented, less concerned with future generations, beginning about 1970. This change has persisted. The roughly monotonic decline in infrastructure as a percent of GDP since 1970 is remarkable. The government began consuming more relative to its income and investing less around 1970."[4] Although Fair is interpreting economic data here, it is clear that there is more at stake than bare economic investment. The decline in federal infrastructure investment has become a metric of the nation's priorities, political commitments, and faith in its future. For many thinking about infrastructure today, those priorities seem to have been misaligned for decades, focused on short-term growth rather than on long-term planning and collective action.

The drop-off in federal investment beginning in the 1970s brought infrastructure to the public's attention. At the bicentennial, the American Public Works Association invited us to recall that "[t]he vast network of public works facilities which extends from coast to coast provides the life-support systems for the most productive nation in the world."[5] Soon after Ronald Reagan took office, politicians and experts took to the stage to make the case for renewed infrastructure investment.[6] In 1981, the Council of State Planning Agencies issued a report turned into a book with the title *America in Ruins: Beyond the Public Works Pork Barrel*, which received positive reviews from mainstream media outlets. Seymour Melman, a professor of industrial engineering, reviewed the report in a piece titled "Looting the Means of Production," and noted the decline in national infrastructure investment in favor of more investment in military hardware.[7]

America in Ruins lays out a dire case for the state of America's infrastructure in the early 1980s: "America's public facilities are wearing out faster than they are

---

[4] Fair, "U.S. Infrastructure," *supra* note 2, at 26.
[5] *History of Public Works in the United States* (1976).
[6] HENRY PETROSKI, THE ROAD TAKEN: THE HISTORY AND FUTURE OF AMERICA'S INFRASTRUCTURE (2016), 13–15; National Council on Public Works Improvement, FRAGILE FOUNDATIONS: A REPORT ON AMERICA'S PUBLIC WORKS 1 (U.S. Government Printing Office, 1988). ("The quality of a nation's infrastructure is a critical index of its economic vitality. Reliable transportation, clean water, and safe disposal of wastes are basic elements of civilized society and a productive economy. Their absence or failure introduces an intolerable dimension of risk and hardship to everyday life, and a major obstacle to growth and competitiveness.")
[7] Seymour Melman, *Looting the Means of Production*, NEW YORK TIMES, July 26, 1981: E21. When the authors reissued the book two years later, they had made a telling change to its title: it was now *America in Ruins: The Decaying Infrastructure*, without the reference to the "public works pork barrel." Changing the title from "pork barrel" in 1981 to "decaying infrastructure" in 1983 signals an important shift in focus. Infrastructure would now reflect the more positive attitude and a move away from boondoggles, waste, and other longstanding republican themes in public works politics. I am grateful to Petrowski for noting this subtle shift in phraseology. PAT CHOATE & SUSAN WALTER, AMERICA IN RUINS: BEYOND THE PUBLIC WORKS PORK BARREL (1981); PAT CHOATE & SUSAN WALTER, AMERICA IN RUINS: THE DECAYING INFRASTRUCTURE (1983); AMERICA'S INFRASTRUCTURE: AN AGENDA FOR THE 1980S (1984).

being replaced. The deteriorated condition of the basic facilities that underpin the economy presents a major structural barrier to the renewal of national economy. In hundreds of communities, deteriorated public facilities threaten the continuation of basic community services such as fire protection, public transportation, water supplies, secure prisons, and flood protection."[8] A partial list of the systems in need of repair in the early 1980s included: Eisenhower's "deteriorating" interstate highway system, nonurban highways, bridges, railroads, municipal water supplies, water pollution control standards, public works in several major cities (including New York, Cleveland, and Dallas); jails, water resource development, dams, and other public works.[9] The phrase "our crumbling infrastructure" begins to circulate in the 1980s to describe a sense of decline among liberals in the shadow of their defeat and demoralization.[10]

In 1983, Congress established the National Council on Public Works, which was tasked with reporting over the next five years on the state of the nation's infrastructure. In 1988, the council framed its final report to the president, "Fragile Foundations," in the language of historical memory and national patrimony:

> The Eerie Canal; the transcontinental railroads; the great dams and water systems of the west; the airports, seaports, and transit systems that serve our cities; our network of modern highway and soaring bridges—all these are part of this country's great public works inheritance from the generations of Americans who built before us. These massive and sometimes daring achievements supported the growth of the greatest economic power the world has ever known. They have been the envy of other countries and the model for our competitors. Now that inheritance is in danger.[11]

In the midst of our perennial debates over fiscal politics, many have looked to the New Deal as a source of inspiration, a reminder of the possibilities that lie in concerted government action in the public good. More recently, writing for *Smithsonian Magazine*, for example, Andrea Stone pointed readers to the sense of beauty, wonder, and monumentality of New Deal vision:

> Long before "stimulus" became a dirty word in some quarters of Washington, the federal government put people to work building things. Lots of things....The WPA built, improved or renovated 39,370 schools; 2,550 hospitals; 1,074 libraries; 2,700 firehouses; 15,100 auditoriums, gymnasiums and recreational buildings; 1,050 airports, 500 water treatment plants, 12,800 playgrounds, 900 swimming pools; 1,200 skating rinks, plus many other structures. It also dug more than 1,000 tunnels; surfaced 639,000 miles of roads and installed nearly 1 million miles of sidewalks,

---

[8] Choate & Walter, *America in Ruins: The Decaying Infrastructure*, supra note 7, at 1.
[9] Id. at 1–3; *see also* B. Drummond Ayres, Jr., *Public Facilities Held Facing Crisis*, NEW YORK TIMES, Sept. 11, 1981: A17.
[10] *See*, for example, Joan C. Szabo, *Our Crumbling Infrastructure*, NATION'S BUS. 16, 16–24 (Aug. 1989).
[11] NATIONAL COUNCIL ON PUBLIC WORKS IMPROVEMENT, FRAGILE FOUNDATIONS: A REPORT ON AMERICA'S PUBLIC WORKS 1 (U.S. Government Printing Office, 1988).

curbs and street lighting, in addition to tens of thousands of viaducts, culverts and roadside drainage ditches.[12]

The infrastructure catalogue carries us back to the monumental ambition of the past and contrasts that with the shrunken horizons of the present, and the sense you get from this work is that past greatness should guide modern politics. Infrastructure is now, as always, a material link between citizens and government, tying local goods and services to a larger network of capitalism, state, and a normative vision of politics. However, the growing prestige of the New Deal in today's political discourse is built on a search for historical precedent.

The case for infrastructure has always been both obvious (because infrastructure, by whatever name, is a precursor for a functioning modern society) and controversial (because it implicates the politics of finance, taxation, legal norms, environmental, and other concerns). One way to square the circle of fiscal concerns of big government and debt on the one hand and markets on the other has been through the politics of growth. Infrastructure's best centrist case as an object of public investment lies in economic growth and development, supplying a foundation or precursor to other activities that are considered valuable, such as innovation, trade, jobs, etc. Policy debates in the 1980s reveal the abiding connections between infrastructure and the postwar politics of growth, innovation and productivity : "The nation's long-term economic growth will depend heavily on the adequacy of its public works infrastructure. In the past several years, much attention – both public and Congressional – has been drawn to the declining condition of infrastructure systems and to those systems' capacity to accommodate future economic and population growth...."[13] Economists continue to debate the effects of infrastructure on

---

[12] Andrea Stone, *When America Built Infrastructure, These Beautiful Landmarks Were the Result,* SMITHSONIAN MAGAZINE, DECEMBER 10, 2014; *see also* THE LIVING NEW DEAL, https://livingnewdeal.org/; *Opinion: "Boondoggles" Helped to Build America,* NEW YORK TIMES, Nov. 11, 1982, Section A, Page 30 ("With unemployment now at the highest point in 42 years, the Democrats have proposed a public-works program to upgrade our crumbling infrastructure. It is reported, however, that President Reagan is still firmly opposed to any such Government 'make-work' programs.... Are we hearing echoes of their Republican counterparts of the New Deal era, who labeled W.P.A. and related public-works programs as 'boondoggling'? These W.P.A., C.W.A. and P.W.A. 'boondoggles' were responsible for 10 percent of all new roads in America, 35 percent of all new hospitals, 70 percent of all new schools. They created water-supply and flood-control systems, sewers, ports and bridges. They built the Lincoln Tunnel, the Triborough Bridge and Boulder Dam. It was a time when the President of the United States understood that jobs, and not admonitions to 'stay the course,' were needed to restore self-reliance"); *see also* ROBERT D. LEIGHNINGER, JR., LONG-RANGE PUBLIC INVESTMENT: THE FORGOTTEN LEGACY OF THE NEW DEAL (2007); Theda Skocpol, *Legacies of New Deal Liberalism,* 30 DISSENT 33, 33–34 (1983).

[13] CITIES AND THEIR VITAL SYSTEMS: INFRASTRUCTURE, PAST, PRESENT AND FUTURE (Jesse H. Ausubel & Robert Herman, eds., 1988); *see also* William R. Thompson, AMERICAN GLOBAL PRE-EMINENCE: THE DEVELOPMENT AND EROSION OF SYSTEMIC LEADERSHIP 139 (2022) ("Putting aside public safety concerns, infrastructure investment is critical to keeping an economy functioning. The problem is that old bridges, roads, and equipment keep working until they fail.

other economic fundamentals in the United States and around the world.[14] Labor economists point to the number of jobs at stake in infrastructure or related fields.[15] The American Society for Civil Engineers' latest report provides a $5.9 trillion price tag for infrastructure investment.[16] While it is important to note that each of these groups will have their own biases and interests in play for more infrastructure investment, nevertheless more infrastructure spending has been a persistent political theme since the 1980s.

Since the 1980s, privatization and market politics have played an important role in how we argue over infrastructure. Privatization serves as a battlefield where we compete over different normative conceptions of the public good. The general erosion of the public–private divide after the New Deal, the refurbished virtues of corporate capitalism, and the pressure on state and local budgets suggested "public–private partnerships" as a new direction for infrastructure governance. In part, this followed a global trend toward privatization beginning in the 1970s.[17] In the United States, Reagan appointees rewrote administrative regulations to ensure a maximum of "outsourcing" and contracting out of public services to the private sector. During Reagan's first term, the Office of Management and Budget (OMB) updated its Circular A-76, a guidance document for federal procurement policy. The Circular, which had been in place in various forms since the 1950s, sets guidelines for the federal government on how much government work should be outsourced to the private sector: "In the process of governing, the Government should not compete with its citizens. The competitive enterprise system, characterized by individual freedom and initiative, is the primary source of national economic strength. In recognition of this principle, it has been and continues to be the general policy of the Government to rely on commercial sources to supply the products and services the Government needs." In the 1990s, Democrats developed these themes into a program of more efficient government, largely embracing the Reagan revolution as a *fait accompli*.[18] Sidney M. Levy's *Build, Operate, Transfer: Paving the Way for*

This phenomenon encourages decision makers to put off what most observers would acknowledge as necessary investments in sustaining the future of economic activities.")

[14] See, for example, Jeffrey M. Stupak, *Economic Impact of Infrastructure Investment*, CONGRESSIONAL RESEARCH SERVICE, Jan. 24, 2018.

[15] See, for example, *Infrastructure Alternatives for 2005: Employment and Occupations*, MONTHLY LABOR REVIEW, Vol. 117, No. 4 (Apr. 1994): 22–28.

[16] American Society of Civil Engineers lists "surface transportation, drinking water/waste water/storm water, electricity, airports, inland waterways & marine ports, dams, hazardous & solid waste, levees, public parks & recreation, and schools" as its core infrastructure categories. American Society of Civil Engineers, *A Comprehensive Assessment of America's Infrastructure*, 2021 REPORT CARD FOR AMERICA'S INFRASTRUCTURE, 6.

[17] Asli Bâli & Aziz Rana, *Constitutionalism and the American Imperial Imagination*, 85 U. CH. L. REV. 257, 277–79 (2018).

[18] AL GORE, NAT'L PERFORMANCE REVIEW, EXECUTIVE SUMMARY: FROM RED TAPE TO RESULTS; CREATING A GOVERNMENT THAT WORKS BETTER AND COSTS LESS (1993).

Tomorrow's Infrastructure (1996), to take another example from the 1990s, answered the crumbling infrastructure question with a call for more private sector involvement with the provision of infrastructure.[19]

But despite the Reagan restoration and the push for privatization, the troubling question of governance norms remain, and privatization remains controversial. In the early days it was not immediately clear if there was any infrastructure that could not be privatized. The post office? Airports? State parks? These questions will likely remain continuing sources of political controversy, as the question of what is "public" implicates competing political ideologies and complex fiscal questions. One challenge of privatization at scale, however, is public opinion and deep-seated republican norms that government should be responsible to the public at large, as well as wariness at allowing too much control over public things to private parties. It turns out that concepts such as the "public interest," which animated earlier generations, have not quite disappeared in the years since. In the heady days of the 1990s tech boom, for example, many began to worry about accountability to the public and promoted many different solutions to privatization of public goods. Labor unionists have been some of the most vocal critics of privatization, with the argument that contracting out tends to weaken the power of unions with employment of temporary contractors rather than employees with job protections. Scholars and policy analysts have continued to grapple with the privatization phenomenon today, a debate that will likely continue.[20]

Moreover, infrastructure itself continues to contain ambiguities, which reflects modern political ideologies as well as the reach of new technologies. The Congressional Budget Office (CBO) published a report in 1983 that reflected the themes that had become common across the country in the Reagan years, when policy advocates began their calls for more spending on infrastructure. The report provides a fairly standard definition of "public works infrastructure" as "highways, public transit systems, wastewater treatment works, water resources, air traffic control, airports, and municipal water supply." However, it adds in a footnote that this list could also include "social facilities as schools, hospitals, and prisons...."[21] Here we see the two senses of infrastructure from Cold War modernization and development discourse, one that identifies hard facilities with obvious utility for the conduct

---

[19] SIDNEY M. LEVY, BUILD, OPERATE, TRANSFER: PAVING THE WAY FOR TOMORROW'S INFRASTRUCTURE (1996).

[20] *See*, for example, Chiara Cordelli, THE PRIVATIZED STATE (2020); U.S. GEN. ACCOUNTABILITY OFFICE, FEDERAL-AID HIGHWAYS: INCREASED RELIANCE ON CONTRACTORS CAN POSE OVERSIGHT CHALLENGES FOR FEDERAL AND STATE OFFICIALS 1 (2008); MARTHA MINOW, PARTNERS NOT RIVALS: PRIVATIZATION AND THE PUBLIC GOOD (2002); ELLIOTT D. SCLAR, YOU DON'T ALWAYS GET WHAT YOU PAY FOR: THE ECONOMICS OF PRIVATIZATION (2000); Michal Laurie Tingal, *Privatization and the Reagan Administration: Ideology and Application*, 6 YALE LAW AND POLICY REVIEW 229 (1988).

[21] PUBLIC WORKS INFRASTRUCTURE: POLICY CONSIDERATIONS FOR THE 1980S (Congressional Budget Office, 1983).

of everyday life and others that are classified as "social facilities," which potentially imply contentious normative disagreement (e.g., do we need prisons in the same way we need transportation infrastructure?). In this sense, then, there is bound to be at least some disagreement about definitions of infrastructure because there is not a clear answer to the dilemma of what is "economic" and what is "social" and how they are linked together in an agreed-upon sense of development. I would like to suggest here that this division gives us a glimpse of infrastructure as a modern political ideology, a tension with different visions of fiscal politics, federalism, and attitudes toward government at its center.

Brett Frischmann makes the economic case in *Infrastructure: The Social Value of Shared Resources* (2012) that infrastructure should be viewed through the lens of the commons and reminds us of what many have argued since the time of Adam Smith that infrastructure has "been an important factor in the prosperity and growth of human civilization and [is] integral to modern society."[22] Frischmann also provides an extended discussion of "nontraditional infrastructures," in which he includes the environment and ecosystems, including "cultural, economic, and social" systems. Frischmann's case is that infrastructure produces numerous "positive externalities," which nevertheless "may not be as easy to identify, discuss, quantify, and appreciate" as private goods.[23] Moreover, Frischmann expands the category of infrastructure to include "intellectual infrastructure," which he defines as "basic research, ideas, general purpose technologies, and languages, creates benefits for society primarily by facilitating a wide range of downstream productive activities, including information production, innovation, and the development of products and services, as well as education, community building and interaction, democratic participation, socialization, and many other socially valuable activities."[24] This sense of infrastructure points us back to the social liberalism and modernization discourse of the 1950s and 1960s, updated with a sophisticated argument based in welfare economics to replace concepts such as "social" that had fallen into disrepute in the years since. It also reminds us that the case for commons and collective goods can be fought out on the terrain of economic utility.

---

[22] Brett Frischmann, Infrastructure: The Social Value of Shared Resources 211 (2012); *see also* Eric Klinenberg's Palaces for the People: How Social Infrastructure Can Help Fight Inequality, Polarization, and the Decline of Civic Life 15 (2018) is a useful guide to the democratic sense of "social infrastructure" that is being revived by the liberalism of our times: "What counts as social infrastructure? I define it capaciously. Public institutions, such as libraries, schools, playgrounds, parks, athletic fields, and swimming pools, are vital parts of the social infrastructure. So too are sidewalks, courtyards, community gardens, and other green spaces that invite people into the public realm. Community organizations, including churches and civic associations, act as social infrastructures when they have an established physical space where people can assemble, as do regularly scheduled markets for food, furniture, clothing, art, and other consumer goods."

[23] Frischmann, Infrastructure, *supra* note 22, at 238.

[24] *Id.* at 253.

At the most general level, perhaps we can say that social liberals will want to broaden the category of infrastructure in ways that fit within their vision of good government as an agent of advance. Fiscal conservatives, on the other hand, may worry that infrastructure is just a "gobbledygook" term for pork barrel, tax-and-spend politics, and a displacement of the private sector by government. In fact, infrastructure is often used as a proxy for concepts such as community or public interest that had grounded the mid-century social democratic project. However, it is worth noting that the social meaning of infrastructure in government discourse has until fairly recently taken a back seat to technology, commerce, and hard infrastructures, always with an emphasis on economic development or utility. Take for example the platform of the Democratic party since infrastructure became a major theme in the 1980s. In 1980, the party platform refers to infrastructure in its two familiar senses, both as hard infrastructure through public works programs and as social programs that build on a "community's unique infrastructure, resources, and support networks."[25] The 1984 platform leans heavily on the term, blaming the Reagan administration for "neglected" infrastructure and making infrastructure investment a major item on their agenda.[26]

The 1988 Democratic party platform speaks of "helping states build a strong child care infrastructure" among more traditional hard infrastructure themes.[27] In 1992, the platform makes a passing mention of "a national public works investment and infrastructure program" but by 2000, we are talking about bridging the digital divide, rural development, and an "information infrastructure" to spread development around the networked globe.[28] The elasticity of "infrastructure" would soon expand across the digital age to encompass a new sense of a networked society. Moreover, the attack on the World Trade Center on September 11, 2001, and subsequent events, made infrastructures "critical," lending new weight to the concept in public discourse.[29] The year 2004 brought new themes of energy independence but also called for international aid so that Iraqis could see "the tangible benefits of reconstruction: jobs, infrastructure, and services."[30]

The 2008 agenda looked back to the past for inspiration, folding infrastructure into a vision of Progressive era: "A century ago, Teddy Roosevelt called together leaders from business and government to develop a plan for the next century's infrastructure. It falls to us to do the same. Right now, we are spending less than at any time in recent history and far less than our international competitors on this critical

---

[25] 1980 Democratic Party Platform, www.presidency.ucsb.edu/documents/1980-democratic-party-platform.
[26] 1984 Democratic Party Platform, www.presidency.ucsb.edu/documents/1984-democratic-party-platform.
[27] 1988 Democratic Party Platform, www.presidency.ucsb.edu/documents/1988-democratic-party-platform.
[28] 1992 Democratic Party Platform, www.presidency.ucsb.edu/documents/1992-democratic-party-platform; 2000 Democratic Party Platform, www.presidency.ucsb.edu/documents/2000-democratic-party-platform.
[29] See, for example, Kathi Ann Brown, "Critical Path: A Brief History of Critical Infrastructure Protection in the United States," Critical Infrastructure Protection Project, 2006, https://cip.gmu.edu/wp-content/uploads/2016/06/CIPHS_CriticalPath.pdf.
[30] 2004 Democratic Party Platform, www.presidency.ucsb.edu/documents/2004-democratic-party-platform.

component of our nation's strength."³¹ The platform calls for a national infrastructure bank, modernized power grid, high-speed rail, more investment in roads, bridges, schools, and public transport as well as wider broadband access to achieve "a connected America."³² In 2012 and 2016, Democrats were touting "the largest infrastructure investment since President Eisenhower" and promoting "green and resilient infrastructure," as well as promising to increase federal funding for state and local infrastructures.³³

However, conservatives have also acknowledged the infrastructure issue since the Reagan years, suggesting that it is a political theme with some enduring popular appeal: "The Republican Party believes that the nation's long-term economic growth will depend heavily on the adequacy of its public works infrastructure. We will continue to work to reverse the long-term decline that has occurred."³⁴ They also used the concept metaphorically to refer to the "infrastructure of democratic capitalism so essential to economic growth" and "the infrastructure of democracy," following Ronald Reagan's Cold War sense of the term. By 1988, the GOP asks for waiver "Davis-Bacon wage requirements for cities with severe deterioration of the public infrastructure," focusing on labor costs for federal projects and advocating for more privatization.³⁵ Public–private partnerships become a more prominent theme from the 1990s to the present.

President Biden's infrastructure legislation has placed America's perennial infrastructure politics back on the national agenda again. The Infrastructure Investments and Jobs Act, which passed in November 2021, represents the culmination of themes circulating since the 1980s, and the legislation foregrounds investment in the classic menu of hard infrastructures (e.g., transportation, energy, and digital networks). The progressive wing of the Democratic party, however, had wanted to expand the spending package to include soft infrastructure through "Build Back Better Act," which would have included much larger social spending investment and would have implicated the social sense of infrastructure. For example, Senator Bernie Sanders was a proponent of expanding the infrastructure concept to include "health care, education, climate change."³⁶ Elsewhere he urged the public to see infrastructure in the broader frame that social liberals and modernization theory had since the 1960s: "Now is the time to begin addressing our physical infrastructure as well as our human infrastructure. Let's get it done."³⁷

---

[31] 2008 Democratic Party Platform, www.presidency.ucsb.edu/documents/2008-democratic-party-platform.
[32] 2008 Democratic Party Platform, www.presidency.ucsb.edu/documents/2008-democratic-party-platform.
[33] 2012 Democratic Party Platform, www.presidency.ucsb.edu/documents/2012-democratic-party-platform; 2016 Democratic Party Platform, www.presidency.ucsb.edu/documents/2016-democratic-party-platform.
[34] 1984 Republican Party Platform, www.presidency.ucsb.edu/documents/1984-republican-party-platform.
[35] 1988 Republican Party Platform, www.presidency.ucsb.edu/documents/1988-republican-party-platform.
[36] Bernie Sanders (@SenSanders), TWITTER (Sept, 2, 2021, 7:28 PM), https://twitter.com/sensanders/status/1433572638014640128?lang=en.
[37] Bernie Sanders (@SenSanders), TWITTER (Apr. 6, 2021, 11:00 AM), https://twitter.com/berniesanders/status/1379448812146679809.

The recent infrastructure debate has inspired commentators to search for historical precedent and definitions. Binyamin Applebaum of the *New York Times* notes the 1982 use of "infrastructure" in Reagan's speech before Parliament and what appeared as a sudden revival in 2021, as well as the fact that liberals and conservatives were divided over its definition: "President Biden has proposed a $2 trillion infrastructure plan that includes money for 'community college infrastructure,' for care programs for older and disabled Americans and for electric-car charging stations. Republicans insist that none of this counts as infrastructure. They propose to spend a smaller amount of money on 'real' infrastructure like roads and bridges."[38] Conservative news outlets have criticized the Biden infrastructure plan and its broad definition of infrastructure, reasserting the role of the private sector in creating it.[39] The historical record suggests a more complicated picture of a very elastic concept that shifts over time and in different contexts. As this book has been chronicling, there is no natural boundary between public and private sectors, as much public government activity is undertaken through private contractors, and much commercial activity takes place on infrastructures that have been subsidized or created by governments. The debate over definitions is really a debate over different visions of the relations between citizen and state and between business and government.

While infrastructure spending remains popular with the public, questions of historical precedent hang heavily over our contemporary infrastructure discourse and likely will for the foreseeable future.[40] Journalists and commentators began comparing Biden's ambitious infrastructure agenda to the New Deal and to Lyndon Johnson's Great Society for its vision of federal investment in both hard and soft infrastructure. The historian David B. Woolner praised Biden for wanting to "go big on infrastructure" and reminded his readers that the contemporary debate between liberals and conservatives over the meaning of infrastructure had historical precedent in the New Deal. Woolner criticizes as ahistorical the narrow view of infrastructure that limits the meaning to hard facilities: "But this narrow definition of infrastructure and fear of public investment in multiple facets of the U.S. economy at a time of great need does not square with the nation's history…. As Roosevelt demonstrated, the infrastructure of a nation is much more than paved roads or physical structures. It includes the social and economic well-being of its people and the building of a society that provides a clean environment and equal opportunity for

---

[38] Binyamin Applebaum, *Why the Meaning of "Infrastructure" Matters so Much*, NEW YORK TIMES, April 26, 2021.
[39] Nicole Gelinas, *Joe Biden's Magic Word*, THE WASHINGTON EXAMINER, April 29, 2021: "Until now, modern presidents have defined it as physical: dams, bridges, subway stations, school buildings. The White House wants to expand this definition to include everything from subsidizing electric cars to paying for home health aides. 'Infrastructure' now means just plain old 'spending' – quite a feat for a word that didn't even exist in the American lexicon until after World War II."
[40] Frank Newport, *American Public Opinion and Infrastructure Legislation*, GALLUP, July 2, 2021, https://news.gallup.com/opinion/polling-matters/351815/american-public-opinion-infrastructure-legislation.aspx.

all."[41] The Brookings Institute praised the infrastructure legislation as one step closer to a revived New Deal vision of social investment, while the *Washington Post* argues that Biden's goals would be relatively modest by the standards of the New Deal.[42]

Finally, the idea of "big government" has been in disrepute since the Reagan years, and bipartisan neoliberal politics since the 1990s promised us results judged by market metrics, only to have that equilibrium badly shaken by the financial crisis of 2008. One interesting feature of the Biden infrastructure plan is that it returns us to debates that would have seemed passé only a generation ago. Big government versus small government is our way of framing the issues raised by Biden's infrastructure investment plan. But this framing makes it difficult to see the more complex dynamics that have always been at play in American infrastructure politics. Nevertheless, while the journalist Paul Wald is being ironic when he writes in the *Washington Post* that "Infrastructure is a liberal plot to make you love big government," his joke is not far off the mark.[43] Wald praises Biden's plan for avoiding the sort of problems of corruption and privatization that plagued President Trump's infrastructure plan and lauds the Democrats for a positive vision of governance in the public good. The plan, as he notes, is liberal but in a sense that we can locate in the Progressive Era or the New Deal, precisely the sort of historical examples that American liberals have been evoking, now and again, since the Reagan era. Here is the sense of a confident liberalism embodied by Eisenhower's national highway system, the space program, and other ambitious nation-building projects of the past. All of this illustrates a familiar pattern in American political history, where old debates are remaindered for a time, only to be taken off the shelf and refurbished for present needs. Liberals will argue that "What America Needs Is a Liberalism That Builds," while conservatives will criticize mission creep and boondoggles.[44] Certain issues seem settled, only to return in different form, with a recycled vocabulary repurposed for the present, but bearing the traces of past controversies within them.

---

[41] David B. Woolner, *Biden Wants to Go Big on Infrastructure: History Says That's the Right Call*, THE WASHINGTON POST, Apr. 7, 2021; *see also* Peter A. Schulman, *What Infrastructure Really Means*, THE ATLANTIC, July 13, 2021; Paul Krugman, *Opinion: Republicans Are Mired in Concrete*, NEW YORK TIMES, Apr. 5, 2021; Jim Tankersley & Jeanna Smialek, *Biden Plan Spurs Fight Over What "Infrastructure" Really Means*, NEW YORK TIMES, Apr. 5, 2021.

[42] Adie Tomer, *The Senate Infrastructure Bill Puts America Closer to Another New Deal*, Brookings, Aug. 5, 2021, www.brookings.edu/blog/the-avenue/2021/08/05/the-senate-infrastructure-bill-puts-america-closer-to-another-new-deal/; Andrew Van Dam, *Is It Fair to Call Biden's $3.5 Trillion Plan another New Deal?*, THE WASHINGTON POST, Oct. 2, 2021.

[43] Paul Waldman, *Opinion: Infrastructure Is a Liberal Plot to Make You Love Big Government*, WASHINGTON POST, Nov. 9, 2021.

[44] Ezra Klein, *Opinion: What America Needs Is a Liberalism That Builds*, NEW YORK TIMES, May 29, 2022; David Blackmon, *Infrastructure Bill Implements Green New Deal Via Corporate Welfare*, FORBES Aug. 10, 2021.

Index

Acheson, Dean, 187–88
Adams, John Quincy, 66, 82–83
Administrative Procedure Act, U.S. (1946), 182–83
The Administrative Process (Landis), 182
America in Ruins, 31, 200–201
American Notes on General Circulation (Dickens), 55
Angell, Joseph, 89–90
antebellum era. *See also* turnpikes; *specific topics*
   canal-building during, 111–12
   laissez-faire capitalism during, 18–19
   market revolution of, 18
   turnpikes during, 97–110
Anti-Federalists, 73–74
   arguments over federal power, 64–65
Applebaum, Binyamin, 208
Appleton, John, 147–48
Army Corps of Engineers, 83

Balogh, Brian, 19
Bank of England, 122–23
banking systems. *See also* monetary systems; *specific banks*
   Bank of England and, 122–23
   Deposit and Distribution Act of 1836, 121–22
   Hamilton and
      First Bank of the United States, 70
      Republican opponents of, 70–71
   pet banks, 121–22
   Second Bank of the United States, 81–82
   soft currency in, 121–22
   state banks
      federal bailout of, 124
      growth of, 122
barter economy, 50
Bayard, James A., 76

Bell, Alexander Graham, 161
Bentham, Jeremy, 20–21, 30–31
   on agenda/non-agenda of the state, 37, 181
Benton, Thomas Hart, 123–24
Biddle, Andrew, 121–22
Biden, Joe, 7, 207–208
   Build Back Better Act, 207
   Infrastructure Investments and Jobs Act, 32, 207
Black, Jeremiah S. (Chief Justice), 129–30
Blackstone, William, 22, 27, 38, 93
Bonus Bill, U.S. (1817), 81–82
Booth, Henry J., 30, 151–55
Bowles, Chester Bliss, 195–96
Brewer, John, 63–64
Build, Operate, Transfer (Levy), 203–204
Build Back Better Act, U.S. (2021), 207

C. Knight v. Carrolton Railroad Company, 89
Calhoun, John C., 81–82
Calvo, Christopher, 36–37
canals
   during antebellum era, 111–12
   Erie Canal, 41, 111–12, 118, 192, 201
   in Tenth Census, 134–36
capital. *See* social overhead capital
capitalism. *See* laissez-faire capitalism
Carse, Ashley, 2
CEA. *See* Council of Economic Advisers
Charles River Bridge v. Warren Bridge, 109, 117
Chicago School, 20–21, 36–37
City of Clinton v. Cedar Rapids & M.R.R. Co., 153–54
Civil War, conflict between federal and state governments during, 136
Clarksville & Hopkinsville Turnpike v. T.W. Atkinson, 100

classical liberalism
  corporations and, 52
  definition of, 33
  infrastructure and, 34–35, 52
    competitive, 53–54
    neoclassical fallacy, 37
    police and, 35–46
  in *Wealth of Nations*, 33–46, 54
Clay, Henry, 78, 81
Clinton, DeWitt, 96
Cold War, expansion of infrastructure during, 36–37, 173, 185–97
  government role in, 195
  international involvement in, 187–88
    Common Infrastructure Programme, 187, 188
    as military aid, 189
    SUNFED, 192–94
  Marshall Plan, 31, 173, 186
  modernization theory and, 191–92
  during 1960s, 197
  during 1970s, 197–200
  during 1980s, 199–206
    privatization of infrastructure, 203–204
    under Reagan, 199, 202–204, 207
  public interest and, 197–98
  public utility reform during, 185–86
collective social life, infrastructure as symbol of, 8
Commentaries on the Laws of England (Blackstone), 22, 27, 38, 93
commerce, in *Wealth of Nations*, 40
Commerce Clause, in Fourteenth Amendment, 141, 155–60
  New Deal legislation and, 182
  railroad industry, 158–60
  telegraph industry, 156–57
common good, 164–65. See also public good
Common Infrastructure Programme (NATO), 187, 188
Commonwealth v. Alger, 38–39
Commonwealth v. George Wilkinson, 105
Commonwealth v. Worcester Turnpike Corporation, 106
competition, Smith, A., on, 35
competitive infrastructure, 53–54
Conklin v. Elting, 104
Constitution, U.S., infrastructure development under. *See also* Fourteenth Amendment
  arguments over, 56, 59
  Articles of Federation, 65
  Commerce Clause, 81–82
  Convention of 1787, 62
  Federalist readings of, 60–66
  Federalists and, 60–66
  General Welfare Clause, 81–82
  Necessary and Proper Clause, 72–73
  political battle over, 71–75
    for public works, 71, 73–74
  Postal Clause, 157
  Preamble, 65
  purpose of, 61–62
  small-state, 60
  Supremacy Clause, 65
  Takings Clause, 99–100
  under Tenth Amendment, 115
Constitutional Coup (Michael), 11–12
Continental Dollar, 56
Cooley, Thomas, 131–32, 136, 144, 146–48
core infrastructure, 1–2
corporate welfare, infrastructure investment as, 5–6
corporations
  classical liberalism and, 52
  infrastructure investment as corporate welfare, 5–6
  investment in turnpikes, 93–94
  Smith, A., on, 51–54
  in state infrastructures, 162–63
Corwin, Edward Samuel, 175
Council of Economic Advisers (CEA), 185–86
Crash of 1929, 181
credit clauses, 126
critical infrastructure, 3–4
  sectors of, 4
"crumbling" infrastructure, 7–8
Curtis, Benjamin, 111, 125
Curtis, Thomas, 196–97

Dartmouth College v. Woodward, 117
Darwin, Charles, 18
Dash v. Van Kleeck, 116–17
De Jure Maris (Hale, M.), 90
debt, sovereign
  Hamilton on
    debtor states, 69–71
    public finance and, 68–70
    Treasury bonds and, 70
  Smith, A., on, 46–51
    growth of debt, 49
    mercantile system and, 48–49
debt repudiation, 117–25
  by state, 120–21

debtor states, 69–71
Declaration of Independence, 33
  Wealth of Nations and, 57
democracy. *See also* classical liberalism; liberalism
  infrastructure as symbol of, 9
  road-building authority and, 94–97
Democracy in America (Tocqueville), 55
Deposit and Distribution Act of 1936, U.S., 121–22
Dicey, A. V., 175–76
Dickens, Charles, 55
Dirksen, Everett McKinley, 189
Donohue, Kathleen G., 19
Douglas, William O., 185–86
Dove, John A., 28, 118–19
Due Process Clause, in Fourteenth Amendment, 137, 140, 142–45, 150
Durfee, Thomas, 89–90

Easterly, William, 197
economic-social infrastructure, 193
Edison, Thomas, 161
Edling, Max M., 19, 61–62
Ely, Richard, 162–64, 172–73
Embargo Act of 1807, U.S., 76
eminent domain, Ohio Turnpike Statute of 1840 and, 99–100
Enabling Act, U.S. (1801), 76–77
Equal Protection Clause, in Fourteenth Amendment, 137, 145
Erie Canal, 41, 111–12, 118, 192, 201

Fair, Ray C., 199–200
Federalists
  Constitution and, 60–66
  on federal power, 64–65
  on road-building authority, 58, 59
Ferguson, Homer S., 189–90
Ferguson, Scott, 51
Fine, Sidney, 17, 143
First Bank of the United States, 70, 118
First Report on Public Credit (Hamilton), 67
Folmsbee, Stanley J., 94–95
Foucault, Michel, 13
Fourteenth Amendment, U.S. Constitution, infrastructural development and, 136–45
  Commerce Clause, 141, 155–60
    New Deal legislation and, 182
    railroad industry, 158–60
    telegraph industry, 156–57
  Due Process Clause, 137, 140, 142–45, 150
  Equal Protection Clause, 137, 145

laissez-faire economics under, 142–45
License Cases, 140
Munn v. Illinois, 139–42
police power under, 141
Privileges and Immunities Clause, 137
property rights under, 167
Slaughterhouse Cases, 137–39
Fragile Foundations, 31
Frankfurter, Felix, 176
Freedom through Law (Hale, R. L.), 184–85
Freund, Ernst, 136, 144, 176
Frischmann, Brett, 205

Gallatin, Albert, 26, 46, 78, 80–81, 92
Gallatin Plan, for U.S. infrastructure
  components of, 79–80
  infrastructural nationalism as element of, 79
  Report of the Secretary of the Treasury on the Subject of Public Roads and Canals, 78
  road-building authority under, 78–81
General Survey Act, U.S. (1824), 83
Gibbons v. Ogden, 138
Gilmore, Joshua, 106
Goodrich, Carter, 183–84
governance
  money as state project of, 50
  Smith, A., on, 46–51
  stakeholder theory of, 48
Governing the American State (Johnson, K.), 17
The Government and the Economy (Goodrich), 184
government debt. *See* debt
A Government Out of Sight (Balogh), 19
Granger Laws, 139
Green, Theodore Francis, 188
Green New Deal, 6
Gruenther, Alfred, 169, 188
Guldi, Jo, 35
Gunderson, Gerald, 87

Hale, Matthew, 90
Hale, Robert Lee, 179, 180, 184–85
Hall, Aaron, 81
Hamilton, Alexander, 25–26, 46, 49, 169
  banking systems and
    First Bank of the United States, 70
    Republican opponents of, 70–71
  Bayard and, 76
  First Report on Public Credit, 67
  on government/sovereign debt
    debtor states, 69–71

Hamilton, Alexander (cont.)
  public finance and, 68–70
  Treasury bonds and, 70
  on infrastructural investment, 134
  on laissez-faire capitalism, 66
  on nation-building, 67–71
  on "necessary and proper" clause, 72–73
  on public finance, 57, 59–60
    government/sovereign debt, 68–70
    monetary systems, 50, 63–65, 68–69
    public borrowing, 68
    reforms on, 66–71
    Treasury bonds, 70
  Report on a National Bank, 67
  Report on the Subject of Manufactures, 67
Harcourt, Bernard, 20–21
hard infrastructure, 42–43
Harrison, Benjamin, 60–61
Hartz, Benjamin, 183
Hartz, Louis, 56, 183
von Hayek, Friedrich, 184
Helvering v. Davis, 169, 182
Hepburn Act, U.S. (1906), 160
highways
  Law of Highways, 89–90
  road-building authority and, 89–90
  turnpikes as public highways, 96–97, 105
Hillhouse, A. M., 135
History of Public Works in the United States, 8–9
Hofstadter, Richard, 169
Hohfeld, Wesley Newcomb, 178–80
Holmes, Oliver Wendell, Jr., 177
Holt, Amos, 106
Hovenkamp, Herbert, 178
Hume, David, 47–48, 59–60, 63–64
Humphrey, Hubert, 192–93

ICC. *See* Interstate Commerce Commission
The Illusion of Free Markets (Harcourt), 20–21
In re Kensington Dist. Division, 108–109
infrastructural nationalism
  Gallatin Plan and, 79
  under Jackson, 85–86
infrastructure. *See also* New Deal; private investment; public infrastructure; Smith, Adam; United States; *specific topics*
  classical liberalism and, 34–35, 52
  competitive infrastructure and, 53–54
  core, 1–2
  critical, 3–4
    sectors of, 4

"crumbling," 7–8
definitions of, 1, 4, 34
  ambiguity in, 1–2
  scope of, 4–5
  traditional, 1
  as embodiment of state power, 16
  etymological origins of, 1–2
  fragility of, 7–8
  hard, 42–43
  human activity and, categories of, 3
  as metaphor, 3
  as national interest, 8–9
  origins of, 31
  physical, 2
  in policy discourse, 3–4
  in political contexts, 5–6, 32
    as corporate welfare, 5–6
    federal investment debates over, 5–6
    Green New Deal, 6
    for Progressives, 5–6
    public governance and, 5
  public capital and, 1–2
  public utilities and, 3
  public works, 3–5, 34
  regional, 2
  self-liquidating, 44, 35–46
  social overhead capital and, 8, 31
  soft, 42–43
  state role in, 17–22
  superstructure and, 2
  as symbol
    of collective social life, 8
    of democracy, 9
    of modernity, 15
Infrastructure (Frischmann), 205
Infrastructure for the 21st Century (National Research Council), 4
Infrastructure Investments and Jobs Act, U.S. (2021), 32, 207
infrastructure studies, 12–17
  Foucauldian approaches to, 13
Interstate Commerce Commission (ICC), 30, 160

Jackson, Andrew, 18–19
  First Bank of the United States and, 118
  road-building authority and, 84–85
  Second Bank of the United States and, 121–22
  U.S. infrastructural development under, 83–86
    expansion of transportation networks, 84–85
    infrastructural nationalism and, 85–86
    laissez-faire capitalism and, 84

James, Edmund J., 162
Jefferson, Thomas, 69–70
  Madison and, 73–74
  on "necessary and proper" clause, 72–73
  on Postal Clause, 157
  on public finance, 77
  on U.S. infrastructure
    establishment of, 71–75
    federal retrenchment of, 75–78
Jevons, William Stanley, 177
Johnson, Kimberly S., 17
Johnson, Lyndon, 208
Jones, Christopher, 9
Joshua Gilmore v. Amos Holt, 106
Judd, Walter Henry, 188
Judiciary Act of 1801, U.S., 75

Kelley, Oliver Hudson, 139
Keynes, John Maynard, 174, 180–81
Klein, Daniel B., 93, 94
Krock, Arthur, 189

Laissez Faire and the General Welfare State (Fine), 143
laissez-faire capitalism
  during antebellum period, 18–19
  decline of, 172–73
  under Fourteenth Amendment, 142–45
  Hamilton on, 66
  Jackson and, 84
  legal realism and, 178–79
  natural monopolies and, 162
  origins of, in U.S., 18
  during Progressive Era, 172–73
  property rights and, 179–80
  public utilities and, 162
  Smith, A., on, 36, 59–60, 66, 184
Land Ordinance of 1785, U.S., 61
Landis, James M., 182
Larkin, Brian, 15
Larson, John Lauritz, 18, 56, 58, 70–71
Law and Public Opinion in England (Dicey), 175–76
Law of Highways (Angell and Durfee), 89–90
Lectures on Jurisprudence (Smith, A.), 23
Lectures on Justice, Police, Revenue and Arms (Smith, A.), 37–40, 45–46
Lee, Timothy B., 87
legal realism, laissez-faire capitalism and, 178–79
Leigh, Susan, 14
Leighninger, Robert D., 171–72

Levy, Sidney M., 203–204
Lew, Jacob, 49
The Liberal Tradition in America (Hartz, L.), 183
liberalism. *See also* classical liberalism
  legal profession critiques of, 176
  during Progressive Era, 174–85
  road-building authority and, 89–91
  as tacit consent to government regulation, 89
License Cases, 140
Lochner v. New York, 139, 149
Locke, John, 21, 26–27, 175
  on road-building authority, 89
Long-Range Public Investment (Leighninger), 171–72

Machiavelli, Niccolò, 47
Macon, Nathaniel, 58–59
Madison, James, 62, 69–70
  Bonus Bill, 81–82
  Jefferson and, 73–74
Mandeville, Bernard, 35
Mann, Michael, 13–14
Mann-Elkins Act, U.S. (1910), 160
marginalism, 177–78
The Market Revolution (Larson), 18
Marshall, Alfred, 177
Marshall, John (Chief Justice), 73, 117
Marshall Plan, 31, 173, 186
Marx, Karl, 3
Mashaw, Jerry, 75–76
McCloskey, Robert, 175–76
McCulloch v. Maryland, 73
M'Clenachan v. Curwen, 99
McNamara, Peter, 67
Melman, Seymour, 200–201
Menger, Carl, 177
mercantile system, debt and, 48–49
Michael, Jon D., 11–12
Mill, John Stuart, 53, 174, 179
Minicucci, Stephen, 83, 86
modernity, infrastructure as symbol of, 15
modernization theory, 191–92
monetary systems
  Continental Dollar, 56
  Hamilton on, 50, 63–65, 68–69
  origins of, as state governance project, 50
  Smith, A., on, 50–51
    in barter economy, 50
    origins of, 49–50
  soft currency, 121–22

monopolies. *See also* natural monopolies
　perpetual, 51–52
Monroe, James, 41
Munn v. Illinois, 29, 131, 139–42, 158–59

National Research Council, 4
nationalism. *See* infrastructural nationalism
nation-building, 78–79
nation-states. *See* the state
NATO. *See* North Atlantic Treaty Organization
natural law constitution, 175
natural monopolies
　laissez-faire capitalism and, 162
　Smith, A., on, 24, 35, 51–54, 162
"necessary and proper" clause, 72–73
neoclassical fallacy, 37
New Deal, 169–72
　Commerce Clause and, 182
　historical coverage of, 169–70
　historical legacy of, 171–72, 201–202
　liberal response to, 169–70
　New Left response to, 170–71
　political success of, 170
　regulatory capture theories, 171
　scope of, 171–72
　social overhead capital and, 186–87
New Left, 170–71
North American Review, 125
North Atlantic Treaty Organization (NATO), 187, 188
Northwest Ordinance (1787), 89–90
Novak, William J., 19–20, 39, 57, 112–13
　on *salus populi* tradition, 152
　on state law reforms, 128

O'Brian, John Lord, 176
Of Commerce (Hume), 48
"Of Public Credit" (Hume), 47–48
Ohio Turnpike Statute of 1840, 97–110
　calculation of damages under, 100
　eminent domain arguments, 99–100
　freeholders and, 100–101
　"shunpiking" under, 102–103
　toll exemptions under, 101–103
On Socialism (Mill), 174

Paine, Thomas, 27, 95–96
Panic of 1837
　Bank of England and, 122–23
　crisis of infrastructure investment before, 121–23
　federal bailouts after, 124
　origins of, 113–14
　sovereign debt as factor in, 113–14
　state law reforms after, 125–26, 128
Parker, Isaac, 106
Parkersburg v. Brown, 149, 150
Parsons, Talcott, 191
pecuniary compensation, 132
Penn, William, 99
Pennsylvania Coal v. Mahon, 109–110
Pensacola Telegraph Company v. Western Union Telegraph Company, 30, 157
People ex. rel. Detroit & Howell Railroad v. Salem, 131–32, 145–46
The People v. Kingston and Middleton Turnpike Company, 107–108
The People's Welfare (Novak), 112–13
physical infrastructure, 2
Pierce, Franklin, 85–86
Pierson, George Wilson, 55
Poinsett, Joel Roberts, 55–56
police power
　Commonwealth v. Alger, 38–39
　under Fourteenth Amendment, 141
　Smith, A., on, 37–41
　economy and, 38–40
　evolution of, 45–46
　regulatory history of, 38–40
　turnpikes and, 106
The Police Power, Public Power and Constitutional Rights (Freund), 144
Postal Clause, U.S. Constitution, 157
Postal Service Act, U.S. (1792), 71, 73–74
Pound, Ezra, 14–15
Pound, Roscoe, 175–76
Prettyman v. Supervisors of Tazewell County, 130–31
Principle of Political Economy (Mill), 53
private investment, in infrastructure, 2–3, 17–22
　during Cold War, 203–204
　criticism of, 11–12
　during 1980s, 203–204
　public debate over, 10–11
　public–private partnership, 11, 34
　Smith, A., on, 35
private property. *See also* property rights
　turnpikes as, 96–97
Privileges and Immunities Clause, under Fourteenth Amendment, 137
Progressive Era
　infrastructural development during, 132–33
　laissez-faire capitalism during, 172–73

Progressive Party
  property rights and, 179–80
  on state infrastructure, arguments for, 5–6, 166–68
property rights
  under Fourteenth Amendment, 167
  laissez-faire capitalism and, 179–80
  Mill on, 179
  police power and, 38–39
  Progressives and, 179–80
  Smith, A., on, 24, 139
public benefit theory of government investment, 130
public borrowing, 68
public capital, infrastructure and, 1–2
public choice theories, 44
public economy, 37
public finance, Hamilton on, 57, 59–60
public finance mechanisms
  Hamilton on, 57, 59–60
    government/sovereign debt, 68–70
    monetary systems, 50, 63–65, 68–69
    public borrowing, 68
    reforms on public finance, 66–71
    Treasury bonds, 70
  Jefferson on, 77
the public good, 133, 136
public goods, 34
public governance, infrastructure and, 5
public infrastructure, 2–3, 17–22
  public–private partnership, 11, 34
    Smith, A., on, 35
public interest, infrastructure as
  during Cold War, 197–98
  states' role in, 161–66
public utilities
  infrastructure and, 3
  innovation of, 134–36
  laissez-faire capitalism and, 162
  public reaction to, 134–36
  reform approach to, 134–36
  reform of, during Cold War, 185–86
  Smith, A., on, 51–54
public utilities theory, 133, 161–66
  common good argument, 164–65
  pricing guide for utilities, 165–66
public works, 3–5, 34
  political battle over, 71, 73–74
  Smith, A., on, 40–41, 192, 193
public-private partnership, in infrastructure, 11, 34
  Smith, A., on, 35, 192
  for turnpikes, 87
    private property rights and, 96–97

railroad industry
  federal classification of, 142
  franchise rights for, 154
  under Granger Laws, 139
  Interstate Commerce Commission and, 160
  Munn v. Illinois, 29, 131, 139–42, 158–59
  pecuniary compensation and, 132
  regulation of, 158–60
  subsidies for, 147
  in Tenth Census, 134–36
  Treatise on the Law of Street Railways, 30
  Wabash, St. Louis & Pacific Railway Company v. Illinois, 158
Reagan, Ronald, 9, 199, 202–204, 207
regional infrastructure, 2
regulatory capture theories, 171
Reinecke, David, 9
The Relation of the Modern Municipality to the Gas Supply (James), 162
Report of the Secretary of the Treasury on the Subject of Public Roads and Canals (Gallatin), 26, 78
Report on a National Bank (Hamilton), 67
Report on the Subject of Manufactures (Hamilton), 67
republicanism, road-building authority and, 94–97
A Revolution in Favor of Government (Edling), 19
road-building authority, 57–60, 76–77. *See also* turnpikes
  expansion of transportation networks, 84–85
  Federalists and, 58, 59
  under Gallatin plan, 78–81
  highways, 89–90
  Jackson and, 84–85
  liberal governance and, 89–91
    tacit consent to government regulation, 89
  local democracy and, 94–97
  Locke on, 89
  under Northwest Ordinance, 89–90
  pecuniary compensation and, 132
  during privatization craze, 87
  publicness of, 90–91
  republicanism and, 94–97
  Smith, A., on, 91–92
Robbins, Bruce, 14–15
Roberts, Alasdair, 123
Roosevelt, Teddy, 206–207
Rostow, Walt Whitman, 31, 173, 191–92

salus populi tradition, 152
Sanders, Bernie, 7, 207

Savings and Loan Association v. City of Topeka, 132, 148–49
Scheiber, Harry, 135, 183
Schlesinger, Arthur, 169
Schumacher, Ernst, 197
Scott, James C., 13, 59
Second Bank of the United States, 81–82, 121–22
Second Treatise on Civil Government (Locke), 89
Sedgwick, Theodore, 130–31
seignorage, 46–47
self-liquidating infrastructure, 44, 35–46
  turnpikes as, 93, 94
Sen, Amartya, 36–37
Sharpless v. Mayor of Philadelphia, 128–29
Shaw, Lemuel (Justice), 38–39
"shunpiking," 102–103
Skinner v. Anderson, 104
Skousen, Mark, 33
The Slaughterhouse Cases, 29, 137–39
Small Is Beautiful (Schumacher), 197
Smith, Adam, 5, 22–26. *See also* classical liberalism; *Wealth of Nations*
  on competition, 35
  on corporations, 51–54
  on debt, 46–51
    growth of, 49
    mercantile system and, 48–49
  on functions of state, 40–41
  Gallatin and, 80–81
  on governance, 46–51
    stakeholder theory of, 48
  on infrastructure
    benefits of, 41–45
    competitive infrastructure, 53–54
    as condition of advanced society, 159
    corporate involvement in, 162–63
    government role in, 113, 134
    hard infrastructure, 42–43
    privatization of, 35
    public-private partnerships over, 35
    purpose of, 42–43, 205
    seignorage and, 46–47
    as self-liquidating, 35–46, 93, 94
    soft infrastructure, 42–43
    state financing of, 42–44
  on laissez-faire capitalism, 36, 59–60, 66, 184
  Lectures on Jurisprudence, 23
  Lectures on Justice, Police, Revenue and Arms, 37–40, 45–46
  on money, 50–51
    in barter economy, 50
    origins of, 49–50
  on nation-building, 78–79
  on natural monopolies, 24, 35, 51–54, 162
  on police power, 37–41
    economy and, 38–40
    evolution of, 45–46
    regulatory history of, 38–40
  on promotion of public interest, 36
  on property rights, 24, 139
  on public choice theories, 44
  on public economy, 37
  on public utilities, 51–54
  on public works, 40–41, 192, 193
  on road-building authority, 91–92
  on statelessness, 36–37
  truck and barter theory and, 179
Smith, Jason Scott, 169
social benefit theory, 149
social Darwinism, 18
social overhead capital, 8, 31, 186–87
socialism
  Mill on, 174
  states' role in infrastructure and, 166
soft currency, in banking systems, 121–22
soft infrastructure, 42–43
sovereign debt. *See* debt
Special United Nations Fund for Economic Development (SUNFED), 192–94
Spencer, Herbert, 174
The Spirit of the Common Law (Pound, R.), 175
Sprague, Frank, 161
St. Louis & Pacific Railway Company v. Illinois, 30
The Stages of Economic Growth (Rostow), 31, 191–92
stakeholder theory, of governance, 48
the state. *See also* debtor states; nation-building; states' role in infrastructure
  agenda of, 37, 181
  financing of, 42–44
  functions of, 40–41
  infrastructure as embodiment of, 16
  non-agenda of, 37, 181
  statelessness, 36–37
  state–market relations, 35
state commissions, on state infrastructure, 165–66
state courts
  pro-development legal model and, 116
  role in infrastructure, 114–16
statelessness, 36–37
states' role in infrastructure
  chartered corporate ventures, 162–63
  under Commerce Clause, 155–60

Index

railroad industry, 158–60
telegraph industry, 156–57
crisis of infrastructure investment, 117–25
 before Panic of 1837, 121–23
Dash v. Van Kleeck, 116–17
debt repudiation and, 117–25
 by state, 120–21
debt-financed investment, 132–33
expansion of infrastructure, 112–13
franchise systems, 163
law reforms for, 125–31
 constitutional reforms, 127–29
 credit clauses, 126
 debt provisions, 126–27
 after Panic of 1837, 125–26, 128
 municipal finances and, 128
Panic of 1837 and
 Bank of England and, 122–23
 crisis of infrastructure investment before, 121–23
 federal bailouts after, 124
 origins of, 113–14
 sovereign debt as factor in, 113–14
 state law reforms after, 125–26, 128
 under Postal Clause, 157
pro-development legal model, 115–17
 private interests in, 117
 role of state courts, 116
 under Tenth Amendment, 115
Progressive arguments about, 166–68
public benefit theory of government investment, 130
public good and, 133
public interest and, 161–66
public purpose and, 128–29
 definition of, 114–15
 limits on state investment, 125–31
 state investment and, limits on, 125–31
 taxation, limits on, 145–51
public utilities theory and, 133, 161–66
 common good argument, 164–65
 pricing guides in, 165–66
regulated industries and, 155–60
 railroad industry, 158–60
 telegraph industry, 156–57
socialist arguments about, 166
state commissions, 165–66
state courts and, 114–16
in state's agenda/non-agenda, 37, 181
through taxless financing, 117–25
vested rights theory and, 117
Stone, Andrea, 201–202

subsidies, for railroads, 147
SUNFED. *See* Special United Nations Fund for Economic Development
superstructure, infrastructure and, 2

Takings Clause, U.S. Constitution, 99–100
taxless financing, states' role in infrastructure and, 117–25
Taylor v. Ross County Commissioners, 148
telegraph industry
 Pensacola Telegraph Company v. Western Union Telegraph Company, 157
 regulation of, 156–57
Tenth Census, 134
Thomas, David, 57
Tiedemann, Christopher, 30, 136, 143
Tocqueville, Alexis de, 55–56
tolls, on turnpikes, 101–103
 evasion of, 102–103
 property damage against, 103–104
 "shunpiking" and, 102–103
Travels through the Western Country in the Summer of 1816 (Thomas), 57
treasury bonds, 70
Treatise on The Constitutional Limitations Which Rest upon the Legislative Power of the States of the American Union (Cooley), 132, 144
Treatise on the Law of Street Railways (Booth), 30, 151–55
A Treatise on the Limitations of Police Power in the United States (Tiedeman), 30, 143
truck and barter theory, 179
Truman, Harry, 185–86
turnpikes, 87–88
 during antebellum era, 97–110
 Charles River Bridge case, 109
 Commonwealth v. George Wilkinson, 105
 Commonwealth v. Worcester Turnpike Corporation, 106
 Conklin v. Elting, 104
 corporate investment in, 93–94
 economics of, 91–94
 Gallatin on, state construction of, 92
 Joshua Gilmore v. Amos Holt, 106
 M'Clenachan v. Curwen, 99
 Ohio Turnpike Statute of 1840, 97–110
  calculation of damages under, 100
  eminent domain arguments, 99–100
  freeholders and, 100–101
  "shunpiking" under, 102–103
  toll exemptions under, 101–103

turnpikes (cont.)
    Paine on, 95–96
    pecuniary compensation and, 132
    Pennsylvania Coal v. Mahon, 109–110
    The People v. Kingston and Middleton Turnpike Company, 107–108
    police power and, 106
    political contexts for, 91–94
    private rights of, 105
    as public highways, 96–97, 105
    public regulation of, 106
    as public–private partnership, 87
    private property rights and, 96–97
    In re Kensington Dist. Division, 108–109
    as self-liquidating infrastructure, 93
    Skinner v. Anderson, 104
    state support for, 91–92, 97–110
    under Takings Clause, 99–100
    tolls on, 101–103
        evasion of, 102–103
        property damage against, 103–104
        "shunpiking" and, 102–103
    vested rights theory and, 109
    Wales v. Stetson, 103–104
Two Treatises on Government (Locke), 26–27
Tyler, John, 124

United States (U.S.), infrastructural state in, 57–86. *See also* Constitution; Hamilton, Alexander; Jefferson, Thomas
    Administrative Procedure Act, 182–83
    Anti-Federalists and, 73–74
        arguments over federal power, 64–65
    Army Corps of Engineers' role in, 83
    Bonus Bill, 81–82
    Build Back Better Act, 207
    constitutional battle over, 71–75
        for public works, 71, 73–74
    Deposit and Distribution Act of 1936, 121–22
    Embargo Act of 1807, 76
    Enabling Act, 76–77
    expansion of, 111–115
        role of state governments in, 112–113
    federal power over, 58
        Anti-Federalists on, 64–65
        Federalists on, 64–66
    Federalists and
        constitution and, 60–66
        on federal power, 64–65
        on road-building authority, 58, 59

    fiscal state and, 60–66
        political economy of, 66
    Gallatin Plan, 78–81
        components of, 79–80
        infrastructural nationalism as element of, 79
        Report of the Secretary of the Treasury on the Subject of Public Roads and Canals, 78
    General Survey Act, 83
    general welfare questions, 62
    Hepburn Act, 160
    infrastructural nationalism and
        Gallatin Plan and, 79
        under Jackson, 85–86
    Infrastructure Investments and Jobs Act, 32, 207
    internal improvements, 56
        Jackson role in, 83–86
        expansion of transportation networks, 84–85
        infrastructural nationalism and, 85–86
        laissez-faire capitalism and, 84
    Judiciary Act of 1801, 75
    laissez-faire theories of, 56–57
    Land Ordinance of 1785, 61
    Mann-Elkins Act, 160
    Northwest Ordinance, 89–90
    Postal Service Act, 71, 73–74
    public response to, 86
    regional divisions over, 58–59
    road-building authority and, 57–60, 76–77
        expansion of transportation networks, 84–85
        Federalists and, 58, 59
        under Gallatin plan, 78–81
        Jackson and, 84–85
        Tocqueville and, 55–56
    U.S. postal service, 112
    Valuation Act, 160
    War for Independence, 62–63, 67
U.S. postal service, 112

Valuation Act, U.S. (1910), 160
Veblen, Thorstein, 172–73, 178
vested rights theory, 109
    states' role in infrastructure and, 117

Wabash, St. Louis & Pacific Railway Company v. Illinois, 158
Waite, Morrison (Justice), 29
Wald, Paul, 209
Wales v. Stetson, 103–104
Walker, Pinkney A., 130
Walker v. Cincinnati, 148
Walras, Léon, 177

War for Independence, 62–63, 67
Waring, George E., Jr., 165
Washington, George, 58, 60–61
Wealth of Nations (Smith, A.), 22, 23, 33. *See also* classical liberalism
  classical liberalism in, 33–46, 54
  commerce in, 40
  on costs of infrastructural projects, 80
  Declaration of Independence and, 57
  financial systems in, 63–64
  police power in, 37–41
    economy and, 38–40
    evolution of, 45–46
    regulatory history of, 38–40
    public works in, 40–41
    state–market relations in, 35
Weber, Max, 191
Webster, Daniel, 123
West Coast Hotel v. Parrish, 182
Woolner, David B., 208

Ingram Content Group UK Ltd.
Milton Keynes UK
UKHW020641050723
424512UK00024B/205